# ECONOMIC ASPECTS OF DISABILITY BEHAVIOR

# CONTRIBUTIONS
# TO
# ECONOMIC ANALYSIS

207

*Honorary Editor:*
J. TINBERGEN

*Editors:*
D. W. JORGENSON
J. J. LAFFONT

NORTH-HOLLAND
AMSTERDAM • LONDON • NEW YORK • TOKYO

# ECONOMIC ASPECTS OF DISABILITY BEHAVIOR

Leo J. M. AARTS
Philip R. DE JONG

*Faculty of Law*
*University of Leiden*
*Leiden, The Netherlands*

1992

NORTH-HOLLAND
AMSTERDAM • LONDON • NEW YORK • TOKYO

ELSEVIER SCIENCE PUBLISHERS B.V.
Sara Burgerhartstraat 25
P.O. Box 211, 1000 AE Amsterdam, The Netherlands


**Library of Congress Cataloging-in-Publication Data**


Aarts, L.
    Economic aspects of disability behavior / Leo J.M. Aarts, Philip
R. de Jong.
        p.   cm. -- (Contributions to economic analysis ; 207)
    Includes bibliographical references and index.
    ISBN 0-444-89462-4
    1. Insurance, Disability--Netherlands.  2. Disability evaluation-
-Netherlands.   I. Jong, Philip R. de, 1949-   . II. Title.
III. Series.
HD7105.25.N4A27   1992
368.4'2'009492--dc20                                      92-25774
                                                               CIP


ISBN: 0-444-89462-4

368.42
Alle

This book is printed on acid-free paper.

PRINTED IN THE NETHERLANDS

# INTRODUCTION TO THE SERIES

This series consists of a number of hitherto unpublished studies, which are introduced by the editors in the belief that they represent fresh contributions to economic science.

The term "economic analysis" as used in the title of the series has been adopted because it covers both the activities of the theoretical economist and the research worker.

Although the analytical methods used by the various contributors are not the same, they are nevertheless conditioned by the common origin of their studies, namely theoretical problems encountered in practical research. Since for this reason, business cycle research and national accounting, research work on behalf of economic policy, and problems of planning are the main sources of the subjects dealt with, they necessarily determine the manner of approach adopted by the authors. Their methods tend to be "practical" in the sense of not being too far remote from application to actual economic conditions. In additon they are quantitative.

It is the hope of the editors that the publication of these studies will help to stimulate the exchange of scientific information and to reinforce international cooperation in the field of economics.

*The Editors*

# ACKNOWLEDGEMENTS

This book builds on a series of studies that were part of a research program called *Determinantenonderzoek WAO* (Dutch Disability Study). This Disability Study sought to determine the causes of the impressive and unanticipated growth of benefit recipiency under the Dutch Social Insurance Disability (DI) Act which became manifest in the early 1970s, not long after this comprehensive insurance scheme had been enacted.

Han Emanuel, at the time Secretary to the Dutch Social Security Council for Financial and Economic Affairs, initiated the study. His views on the potential contributions of research to social security policy were shared by the Council that approved the project in 1975. The project was set up as a joint venture of the Council and the Center for Research in Public Economics at Leiden University. Bernard van Praag, then Professor of Economics at Leiden and Director of the Center, and Han Emanuel directed the research team consisting of a sociologist, Hilbrand Bruinsma, a data-analyst/computer scientist, Peter Hop, and two economists, Philip de Jong and Leo Aarts, who joined the team in 1977 and 1979 respectively.

Our prime acknowledgements regard our fellow team members:

First of all, Han Emanuel, whose involvement with the project has been crucial. If not for his rampant enthusiasm, his relentless efforts to make the project a unique enterprise, and his rare talent to crash through the gates of bureaucracy, there would have been no such thing as a Dutch Disability Study.

The design and management of a large research project is one thing, its execution is quite something different. Apart from specialized skills it requires patience and precision. Peter Hop proved to combine all of these attributes. In the first stage of the project he designed the lay-out of the questionnaires, coordinated their coding and, most importantly, transformed a mash of data into workable, well-organized, sets. After that he was not only invaluable in quickly and faultlessly satisfying all our analytic desires, he also commented on our models and so contributed to their improvement. His impeccable administration and documentation enabled us to stay in touch with the data after the project had ended.

We are also indebted to Hilbrand Bruinsma, the sociologist on the team. His contributions to the project and hence, indirectly, to this book have been manifold. He taught us that behavioral approaches to such seemingly random malfortunes as disability have a much longer history in sociological than in economic thought, and made us familiar with both the theoretical and empirical literatures on medical sociology. He stressed the importance of certain non-monetary job aspects and operationalized abstract concepts related to the social and psychological meaning of work and disability. Moreover, thanks to his affiliation with the Joint Medical Service (GMD) he was able to provide us with real world information on administrative routines regarding disability determinations, and to help convince the board of the GMD to carry out large parts of the data-collection. He left the team in 1983 because his research activities at the GMD prevented him to continue his collaboration.

The project was co-directed by Bernard van Praag. Being a forerunner in the fields of both theoretical modelling of individual behavior and econometric analysis of micro-data his comments and suggestions have greatly stimulated us and helped to improve the modelling of the complex causalities under study. His scholarly qualities, however, have not prevented him from reminding us to emphasize the policy relevance of our data and analyses. His patience and confidence helped us through the dark stages of the production process of this book. We gratefully acknowledge his contributions.

By successive decisions taken in 1975, 1979, and 1981, the Social Security Council covered all of the project expenses, including such disparate matters as the salaries of two economic researchers, the costs of two large-scale surveys, of computational and secretarial assistance, and of the restoration of two rooms at Leiden to help the university host the project. The generosity of the Council is gratefully acknowledged.

The care of the Council also included immaterial matters. During its full length, the project was guided by a scientific advisory committee which consisted of three scholars each representing a different discipline; a Professor of Law - Jaap Rang, succeeded by Frits Noordam; a Professor of Economics - Cees Nieuwenburg; and a Professor of Psychology - Jacques Allegro; a representative of the trade unions - Jelle Hoogland, succeeded by Chris Driessen; and a representative of employers' organizations - Jan Haverhals. In all stages of the project their comments and suggestions have been most helpful.

The unique dataset on which this book is based, has involved the magnanimous collaboration of the social security administrators: Thanks to the support of the Joint Medical Service and the Industrial Associations, and to the dedication of insurance doctors and ergonomists at the regional offices of the Joint Medical Service, we were able to solve a major problem in disability research - adequate measurement of health status. Moreover, numerous staff members at regional branches of the Industrial Associations were instrumental in monitoring an initial sample of more than 9,000 employees on sick leave. Their contributions were indispensable.

Finally, we should like to thank the thousands of people who participated in the surveys. The very detailed information they provided is the fundament of our study.

*Leo Aarts*
*Philip de Jong*

# CONTENTS

# LIST OF TABLES, SCHEMES (S), AND FIGURES (F)

Chapter 1

# ECONOMIC ASPECTS OF DISABILITY BEHAVIOR; INTRODUCTION

## 1.1 Introduction

Through social security primary incomes are transferred from the active to the non-active population, equalizing the income distribution and alleviating economic hardship for the needy.

Social insurance programs covering the risk of earnings' losses due to disability are at the core of all modern social security systems. The disability risk, however, is ill defined and hard to measure. The vagueness of the disability concept may have contributed to increasing income support from Social Disability Insurance Schemes (hereafter referred to as DI-programs) which has been observed in most Western countries since the 1970s when, at the same time, their economies faltered and the baby boom generation entered the labor market. National DI-programs came to serve as a shelter for older, low-skilled, workers who could be easily replaced by better educated youths [Haveman et al. (1984)].

While most OECD countries have witnessed similar developments the Dutch disability experience may serve as the epitome of the problems encountered in designing social security programs that are both equitable and efficient. Here, a combination of lax eligibility criteria and lenient administrative routines have facilitated a program growth that, both in terms of DI-beneficiaries and expenditures, is matched by no other national social security system. Whatever the merits of such a disability policy may be, the Dutch experience provides an interesting case and an adequate framework to study the economic aspects of disability behavior.

Dutch disability insurance policy is as conspicuous internationally as it is contentious nationally. The incessant growth of the disability beneficiary volume has been subject to public debate ever since the early seventies. Public attention may have been fluctuating over the years, disability never disappeared from the agenda. Now that it has become clear that the major program adjustments of 1987 have not yielded the intended cost reducing effects, public interest is booming again.

Today, 13 out of each 100 workers covered are receiving earnings replacing benefits from the Dutch Disability Insurance Scheme. Among older workers (over 55 years), more than 50 percent have left the labor force to enter the DI-program. Annually, 15 out of each 1,000 workers insured become eligible for disability benefits. The average age of newly awarded beneficiaries is 47. Most of them, some 80 percent, will stay on the DI-rolls until 65 when eligibility runs out. Although disability growth was even worse in the late seventies, the current size of the DI-volume is considered a social and financial problem, just as it has been over the past two decades.

In nearly all modern Western societies expenditures on social security have increased over the last decades. Since coverage has been extended, both in terms of eligibility and benefit income, these increases are a direct consequence of the maturation of the Welfare State. Paradoxically, however, the increase in social security expenditures itself may have induced further growth. The increasing unemployment and disability outlays have been financed by burdening the payroll. This made labor more expensive. As a consequence, employers tried to dismiss increasing numbers of workers whose productivity did not match the increased wage bill anymore. As these "non-employable" workers came to depend on social security, the result has been a further burdening of the wage bill, a further reduction of the demand for labor, and, a further increase of benefit entitlements, etcetera.
The danger of gradually slipping into this "social security trap"[1] has elicited public debate on the need to reshape the existing national social security systems into systems with a size and design society is able to sustain. Such reforms have fuelled a renewed interest in the balance of social costs and benefits of social security. Many economic issues have been raised, all boiling down to the old efficiency - equity controversy. All of these issues can be studied in the framework of the DI-program. Its steady growth is illustrative of the positive and negative aspects of the Welfare State in general.

Our book is about the economic aspects of disability behavior, i.e., disability program participation. In this first and introductory chapter we will raise some of the issues at stake. In section 1.2, we briefly introduce some general welfare theoretical features of social insurance in general and disability insurance in particular. In section 1.3, we will elaborate on the efficiency and equity aspects of social disability insurance. Here, we introduce the behavioral aspects of social disability insurance programs and raise the main questions to be addressed in our analysis. Section 1.4 concludes with an outline of the book.

## 1.2    Social Disability Insurance

Social disability insurance is designed to provide an insurance against the risk of earnings' loss due to functional impairments. Surely, the full private and social cost of disability exceed the losses related to reductions in productivity alone. They also include expenses for medical care and special aid, and losses of social and psychological well-being. Secondly, the presence of an impairment will also affect the well-being of others. Family members and acquaintances may have to make practical, financial, and psychological adjustments to accommodate their handicapped relative or friend. Thirdly, the presence of impaired persons in a society will also have more widely felt impacts. Depending on their degrees of risk-aversion, others will become aware of the risk of losing their livelihood due to impairments. Finally, society at large may suffer some loss of well-being simply by knowing of, or observing, the impaired person's situation. Such external effects are denoted as "collective compassion" costs. They introduce feelings of solidarity as motives to establish charitable funds and collective arrangements.[2]

In the absence of any form of compensation, this gamut of impairment costs would fully impinge on the handicapped, their relatives and acquaintances, and other individual members of society. Under such primitive circumstances social welfare, being the aggregate of individual utilities, would probably be lower than in societies that have some form of compensatory system. From a welfare-theoretical point of view, then, the efficiency of these systems is judged by their contributions to increasing social welfare.

Compensation means transferring income from one party (DI-program contributors) to the other (DI-benefit recipients). Social insurance is just one way to organize these income transfers. Private insurance, and juridical liability assignments, are conceivable alternatives to public arrangements. Each compensatory system will have its utility-winners and losers, as compared to the counterfactual of no compensation whatsoever. Under a social disability insurance system, the beneficiaries and their families are obvious winners, whereas all others may be net-winners or net-losers. To the risk-averse consumer or to the altruist, the utility-gains resulting from insurance coverage and coverage of "collective compassion" costs may more than offset the utility-losses resulting from compulsory contributions to the DI-fund. These losses may even be zero, if the risk-averse consumer would have purchased a comparable coverage voluntarily, were he not covered by social insurance, or if the altruist would have donated a yearly sum to a charitable fund for the handicapped, were he not obliged to contribute to the DI-program.

Using a social welfare concept based on interpersonally comparable utility, social insurance can be proven to be the optimal compensation system, provided the aggregate net utility-gain it yields exceeds the social welfare contributions of all of its alternatives.

**Private versus Social Disability Insurance**
In theory, the utility framework could be employed to derive optimal coverage and eligibility criteria, and optimal benefit sizes.[3] This introduces the theory of efficient insurance contracts as an additional approach to the design of the optimal disability policy. Under an efficient contract policyholders maximize their expected utilities, subject to the constraint that the insurer should, at least, break even. Such a contract provides full coverage against income loss, which equals the present value of foregone earnings during the period of disability. Each individual is charged a total premium equal to his or her expected loss. Premiums, then, differ according to probabilities of disability, as indicated by age, health, and occupation. They should also reflect differences in earnings potential, as indicated by current and previous earnings, schooling, skills, and labor market conditions.[4]
Under such a purely private, purely individualized, insurance system, the worst risks would be charged the highest premiums. Workers with high disability probabilities would be confronted with correspondingly high insurance expenses. Among such workers, however, the prevalence of low earnings and weak employment positions is relatively high. They will mostly remain uninsured, as they will be unable, or reluctant, to purchase disability coverage. Efficient as it may be, private insurance is likely to turn out to be inadequate.
Other problems, all pertaining to the unpredictability of the disability incidence, actually preclude private provision of an adequate disability coverage. To the insurer, whether private or social, the first and basic problem is the definition and verification of the insured risk - income loss due to disability. Except in extreme cases, the severity of impairments, their incapacitating effects, and their curability, are not accurately assessable. Only if the insurer were to limit coverage to clear-cut cases, this informational problem could be contained to manageable proportions.

Adequacy, however, requires coverage of all medical contingencies, and so introduces a potentially sizeable amount of error into disability determinations. Two types of error can be distinguished: erroneous denials (Type I errors, or false negatives) and erroneous admissions (Type II errors, or false positives). Both kinds of error have adverse effects on social welfare. An insurance contract which has excessively strict eligibility rules, will be biased toward a significant number of erroneous denials. The denied disabled, their households, and society at large, would all suffer welfare losses due to deficient coverage.
At the opposite extreme one may imagine a contract which is so lenient as to provide an (initial) award to anyone who claims to be disabled. Such a contract might be based on the legal rule that a man is innocent (incapacitated) until proven guilty (healthy). This, in fact, is a common decision rule in medicine: "When in doubt suspect illness". Such a liberal contract rules out all Type I errors, at the

expense of a, potentially, significant amount of Type II errors, i.e., erroneous awards. Such insurance contracts will be considered prohibitively expensive, even when publicly provided.

Associated with the delicate trade-off between Type I and Type II errors, we may list three insurance-specific problems to support the case for public provision of disability insurance contracts.[5] First, individual disability risks may collectively depend on labor market conditions, thereby introducing **risk-dependence**. A market for private insurances is only viable if the risk is shared among a heterogeneously composed population of policyholders. Private funds are likely to collapse under an unexpected surge of disability claims, provoked by an epidemic, high unemployment, or an increase in preferences for retirement. The unanticipated growth of Dutch DI-recipiency in the 1970s, may be illustrative of the prediction problems engendered by dependent risks (see table 2.15).

Second, the extent of risk may be influenced by individual decisions based on work-leisure preferences. The possibility that the insured individual can affect both the probability of incurring a loss and the amount of the loss, is usually referred to as the problem of **moral hazard**. Moral hazard emerges if, upon full coverage, the insured act as if damages were costless.[6] The insurer may try to contain the resulting excessive amount of loss by coverage reductions, and/or provision of appropriate incentives for rehabilitation. At the expense of adequacy, the insurer may supply policies with partial (less than 100%) coverage (coinsurance), or may deduct a fixed amount of money from each compensation (deductibles). Policies may also exclude contingencies that are directly attributable to risky habits, such as sport accidents or diseases related to nicotine and alcohol consumption. As concerns containment of the duration of disability, the insurer may prescribe engagement in a rehabilitative program and subsequent reentry into the labor force. Or, the policy may provide compensation for a limited period only.

And, third, the informational problems that surround disability determinations prohibit reliable estimates of individual risks, and corresponding premiums, or even adequate grouping of the insured population into risk categories. If premiums do not closely reflect differences in expected losses, **adverse selection** can be a significant problem to the private insurer. Low-risk people will tend not to buy insurance, unless they are extremely risk-averse, whereas high-risk individuals will only buy insurance as long as they can afford it. The resulting high average risk will compel a correspondingly high premium, and participation in the insurance will dwindle. In sum, the three insurance problems of risk dependence, moral hazard, and adverse selection, preclude private provision of adequate disability insurance contracts.

## 1.3     Efficiency and Equity Aspects of Social Disability Insurance

In industrialized democracies people turn to government, if the market fails to provide adequate coverage of risks which have pervasive and drastic consequences. To these urges, government may respond by regulating the private insurance industry, say, by mandating insurance purchases. But if such regulated markets are still deemed deficient, government may intervene by launching a social insurance program.

Social insurance schemes can take many forms. The history of Dutch social insurance witnesses a development from privately organized funds covering only certain groups and certain risks in the 19th century, to the current system which legally establishes nationwide coverage of all kinds of risks. As in other industrialized countries, the birth of social insurance in the Netherlands is marked by the creation of risk funds covering the consequences of occupational hazards, both in terms of health costs and loss of earnings. These funds were organized per branch of industry, and coverage differed accordingly. Extent of coverage depended on the size of risk, and on the coercive power of the labor movement in a specific branch. Contributions were levied on a pay-as-you-go basis, and participation was compulsory.[7]

Government started to intervene in disability coverage with the enactment of the Industrial Accidents Act, the first Dutch social insurance program, in 1903. This Act merely assigned liability for certain accidents in certain jobs to the employer, and established wage-related benefit amounts and benefit durations. From then on, coverage was gradually made more comprehensive. The present state of the social (disability insurance) system is described in chapter 2.

The common denominator of all of these collective coverage arrangements, whether primitive and stringent, or comprehensive and lenient, is the compulsory participation of both employers and employees. A mandatory scheme may correct some of the equity and efficiency problems that are inherent in private disability coverage, and so may add to social welfare.

In the literature on the meritorious aspects of social insurance a number of advantages and disadvantages are listed.[8] First, a collective arrangement solves the adverse selection problem by charging an average premium on a pay-as-you-go basis. High-risk individuals, then, are subsidized by low-risk contributors. These compulsory subsidies may imply potential welfare gains and losses. High-risk groups that, in a market setting, would be charged considerably higher premiums, may gain, whereas low-risk individuals may lose, if they would have preferred to buy smaller amounts of coverage, were they free to choose.

The argument applies to employees as well as employers. A social disability insurance covers, at least part of, the liability damages resulting from job-related accidents and diseases that would otherwise fully impinge on the employer. The insurance system produces a subsidy from low-risk industries, e.g., banking, to high-risk branches, e.g., construction. These intra-industry subsidies may introduce ineffi-ciencies, as they shield high-risk firms from the full extent of their disability liabilities. As an alternative, premiums may be calculated so as to differ according to the average risk within an industry. Such, experience-rated, risk-groups are distinguished under the Dutch Sickness Benefit program.

Second, by eliminating adverse selection, a compulsory insurance scheme greatly enhances the insurance base on which premiums are calculated. Therefore, the average premium will be lower than the private market equilibrium. Moreover, mandatory participation reduces selling costs, and introduces economies of scale. These efficiency gains of collective supply should be weighed against the individual welfare losses engendered by compulsory consumption of a standard insurance package. Collective arrangements do not take account of variations in individual preferences.

Third, given the informational problems inherent in disability risk assessment, individuals may be myopic with respect to their disability risks. Mandatory partici-pation in a social insurance scheme may correct erroneous perceptions or harmfully risk-loving preferences. Paternalistic intervention by collective compulsory arrange-ments may prevent myopic, or irresponsible, individuals from incurring large disability damages.

Fourth, to the extent that disability risks and earning capacities are negatively correlated, a social disability insurance scheme redistributes income from affluent contributors to poor beneficiaries. Income redistribution enhances equity, and so altruists enjoy utility gains. Moreover, since the disability risk increases with age, social insurance produces an inter-generational redistribution, through which the younger cohorts subsidize the elderly.

Fifth, from a macro-economic perspective one may argue that, if the aggregate disability risk depends on macro-economic circumstances, social insurance benefits may act as a built-in stabilizer by maintaining the purchasing power of the disabled in times of economic slackness.

The above listing suggests that the welfare gains of a social disability scheme are likely to outweigh losses, and that the social welfare contribution of a collective arrangement outweighs that of its market alternatives. Social insurance, however, creates legal and institutional constraints on the operation of the labor market, which may affect labor demand as well as labor supply. Payroll taxes, necessary to finance program expenditures, widen the gap ("wedge") between the gross wage paid by employers and the net wage received by workers. Employer-borne gross wage costs are increased relative to the perceived marginal product of employees, and the net wage received by workers is reduced relative to their supply price of labor. To the extent that employers and employees perceive their social insurance contributions as losses, both labor demand and supply diminish. As a result of social insurance legislation, then, a less favorable market equilibrium is obtained where the employment volume and net wages are lower, and gross wage costs are higher as compared to private arrangements.

In times of economic slack, the aggregate unemployment and disability risks rise. So do the necessary employer-borne contributions, entailing increased productivity demands. Impaired workers are disproportionally hit by these adverse demand side effects; their worsened job security and employment opportunities upon dismissal, will increase the benefit recipiency volume further. Therefore, during an economic downturn, a pay-as-you-go insurance system is liable to degenerate into a destructive spiral, fuelled by ever expanding beneficiary volumes.[9]

On the supply side, two mutually reinforcing effects may discourage work effort. First, social insurance taxation of earnings lowers net wage rates, and, therefore, may change the relative prices of leisure and other commodities. If leisure is a normal good, and substitution elasticities outweigh income elasticities, wage losses will result in reductions of supply of working hours. Second, benefit eligibility, based on inaccurate or lenient disability determinations, enables mildly impaired workers to opt for benefit recipiency, if they prefer so. Generally, an intrinsically inaccurate award system such as disability insurance, enlarges the set of behavioral options. Hence, if disability awards are granted by inaccurate or lenient, routinized, procedures, the insured may be able to influence their award probabilities, benefit amounts, and benefit durations, according to their preferences and circumstances.

Moreover, under a collective arrangement neither the insured employees, nor their employers, will bear the full expected costs and benefits of their preventive or curative actions. Too little effort will be devoted to risk prevention and loss reduction, and program costs will be higher than they would be if rigorous risk verifications were possible, or if stringent award conditions were acceptable. Adequate collective arrangements, therefore, are liable to aggravate the moral hazard problem.

The potential presence of a significant moral hazard component within socially insured risks, poses considerable, and abundantly studied, efficiency problems.[10] The moral hazard component can be defined as that part of the aggregate disability risk which is attributable to program disincentives to engage in preventive and rehabilitative activities.

Our study endeavors to analyze the transition from work to DI-program participation in the Netherlands. We will describe the medical and non-medical factors that contribute to this transition, acknowledging the intricate causalities that govern DI-enrolment. At the end of this book we have hopefully collected enough material to be able to give a solid judgement on the relative efficiency of the Dutch disability insurance system. Reporting on a Dutch case study we nevertheless hope to provide building blocks for the study of similar programs in other countries as well. Moreover, we hope our study will contribute to the policy makers' awareness of the behavioral responses elicited by social policy.

## 1.4 Outline of the Book

Although the central focus of our study is on the behavioral responses of individual employees to the Dutch DI-program, we will also study the behavior of the employing firms, or rather the determinants of firm specific DI-incidence rates.

In chapter 2 we set the stage. Here, we provide a background against which the DI-program can be appreciated, and the behavioral responses it prompts. The performance of the Dutch social security system, in terms of outlays, participants, and distributional impact, will be compared with those of other Western economies. The main institutional features of the Dutch social security system are introduced and a comprehensive record of the Dutch social security system, and the Disability Insurance program in particular, is presented. Chapter 2 also includes a brief international comparison of Social Disability Insurance arrangements and an overview of the main features of the Dutch Social Security System Reform that was introduced in 1987.

In chapter 3 we elaborate on disability as a behavioral phenomenon. The behavioral approach is based on the inevitable subjectivity of disability assessments which is likely to introduce individual tastes, social values, and financial evaluations into the definition and perception of disability. Starting from the early and pathbreaking work in conceptualizing and structuring the complex notion of disability by medical sociologists and psychologists, we choose to elaborate disability behavior along micro-economic lines. In combination, both disciplinary angles introduce a host of non-medical factors as determinants of disability behavior. In this study, we employ the micro-economic paradigm of utility maximization to construct a formal model of disability behavior, more specifically, of DI-program participation. This model states that workers will apply for DI-benefits if they expect the difference between the lifetime utilities in the DI and the WORK options to be positive. It provides a framework for the analysis of financial considerations and program disincentives to (re)employment. The formal DI-model is transformed into an operational form which also includes the medical-sociological perspective.

The study reported in this book is the offspring of a research program on the Determinants of Growth in Disability Income Support in the Netherlands. The program was initiated by the Dutch Social Security Council in 1975 and carried on until 1987. As part of this program two large samples were surveyed in 1980. From those are our data. In chapter 4, we will briefly describe the history of the research

program. We will also elaborate on the sampling procedures and present a
preliminary summary of the major characteristics of the samples used. The nonresponse is analyzed and some other limitations of the databases are discussed.

After having introduced the Dutch social security system, the theoretical approach
and the databases in the preceding chapters, we present the empirical part of our
analysis of disability behavior in the chapters 5 through 10.

In chapter 5, we make an attempt to determine the amount of Type II errors in
disability assessment, i.e., the amount of "erroneous awards". Using the ratings of
social insurance physicians and ergonomists, we describe the objective prevalence
of disability among our 1980 sample of Dutch DI-entrants. We use a dichotomous
version of the formal definition of disability under the DI-program; disabled are
those who are unable to perform commensurate work for the usual, pre-disability,
number of hours. This measure is analyzed, and compared with self-definitions,
in chapter 10. In chapter 5, we also speculate on how the 1987 Social Security
System Reform may have affected the amount of work capacity sheltered in the
DI-program today.

In chapter 6, we analyze the endogeneity problems related to the databases used
for investigating the probability of DI-entry. Specifically, variables measured by
subjective scales may be blurred by preferences or legitimation, which we denote
as endogenous measurement errors. We will propose a model that is fit to test for
the presence of these errors and that provides a method to correct the afflicted
variables.

Chapters 7 and 8 deal with employment opportunities. In chapter 7, the competitive
power in the labor market of different groups of employees is analyzed, while
chapter 8 focuses on the within firm prospects under their current employment
contract. Chapter 7 deals with the modelling and estimation of individual labor
market histories. Theoretical aspects are summarized and a statistical duration model
is estimated. The empirical analysis of work histories enables the development of
valid, individually varying, instruments measuring the probability of becoming
unemployed and the probability of re-employment.

In chapter 8, we will focus on the firm's influence on the process leading to the
disability status of its employees. We try to assess to what extent the inter-firm
variance in DI-incidence rates, i.e., the relative number of employees enrolling the
DI-program, is accounted for by indicators related to the probability of occurrence
of functional limitations and by indicators related to the firm's response to these
functional limitations. We will argue that the firm's response depends on the cost-
benefit balance of retaining (or replacing) functionally impaired employees. A model
to examine the determinants of the variation in DI-incidence rate among firms is
proposed, estimated and discussed. From the estimation results, a measure for the
firm specific risk of DI-program enrolment is derived. This instrument encompasses
the firm's employment outlook as well as the occupational risks to which the employees are exposed, and the firm's policy with regard to impaired employees. In

the individual disability probability model (chapter 10), this measure will be included as an indicator of the DI-risk to which an individual employee is exposed.

In chapter 9, we make an attempt to determine the expected income streams associated with either of two options; DI-program enrolment or continued labor force participation. A central variable is of course the expected lifetime wage trajectory. We suspect the wage rate to be jointly determined with the disability risk under study by unobserved factors like innate abilities and social background. To test the simultaneity proposition we estimate an endogenous switching model that allows for control of selection mechanisms in wage determination.

The chapters, 7, 8, and 9, then, are devoted to the estimation of separate submodels, each covering one part of the multicausal process governing DI-enrolment. The instrumental variables resulting from these submodels intend to summarize comprehensive sets of socio-medical and economic factors. In chapter 10, we use these instrumentals, the residual work capacity measure derived in chapter 5, and the attitudinal variables adjusted for endogenous measurement errors in chapter 6, as building blocks for the definitive version of the three structural probability models under scrutiny:

- a model describing the unconditional probability of DI-program enrolment, Pr{DI}, i.e., the probability that, within a year, a DI-insured worker reports sick, remains unable to work during the mandatory waiting period for DI-eligibility of 12 months and, subsequently, is awarded a DI-benefit;
- analogously, a model for the unconditional probability of a DI-insured worker reporting sick and remaining sick for at least 5 months, Pr{5M.SICK};
- a model for the conditional probability of DI-enrolment given 5 months sickness, Pr{DI|5M.SICK}.

While the probability model for Pr{DI} stands on its own in that it aims to describe the full transition from work to DI-enrolment, the other two probability models are linked as P{5M.SICK} and Pr{DI|5M.SICK} represent successive stages in the DI-process. By shifting the perspective from the global unconditional probabilities to a more detailed description of the DI-probability conditional on 5 months sickness, we focus on the last stage in the DI-process. Here, we will be able to confront self-perceptions of work limitations and residual capacities with the views of the gatekeepers of the DI-program.

Finally, in chapter 11, we will present 1990-2050 forecasts of the number of disability beneficiaries under a diversity of scenarios. In the first scenario - the "central variant" - we assume that both disability and labor market behavior remain unaltered. This allows us to study the full effects of population ageing. The other scenarios stage 6 alternatives to turn the demographic wave.

Chapter 12 summarizes and concludes.

**Notes**

1. This label was introduced by Van Praag et al. (1980, 1982).

2. See Culyer (1974).

3. See for instance Orr (1976).

4. In this section we cite freely from Weaver (1986).

5. See Carrin (1979) and Diamond (1977).

6. See Pauly (1968).

7. For the history of Dutch social disability insurance, see Van den Bosch and Petersen (1983, chapter 3)

8. For a comprehensive listing of the welfare gains and losses associated with social security see Haveman (1985).

9. For a verbal treatment of the (insurance) economic problems encountered by the Dutch Disability Social Insurance system, see Van Praag (1981).

10.See e.g. Danziger et al. (1981) and Berkowitz and Hill (1986) for reviews of the literature. For a survey of the literature on the effects of social security on saving, labor supply and income distribution in the USA, see Aaron (1982).

Chapter 2

# THE DUTCH DISABILITY PROGRAM IN NATIONAL AND INTERNATIONAL PERSPECTIVE

## 2.1 Introduction

In this chapter we provide a background against which one may appreciate the Dutch Social Disability Insurance program and the ways in which workers, firms, and program administrators respond to it.

In section 2.2 we describe how Dutch social security compares with other Western economies in terms of outlays, participants, and distributional impact. Section 2.3 introduces the main institutional features of the Dutch Social Security System. A comprehensive record of the Dutch Social Security System, and the Disability Insurance Program in particular, are presented in section 2.4. That section also includes a brief international comparison of Disability Social Insurance arrangements. Section 2.5 documents the main features of the 1987 Reform of the Dutch Social Security System. In section 2.6 we summarize the conclusions of this chapter.

## 2.2 Dutch Social Security in International Perspective

### 2.2.1 International Comparison of Expenditures and Financing

In all modern Western societies expenditures on social security have increased over the last decades. Table 2.1 summarizes some cross-national OECD statistics of government expenditures on income maintenance over the 1970 and 1980 decade. Although these figures are troubled by inter-country differences in the categorization of expenditure items they clearly show an increase in public income support in all countries listed.[1]

In the late 1980s, the European governments included spent 13 to 24 percent of Gross Domestic Product (GDP) on Pensions, Sickness Benefits, Family Allowances, and Unemployment Compensation. Compared with 1970, the increase varies from

3 percentage points of GDP in Germany to 11 percentage points in France.[2] In the non-European member states government spending on income maintenance was at a relatively modest level of 2 to 6 percent of GDP in 1970 and has been increasing to about 8 percent towards the end of the 1980 decade. At that time, within OECD-Europe, spending on the selected programs was relatively high in France and the Netherlands and relatively low in the United Kingdom.

Table 2.1    General Government Expenditures on Income Maintenance[a] as a Percentage of GDP in Several OECD-countries, 1970-1988

|  | 1970 | 1979 | 1988 |
|---|---|---|---|
| Germany | 13 | 17 | 16[e] |
| France | 13[b] | 17 | 24[f] |
| Italy | 11 | 16 | - |
| Netherlands | 13 | 19 | 19 |
| United Kingdom | 7 | 11 | 13[f] |
| Denmark | 11[c] | 15 | 15 |
| Sweden | - | 17[d] | 17[e] |
| Australia | 4 | 7 | 7[e] |
| Japan | 2 | 6 | 8 |
| United States | 6 | 8 | 8[e] |

[a]  Included are Pensions, Sickness Benefits, Family Allowances and Unemployment Compensation administered by Central Government (including the Social Security System) and regional and local authorities.
[b]  Figure refers to 1975.
[c]  Figure refers to 1971.
[d]  Figure refers to 1981.
[e]  Figure refers to 1987.
[f]  Figure refers to 1986.
Sources: Saunders & Klau (1985, pp. 51, 52), Oxley, Maher et al. (1990, pp. 44-46).

An inter-country comparison of social security spending within the European Community (EC) is presented in table 2.2. The figures are provided by the statistical bureau of the EC, Eurostat. They are not directly comparable with the OECD figures due to differences in definitions. The general picture is the same, however, showing an increase in social security outlays throughout the European Community. Within the European Community the total amount of social security expenditures in 1989 ranges from 21 percent of GDP (in Ireland and the United Kingdom) to 30 percent (in the Netherlands and Denmark).

The major growth took place in the early seventies. In Germany, the country with the highest level of social security spending in 1970, the increase apparently turned into a gradual decrease by 1975. In most other countries expenditures kept rising until 1985. The late 1980s reveal a decrease from 26 to 25 percent for the EC at large. Throughout the two decades, the Dutch level of spending has been fairly high. Its deviation from the EC average has increased from 3 points in 1970 to 5 points in 1989.

Table 2.2    Social Security Expenditures in the European Community, 1970-1989, as Percentage of GDP

|  | 1970 | 1975 | 1980 | 1985 | 1989 |
|---|---|---|---|---|---|
| Germany | 22 | 30 | 29 | 28 | 27 |
| France | 19 | 23 | 25 | 29 | 28 |
| Italy | 14 | 18 | 19 | 23 | 23 |
| Netherlands | 20 | 27 | 30 | 31 | 30 |
| Belgium | 19 | 24 | 28 | 29 | 27 |
| Luxembourg | 16 | 22 | 27 | 26 | 26 |
| United Kingdom | 14 | 20 | 22 | 24 | 21 |
| Ireland | 14 | 20 | 22 | 24 | 21 |
| Denmark | 20 | 26 | 29 | 28 | 30 |
| EC | 17 | 23 | 24 | 26 | 25 |

Source: Eurostat (1990).

Whatever definition of social security one applies, at the core of each modern social security system is a set of programs aimed at the provision of income to replace earnings when interrupted by unemployment, sickness, or disability and to support retirement. In table 2.3 we compare the relative shares of expenditures on coverage of these risks. In 1989, within the EC as a whole, 11 percent of total social security expenditures is allocated to disability programs. Old age schemes account for 37 percent while unemployment insurance takes 7 percent of the budget.

Table 2.3    Disability[a], Unemployment and Old Age[b] Social Security Expenditures as a Percentage of Total Social Security Expenditures[c], European Community 1980-1989

|  | Disability | | Old Age | | Unemployment | |
|---|---|---|---|---|---|---|
|  | 1980 | 1989 | 1980 | 1989 | 1980 | 1989 |
| Germany | 11 | 12 | 29 | 30 | 5 | 6 |
| France | 9 | 9 | 37 | 37 | 5 | 7 |
| Netherlands | 20 | 21 | 28 | 30 | 6 | 10 |
| Belgium | 12 | 12 | 29 | 31 | 12 | 12 |
| United Kingdom | 10 | 11[d] | 41 | 41[d] | 10 | 6[d] |
| Ireland | 7 | 7 | 28 | 25 | 9 | 15 |
| Denmark | 9 | 10 | 36 | 36 | 13 | 15 |
| EC | 10 | 11[d] | 36 | 37[d] | 6 | 7[d] |

[a]    Disability including sickness, excluding health care.
[b]    Old Age including supplementary private pensions.
[c]    See table 2.2.
[d]    Figure refers to 1988.
Source:   see table 2.2.

Differences among the EC member states appear to be quite substantial.
The Netherlands, for instance, spend twice as much on disability and sick leave than their EC partners. Expenditures on old age are relatively high in the United Kingdom where they account for 41 percent of the budget, whereas in Germany and the Netherlands only 30 percent is allocated to this category. The share of unemployment outlays ranges from 6 percent in Germany to 15 percent in Ireland and Denmark. In 1989, unemployment expenditures take 10 percent of the Dutch social security budget which is high both compared to the 1980-level and to the EC-average.
While there are important differences among the EC-countries in the amounts of social security spending, table 2.3 suggests that the program wise variation between the countries is even larger. This would imply the existence of certain trade-offs between the programs listed. Across the selected countries individuals that run similar risks seem to be covered by different schemes depending on nationally varying definitions of unemployment, disability and old age.

In addition to international differences in social security spending there are also differences in social security financing. While all European social security systems are mainly financed on a pay-as-you-go basis, the financial burden appears to be differently distributed among employers, employees and the general government budget. Table 2.4 presents a cross European comparison of social security financing.

**Table 2.4**   Social Security Contributions by Employers, Employees (Protected Persons) and by Government as a Percentage of Total Social Security Receipts, European Community 1980-1989.[a]

| | Employers' Contributions | | Employees Contributions | | Public Contributions | | Total current Receipts (Bill. ECU) | | Average Annual Rate of Change (percentages) |
|---|---|---|---|---|---|---|---|---|---|
| | 1980 | 1989 | 1980 | 1989 | 1980 | 1989 | 1980 | 1989 | |
| Germany | 41 | 40 | 28 | 31 | 27 | 26 | 176 | 312 | 6.6 |
| France | 56 | 52 | 24 | 29 | 17 | 17 | 127 | 247 | 7.7 |
| Italy | 60 | 53 | 14 | 15 | 24 | 30 | 69 | 190 | 11.9 |
| Netherlands | 37 | 31 | 31 | 35 | 20 | 17 | 45 | 72 | 5.4 |
| Belgium | 45 | 41 | 18 | 26 | 34 | 28 | 24 | 38 | 5.3 |
| Luxembourg | 35 | 33 | 23 | 23 | 33 | 38 | 1 | 2 | 8.0 |
| Un. Kingdom | 33 | 29 | 15 | 17 | 43 | 41 | 99 | 193 | 8.8 |
| Ireland | 25 | 24 | 11 | 15 | 63 | 60 | 3 | 6 | 9.2 |
| Denmark | 10 | 9 | 2 | 5 | 83 | 80 | 15 | 31 | 8.6 |
| EC | 45 | 42 | 22 | 24 | 28 | 28 | 588 | 1168 | 9.0 |

[a]   For the UK and EC the 1989 figure refers to 1988.
Source: see table 2.2.

Within the Community at large, total receipts have increased at an annual rate of 9 percent during the 1980s. In the Netherlands and Belgium, total receipts increased at a annual rate of over 5 percent. Italy on the other hand experienced an annual, nominal, increase of nearly 12 percent.

In Denmark, 80 percent of the budget is financed out of general revenue. To a lesser extent, general revenue is the main source also in Ireland and the UK. In the Netherlands and France, on the other hand, government is charged for only 17 percent of total expenses. Here, the bulk of the system is financed by burdening the wage bill. Employer borne contributions are relatively dominant in Belgium, France, Germany and Italy. The insured persons themselves pay the largest share in the Netherlands, where their contributions cover 35 percent of social security expenditures.

The relative share of government in financing social security may be indicative of the character of National Social Security Systems. A large share of wage bill financing stresses the insurance character of the system, whereas systems with more of a welfare character are largely financed by general revenue.

More important perhaps is the effect of the share of government contributions on the national economy in general and the labor markets in particular. A relatively large government share implies an equally large "tax-base" for social security contributions, since the burden is spread over the complete range of economic activities, whereas a large share of employer and employee borne contributions implies that social security expenditures put a disproportionate weight on the wage bill. In that case the wedge between gross labor costs and net earnings will be relatively wide with assumedly adverse impacts on the national economy.

### 2.2.2    Labor Market and Income Distribution

Standard neoclassical economic theory claims that the redistribution of primary incomes through the tax-transfer system will elicit behavioral effects, both on the supply side and the demand side of the labor market. Most obvious are the income effects, inducing people to seek benefits when replacement rates go up. Next, there may be entitlement effects, causing some to design their work patterns and living arrangements so as to become eligible for social security. Finally, employer- and employee-borne social insurance contributions add to income tax to produce a sizeable gap between labor costs and net earnings, which is assumed to work as a disincentive for both sides of the labor market. Obviously, social security will also have positive welfare effects. It may contribute to increase welfare by reducing uncertainty, by creating a more equitable income distribution, and by its positive impact on macro-economic stability.[3] Below we will picture some of the phenomena that may be affected by the size and structure of social security.

## Labor Force Participation

Since the bulk of social security spending involves the transfer of incomes from the active to the inactive population, the observed growth of social security systems coincided with increasing inactivity and decreasing labor force participation rates. Table 2.5 presents some international key figures. Note that international differences in the definition of labor force participation may bias these inter-country comparisons.

Table 2.5    Labor Force Participation Rates by Sex and Age in Several OECD Countries. 1970-1990

| | Males | | | | | Females | | | | |
|---|---|---|---|---|---|---|---|---|---|---|
| | 1970 | 1975 | 1980 | 1985 | 1990 | 1970 | 1975 | 1980 | 1985 | 1990 |
| *a. Age 55-64* | | | | | | | | | | |
| Australia | 85 | 79 | 69 | 60 | 63 | 23 | 24 | 22 | 19 | 25 |
| Canada | 84 | 79 | 76 | 70 | 65 | 30 | 31 | 34 | 34 | 36 |
| Finland | 74 | 66 | 57 | 52 | 45 | 46 | 43 | 44 | 46 | 40 |
| France | 75 | 69 | 69 | 50 | 46 | 40 | 36 | 40 | 31 | 31 |
| Germany | 82 | 68 | 66 | 57 | 63[a] | 30 | 25 | 27 | 23 | 26[a] |
| Ireland | 91[b] | 84 | 79[b] | 75 | 71[d] | 21[b] | 21 | 20[c] | 18 | 17[a] |
| Japan | 87 | 86 | 85 | 83 | 83 | 44 | 44 | 45 | 45 | 47 |
| Netherlands | 81[b] | 72 | 63 | 47 | 43 | 15[b] | 14 | 14 | 14 | 17 |
| Spain | 84[e] | 80 | 76 | 67 | 62 | 22[e] | 23 | 21 | 20 | 20 |
| Sweden | 85 | 82 | 79 | 76 | 75 | 45 | 49 | 55 | 60 | 66 |
| United Kingdom | 88[b] | 88 | 82 | 69 | 68 | 40[b] | 40 | 39 | 35 | 39 |
| United States | 81 | 75 | 71 | 67 | 67 | 42 | 41 | 41 | 42 | 45 |
| *b. Total* | | | | | | | | | | |
| Australia | 92 | 90 | 88 | 85 | 86 | 46 | 50 | 53 | 54 | 62 |
| Canada | 87 | 87 | 88 | 86 | 86 | 41 | 51 | 58 | 64 | 69 |
| Finland | 88 | 84 | 83 | 82 | 81 | 64 | 68 | 70 | 74 | 73 |
| France | 87 | 85 | 83 | 79 | 73 | 50 | 53 | 56 | 56 | 58 |
| Germany | 93 | 87 | 84 | 80 | 83[a] | 48 | 50 | 50 | 50 | 55[a] |
| Ireland | 97[b] | 91 | 89[c] | 86 | 83[d] | 35[b] | 35 | 36[c] | 37 | 38[d] |
| Japan | 89 | 90 | 89 | 88 | 88 | 55 | 52 | 55 | 57 | 60 |
| Netherlands | 86[b] | 82 | 78 | 76 | 76 | 30[b] | 32 | 36 | 41 | 45 |
| Italy | 82 | 80 | 81 | 78 | 77 | 29 | 30 | 39 | 41 | 44 |
| Spain | 93[e] | 91 | 88 | 83 | 79 | 32[e] | 34 | 34 | 35 | 42 |
| Sweden | 91 | 91 | 90 | 88 | 89 | 61 | 69 | 76 | 80 | 84 |
| United Kingdom | 94[b] | 93 | 92 | 88 | 89 | 56[b] | 59 | 62 | 63 | 68 |
| United States | 90 | 88 | 88 | 87 | 88 | 50 | 55 | 61 | 66 | 70 |

[a]  1987.
[b]  1971.
[c]  1981.
[d]  1989.
[e]  1972.
Source:   OECD (1991, pp. 468-499).

Among the countries listed male labor force participation rates indeed have decreased over the period considered. The mid-1980s however mark a turning point in most countries. As of then, the decline of male labor force participation has been stabilized in many countries and even turned into an increase in some.

Canada and Japan, both countries with relatively low participation rates in 1970, showed a very small decrease. The sharpest initial reduction, 13 percentage points, can be observed in Germany and Spain. With an initial reduction of 10 points, the decrease has not been extremely large in the Netherlands. However, since Dutch male participation rates came down from a rather low level in 1970, the result has been a position at the bottom line in 1985.

During the late 1980s, male participation rates went up in four of the countries listed, most notably in Germany (up 3 points). The decline continued in five countries. In France and Spain, with a decline of 6 and 4 points, respectively, no reversal of the historical trend occurred. Although the Dutch male participation rate did not go down any further, by the end of the decade, it still is among the lowest rates observed internationally.

Among the older male population participation rates have fallen dramatically in most countries. The largest decline in older male labor force participation can be observed in the Netherlands where participation diminished with 38 points to a level of 43 percent. Finland and France also show sizeable reductions of 29 points. The other countries rank somewhere in between with reductions varying from 14 points in the USA to 22 points in Australia. Japan, showing a decrease of only 4 points, and Sweden, where older male participation fell no more than 10 points, are the exceptions to this general picture. Some countries showed a gradual decrease in older male participation. In Germany, however, the major part of the decrease has been realized in the early seventies, whereas in France and the United Kingdom the decline is largely concentrated in the early eighties. Although, in the late 1980s, older males' participation rates went up again in Australia (up 3 points) and, most notably, in Germany (up 6 points), the general picture is one of continuing decline be it at a lower pace. By the end of the 1980 decade, older male participation rates range from 43 percent in the Netherlands to 83 percent in Japan. Note that the difference between the Dutch and German rates is no less than 20 points.

Female participation rates show a rather different pattern. In all countries listed female participation rates have increased over the period considered. Large increases can be observed in Canada (29 points), the United States (20 points) and Sweden (23 points). The Swedish increase is particularly remarkable since already in 1970 Swedish female participation rates were the highest among the countries listed. With 84 percent of the female population participating in 1990, Swedish women appear to be far more involved in labor market activities than French, Dutch, or Italian men. In 1970, Dutch female labor participation was no more than 30 percent and apart from the Italian rate the lowest of all countries listed. By 1990, it had increased to 45 percent, which still is a rather low figure with only Ireland,

Spain and Italy showing lower rates. An adjustment of the female participation rates to take account of the actual number of work hours would seriously affect this picture. Female parttime work is a wide spread phenomenon in the Netherlands and the Scandinavian countries. With 55 percent of all Dutch participating women working parttime, as opposed to for instance, 30 percent in Germany or 26 percent in the United Kingdom, the adjusted Dutch 1990 female participation rate would reduce to about 33 percent. In 1987, in an EC ranking based on actual work hours instead of working persons, Dutch female labor force participation amounted to no more than 26 percent. Only Spanish females put in less market hours (24 percent).[4]

Among older women participation patterns differ more strongly. In 1990, older female rates range from 17 percent in the Netherlands and Ireland to 66 percent in Sweden. Over the 1970-1990 period, decreases (France: - 9 points) as well as increases can be observed. Again, the Swedish figure, showing an increase of 21 points, is remarkable. The labor force participation rate among older Dutch females has been at the bottom line throughout the entire period.

As compared to the countries listed in table 2.5, Dutch labor force participation rates, both male and female, are among the lowest. This was true in 1970 and still was the case in 1990. It holds for the population in the 55-64 age group as well as for the entire population of working age years. The decrease in Dutch male participation rates is among the largest observed, and is reflected by an internationally high level of Disability program participation (see section 2.4.2 below). Dutch female rates, although substantially increasing, still appear to be fairly low too.

### Income Policy Aspects

Social security financing and spending affect the income distribution. Some of these distributional effects will be reviewed below.

In 1985, the Dutch tax-transfer system produced a wedge between gross labor costs and net earnings, amounting to 50 percent of gross labor cost for a modal worker. Employer borne social insurance contributions account for about half of the wedge, the other half is borne by employees through income tax and social insurance contributions. The marginal wedge, i.e., the marginal burden of income tax plus social insurance premiums, amounted to nearly 50 percent at the minimum wage level and 61 percent at the modal wage level. This implies that a one guilder rise in net earnings leads to a rise in labor cost by Dfl. 2.00 at the minimum, and by Dfl. 2.56 at the modal level. In 1980, the marginal wedge amounted to 49% for the minimum wage and to 53% for the modal wage. Tax-reforms have brought about a decline in marginal rates to 46% for both the modal and the minimum wage level in 1990 (table 2.6, panel a).

The wedge between labor costs and net earnings is created by taxes and social security contributions levied over the wage bill. Table 2.6 (panel b) illustrates how income tax and social security contributions affect the net hourly wages of industrial

workers in the European Community in 1988/1989. The comparison is based on
hourly wage rates in the industrial sector expressed in Purchasing Power Parities.
The Dutch tax and social security burdens appear to be rather similar to that of
Germany. In Germany, gross hourly labor costs are 3 points higher, gross earnings
are 1 point higher, whereas a single person's net income is about the same. The
main difference is the 5 points extra net wage for the German one-income couple
with two children. In both countries the total wedge is about 10 points higher than
in the United Kingdom. The difference with France is approximately 5 points.

Table 2.6    Gross Labor Costs, Gross Wages and Net Wages in the Netherlands
(1980-1990) and in Selected EC-countries (1988/1989)

a.  **Annual Labor Costs, Gross and Net Earnings for a Modal Worker (Single Earner, Family
Allowances Excluded) in the Netherlands 1980-1990**

|  | 1980 | 1985 | 1990 |
|---|---|---|---|
| gross labor costs (Dfl) | 42,718 (100) | 51,123 (100) | 53,562 (100) |
| gross earnings (Dfl) | 33,500  (78) | 40,000  (78) | 42,000  (78) |
| net earnings (Dfl) | 22,760  (53) | 25,375  (50) | 28,607  (53) |
| employee borne contributions as a percentage of gross earnings | | | |
| - average rate | 32 % | 37 % | 32 % |
| - marginal rate | 53 % | 61 % | 46 % |

b.  **Gross Hourly Labor Costs, Gross and Net Earnings of Average Fulltime Industrial Workers
in Selected EC-Countries in PPS 1988/1989 (NL=100)**

|  | Netherlands | Belgium | France | Germany | United Kingdom | Denmark |
|---|---|---|---|---|---|---|
| labor costs[a] (PPS) | 11.53 (100) | 92 | 89 | 103 | 94 | 97 |
| gross earnings (PPS) | 9.57 (100) | 93 | 81 | 101 | 99 | 111 |
| net earnings[b] (PPS) | | | | | | |
| - single person | 6.17 (100) | 94 | 96 | 100 | 112 | 93 |
| - one-income couple with 2 children | 7.15 (100) | 113 | 97 | 105 | 110 | 101 |
| wedge (% of labor costs) | | | | | | |
| - single person | 46.5 | 45.1 | 42.5 | 47.9 | 36.4 | 48.8 |
| - one-income couple with 2 children | 38.0 | 23.6 | 32.3 | 37.0 | 27.6 | 35.3 |

[a]   Calculated applying the macro-proportion of employer borne social security contributions.
[b]   Family allowances included. Calculated applying the 1989 rates on the 1988 values of gross
hourly wages.
Sources:  Tweede Kamer A (1991); Tweede Kamer B (1987); Eurostat (1991); OECD (1990).

In Belgium the one-earner family appears to be relatively mildly taxed at least when the comparison is based on hourly industrial wages as is the case here. In Denmark the single person wedge is larger and the one-earner family wedge smaller than in the Netherlands. The composition of the wedge differs among the countries listed. The employers' share is is comparatively high in France, while in the United Kingdom and Denmark the employers' wedge is relatively small (see also table 2.4).

Another important distributional aspect of the social security system is the extent to which it succeeds at guaranteeing an adequate minimum income level. Table 2.7 shows how the net amount of (welfare) benefits at this minimum level in the Netherlands compares with five other EC-countries. The figures refer to 1988. The comparison can only be tentative due to international differences in welfare program definitions that are not accounted for.[5]

Table 2.7    Net Social Minimum (Welfare) Benefits in EC-Countries, Relative to the Netherlands (1988)[a]

|  | Netherlands | Belgium | France | Germany | United Kingdom | Denmark |
|---|---|---|---|---|---|---|
| Household type: |  |  |  |  |  |  |
| Single person | 100 | 78 | 61 | 70 | 57 | 53 |
| One parent family with 2 children | 100 | 84 | 72 | 94 | 73 | 92 |
| Married couple |  |  |  |  |  |  |
| - no children | 100 | 73 | 64 | 76 | 62 | 74 |
| - 2 children | 100 | 90 | 77 | 101 | 81 | 104 |

[a]    Based on the EC Purchasing Power Standard, Childcare Allowances are included, Rent subsidies are excluded.
Source: Tweede Kamer A (1990, p. 97); Korpel et al. (1989, pp. 45-52).

In the Netherlands, social security benefits at the minimum level appear to be relatively high. The amount of minimum benefits provided to single person households is considerably higher than elsewhere. One parent families also appear to be relatively well off in the Netherlands. On the other hand, the differences for married couples with dependent children are relatively small. They receive a similar amount of benefits in Germany, and a 4 percent higher amount in Denmark. In general, the differences with the neighboring countries range from 27 to 10 percentage points in Belgium, and from 30 to 0 percentage points in Germany.

The social minimum puts a floor in the distribution of (net) wages. In the Netherlands the net minimum benefit amount for families was equated with the net minimum wage in the early seventies. Since Dutch wages, including the minimum wage, are heavily taxed, labor costs at the minimum wage level are rather high, thus causing a high floor in the distribution of gross wages. This high level of gross minimum wages may have a compressing effect on the wage distribution as is suggested by table 2.8 that shows an inverse relation between the inter-sector variation of wage costs and the relative size of the minimum wage. The Dutch, Danish, and Swedish wage distributions are characterized by small coefficients of variation and relatively high minimum wage levels, whereas in France, where the social minimum is relatively low, the coefficient of wage variation is rather high.

Table 2.8    The Inter-Sector Variation of Wage Costs and the Relative Size of the Minimum Wage in Several OECD Countries, 1985.

| | Coefficient inter-sector variation of wage costs | minimum wage as a percentage of average wage costs |
|---|---|---|
| Netherlands | .19 (2)[a] | .54 (2)[a] |
| Germany | .21 (4) | .39 (4) |
| Denmark | .17 (1) | .56 (1) |
| Sweden | .19 (3) | .47 (3) |
| France | .26 (5) | .36 (5) |
| United States | .37 (6) | .32 (6) |
| Japan | .72 (7) | .29 (7) |

[a]  Ranking between parentheses.
Source: Tweede Kamer B (1991, p. 82).

### Distributional Aspects
A comparative analysis of the impact of the tax-transfer system on the size distribution of income among a number OECD countries shows that cash transfers indeed play an important role in reducing income inequality by providing income support to the lowest income households [Saunders & Klau (1985, pp. 207-228)].[6] In the Netherlands too, the system of transfers to and from government and social insurance funds reduces income inequality. In 1977, the Dutch tax-transfer system causes a decrease of the Gini-coefficient by 47 percent, from .508 to .270. Social security transfers alone reduce the Gini by 37 percent [Odink (1983)]. In terms of the Gini-coefficient, the Dutch size distribution of net household income in the late 1970s probably is flatter than that of any other OECD country. At least it seems to be flatter than that of Sweden (.30, in 1979), Denmark (.30, in 1976), the United Kingdom (.32, in 1979), Germany (.37, in 1974), Ireland (.32, in 1973), Spain (.37, in 1973-74) and France (.39, in 1975).[7]

## 2.3      Outline of the Dutch Social Security System

### 2.3.1      Introduction

Within the Dutch Social Security System a distinction is made between social insurance programs and social, or "welfare", provisions. The difference between these two kinds of arrangements lies in their administration and financing modes. Social insurance benefits are financed by compulsory contributions. The premiums are determined under a pay-as-you-go system. Social Insurance administration rests with trade-unions and employers' organizations. Social provisions, on the other hand, are financed by general revenue, and administered by (local) government. Social insurance schemes can be further divided into national programs, covering all residents, and programs that only cover private sector employees. Civil servants have their own arrangements, which are partly capital-funded.

The principle of solidarity, and the constitutionally established responsibility of the state to protect its residents from poverty, may be regarded as the fundament of the Dutch Social Security System. The plight to protect is represented by two functions of the social security system: wage-replacement, and minimum income (basic needs) guarantees. The wage-replacing function is based on mutual solidarity among private sector employees and their employers to protect the employees' acquired standards of living. Wage-replacing schemes for private sector employees are social insurance programs covering loss of earnings due to unemployment (WW), sickness (ZW), or disability (AAW and WAO).

National insurance and welfare programs safeguard the subsistence levels (basic needs) of all residents in case of old age (AOW, if over 65, national insurance), disability (AAW, national insurance), death of breadwinner (AWW, national insurance), insufficient means (ABW, welfare), and unemployment not covered by social insurance (RWW, welfare). National insurance programs are financed by mandatory contributions of all income recipients; welfare provisions are funded by general revenue.

Next to income maintenance, medical and child care expenses are also covered by social insurance schemes. The health costs of private sector employees earning less than a certain gross wage (currently Dfl 50,150 per year) are covered by the Health Cost Insurance program (ZFW, social insurance). Exceptional medical expenses, such as institutionalization, are covered by national insurance (AWBZ). Finally, a quarterly child care allowance (AKW) is financed by general revenue.

### 2.3.2      The Social Minimum

The social minimum is defined as the amount of money considered necessary to provide for one's basic needs. Basic needs are assumed to depend on age and household composition. The social minimum is directly linked to the after tax statutory minimum wage. It establishes a safety net in the social security system. The social minimum for a two person household, with or without children, is 100 percent of the net minimum wage; for single parent families the social minimum amounts to 90 percent; for single persons it is 70 percent.[8] Before the 1987 System Reform, the wage-replacing schemes contained a minimum income guarantee, at least for married employees. Hence, if a disability or unemployment benefit for an employee with dependents would fall short of the net minimum wage, he or she would get a minimum income allowance. During the 1970s, these allowances were granted to all disability and unemployment beneficiaries, whether breadwinner or not. Making these allowances dependent on household composition, was one of the earlier retrenchments (see section 2.5 below).

Consequently, the generosity of the Dutch Social Security System strongly hinges upon the level and development of the statutory minimum wage. When, in the early 1970s, the purchasing power of minimum wages was raised faster than average wages, real benefits went along. When, in the late 1970s, minimum wages were adjusted yearly to changes in the cost of living, so were benefits.

### 2.3.3  Early Retirement

A strict definition of the social security system would not include early retirement programs. However, since its introduction in 1975, early retirement has become an important alternative both to continued labor force participation and to enrolment in unemployment or disability programs for the older members of the labor force. The Early Retirement Program (the "Vervroegde Uittredingsregeling", VUT) was introduced as an element of collective bargaining agreements between trade unions and employers. It was designed to increase employment opportunities for unemploy- ed youth by stimulating the early retirement of elderly employees. While all civil servants are covered by an early retirement scheme, coverage among privately employed is restricted to approximately 70 percent (1986). Coverage appears to be associated with the size of the employing firms since only 50 percent of all firms are participating in an early retirement program. Eligibility criteria differ among industries. The average minimum age of entitlement has declined from 63, original- ly, to 61 in most industries. ER-benefit entitlements further depend on duration of current employment. Under most ER-programs a minimum employment duration of 10 years is required. The after tax benefit-wage ratio differs between the various programs ranging from 85 to 100 percent.[9] ER-benefits are earnings tested.

Indicative of the relevance of early retirement schemes may be the fact that 48 percent of all non-participating males in the relevant age group of 60-64 years are receiving Early Retirement Benefits, whereas 12 percent are receiving Unemployment benefits and 40 percent DI-benefits. These figures refer to 1988. In 1980 the ER-share in non-participation was only 9 percent and the DI-share still was about 78 percent.[10]

Most Early Retirement provisions are financed on a pay-as-you-go basis. In the public sector they are administered by pension funds. In the private sector their administration is in the hands of private pension funds, or single employers, or they are clustered into branch-wise, specialized, Early Retirement funds. In 1985 the pension funds accounted for 50 percent of the ER outlays, branch-wise ER-funds administered 30 percent, and single employer funds accounted for the remaining 20 percent. ER provisions are covered by a 1.5 percent wage bill contribution. Less than two thirds of this contribution is employee borne [Bolhuis et al. (1987)].

### 2.3.4   Unemployment

Until 1987, a private sector employee's risk of earnings' loss due to unemployment was covered by three unemployment programs. The first six months of an unemployment spell were, and still are, covered by Unemployment Insurance (UI, in Dutch WW). Unemployment Insurance benefits replace a fixed percentage (80 percent in 1980, currently 70 percent) of pre-unemployment earnings up to a maximum of Dfl. 260 per work day. To obtain UI-coverage an employee should have been gainfully employed for at least 130 days in the course of the year preceding unemployment.[11] Eligibility is contingent on coverage, and on the absence of liability of the insured for his or her job loss. The latter requirement implies that the unemployed should be laid off against their will and, second, that they are obliged to search for re-employment opportunities, and to accept all "commensurate" job offers. Whether a particular job offer is considered "commensurate" depends on education, work history, age, previous income, area of residence, and actual duration of the unemployment spell. The law is not very explicit about these criteria. The implication of particular aspects of "commensurateness" is determined by jurisprudence and, moreover, seems to depend on general economic and other societal conditions. Discharges are subject to the approval of local labor market agencies ("Gewestelijke Arbeidsbureaus"). In general, employers will not be granted a permit for a lay-off unless the job -not the worker- has become redundant or unless personal work relations have been seriously damaged.

After lapse of the UI-period, the jobless employee could apply for Unemployment Provision (UP, in Dutch WWV). Coverage under UP was defined somewhat broader than UI-coverage, as it also took care of workers who had not (yet) gained full coverage under civil servant schemes. Due to its welfare character, UP, in flagrant contradiction with equal treatment, excluded married women from entitlement, unless they were breadwinners. After successful litigation, married women were granted full UP-entitlements as of 1985.

During this second stage of the unemployment spell the benefits-wage ratio was 75 percent until 1985, and 70 percent hence. Originally, until a few years before the System Reform, the maximum duration of UP-benefits was two years for all entitled. As of 1975, employees over 58 remained eligible until age 65. In 1983, preluding the Reform, maximum UP-duration was limited to 6 months for those under 23. In 1985, the age-dependency of maximum UP-durations was further emphasized by introducing a one year maximum for 23-30 year olds and 1.5 year maximum for 30-35 year olds. Only those 35 and over kept their entitlements for two years. The involuntariness of unemployment is not an absolutely necessary requirement for UP-entitlement. Wilful unemployment, however, can be penalized by reducing the benefit, or by temporarily suspending benefit payment. By the 1987 Reform the UP-program was abolished or, rather, integrated into the UI-program. As a consequence, the UI-benefit duration, now, depends on age with a maximum of 5 years for those over 59 (see also section 2.5).

After lapse of the UP- or UI-period, those still unemployed may turn to social assistance under the Unemployment Welfare Provisions scheme (UWP-scheme, in Dutch RWW). The UWP is a welfare provision at the subsistence level defined by the social minimum. Every job seeking resident over 16 is entitled to UWP-benefits, independent of work history. UWP-benefits are fully means tested. The test includes income and wealth, both of the job seeker, and his or her household members.

Entry to any of the above unemployment schemes is contingent upon the availability of the applicant for work. Continuation of unemployment benefits depends on evidence of regular, unsuccessful, job search activities. To obtain, and keep, eligibility, therefore, a job seeker should register at a local labor market agency. These governmental agencies aim at mediating between employers and job seekers.

### 2.3.5   Ill Health: Sickness and Disability

Private sector employees who are incapable to perform their current jobs because of illness or injury, are entitled to Sickness (ZW) Benefits. Until 1985, Sickness Benefits replaced 80 percent of earnings. As of 1985, the replacement rate is 70 percent but collective bargaining agreements between employers and employees normally stipulate that Sickness Benefits should be supplemented up to the level of net earnings.[12] 95 percent of all employers provide supplementary Sickness Benefits. Sickness Benefits run out after twelve months. They are not means tested.

Most of the sickness spells are of relatively short duration; 80 percent take no more than a fortnight. The share of long-term spells in the Sickness Benefit outlays, however, is substantial. Nearly 30 percent of all sickness days are accounted for by 2 percent of the spells of at least 365 days. These spells usually result in enrolment in the DI-program. Another 20 percent of all sickness days are accounted for by spells that last between 92 and 365 days [Groothoff (1986)].

After the mandatory waiting period of twelve months, one can apply for Disability Insurance benefits (DI-benefits, in Dutch AAW/WAO). The risk covered by the DI-program is defined as the income loss due to the incapacity to perform *any* commensurate employment, not just the incapacity to perform one's current work. Dutch law defines as disabled "a person who -as a consequence of illness or injury-, fully or partly, is unable to earn -with labor which is commensurate to his strength and capabilities and which, with respect to his training and work history, he can reasonably be asked to perform at the place where he works or at a similar place-what physically and mentally healthy persons in otherwise similar circumstances usually earn" [Emanuel et al. (1984)]. As a consequence, the extent to which a particular person is considered disabled does not only depend on physical and mental health status, but also on education, work history, previous income, and other factors.

The degree of disability is determined by measuring an applicant's "earning capacity", i.e., the amount of labor income a disabled person would be able to earn with commensurate work, expressed as a percentage of the income earned by healthy, but otherwise similar, persons. The degree of disability, then, is the complement of earning capacity.

The first tranche of DI-benefits is provided under the National Disability Pensions Act (AAW) enacted in 1976. Its introduction concluded the era of expansion of the social security system. The AAW-program covers all residents, aged 18-64, whether privately, publicly, or self-employed. Moreover, AAW also covers the supply of provisions in kind. These provisions may be work-oriented, i.e. aiming at maintenance or recovery of productive potential, or oriented towards improvement of conditions for independent living. Such provisions which account for only 4 percent of total AAW-expenditures are left unconsidered in this study.[13]

AAW-benefit entitlement depends on gainful activity as witnessed by the claimant's earnings in the year preceding disablement. This eligibility criterion does not apply to those who are handicapped congenitally, or who became handicapped in early childhood.

AAW-benefit size is derived from the social minimum. Before the 1987 Reform, the base amount determining AAW-benefit entitlements depended on household composition and household earnings. From the inception of the AAW-program, the existing disability provisions for private and public sector employees (WAO and ABP-pensions), which are earnings related, became supplementary to the minimum AAW-benefit. If a disabled worker were to be granted a full disability benefit, equalling 80 percent of his gross wage in 1980, then the base minimum part of his benefit would be financed by the general disability (AAW) fund, while only the above minimum part, from the minimum up to 80 percent of the gross wage, would be supplemented by the WAO and ABP funds.

The AAW-program distinguishes six disability classes, contingent on severity of disability, ranging from 0%-25%, 25%-35%, etc., via 65%-80%, to 80%-100%. Hence, the minimum degree of disability yielding entitlement to AAW-benefits is 25 percent. Before 1985, partial AAW-benefits ranged from 20 percent of full (social minimum) benefits in the 25-35 category, to 80 percent of the social minimum in the 80-100 category.

Next to AAW-coverage, privately employed workers enjoy supplemental coverage through the WAO-program, that provides the second tranche of DI-benefits. Under this program, seven disability categories are being distinguished, ranging from 0%-15%, 15%-25%, etc., via 65%-80%, to 80%-100%. The minimum degree of disability yielding entitlement to WAO-benefits is 15 percent. In 1980, wage replacement rates ranged from 9 percent of gross earnings in the 15-25 category, to 80 percent of gross earnings in the 80-100 category. During the first year of DI-entitlement, 56 percent of all employers provide supplementary disability benefits up to between 90 to 100 percent of after tax earnings.

Disability assessments are made by an independent medico-vocational body, the Joint Medical Service (JMS, in Dutch, Gemeenschappelijke Medische Dienst, GMD). On matters of disability (AAW or WAO) insurance claims, whether benefits or provisions in kind, the relevant insurance boards ("Industrial Associations", see below) are obliged to consult the JMS.

As Sickness and Disability Insurance benefits are administered by the same insurance boards, application for DI-benefits by privately employed workers is only a matter of form. At the end of the one year DI-waiting period - covered by Sickness Benefits - DI-benefit application, and the documentation needed by JMS to make a disability assessment, is administratively prepared, without a beneficiary's interference.

### 2.3.6   The Labor Market Consideration in Disability Assessment

Under the definition of disability used in the AAW/WAO-programs, adjudicators of disability benefits find it difficult to make disability assessments as accurate as suggested by the number, and width, of the legal disability categories. Theoretically, estimates of remaining earning capacities should be made on the basis of a claimant's medical and vocational characteristics, and a catalogue of commensurate jobs, whether vacant or not. Such theoretical assessments, however, will diverge from "actual" earning capacities if commensurate jobs are not made available to partially disabled persons. A disabled person's poor employment opportunities, then, may result from discriminatory behavior of employers, and, therefore, may be indirectly attributable to the claimant's mental or physical impairment. Moreover, reluctance to employ the partially disabled will be reinforced under conditions of general unemployment. A second problem in disability assessment, then, is to determine whether unemployability of the partially disabled is due to impairment proper, or to, often inextricable, combinations of impairment and unemployment.

Before Reform, the law recognized the potential discrepancy between theoretical and actual earning capacities. It stipulated that the adjudicators, in their assessments of the degree of disability, should take account of the difficulties partially disabled persons might experience in finding commensurate employment. This legal provision is usually referred to as the "labor market consideration" ("Verdiscontering van werkloosheid") in the AAW- and WAO-programs.

In daily practice, however, proper application of this provision turned out to be impossible for the two assessment problems mentioned above. As of 1973, this administrative problem was solved by coarsely assuming that poor employment opportunities result from discriminatory behavior, unless the contrary can be proven. As a rule, the ensuing administration practice was equally coarse; partially disabled applicants were treated as if they were fully disabled.

This interpretation of the law made accurate assessments of theoretical earning capacities unnecessary as a minimum degree of 25 percent (for self-employed claimants under AAW) or 15 percent (for privately employed claimants under WAO) would be sufficient to entitle a person to full DI-benefits. As a matter of fact, the JMS is not equipped to examine all "applications" for DI-benefits explicitly and to provide the Industrial Associations with comprehensive recommendations on the disability status and rehabilitative potential of ailing workers. Therefore, the mandatory consultation procedure is often reduced to a formal, paper, announcement of application by the Industrial Associations. On agreement, this condensed procedure suffices in "clear cut" cases, i.e., cases in which the Industrial Associations have reason to assume that the worker involved will either be able to resume his current job within the near future or will never be able to perform any commensurate work at all. In practice, approximately 50 percent of all annual DI-benefits awards are dealt with following this reduced procedure (see chapter 5).

### 2.3.7     Social Security Administration and Financing

The administration of social security in the Netherlands is allocated to two kinds of bodies. In general, social insurances are administered by autonomous insurance boards, and financed through separate funds, whereas the administration of social provision (welfare) schemes rests with (local) government agencies, their expenditures being covered by general revenue.

As concerns their administration, social insurance programs can be broken down into two categories:
- schemes covering the work-related risks of unemployment, sickness, and disability;
- schemes covering the "demographic risks" of old age and loss of spouse or parents.

The administration of the work-related social insurances (Unemployment Insurance, Sickness Benefits, Disability (AAW/WAO) Insurance) is delegated to 23 insurance boards, representing different branches of industry. These "Industrial (Insurance) Associations" (bedrijfsverenigingen) are managed by representatives of employer organizations and trade unions. They have discretion to develop autonomous benefit award policies. Collective strategies are formed through directives of the Federation of Industrial Associations.

The Industrial Associations are supervised by the Social Security Council (Sociale Verzekeringsraad). Trade unions, employer organizations, and independent government appointees, have equal shares in the membership of the Social Security Council. The Council effectuates its supervisory power by issuing directives to the Industrial Associations. The Council also supervises the boards of the Unemployment and Disability Insurance Funds (in Dutch, Algemeen Werkloosheidsfonds, AWF and Algemeen Arbeidsongeschiktheidsfonds, AOF). These boards make bi-yearly calculations of the payroll tax rates necessary to cover program expenditures. Next to supervision, the Council also has advisory tasks. Government is obliged to consult the Council on matters of social security policy, part of which is the bi-yearly assessment of social insurance premiums.[14] Government may, however, depart from, or downright ignore, the Council's recommendations. Moreover, the Minister of Social Affairs and Employment autonomously determines the division of the burden of social insurance contributions between employers and employees.

The National Insurance programs for old-age and survivors' benefits (AOW and AWW), are administered by the Social Security Institute (Sociale Verzekeringsbank). This administrative body is also run by employers' and employees' representatives. Management of the Old Age and Survivors' Pension Funds, rests with the Social Security Institute, under supervision of the Social Security Council.

National Assistance (welfare) programs (Welfare, Unemployment Provisions, Unemployment Welfare Provisions, etc.) are administered by municipalities under supervision of the Minister of Social Affairs and Employment.

Claimants may appeal against award determinations at independent, administrative, Courts of Appeal, and, in last instance, at the Central Court of Appeal. Formally, the decisions of this highest instance cannot create law. Their authority, however, is such that they usually have legal precedence.

**Financing**

The pay-as-you-go contribution rates necessary to finance program expenses in 1986 and 1988, are listed below (table 2.9). Some of the contributions are split between employers and employees, others are fully incumbent on one of both parties. Total employers' contributions as a percentage of gross wages amounted to 22.1 percent in 1986 and 19.7 percent in 1988. In 1986 total employees' contributions were 21.6 percent of gross wages (22.1 in 1988). The base amount of earnings covered by AAW was Dfl. 91 per work day. Hence, earnings up to Dfl 91 are exempted from WAO-contribution levies.

Contributions to the Sickness Benefit program (ZW) and to the Unemployment Insurance Program (WW) differ according to branch wise risk groups. In construction, for instance, Sickness Benefit contributions amount to 15 percent, whereas in in the banking sector the rate is about 3 percent (1988). The other insurance funds are fed through uniform contribution levies.

Under the 1987 social security reform, the Unemployment Provision (WWV) scheme, which used to cover medium term (6 to 30 months) unemployment and was financed by general revenues, has been integrated into Unemployment Insurance. UI contribution rates, therefore, have been raised. For 1989, the average UI contribution rates are 1.58 for employers, and 2.98 for employees.

Table 2.9     Social Security Contribution Rates in 1992 as Percentages of Gross Income

|  | | Employers | Employees | Maximum taxable amount of income |
|---|---|---|---|---|
| *National Insurances* | | | | |
| AOW | (Old Age) | | 14.40 | |
| AWW | (Survivors) | | 1.15 | |
| AWBZ | (Medical Expenses) | | 8.30 | 42,966[a] |
| AAW | (Disability) | 6.60[b] | 2.75 | |
| *Employees' Insurances* | | | | |
| ZW[c] | (Sickness Benefits) | 4.00 | 1.20 | |
| WAO[d] | (Disability) | | 13.00 | 284[e] |
| WW[c] | (Unemployment) | 1.20 | 1.20 | |
| VUT[c] | (Early Retirement) | 0.85 | 0.45 | |
| ZFW | (Medical Expenses) | 5.15 | 0.10 | 178[e] |

[a]  Per year.
[b]  This employers' contribution is fictive because it is financed out of general revenue as part of the 1990 tax reform.
[c]  Averaged over branchwise risk groups.
[d]  The first Dfl. 98 per day is exempted from the WAO-premium levy.

## 2.4       The DI-program in National and International Perspective

### 2.4.1       The DI-program in National Perspective

As documented in section 2.2, both the level of spending and the pace of expenditure growth of Dutch social security rank among the highest of all OECD countries. Dutch social security grew in many directions. Between 1965 and 1976 a number of new programs were enacted, extending coverage both in terms of risks and people. During that same decade, benefits rose faster than wages. Hence, real benefits increased.

Table 2.10       Income Recipiency by Work Status, Recipiency Years, Annual Averages (Thousands), 1970-1990

|  | | 1970 | 1975 | 1980 | 1985 | 1990 |
|---|---|---|---|---|---|---|
| *Labor income recipiency:* | | | | | | |
| Employees: | private sector | 3,142 | 3,072 | 3,152 | 3,032 | 3,323 |
|  | public sector[a] | 572 | 637 | 714 | 736 | 734 |
| Self-employed | | 737 | 676 | 625 | 607 | 618 |
| Total | | 4,451 | 4,385 | 4,491 | 4,375 | 4,675 |
| *Transfer income recipiency:* | | | | | | |
| Old age and survivors | | 1,179 | 1,321 | 1,448 | 1,570 | 1,674 |
| Disability | | 196 | 310 | 608 | 698 | 766 |
| Sickness | | 258 | 280 | 306 | 257 | 330 |
| Unemployment | | 58 | 197 | 235 | 650 | 526 |
| Social Assistance | | 70 | 117 | 117 | 183 | 182 |
| Total | | 1,761 | 2,225 | 2,714 | 3,358 | 3,478 |
| *Total income recipiency* | | 6,212 | 6,610 | 7,205 | 7,733 | 8,153 |
| Transfer recipiency as % of total income recipiency | | 28.3 | 33.7 | 37.7 | 43.4 | 42.7 |
| of which: | | | | | | |
| disability recipiency | | 3.1 | 4.7 | 8.4 | 9.0 | 9.9 |
| unemployment recipiency | | 0.9 | 3.0 | 3.3 | 8.4 | 6.5 |

[a]   Including Sickness Payments to civil servants.
Sources: Min. SoZaWe (1991); Tweede Kamer A (1991); Centraal Planbureau (1991).

The behavioral effects that are prompted by the presence of social security per se were presumably exacerbated by exogenous factors, such as the economic recessions of 1975 and 1981-83, population aging, increasing female labor force participation, stronger preferences for part-time work, and changing family structures. The combined effect of these socioeconomic factors has been an impressive growth of transfer recipiency man-years from 1.76 million in 1970 to 3.48 million in 1990 (see table 2.10).[15] Over these two decades the transfer recipiency rate, defined as the number of transfer recipiency years per 100 income recipiency years, grew from 28 to 43 percent. Disability transfer recipiency has increased from 3.1 to 9.9 out of every 100 income recipiency years. It grew sharply in the late 1970s (from 4.7 to 8.4). In the early 1980s, when the growth of disability income recipiency flattened, unemployment started soaring so that by 1985 8.5 out of each 100 income recipients were receiving unemployment benefits. In the second half of the 1980 decade, an unprecedented employment growth - mainly brought about by a concerted effort of labor unions and employers' organizations to contain labor costs - has induced a decline in unemployment benefit recipiency to 6.5 percent. Overall, the steady growth of transfer recipiency faltered in the mid-1980s and stabilized (with a tendency of decline) at the level of 43 percent in the years thereafter.

As documented before in section 2.2.1, this growth is parallelled by a rapid growth of social security expenditures in the 1970s that leveled off during the 1980 decade. A detailed, programwise, composition of Dutch social security expenditures is presented in table 2.11. In the definition of social security employed here, we include schemes that cover the risk of income loss due to unemployment, sickness, disability, early retirement, old age, and death of breadwinner; and provisions that contribute to the coverage of specific costs, such as medical expenses to prevent or cure illnesses, and child care expenditures. Excluded are the host of other grants and subsidies, such as those for housing, education, and the arts. However, to the extent that income maintenance is the core element of social security, the programs listed in table 2.11 provide a rather complete picture.

Between 1965 and 1975 total expenditures jumped from 12.4 percent of GNP to 23.4 percent. Those were the years of quick expansion. Its budgetary consequences, its effects on disposable income and labor cost, and the mid-seventies recession, made policymakers hesitant to expand the system any further. The 1976-1980 period, then, may be denoted as the years of consolidation. Real growth of social security was less than half the increase in the previous five years. During the 1980-1985 period, social security policy changed from reluctance to expand into an urge to save.[16] As a result, the GNP share of social security stopped growing.

Social Insurance consists of general programs, and programs that only cover wage earners. Civil servants are entered as a separate category since they have special, partly capital-funded, provisions that cover income loss and medical expenses.

The risk of income losses due to disability is covered by the already introduced AAW- and WAO-programs. The AAW-program, enacted in 1976, covers all residents providing minimum disability benefits to self-employed, civil servants, and privately employed workers, whereas the WAO-program covers only privately employed workers, providing DI-benefits supplementary to the AAW base amount. Prior to the introduction of the AAW-program, DI-benefits awarded to private and public sector employees were completely financed through the WAO- and ABP-programs.

As of 1976, the base amount of DI-benefits is financed through AAW, whereas the WAO- and ABP-programs provide for the above minimum amount of DI-benefits. This explains why WAO and ABP expenditures first rise, and then, after 1975, decline.

Table 2.11    Expenditures on Major Social Security Programs in the Netherlands, as Percentage of GNP, 1965-1990

| | 1965 | 1970 | 1975 | 1980 | 1985 | 1990 |
|---|---|---|---|---|---|---|
| *Social Insurance Programs* | | | | | | |
| *General Coverage* | | | | | | |
| Old Age (AOW) | 4.2 | 4.3 | 5.3 | 5.7 | 5.8 | 5.9 |
| Survivors (AWW) | 0.6 | 0.6 | 0.7 | 0.7 | 0.6 | 0.8 |
| Child Allowances (AKW) | 1.9 | 1.9 | 2.0 | 2.1 | 1.8 | 1.2 |
| Disability Insurance (AAW) | n.e[a] | n.e | n.e | 2.0 | 2.6 | 2.8 |
| Exceptional Medical Expenses (AWBZ) | n.e | 0.9 | 1.7 | 2.0 | 2.1 | 2.7 |
| *Private Sector Employees* | | | | | | |
| Unemployment Insurance (WW)[b] | 0.2 | 0.4 | 0.8 | 0.7 | 0.7 | 0.9 |
| Early Retirement | n.e | n.e | n.e | 0.2 | 0.5 | 0.4 |
| Sickness Benefits (ZW) | 1.2 | 1.9 | 2.2 | 2.2 | 1.7 | 2.1 |
| Disability Insurance (WAO) | 1.2[c] | 1.6 | 2.7 | 2.4 | 1.6 | 1.6 |
| Medical Expenses (ZFW) | 2.0 | 2.7 | 3.6 | 3.8 | 3.9 | 3.3 |
| *Public Sector Employees* (ABP)[d] | n.a[e] | 1.3 | 1.7 | 1.5 | 1.2 | 1.2 |
| *Total Social Insurance* | 11.3 | 15.7 | 20.7 | 23.5 | 22.6 | 22.9 |
| *Welfare Programs* | | | | | | |
| Unemployment Provision (WWV)[b] | 0.0 | 0.1 | 0.6 | 0.6 | 1.1 | - |
| Social Assistance for | | | | | | |
| - long term unemployed (RWW) | 0.0 | 0.0 | 0.2 | 0.4 | 1.7 | 1.5 |
| - other contingencies (ABW) | 0.9 | 0.8 | 1.4 | 1.3 | 0.9 | 0.9 |
| Sheltered Employment (WSW) | 0.2 | 0.4 | 0.6 | 0.5 | 0.4 | 0.4 |
| *Total Welfare* | 1.1 | 1.4 | 2.8 | 2.8 | 4.2 | 2.8 |
| *Total Social Security* | 12.4 | 17.0 | 23.4 | 26.4 | 26.8 | 25.9 |
| *Total Social Security + Private Pensions* | n.a | 19.9 | 26.8 | 29.9 | 31.0 | 30.4 |
| *GNP (billions current guilders)* | 68.6 | 121.7 | 219.6 | 335.8 | 413.8 | 509.0 |

[a] n.e.: non existent.
[b] As of 1987, the old UI and UP programs have been replaced by a new unemployment insurance scheme.
[c] IWI and OW (WAO was introduced in 1967).
[d] Includes Unemployment, Early Retirement, Disability, and Old Age Pensions awarded to (former) public sector employees.
[e] n.a.: data not available.
Sources: Tweede Kamer A (various years); CPB (various years).

To get a better picture of disability benefit costs, AAW and WAO expenditures should be summed. Similarly, one should sum the unemployment expenditures of the UI (WW), UP (WWV), and UWP (RWW) programs to get a full grasp of total unemployment benefit outlays. Since these programs cover disjoint contingencies they can be faultlessly added. The same argument holds for the two health cost programs, ZFW (medical expenses) and AWBZ (exceptional medical expenses), and the so-called demographic risks, old age (AOW) and survivors (AWW) benefits and child allowance (AKW), where summation also clarifies the picture.

Table 2.12      Summed Expenditures on Unemployment, Sickness, Disability, Health Cost, Early Retirement and Demographic Programs, as Percentage of GNP, 1965-1990

|  | 1965 | 1970 | 1975 | 1980 | 1985 | 1990 |
|---|---|---|---|---|---|---|
| Unemployment (WW, WWV, RWW) | 0.2 | 0.5 | 1.6 | 1.7 | 3.5 | 2.4 |
| Early Retirement | n.e | n.e | n.e | 0.2 | 0.5 | 0.4 |
| Disability (AAW, WAO) + Sickness (ZW) | 2.4 | 3.5 | 4.9 | 6.6 | 5.9 | 6.5 |
| Medical Expenses (AWBZ, ZFW) | 2.0 | 3.6 | 5.3 | 5.8 | 6.0 | 6.0 |
| Demographic (AOW, AWW, AKW) | 6.7 | 6.8 | 8.0 | 8.5 | 8.2 | 7.9 |
| Total | 11.3 | 14.4 | 19.8 | 22.8 | 24.1 | 23.2 |

Source: See table 2.11

Table 2.12 unambiguously reveals the chronology and composition of expenditure growth; Due to the introduction, in 1968, of the AWBZ program, social security expenditures on health costs rose sharply between 1965 and 1975. Disability expenditures exploded during the seventies and stabilized in the early 1980s, when total expenditure growth was dominated by the increase of unemployment and, to a lesser extent, early retirement expenditures. Between 1985 and 1990, the overall share of the programs included in table 2.12 has been declining from 24.1 to 23.2 percent of GNP. This reduction resulted from a substantial decrease in unemployment outlays and child allowances, large enough to compensate for the renewed increase in disability and sickness expenditures.

With the exception of the demographic risks, the contingencies listed have one characteristic in common. To some extent, each of these risks can be influenced by the choice behavior of the individual members of the insured population. Part of their growth, therefore, may be labelled endogenous and is reflected by the decreasing labor force participation rates that we have documented in section 2.3.

A more detailed breakdown of trends in employment and labor force participation between 1971 and 1990 in the Netherlands is presented in table 2.13. Total labor supply is determined by the potential labor force - i.e., the population aged 15-64, or the participation base - and the participation rates. During the period under study, the baby boom generation entered the potential labor force causing it to grow

Table 2.13          Employment, Labor Force, and Total Population by Sex, in Thousands, Yearly Averages, 1971-1989

|  |  | 1971 | 1975 | 1980 | 1985 | 1989 |
|---|---|---|---|---|---|---|
| *Males* | | | | | | |
| 1 | Employed[a] | 3,507 | 3,423 | 3,527 | 3,363 | 3,643 |
| 2 | Unemployed[a] | 51 | 197 | 209 | 498 | 288 |
| 1+2 | Labor Force | 3,558 | 3,620 | 3,736 | 3,861 | 3,931 |
| 3 | Disabled | 198 | 285 | 442 | 493 | 580 |
| 4 | Students (15-30) | 444 | 519 | 604 | 659 | 657 |
| 5 | Early Retirees (61-64) | n.e | n.e | 21[b] | 59 | 103 |
| 1,2,3,4,5 | Subtotal | 4,200 | 4,424 | 4,804 | 5,072 | 5,271 |
| 6 | Population (15-64) | 4,170 | 4,406 | 4,735 | 5,023 | 5,182 |
| 1/6 | Employment Rate | .84 | .78 | .74 | .67 | .70 |
| (1+2)/6 | Participation Rate | .85 | .82 | .78 | .77 | .76 |
| 7 | Population over 64 | 591 | 626 | 670 | 703 | 749 |
| 8 | Total population | 6,587 | 6,804 | 7,021 | 7,167 | 7,316 |
| *Females* | | | | | | |
| 1 | Employed[a] | 1,268 | 1,354 | 1,608 | 1,814 | 1,979 |
| 2 | Unemployed[a] | 11 | 63 | 117 | 263 | 231 |
| 1+2 | Labor Force | 1,279 | 1,417 | 1,724 | 2,077 | 2,210 |
| 3 | Disabled | 59 | 85 | 138 | 179 | 264 |
| 4 | Students (15-30) | 260 | 349 | 458 | 535 | 533 |
| 5 | Early Retirees (61-64) | n.e | n.e | 1[b] | 1 | 4 |
| 1,2,3,4,5 | Subtotal | 1,598 | 1,851 | 2,321 | 2,792 | 3,011 |
| 6 | Population (15-64) | 4,102 | 4,322 | 4,627 | 4,900 | 5,037 |
| 1/6 | Employment Rate | .31 | .31 | .35 | .37 | .39 |
| (1+2)/6 | Participation Rate | .31 | .33 | .37 | .42 | .44 |
| 7 | Population over 64 | 764 | 848 | 959 | 1,047 | 1,127 |
| 8 | Total population | 6,608 | 6,862 | 7,128 | 7,324 | 7,489 |
| *Total* | | | | | | |
| 1 | Employed[a] | 4,775 | 4,777 | 5,135 | 5,177 | 5,622 |
| 2 | Unemployed[a] | 62 | 260 | 325 | 761 | 519 |
| 1+2 | Labor Force | 4,837 | 5,037 | 5,461 | 5,938 | 6,141 |
| 3 | Disabled | 258 | 370 | 580 | 672 | 845 |
| 4 | Students (15-30) | 704 | 868 | 1,062 | 1,194 | 1,190 |
| 5 | Early Retirees (61-64) | n.e | n.e | 22[b] | 61 | 107 |
| 1,2,3,4,5 | Subtotal | 5,799 | 6,275 | 7,125 | 7,865 | 8,283 |
| 6 | Population (15-64) | 8,272 | 8,728 | 9,362 | 9,922 | 10,219 |
| 1/6 | Employment Rate | .58 | .55 | .55 | .52 | .55 |
| (1+2)/6 | Participation Rate | .58 | .58 | .58 | .60 | .60 |
| 7 | Population over 64 | 1,355 | 1,475 | 1,629 | 1,749 | 1,876 |
| 8 | Total Population | 13,195 | 13,666 | 14,150 | 14,491 | 14,805 |

[a] Including recipients of Sickness Benefits.
[b] Figure refers to 1981; n.e = non existent.
Sources: Min. SoZaWe (various years); Bolhuis et al. (1987).

by 1.95 million persons, or 24 percent. Overall participation expanded only marginally, to 60 percent of the potential labor force. As a result, labor supply grew by 1.3 million persons, or 27 percent. As witnessed by the (un-)employment figures, the Dutch labor market has had steadily increasing difficulties to absorb the growing supply of labor. Total employment, excluding vacancies, grew by 400,000 persons from 1971 to 1985. This growth is fully accounted for by female employment which increased by 550,000, while male employment decreased. The rise in female employment was accompanied by a growing preference for part-time work. Hence, a growing discrepancy between employment in persons and in man-years (see also table 2.10). Although female employment grew impressively, the market was unable to completely digest the increase in women's labor supply. In the period 1971-1985, female labor supply grew by 800,000 and caused an increase in female unemployment of 250,000. In the second half of the last decade the market's ability to absorb labor supply substantially improved. Employment increased at a rate of over 100,000 per year and, while labor force growth faltered, unemployment came down from 761,00 to 519,000.

The increase in female participation to 44 percent, although substantial, has failed to close the gap with female participation rates in other OECD countries as was shown in table 2.5.

Male participation rates have decreased. As an effect of the baby boom generation entering the labor market, male labor supply still grew by 373,000 or 10 percent. The reduction in male participation is concentrated among older workers (over 45), who, during the 1970s, massively retired through the disability program. The latter may be regarded as a grand, and sustained, process of purging the labor force of low productivity workers that otherwise would have been laid off. By entering the DI-program these workers were able to avoid unemployment. Thus, a substantial amount of unemployment has been sheltered in the DI-program.

To an individually variable extent, then, disability and unemployment coincide. Although this coincidence is a general problem in disability insurance, as the disability risk cannot be adequately defined without reference to vocational characteristics,[17] in the Netherlands, this problem was strongly aggravated by the administrative interpretation of the explicit "labor market consideration" in the DI-program. In practice any worker with a chronic ailment was entitled to a full benefit as long as he was unable to find a commensurate job (see the preceding section). This put the gates of the DI-program wide open, while the exits stayed shut as the usual competitive disadvantages of disabled workers were enhanced by vast supply surpluses.

In absolute numbers, the surge of disability was even more prominent among older women. The ensuing reduction of female labor supply, however, was compensated by an increased preference for paid work of women in all age-groups, except those over 60. The older worker's participation trends reflect the increases in both early retirement and disability entitlements.

Due to the traditionally low labor force participation of Dutch married women,[18] overall participation used to be comparatively low too. The recent increase in female labor supply has been counterbalanced by an equally steep decrease in the labor supply of older workers, yielding an overall participation rate which, at 60 percent, has been the lowest among the OECD-countries throughout the decade.

As a consequence of the surge of unemployment in the early 1980s, the employment rate came down to 52 percent in 1985.[19] This is 6 points under the European Community average and 12 points under that of the OECD territory.[20] Although the employment rate had improved by the end of the decade, it is still well below the EC and OECD averages.

### The Disability Insurance Program 1967-1988

In the remainder of this section we will focus on the Dutch Disability Insurance programs for private sector employees (AAW/WAO).

At the end of 1990, the Social Security Council counted 881,600 Disability Social Insurance beneficiaries: 633,200 (or 72 percent) used to be privately employed; 91,200 (or 10 percent) had a history of public sector employment; 58,900 (or 7 percent) were self-employed; and 90,800 (or 10 percent) were registered as "early handicapped". The latter have no work history since their disability occurred prior to working age.

As expected, older workers are vastly overrepresented among the DI-recipients: Almost 70 percent are over 45, and about 40 percent are over 55 (table 2.14). Obviously, the age distribution of DI-beneficiaries strongly contrasts with that of the insured population, consisting of privately employed and (short term) unemployed workers. For instance, among the population at risk only about 20 percent is older than 45.

Table 2.14   Age Distributions of the DI-Beneficiaries and the Insured Population, and Age Specific DI-Dependency Rates, 1980-1990

| Age brackets | DI-beneficiaries | | Insured population | | DI-Dependency rate[a] | |
|---|---|---|---|---|---|---|
| | | | (percentages) | | | |
| | 1980 | 1990 | 1980 | 1990 | 1980 | 1990 |
| 15 - 24 | 2.1 | 1.6 | 25.0 | 25.1 | 1.2 | 0.3 |
| 25 - 34 | 10.2 | 9.7 | 313 | 30.4 | 4.4 | 4.2 |
| 35 - 44 | 16.2 | 19.9 | 21.6 | 24.7 | 9.6 | 10.0 |
| 45 - 54 | 28.0 | 29.5 | 14.8 | 15.3 | 21.1 | 21.1 |
| 55 - 64 | 43.5 | 39.4 | 7.2 | 4.4 | 46.2 | 55.5 |
| Total | 100 | 100 | 100 | 100 | 12.4 | 12.2 |

[a]   Number of DI-beneficiaries as a percentage of the population at risk including the DI-beneficiaries.
Sources:  Annual Reports of AAf and GMD; own calculations.

The dependency rate, reported in the third pair of columns, is defined as the number of beneficiaries as a percentage of the population at risk, including beneficiaries.

In the oldest age-bracket the dependency rate was 46 percent in 1980 and increased to 55 percent by 1990. Presently, in this age-group, more workers are disabled than at work which illustrates the "early retirement" character of the disability scheme.

Table 2.15 contains detailed information on the growth of the DI-program since its introduction in 1967. Its enactment implied the abolition of two more restrictive health-related income replacement programs.[21] Right from the beginning, the program started growing. Indeed a moderate increase up to 200,000 beneficiaries had been anticipated. However, its continued growth far beyond the initial prognosis came as a surprise when it occurred. At an average annual rate of 9 percent in the 1970s and 2 percent in the 1980s, the number of DI-beneficiaries increased to 633,200 by the end of 1990.

Table 2.15      The DI-Program, 1969-1990

| | Average number of benefits (x1,000) | Full Awards as perc. of total | Disability dependency rate per 1,000[a] | Disability incidence rate per 1,000[b] | Terminations through recovery per 1,000 | Disability expenditures as perc. of GNP[c] | After tax repl. rate for modal workers |
|---|---|---|---|---|---|---|---|
| 1969 | 194 | 79.5 | 53 | 13.4 | 38 | 1.4 | –.– |
| 1970 | 215 | 80.6 | 60 | 15.5 | 33 | 1.6 | –.– |
| 1971 | 237 | 81.2 | 61 | 16.0 | 33 | 1.8 | –.– |
| 1972 | 261 | 81.7 | 71 | 16.5 | 31 | 2.0 | –.– |
| 1973 | 287 | 82.8 | 76 | 17.1 | 33 | 2.1 | 80.4 |
| 1974 | 313 | 83.7 | 83 | 18.3 | 30 | 2.3 | 82.3 |
| 1975 | 349 | 84.0 | 92 | 22.1 | 32 | 2.6 | 83.0 |
| 1976 | 383 | 84.3 | 101 | 22.1 | 35 | 2.9 | 85.1 |
| 1977 | 432 | 85.3 | 110 | 21.9 | 34 | 3.5 | 85.0 |
| 1978 | 461 | 85.2 | 117 | 22.6 | 38 | 4.0 | 86.9 |
| 1979 | 486 | 85.0 | 122 | 21.4 | 40 | 4.2 | 86.8 |
| 1980 | 508 | 84.6 | 124 | 20.4 | 42 | 4.4 | 87.0 |
| 1981 | 523 | 84.0 | 125 | 18.7 | 40 | 4.4 | 86.7 |
| 1982 | 535 | 83.3 | 131 | 18.0 | 36 | 4.5 | 84.5 |
| 1983 | 545 | 83.4 | 130 | 14.0 | 32 | 4.4 | 81.3 |
| 1984 | 557 | 83.3 | 130 | 13.9 | 27 | 4.4 | 78.2 |
| 1985 | 563 | 83.2 | 129 | 14.3 | 28 | 4.2 | 72.1 |
| 1986 | 571 | 83.1 | 129 | 13.8 | 24 | 4.1 | 71.3 |
| 1987 | 579 | 81.7 | 129 | 13.7 | 25 | 4.2 | 71.0 |
| 1988 | 592 | 81.1 | 129 | 14.6 | 23 | 4.1 | 70.3 |
| 1989 | 611 | 80.1 | 124 | 16.0 | 27 | 4.0 | 70.0 |
| 1990 | 633 | 79.5 | 122 | 17.6 | 31 | 4.4 | 70.0 |

[a]   DI-beneficiaries included.
[b]   DI-beneficiaries excluded.
[c]   Total expenditures.
Sources: AAf (various years); GMD (various years); Tweede Kamer A (various years); CPB (1990); SVr (various quarters); own calculations.

In the first year after its enactment about 80 percent of beneficiaries were categorized as fully, i.e., 80 - 100 percent, disabled. Hence, they were entitled to full benefits which, until 1985, amounted to 80 percent of before tax earnings. The remaining 20 percent received partial benefits usually as a supplement to reduced earnings. Due to application of the "labor market consideration" the relative number of full beneficiaries gradually increased from 80 in 1970 to around 85 percent in 1980. Since then, the full benefit share gradually declined. In 1990 it was back at its pre-1970 level of 79,5 percent. From these data the 1987 disability amendments aiming at full elimination of labor market considerations from disability assessments appear to have had only a marginal effect.

The DI-dependency rate grew from 53 DI-beneficiaries per 1,000 workers insured in 1969 to 131 per 1,000 in 1982. Since then, DI-dependency gradually declined to a level of 122 per 1,000 in 1990. DI-benefit expenditures grew along to 4.5 percent of GNP in 1982, and subsequently declined to 4.0 percent in 1989. The 0.4 increase in 1990 is mainly caused by an increase in the number of AAW-beneficiaries. While the DI-dependency rate hardly declined, the substantial decrease of the GNP-share of DI-benefit expenditures in the mid-1980s reflects the retrenchments on real DI-benefit income as of 1982 (see section 2.5).

Although both the DI-dependency rate and the GNP-share of DI-benefit expenditures are valid measures of program growth, a more precise index is the "DI-incidence rate", defined as the relative frequency of new DI-awards, and the "termination incidence rate", analogously defined as the annual rate at which DI-beneficiaries leave the DI-program. The annual flows in and out of the DI-program explain the trends in DI-dependency and DI-expenditures. After a steady increase from 13.4 new awards per 1,000 insured in 1969 to 22.6 per 1,000 in 1978, the DI-incidence rate dropped to 14 per mill within less than five years, which is lower than ever during the 1970 decade. In the late 1980s, DI-incidence rates started growing again, partly as a consequence of aging of the insured population.

The recovery rate shows a pattern that corresponds to the award incidence rate. First an increase from over approximately 33 per 1,000 beneficiaries in 1970 to 42 per 1,000 in 1980, than a decrease to reach a minimum of 23 per mill in 1988. Probably as a result of the 1987 amendments, the relative number of recoveries increased again to 31 over the last years of the decade.

Until 1985, before-tax DI-benefits replaced 80 percent of gross pre-disability earnings. The after tax replacement rate steadily increased until 1980 when the first benefit cuts were implemented. The increase was mainly due to the fact that, until 1980, DI-beneficiaries were exempted from paying correspondingly increasing DI-program contributions. As a result, the purchasing power of a modal DI-beneficiary grew by 16 percent whereas real modal wages increased by only 7 percent during the late seventies.

The data in the fourth and last columns of table 2.15 reveal a remarkable concurrence of real benefit cuts and reduced DI-incidence rates in the early 1980s.

These simultaneously occurring reductions suggest that benefit cuts have discouraged workers to claim, or accept, DI-benefits. As will be argued in section 2.5,
the decrease in DI-incidence probably also results from a gradually less lenient
attitude of the gatekeepers of the DI-program. A further explanation for the decline
may be found in the process of purging the labor force of older cohorts of low
productivity workers through disability enrolment. This purgatory process should
have gradually improved the average health status of the population at risk, hence
reducing the DI-incidence rate.

### 2.4.2   The DI-program in International Perspective

In almost all industrialized Western countries social disability insurance programs
have substantially contributed to growing social security expenditures. In the
Netherlands a comparatively large share of the social security budget is devoted
to disability. The already high level of disability spending in the late 1960s combined with the steep growth during the 1970s gave the Netherlands an internationally prominent position as far as disability expenditures are concerned.

In a comprehensive cross-national study of disability policy, Haveman, Halberstadt
& Burkhauser (1984) examine the basic economic issues surrounding public support
for disabled workers. They also provide a systematic review of national disability
policies in eight modern Western economies.[22] The first column in table 2.16
(panel a) originates from this survey. The authors observe similar tendencies in the
countries reviewed, especially in the countries with a mature social security system.
The latter category includes Germany, the Netherlands and Sweden. The observed
adjustments in national disability policies and the consequential program growth
over the 1968-78 decade, lead them to suggest that the common scenario for the
generally observed growth of disability income support runs as follows:

> "As economic growth faltered in the mid-1970s, older workers with more or less serious
> impairments became targets for layoffs and, if out of work, found obtaining a job increa-
> singly difficult. Public officials responded by introducing relaxed eligibility criteria into
> disability programs, making access to them less difficult. They became a form of extended
> unemployment benefits. This option was attractive to older workers, as benefit payments
> became increasingly more adequate, and little stigma was attached to receipt of disability
> income support. Employers, likewise, found this development attractive, as it made release
> of long-term older, low-skilled, or impaired workers less difficult. With large cohorts of
> better educated youths and women entering the labor market, replacement of older workers
> was not difficult. Disability income support programs became an instrument to encourage
> early retirement." (p. 114)

To a varying extent, this scenario is likely to hold for all countries reviewed.

In a comparative study of the income replacing disability programs of five European
countries, Copeland (1981) reaches similar conclusions. She, too, observes the
program increase in the 1966-77 period in all five countries with the Netherlands
on top.

Table 2.16    Real Social Security Disability Expenditures and Disability Benefits Dependency in Selected Countries.

**a. Annual Rate of Growth of Real Social Security Disability Expenditures 1968-1989.**

|  | '68-'78[a] | percentages | '80-'89[b] |
|---|---|---|---|
| Netherlands | 18.6 | | .7 |
| Belgium | - | | .7 |
| Germany | 5.3 | | 1.1 |
| France | 6.7 | | 3.2 |
| Italy | 12.7 | | 5.0 |
| Sweden | 11.7 | | - |
| United Kingdom | .5 | | 2.2 |
| United States | 6.3 | | - |
| EUR | - | | 2.4 |

[a] Source: Haveman, Halberstadt and Burkhauser (1984 p. 84).
[b] Including sickness, disability-invalidity; Source: Eurostat *Rapid Reports*, 1991, no 4.

**b. Social Security Disability Benefits Dependency per 1,000 Persons in the Labor Force (beneficiaries excluded) 1970-1989.**

|  | 1970 | 1980 | Average Annual Change in the 1970s | 1989 | Average Annual Change in the 1980s |
|---|---|---|---|---|---|
| Netherlands | 49 | 126 | +7.7 | 139[a] | +1.4 |
| Germany | 51 | 59 | +0.8 | 55 | - 0.4 |
| Sweden | 49 | 68 | +1.9 | 78 | +1.1 |
| United States | 27 | 41 | +1.4 | 43 | .2 |

[a] Figure refers to 1990.
Source: Aarts, Burkhauser and De Jong (1992)

**c. Standardized DI-Award Rate, DI-Dependency Rate, and Termination Rate among Privately Employed Workers, Averaged over the 1980-87 Period.**

|  | Award Rate | DI-benefits dependency | DI-benefits termination rate | of which through: recovery | old age |
|---|---|---|---|---|---|
| Netherlands | 16.6 | 139 | 68 | ( 21 | 37 ) |
| Belgium | 8.8 | 50 | 136 | ( 58 | 47 ) |
| Germany | 9.5 | 74 | 58 | ( 8 | 35 ) |

Source: Prins (1991).

Copeland suggests that besides the factors in the Haveman et al. scenario, other determinants may have been at work too, such as aging of the insured population and, more specifically, decreasing mortality. She documents a decrease of mortality among the population at large during the late sixties and early seventies of 3.1

percent in Germany to 4.8 percent in the Netherlands. The decrease in mortality among disability pensioners, however, has been substantially higher and ranges from 15.1 percent in the Netherlands to 19.7 percent in Germany. Since decreasing mortality among DI-beneficiaries leads to an extension of the average period of benefit entitlement, it probably has contributed to the growth in disability income support. The substantial decrease of mortality among DI-beneficiaries indicates that on average the health status of DI-beneficiaries has improved, partly perhaps as a result of relaxed entitlement requirements.[23]

Along with real expenditure growth the total number of Disability benefit recipients has substantially increased. At the start of the 1970 decade, the Netherlands, Germany and Sweden counted approximately 50 beneficiaries per 1,000 persons in the labor force (table 2.16, panel b).[24] By the end of the decade, dependency had increased to 127 per 1,000 in the Netherlands, 59 per 1,000 in Germany and 68 per 1,000 in Sweden. The annual increase of 7.7 beneficiaries per 1,000 labor force participants in the Netherlands is yet another indication of the exuberant growth of the Dutch disability program. In the 1980s, real expenditure growth slowed down to an annual 0.7 percent in the Netherlands.

The successful containment of program outlays, however, did not coincide with a stabilization of benefit dependency. During the 1980s the beneficiary volume kept increasing, be it at a much lower rate of 1.4 per 1,000 persons in the labor force. In Germany, where real expenditures increased at an annual rate of 1.1 percent during the 1980s, the relative number of disability beneficiaries decreased at an average rate of .4 per 1,000 labor force participants.

Recently, Prins (1991) has provided standardized figures of disability program in- and outflows among privately employed workers in the Netherlands, Germany and Belgium that are reported in table 2.16, panel c. After demographic differences have been taken into account the average Dutch DI-program inflow rate of 16.6 per 1,000 workers insured appears to exceed those of Belgium and Germany by more than 75 percent. Over the period considered, the average standardized DI-dependency rate in Belgium was 64 percent below the Dutch level. The difference with Germany was almost 50 percent.

Despite cross-national similarities in the disability policy records, one may wonder why disability program growth in the Netherlands has been (much) higher than elsewhere. What are the distinctive features of the Dutch DI-program that can account for its prominent position?

Looking for explanations one has to conclude that the Dutch disability system is not unique for its broad definition of disability. Other countries, such as Belgium, Germany, and France, have similar eligibility standards according to which the main criterion for disability assessment is a person's ability to earn what similar healthy persons with similar training and vocational histories use to earn. Nor is the Dutch system unique in its consideration of labor market opportunities since, in the early seventies, also other European countries (Belgium, Germany, Finland, Sweden) started to take account of the availability of gainful employment opportunities. Not even the high replacement rates are an exclusive characteristic of the Dutch disability program, since Sweden, Germany, and even the United States, under the Workers' Compensation schemes, have net replacement rates up to 90 percent of pre-disability earnings.

We think of four explanations for the exuberant growth of the Dutch DI-program. First, while neither the broad definition of disability, nor the consideration of labor market opportunities nor the high replacement rates per se are unique features of the Dutch system, it is rather the concurrence of these enrolment incentives which makes the Dutch system a special case.

A second explanation is provided by the fact that the Dutch DI-program does not distinguish between job-related and other impairments. By equal treatment of impaired persons irrespective of the cause of their impairments the Dutch DI-program stresses the consequences rather than the causes of disablement, thus reinforcing the solidarity base of the DI-system. Obviously, by this interpretation of solidarity the Dutch system is not only more equitable but also more expensive. On the other hand, by disregarding the causes of impairment costly legal liability assessments are circumvented. Moreover, the impact of this fundamental difference in disability policy on the size of the program may be limited as in many countries the financial consequences of differentiation with respect to cause are mitigated by awarding supplementary entitlements to disabled people from low income groups and families with dependent children.

A third possible explanation is the very low minimum requirement for benefit entitlement. The minimal loss of earning capacity of 15 percent is low, even when compared with the minimum requirements that are applied in foreign disability schemes that cover the consequences of work-related impairments.[25]

The fourth, and possibly most important, explanation for the prominent Dutch DI-program growth is provided by the lenient application of the labor market consideration. The presumption of poor labor market opportunities when partially disabled, has led to an administrative practice in which most applicants with residual earning capacities up to 85 percent, are granted full DI-pensions.

It is important to note that this distinguishing feature of the Dutch DI-system has been a matter of administrative routine rather than conscious legislation. As mentioned in section 2.3.7 the administration of the Sickness Benefit program, and the Disability and Unemployment Insurances is in the hands of branche-wise organized, autonomous, boards consisting of representatives of employers' and trade unions. The common interest of both these market parties in a high productivity/ high wage policy has induced them to use the DI-program exclusively as a generous retirement scheme for those who do not meet productivity standards or are redundant at any rate.

While disability expenditures have been growing in all Western economies the Dutch program grew excessively fast and large, due to the fact that the program incentives affected all privately employed people instead of limited segments of the labor force; and that eligibility was neither contingent on the cause of impairment nor on its severity. Comparatively high replacement rates and lenient assessment procedures probably did the rest.

## 2.5   The 1987 System Reform[26]

It took some time before it was widely recognized that the growth in social security expenditures during the seventies called for a change of policy. Until 1973-74, it was growing prosperity that facilitated an increased supply of Welfare State programs in general and social security in particular. Then, the fourfold oil price increase triggered a deep economic crisis. Profits fell, and so did employment. Social security spending kept rising, however, and this time expenditure growth was caused, at least partly, by increased unemployment and disability induced by the economic crisis.

According to Haveman et al. (1986) the failure to timely recognize the distinctive sources of public expenditure growth is the major cause of the problems that European countries had to face in the mid-eighties. Unlike their European counterparts, US policymakers were soon aware of the structural changes and readily introduced measures to bend the growth of welfare state programs. However, US experience in re-designing their Social Disability Insurance program shows that retrenchments are difficult to effectuate [see Weaver (1986)].[27]

In the Netherlands, the social security system became subject to serious criticism in the late seventies. By then the steadily rising, and seemingly uncontrollable, social security expenditures had started to worry both politicians and administrators. In 1986, after sustained public debates, Dutch Parliament passed seven bills on social security. This new legislation, constituting the Social Security Reform, became effective as of January 1987.

The explicit purpose of this Reform was threefold:
- Elimination of certain imbalances and iniquities, for instance in treatment of males and females and of long-term unemployed and disabled;
- Adjustment to social and cultural changes, such as the increase in female labor force participation and in the number of two-earner and one-person-households;
- Retrenchment of social security expenditures;

The main features of the 1987 Reform are:
- Integration into one Unemployment Insurance Program of the WW and the WWV schemes;[28]
- Eligibility for Unemployment Benefits beyond the 26th week of unemployment for women whose husbands are main breadwinners (in conformity with European Community directives);

- Introduction of work experience as a criterion for Unemployment Benefit duration;
- Disentanglement of the "true disability" and "unemployment" components in the DI-program by eliminating labor market considerations from disability assessments. As a consequence, the total amount of benefits payable to non-working partially disabled persons, should be a mixture of DI-benefits and unemployment benefits in proportion to the degree of disability;[29]
- Reduction of the benefit-wage ratios to 70 percent in the Unemployment Insurance program, the Sickness Benefit program and the Disability Insurance program (already effective as of 1985). Elimination of the indexation of after-tax minimum benefits to after-tax minimum wage. Introduction of a system of supplemental benefits (the "Toeslagenwet") to guarantee unemployed and disabled beneficiaries a minimum household income.[30]

The 1987 Reform has not affected the fundamental and institutional characteristics of the Dutch Social Security System summarized in section 2.3. The principle of solidarity, the modes of financing and administration have survived the Reform. Several measures that were in line with the eventual amendments anticipated the actual enactment of the revisions. One of the prevailing iniquities had been the different financial treatment of older unemployed and older partially disabled persons, despite the similarities of their labor market positions. In 1980, this "generosity gap" was reduced by entitling unemployed workers aged 60 to 65 to continued WWV-benefits after two and a half years of unemployment (see section 2.3.4). By this measure older unemployed are protected from having to rely on wealth-tested Welfare Benefits (RWW).

In anticipation of the disentanglement of the "true disability" and unemployment components in DI-eligibility, the "labor market consideration" was applied more strictly from 1979 onwards. Specifically, newly awarded beneficiaries with considerable residual earning capacities, were subject to this enhanced scrutiny. The change implied that entitlement to full DI-benefits was made dependent on substantial evidence that poor employment opportunities resulted from discriminative behavior towards partially disabled rather than from a general lack of vacancies. These pre-reform policy adjustments are likely to have contributed to the earlier observed decrease in the DI-incidence starting in 1979 (table 2.15).

Furthermore, a series of substantial retrenchments have preluded the System Reform. Starting in 1980, the earnings replacing social insurance benefits for disability and unemployment suffered a series of severe cuts. First, the calculation of after tax benefit amounts was changed by levying social insurance contributions on benefit income. In 1982 and 1983 the after-tax DI-benefit level was reduced through the abolition of certain tax exemptions for the disabled. Then, in 1984, the statutory earnings base was reduced, yielding lower gross benefits. Moreover, all incomes under government control - transfers, civil servant salaries, and the statutory minimum wage - suffered a 3 percent cut. Finally, in 1985, the unemployment and disability replacement rates were lowered from 80 to 70 percent of last earnings. These direct cuts were accompanied by the elimination of the system of automatic indexation (adjustment) of government controlled incomes. In fact, the minimum wage, and, therefore, the minimum benefits were frozen as of 1982.[31]

The last column of table 2.15 documents the cumulated effect of these retrenchments on the after tax disability benefit-wage ratio. The pre-reform retrenchments caused a steep decrease of real DI-benefits starting in 1980. Within six years, the modal beneficiaries lost almost 25 percent of their purchasing power, whereas modal wages suffered a reduction of 10 percent.

Furthermore, as a result of the reduction of benefits, the share of above-minimum benefit recipiency in the earnings related unemployment and disability programs dropped from 90 percent in 1983 to 74 percent in 1986. Since all other social security transfers, except sickness benefits, are minimum benefits, the share of above-minimum benefit recipiency in social security as a whole dropped from 26 to 17 percent.[32] The purchasing power of minimum benefits dropped by about 10 percent between 1981 and 1987.[33] Surely, the distributional consequences of these savings are a widened gap between transfer and labor incomes.[34] Due to the transfer reductions, an increased share of the beneficiaries find themselves in the "safety net" of minimum income guarantees. This illustrates the fact that the recipients of above-minimum transfers had to endure the severest cuts of all socioeconomic groups.


## 2.6   Summary and Conclusions

A cross national survey of social security systems shows that during the seventies and early eighties real social security expenditures increased in all major capitalist economies. The level of spending appears to be substantially higher in Europe than in the USA and Japan, and among the European countries the Netherlands rank first, both in terms of spending and transfer recipiency.

The Dutch Social Security System grew in many directions. Between 1965 and 1976, coverage, both in terms of risk and people, was extended, while benefits rose faster than wages. The behavioral effects prompted by this growth, exacerbated by exogenous factors such as the economic recessions of 1975 and 1981-83, have induced a massive increase of transfer recipiency.

A major part of this growth is accounted for by the DI-program. During the 1970 decade, disability income support became an instrument to encourage early retirement. As a reaction the 1980s witnessed a series of amendments and retrenchments inducing small decreases in the level of social security spending, not only in the Netherlands but also in other EC member states.

In the Netherlands a comparatively large share of the sizeable social security budget is devoted to disability. This gives the DI-program a prominent place in the system. Alarmed by its prominence, government took a series of measures to reduce the amount of DI-benefits and to strengthen DI-eligibility requirements after 1980. These policy changes culminated in the 1987 Social Security System Reform whose main feature is the elimination of labor market considerations from DI-eligibility assessments. This major amendment is discussed further in chapters 5 (section 5.9) and 11 (section 11.4.2). Notwithstanding these changes the Dutch DI-benefit dependency rate of 139 beneficiaries per 1,000 labor force participants was, by the start of the 1990 decade, substantially higher than that in Sweden (78), Germany (55), or the United States (43).

The financial burden of the Dutch Social Security System weighs heavily on the wage bill, more so than in most other countries. The Dutch minimum benefit level is comparatively high, causing an upward pressure from the bottom of the wage distribution. Transfers to and from the government flatten out the overall income distribution further to become one of the flattest in the modern capitalist world. The assumedly adverse impacts of a relatively large wedge between gross labor cost and net earnings and the relative generosity of the DI-programs have contributed to the relatively low Dutch labor force participation rates. Despite the fact that female participation has been growing steadily and the decline in male participation had stopped by the end of the 1980 decade, both male and female rates are still among the lowest to be observed internationally.

The comparatively exuberant growth of the Dutch disability programs is considered to be partly the result of specific program principles, such as the absence of a distinction between job related and other impairments in disability assessment, and the very low minimum requirement for benefit eligibility. However, the administrative practice to award full DI-benefits to the partially disabled on the assumption of poor labor market opportunities may be regarded as the major source of the substantial growth in DI-expenditures.

It is within this, "morally hazardous", institutional framework that the research reported in this book is cast.

## Notes

1. Such as differences in financing method (funded versus pay-as-you-go) and administration. For example, in some countries family allowances are provided through tax reductions and therefore do not enter the accounts, while in other countries government child support is paid in cash and shows up as a direct government expenditure.

2. The figures in table 2.1 include income maintenance expenditures by central government (including the social security administration) as well as those by regional and local authorities. In the Dutch figures, however, Welfare expenditures by local government are excluded. They are recorded in the category "General Public Services". In the Netherlands, total expenditures in the latter category account for 19 percent of GDP (1981), while in the other countries listed these expenditures take only 4 percent on average [Saunders & Klau (1985, pp. 28, 52)].

3. For an elaboration of the pros and cons of the welfare state, including social security, see [Haveman (1985)].

4. Source: OECD, Historical Trends 1960-1988, Paris: OECD (1990) and Eurostat, Labour Force Survey, Luxembourg: Eurostat (1988) as cited in WRR (1990).

5. An important difference is the treatment of housing and rent subsidies. In the Netherlands, Denmark, France and the UK, welfare beneficiaries may be eligible for such subsidies in addition to the welfare benefit they receive, while in other countries such subsidies are incorporated in the welfare program. With respect to the comparison in table 2.7, this implies that the minimum income levels in the three countries mentioned are downwardly biased.

6. The analysis includes Japan, Finland, Denmark, France, Ireland, Germany, Canada, United States and United Kingdom.

7. See Goudswaard & De Jong (1985) and Van Ginneken & Park (1985) referred to in Tweede Kamer B (1987, p. 26).

8. With a reduction for every year the single person is younger than 23.

9. See Aarts & De Jong (1992), table 3. Blomsma & De Vroom (1988) present a survey of early retirement provisions in Sweden, the USA and the Netherlands.

10. Sources: Bolhuis et al. (1987); GMD (1980, 1985); CBS (1980, 1985).

11. This is not required in other schemes, like the Sickness Benefits, Disability and Welfare programs.

12. As employers usually continue to pay wages during spells of sickness, the program can be considered to be an insurance for employers. Employers pay out the Sickness Benefits and often supplement them up to 100% of the pre-sickness wage. They are partly, up to the statutory replacement rate, reimbursed by the Industrial Association that administers the Sickness Benefit, UI and DI-schemes [Emanuel (1985)].

13. The 4 percent number is calculated from Social Security Council, Quarterly Report on Disability, S91/11, p. 34.

14. The Social Security Council's specific task is in testing governmental policy proposals against the legal foundations of the social security system, and by administrative feasibility.
    On matters of social (security) policy, Government has to consult the Social Economic Council (SER) also. The task of this Council, which is composed of the same social groups

(employers, trade unions, and independent government appointees) as the Social Security Council, is to judge policy proposals on income and labor market consequences.

15. Note also the growth in public sector employment, from 12 percent of total employment in 1970 to 16 percent in 1985. Hence, the public sector income recipiency share grew from 33 percent in 1970 to 52 percent in 1990. The jump in social assistance transfer recipiency is mainly due to a surge in the divorce rate, giving single mothers entitlement to these transfers.

16. In section 2.5 these early proposals for retrenchment are described.

17. See for instance Nagi (1969).

18. Excluding women collaborating in their husbands' businesses, the participation rate of Dutch married women grew from 2 percent in 1947, to 4 percent in 1960, to 12 percent in 1971, to 22 percent in 1979, to about 40 percent in 1990. See Hartog and Theeuwes (1985) and *Rapportage Arbeidsmarkt 1991*.

19. 52 percent in persons, and 46 percent in man-years.

20. Given the fact that the Netherlands, in terms of per capita GNP, range among the richest countries of the world, this low employment rate suggests high labor productivity. See WRR (1990).

21. See Emanuel (1979), pp. 98-102, on the disability schemes that preceded the 1967 Disability Insurance Act (WAO).

22. The authors have included the United States, Germany, France, Israel, Italy, the Netherlands, Sweden and the United Kingdom.

23. It is interesting to note that, according to the data in Copeland (1981), the decrease in Dutch DI-incidence rates from 1979 on (see table 2.15), can also be observed in other European countries. In Belgium the annual incidence of disability pension awards peaked in 1973 (with 12.3 awards per 1,000 persons insured). Germany reached a top of 13.2 in 1975.

24. Contrary to those in table 2.14 these dependency rates count the beneficiaries of *all* disability programs irrespective of past work status.

25. For impairments that are not employment-related, a minimum loss of earning capacity is required of 50 percent in Germany, 66 percent in Italy and Belgium, 33 percent in France. In most countries, non-work-related impairments yield a lower replacement rate than work-related impairments.

26. This section is based on De Jong et al. (1990).

27. Weaver (1986) shows how after the implementation of a new requirement in the law that all SSDI beneficiaries be reviewed at least once every three years, nearly half the reviewed beneficiaries were found ineligible. The uproar triggered by this outcome led to new legislation in 1984 that expanded benefit eligibility, secured protection for people on the rolls and allowed the generally liberalizing actions of the courts to influence disability policy (pp. 29-45).

28. The new Unemployment Insurance Act (new WW) covers both short-and medium-term unemployment. The definition of unemployment, eligibility requirements, and benefit durations, have undergone drastic changes.
Under the new WW, employees are considered to be unemployed if they lose at least 5 hours, or half, of their usual number of weekly workhours. Moreover, A system of sanctions has been created to reduce the benefit award according to degrees of culpability to the unemployment status; and to reduce or suspend benefit continuation if the require-

ments of availability for commensurate work and active job search are being violated. These modifications warrant increased flexibility, and compatibility with contemporary work patterns, of the unemployment insurance scheme.
- Under the new WW, a benefit spell can be divided into three parts:
A six months' wage-related benefit yielding 70 percent of last earnings. Eligibility is obtained after 26 weeks of gainful employment during the year preceding unemployment, irrespective of the number of hours or days worked in those 26 reference weeks.
- An extension of the wage-related benefit period, depending on work record. The minimum extension is three months with a record of 5-10 years, The maximum extension of 4.5 years is granted to those with a history 35-40 years. Qualification for extension is obtained if one has been gainfully employed for at least three years during the five years preceding unemployment. Here, gainful employment implies working at least 8 hours per week. Child care periods, and spells of sickness or disability, can be counted as qualifying for an extended benefit.
- After expiry of the wage-related benefit period, unemployment beneficiaries may be entitled to a follow-up benefit ("vervolguitkering"), granting 70 percent of the minimum wage. Qualification for follow-up benefits is subject to the "3-out-of-5-years" rule which also applies to wage-related benefit extension. Follow-up benefits are not wealth-tested. The maximum duration of follow-up benefits is one year, except for beneficiaries who are, at expiry of wage-related benefits, over 58. For these senior beneficiaries the follow-up benefit may continue until 65.
When still unemployed after lapse of the follow-up benefit, one may become eligible for fully means-tested welfare benefits at the social minimum level (see section 2.3).
To those who are 50 or over when becoming unemployed, social assistance under the new Income Provision Act for the Senior and Disabled Unemployed (IOAW) may be granted, after unemployment benefits (including follow-up benefits) have run out. In contrast to RWW, IOAW-benefits are not wealth-tested.

29. Upon expiry of the Unemployment Insurance benefits, a partially disabled beneficiary is entitled to non-wealth-tested social assistance under the Income Provision for the Senior and Disabled Unemployed (IOAW), supplementing the partial disability benefit up to the relevant social minimum.

30. As part of the Reform, a new Supplementary Benefits Act (TW), granting a supplement if an unemployment, sickness, or disability benefit falls short of the statutory social minimum, has been introduced. The amount of supplementary benefits depends on age and household composition. They are tested for household earnings but, contrary to National Assistance, they are not wealth-tested. Since TW-entitlement is contingent upon unemployment, sickness, or disability benefit recipiency, beneficiaries whose award has run out fall down to wealth-tested National Assistance. Wealth-testing, however, is considered unduly harsh for partially disabled workers, and workers who became unemployed after 50. For these categories, then, the separate income provision, IOAW, has been introduced, as part of the Reform program. IOAW acts as a relaxed National Assistance arrangement, granting social minimum benefits which are only tested for household earnings.

31. To warrant subsistence levels, cost of living allowances were given, yearly, to minimum income households ("echte minima").

32. Source: Tweede Kamer (1987, p. 27).

33. Inclusion of the cost of living allowances yields a real income loss of 7 percent.

34. This hypothesis is confirmed by Goudswaard and De Jong (1985). By simulating the, then proposed, benefit cuts on a representative sample they find that the inequality between labor and transfer income recipients, as measured by Theil's intra-group index, increases by 50 percent from 1983 to 1986.

Chapter 3

# THE DISABILITY PROCESS

## 3.1    Introduction

Disability is an ill-defined and complex phenomenon. It is not directly observable but must be inferred from its presumed causes and consequences. The World Health Organization (1980) defines disability as any restriction or lack (resulting from an impairment) to perform an activity in the manner or within the range considered normal.

The assessment of impairments and their limiting consequences involves difficult and painful judgments by the individual afflicted, and equally cumbersome verifications by the members of the individual's social setting. The inevitable subjectivity of these judgments introduces individual tastes, social values, and financial evaluations into the definition and perception of disability. These subjective elements render disability a behavioral phenomenon. It is precisely for these behavioral aspects that disability, and disability insurance, are political issues, and fertile territories for social research.

Medical sociologists were the first to identify illness and disability as behavioral phenomena. It led them to study the differential patterns of behavior emerging from health problems. They observed that people substantially differ in the manner in which they perceive, evaluate, and act upon symptoms and signs of malfunctioning [Mechanic and Volkart (1961)]. Their studies not only explain why patients with similar afflictions behave differently, but also why self-perceptions deviate from professional assessments by doctors and administrators.

Haber (1967) and Nagi (1965) did pathbreaking work by conceptualizing, and structuring, the complex notion of disability. Nagi defines disability as a medically determined reduction of the ability to perform required tasks. These tasks can be classified by spheres of essential activities, such as self-care, education, family relations, employment, and recreation. Since disability insurance (DI) programs are primarily concerned with labor market performance, we shall limit ourselves in this study to **work, or vocational, disability**.

Students of disability may choose from, or combine, several analytic angles. Following Nagi (1969), one can distinguish between clinical, behavioral, and legal approaches. The absence of an economic approach is characteristic of the era in which Nagi developed his analytic tools. As a research topic, disability was still in the realm of sociologists and psychologists. Only after disability program expenditures had become significant, economists entered the scene, starting with Berkowitz and Johnson (1974).

The **clinical** approach involves the medical assessment of the nature, severity, and curability of impairments, and their limiting effects. The following section describes the factors associated with the clinical approach. They form what we denote as the etiological framework.

The **behavioral** approach is concerned with perceptions, evaluations, and coping strategies of the individual afflicted. The research question, here, is why people with clinically comparable ailments behave differently in that some claim to be disabled and others do not. This behavioral approach can be modelled along medical-sociological or micro-economic lines. Both disciplinary angles introduce a variety of non-medical factors as determinants of disability behavior. An impaired worker may, in theory, have a continuum of behavioral options, ranging from complete and permanent withdrawal from the labor market to full restoration of productive potential. The feasibility of these options crucially depends on the clinical characteristics of the impairment. It also hinges upon legal and economic constraints.

The **legal** approach deals with the legitimation of disability claims. If defined narrowly, it concerns the question of eligibility for disability insurance benefits, i.e., whether the disability claim can be substantiated by medical and vocational data. This calls for a separate treatment of the legal characteristics of disability and rehabilitation programs, and the award policies of their gatekeepers. These elements reflect societal responses to disability, and introduce program administrators as separate agents.

The **economic** approach to disability can take diverse forms. Starting from the synonymy of disability with productivity loss, it emphasizes the economic relationships of the impaired worker with employers, program administrators, and household members. More specifically, the economic approach relates to the (re)employability of impaired workers. It introduces non-employability as a distinct aspect of disability, and calls attention for the interlacement of unemployment and disability. This approach stresses the role of employers in transforming impairments into disabilities. To the extent that employers are unwilling to keep or reemploy ailing workers, the scope for choosing a preferred option is constrained.

Second, economics can be used as an analytical tool. In this study, we employ the micro-economic paradigm of utility maximization to construct a formal model of disability behavior.[1] This model states that workers will apply for DI-benefits if they expect the difference between the lifetime utilities in the DI and the WORK options to be positive. It provides a framework for the analysis of financial considerations and program disincentives to (re)employment.

In this chapter, we propose a model of DI-program participation. Program participation results from two contingencies: The probability that an impaired worker will claim to be disabled and, therefore, applies for DI-benefits, and the probability that the claim will be awarded by the program administrators. Or formally,

$$Pr\{DI\} = Pr\{CLAIM\} \cdot Pr\{AWARD \mid CLAIM\}.$$

Claiming to be eligible for DI-benefits is a behavioral consequence engendered by the perceived limiting effects of impairment. Disability behavior, therefore, can be operationally defined by the inclination to apply for DI-benefits. The award probability, on the other hand, represents the external, administrative, judgment of the legitimacy of disability behavior.

The medical-sociological approach to disability behavior is discussed in section 3.2. Given that disability behavior is conditional upon its clinical causes, we commence by describing a conceptual framework for the etiology of disability, in section 3.2.1. Next, in 3.2.2, we deal with the sociological notions and assumptions that surround disability behavior. Then, in 3.2.3, a number of medical and non-medical determinants of disability behavior are derived. In the relation between disability program participation and its clinical causes, two sets of non-medical factors are being distinguished as intermediate elements; one set of vocational, including labor market, factors, and a set of attitudinal characteristics.
In section 3.3, then, we propose a formal, micro-economic, model in which these heterogeneous sets of determinants are being put together. As an introduction, the neoclassical theory of labor supply is used to describe how health may affect work effort. In 3.3.2, this theoretical model is elaborated to encompass the long-term consequences and inherent risks of the two relevant options; continued labor force participation or DI-application. The resulting form reflects the intricate causalities underlying the process of DI-enrolment.
In 3.3.3 and 3.3.4, the abstract, theoretical, version of the DI-model is transformed into an operational form which also restores the link with the medical-sociological perspective. Section 3.4 summarizes and concludes. We argue there that the resulting operational model serves as a framework for the research program that is dealt with in the following chapters of the book.

## 3.2     The Medical-Sociological Approach to Disability Behavior

### 3.2.1     Impairments, Functional Limitations, and Disability: An Etiological Framework

In the definition of disability, health impairments are causally linked with reduced task performance. The presence of an impairment is necessary but not sufficient. Some impairments have no incapacitating effects at all; others prevent performance but their ill effects may be eliminated by certain drugs, aids, or appliances; still others imply total and permanent incapacity.

**Impairment** is defined as a physiological or anatomical loss or other abnormality [Nagi (1969), WHO (1980)]. These losses and abnormalities may stem from diseases, traumatic injuries, congenital deformities, or prolonged disuse of muscles or organs. They remain after the stage of active pathology has passed. The nature and severity of the underlying pathology determine the extent and permanency of impairment.

Impairments become manifest through the limitations in function or capacity they effect. **Functional limitations** can be grouped according to the level of organization at which they are defined and measured. One may discern limitations at the level of molecules, cells, tissues, organs, or the whole organism. Although limitations at a lower level of organization may not be reflected in higher levels, the reverse is not true [Howards et al. (1980)].

To elaborate the concept of disability, high-level definitions and classifications are more useful than low level ones which mostly serve purely medical purposes. A possible classification at the level of organs and systems distinguishes between:

- Energetical limitations, reducing the capacity of metabolic organs (heart, lungs, liver, etc.) to perform physical and mental activities, and endure physical and mental exertion.
- Locomotive limitations, reducing the capacity of the musculo-skeletal and nervous systems to perform physical activities, and endure physical exertion.
- Sensory limitations, such as impaired vision and hearing.
- Mental limitations, reducing intellectual faculties.
- Emotional limitations, impairing the mechanism to cope with life stresses and adjustments.

At an even higher level, activities and tasks may be taken as the basis for classification. One might put, for instance, energetical and locomotive limitations in one class of physical limitations which would include such activities as walking, climbing, lifting and stooping.

Evidently, limitations at the level of activities may result from diverse combinations of lower level limitations. For example, the inability to concentrate may be due to purely emotional factors, may have somatic origins, or both. And the inability to lift a heavy weight may be caused by energetical or locomotive limitations.

The obvious advantage of defining limitations at the level of activities, is that they can be directly related to the demands of task performance. Concerning work disability only those limitations are relevant that interfere with specific job demands. Thus, two people with exactly the same limitations may suffer different degrees of work disability. A hearing limitation is likely to affect a violinist more than a laborer, whilst a foot injury would affect the laborer more than the violinist [Luft (1978)].

Impaired workers that are unable to meet the requirements of their old jobs may create alternatives to DI-enrolment through rehabilitation. Thus they may be able to acquire new skills and/or find a new job commensurate to their limitations.

Scheme 3.1     Etiology of Work Disability

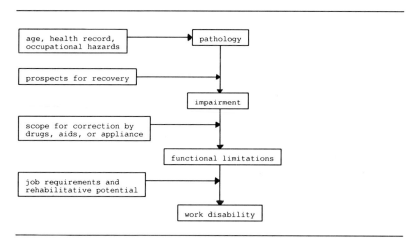

Scheme 3.1 summarizes, from a clinical perspective, the causal chain leading from pathology to disability. According to this scheme, work disability can be defined as the inability to meet specific job demands, due to functional limitations, caused by impairment. Two dimensions along which the elements of this causal chain should be conceptualized are severity and permanency. Other dimensions relate to the nature of impairment, limitations, and disability, e.g., a scale running from somatic to psychological.

### 3.2.2    Behavioral Elements: The Disabled Role

The road from disease to disability is paved with behavioral elements. The recognition of symptoms of impairments, the perception of their incapacitating effects, and the choice of coping strategy with respect to the felt psychological, social, and economic consequences of disability, all involve individual evaluations. Evidently, such evaluations are steered by perceived constraints imposed by remedial, legal, and financial possibilities, and by social forces.

In their seminal paper, Haber and Smith (1971) propose a model of disability behavior which is a modified version of the sick role concept, a concept of long repute in medical sociology.[2] In this sociological tradition, a "role" can be described as a status which evokes a set of expectations defining appropriate norms and behavior. As Nagi puts it lucidly

> "There are general normative patterns governing what society ascribes to, and expects of, the sick, the ill, and the disabled. They are exempted from normal roles, but are expected to seek competent help, co-operate with such help, and resume their usual activities as fully and as soon as their conditions permit. These normative patterns, however, do not identify distinct roles for the disabled in the sense of shared reciprocal expectations to guide interaction with others, as in the case of husband-wife or father-child relationships. Patterns of disability behavior vary considerably (...)." [Nagi (1969, p. 12)].

Consequently, when impairments impose limitations upon workers' capacities and levels of functioning they have some freedom to choose between alternative roles, specifically to either substitute the worker role by the disabled role or not. The assumption of a role, however, is not a gratuitous act. It involves costs and benefits. Their evaluation is a matter of personal and social preferences and conditions.

Application of the role concept to the etiological framework described in the previous section, sets the stage for a model of the process leading from work to disability. Essential elements in this behavioral disability model are recognition, adaptation, and legitimation.

The first step on the road to disability is the recognition of the symptoms of an impairment by the patient and/or significant others. With the exception of impairments at the boundary of survival, recognition depends on individual tastes and cultural norms, on culturally varying "body concepts" [Safilios-Rothschild (1970), pp. 58-59, Zola (1963)]. Such concepts set global, societal, standards for healthiness and normal functioning.

Upon recognition, the impaired worker will try to adapt to his condition in a way that is both socially acceptable and in agreement with his own preferences. Usually, one will seek medical or rehabilitation services to cure or correct the limiting effects of the impairment. A vast literature on medical consumption shows that these search activities are primarily conditioned by the severity of the impairment, and by the quality and accessibility of the health care system. Both factors limit the scope for choice, as they determine the individual time and budget constraints [Andersen (1968), Grossman and Benham (1975), Van de Ven and Van der Gaag (1982)]. To the extent that the impairment collides with regular activities, household members, colleagues, and the employer will exert stronger pressure toward investment in rehabilitative activities.

Whether impairment leads to disability, then, depends on the medical and financial feasibility of correction, and on the intensity of search for these corrective measures. A worker will define himself as disabled, if he perceives himself as being impaired beyond remedy, and if he experiences a substantial reduction in work performance. He will be more inclined to do so, the less painful the financial and psychological consequences of disability.[3]

The consequences of disability are contingent upon the available adjustment strategies. These can be either oriented towards vocational rehabilitation and resumption of one's former worker role, or towards persistent dependency and substitution of the worker role by the disabled role. Rehabilitative adaptations are aimed at reducing the incapacitating effects of an impairment. One may invest in training to obtain a job, commensurate to one's residual abilities. With the help of the employer, one may try to adapt the requirements of the existing job to one's limitations. Vocational rehabilitation, then, is a matter of either fitting the worker to the job, or the job to the worker so as to regain productivity and independence. As an alternative the afflicted worker may try to mollify the financial consequences of disability more directly. He may stop working and try to get income support through public or private transfer payments, or, other household members may act as substitutes in the labor market. This strategy implies unproductivity, and dependency as a consequence. Whereas the first strategy is active and production-oriented, the second strategy is passive and consumption-oriented.

Each of these adjustment strategies involves the approval, often the active collaboration, of other parties. Their success, therefore, primarily depends on the extent to which these others, employers, household members, and program administrators, are willing to confer legitimacy to the disability claim. Legitimation is basically the process of separating the compliant disabled from the willful deviant. As a starting point, the responsibility for incapacity should be attributable to an impairment beyond the control of the individual. However, excusing someone from responsibility for his condition does not relieve him of accountability for his subsequent disability behavior. If, for example, an impaired person claims exemption from work duties, his incapacity should be incorrigible in order to justify his ensuing dependence.

The choice of adaptive strategy is a matter of choosing between the roles of disabled and rehabilitee. Assumption of the disabled role means seeking to be accepted as being unfit for work. It implies dependency upon the work effort of others.

This strategy, then, involves both psychological and pecuniary risks and costs. First, one has to submit oneself to the rules of the legitimation procedure, the outcome of which is uncertain. The disability claim, whereupon the ameliorative strategy is based, may be denied. Or, the claim may be accepted but not the strategy, if the gatekeepers of legitimacy see rehabilitative possibilities. And even if the claim and the strategy are accepted, one has to face the possibility of being stigmatized as a morally inferior person. Being excused from labor force participation, also means cutting oneself off from career prospects. This implies foregoing potential increases in earnings and status.

The benefits of being certified as disabled, on the other hand, are again twofold, financial and psychological. The disabled worker is exempted from work duties, and, given disability insurance, is awarded disability benefits, partially covering earnings lost. The beneficiary status, moreover, provides security from the hazards of labor force participation, such as bad job conditions and unemployment risks. And, finally, it provides an acceptable excuse for lack of labor market success.

### 3.2.3    Determinants of Disability Behavior

Combination of the etiological with the behavioral framework allows us to be more specific about the potential determinants of disability behavior, i.e., the choice of adaptive strategy with respect to recognized functional limitations.

In structuring these determinants, one may distinguish between factors which exogenously influence the choice of behavioral option, such as clinical and vocational data, and attitudinal factors by which these data are filtered to yield perceptions, evaluations, and the eventual behavioral choice. Finally, all of these determinants are conditional upon a set of individual, firm-specific, and societal, background characteristics.

### Clinical Factors

The prime factors which determine the proclivity to choose the disabled role are, of course, those related to the medical condition. The causalities introduced in section 3.2, and summarized in scheme 3.1, induce the following set of hypotheses: The likelihood that a worker will present himself as disabled will be greater
- the more severe the impairment;
- the more prohibitive the ensuing limitations;
- the smaller the medical and technical possibilities for remedy and correction.

Some impairments are caused by random events, such as traffic accidents or viral infections. Many impairments, however, have an identifiable background. They may be related to medical and work histories, living conditions, or lifestyle. It is an oft-observed fact that the prevalence of illness and disability is high in low income,

low education groups [Luft (1978), Howards et al. (1980)]. This may be due to a combination of heavy work, inappropriate diets, and lack of money and information to get adequate medical help. It suggests that, already at the basic level of the etiology of disability, non-medical factors are at work as conditioning elements.
The more severe the impairment, the smaller the scope for corrective action. Severely disabled persons are driven towards dependency, even if they loath it. The success of adjustment by rehabilitative correction, however, does not only depend on the impairment itself but also on a number of vocational aspects which act as conditioning intermediates.

**Vocational Factors**
Apart from the clinical condition, the scope for correction is smaller
   - the more demanding, and specific, the conditions of the current job;
   - the smaller the capacity, or willingness, of the current employer to adapt the job demands to the worker's limitations;
   - the smaller the retraining potential of the disabled worker;
   - the smaller the supply of suitable job alternatives.
Work disability starts when an employee is unable to meet current job demands. Whatever its cause, its nature or its severity, the probability that an impairment will lead to disability is higher the more demanding the job. More specifically, if the impairment is due to an inherent occupational hazard, then, by definition, the resulting limitations will prevent the afflicted worker from keeping that job. For instance, a miner with silicosis will have to find other work, whereas a miner who loses an eye may be able to stay on the job.

Confronted with the inability to do one's usual job, a worker may try to get the job adapted, or to find a suitable alternative, either within the firm, or on the external labor market. He may do so by offering his residual capacities as they are, if there are any. He may also go through a retraining program and offer newly acquired capacities. Obviously, retraining potential depends on human capital, i.e., the productivity base formed by innate abilities, formal schooling and work experience.
The feasibility of these options crucially depends on the internal and external labor market situation. As concerns the internal, firm-specific, opportunities, employers have several instruments to prevent or correct ailing workers' productivity losses. Employers may use regular medical check-ups, workers' consultation procedures, and sickness absenteeism records, to assess the health status of their personnel. Evidently, these data are conditioned by type of production process, and type of personnel. Depending on social concern or economic need, firms may be motivated to act upon these health data by accommodating working conditions or job demands, thus promoting workers' commitment to the firm. Under less favorable

social and economic circumstances employers may seize a reduction in productivity to lay off redundant workers through the DI-program. Such social and economic characteristics of the firm define a specific disability milieu to which employees are exposed.

To the extent that an impairment reduces a worker's productivity and flexibility, it also weakens his competitive power on the labor market. A surplus of labor supply aggravates this competitive disadvantage. The less scarce one's remaining skills, the more difficult it is to keep one's job, or to find an appropriate alternative. Employers will be more inclined to adapt jobs or offer commensurate alternatives, when there is a lack of skilled, healthy substitutes for the impaired employee. On the other hand, impairment is more easily converted into disability when there is a surplus of skills, or when performance standards are raised to reflect the higher level of skills available. The only way to get around these competitive drawbacks is by acquiring new, scarce, skills through retraining.

As a consequence, unemployment and disability are overlapping contingencies. If impaired persons cannot find suitable jobs, health and labor market conditions interact to produce disability. Whether the resulting unemployability is due to unemployment or impairment, may, then, be difficult to tell. In any case, one of the best documented results of disability research is that more people seek disability benefits when and where unemployment is soaring.[4] Under more favorable conditions they might have continued working, despite their ailments.

Other research findings show that many disabled persons, besides their health problems, have productivity characteristics which induce a high unemployment risk (old age, low education, unstable work histories). These findings suggest that proneness to unemployment often coincides with proneness to disability. They indicate that the disability label provides a shelter against labor market frustrations.

**Attitudinal Factors: Work Commitment**

Generally speaking, the proclivity to assume the disabled role is stronger, the lower its perceived costs, and the higher its perceived benefits. Such evaluations can be seen as outputs, using clinical and vocational data as inputs. To the extent that these costs and benefits have an immaterial, psychological, or welfare, dimension too, the factual inputs are filtered by attitudes so as to rationalize a preferred outcome. This implies that attitudes act as intermediates in converting cognitive inputs into perceptions, engendering behavioral choices.

Given our focus on work disability, its consequences, unproductivity and dependency, are perceived as less harmful the lower one's commitment to work in general, and to one's job specifically. The relevant characteristics, then, are work ethic as a general motivational indicator, and satisfaction with one's usual job, as a specific variable. In terms of a micro-economic model such attitudinal elements can be labeled taste factors.

At the social level, work ethic represents the culturally dominant standard for work attitudes. Until the seventies, the traditional role pattern of "husband-breadwinner wife-homemaker" was predominant in Dutch society. This pattern evolved from a puritan, Calvinist, morality, defining idleness as a sin, work, both paid work and homework, as a privilege, and the family as the cornerstone of society. Within this moral system, the husband bore the responsibility to earn a living for his family. Married women were discouraged to do paid work as it was their duty to take care of children and household chores.

The pre-war generation sanctified these traditional values. It had endured hardship during the economic crisis of the thirties and the Second World War. The steady increases in prosperity, henceforth, were generally felt to be associated with these traditional values. The same era of affluence, however, also produced a baby boom generation that had the economic opportunity to challenge the old values, resulting in secularization and emancipatory movements. The modernist morality which went along with the rise of the Welfare State stressed individual freedom, and the multiformity of society. The general tendency was towards more hedonism and less puritanism.

These cultural trends have gradually pushed work ethic away from being a socially imposed category towards an individual choice variable, although still conditioned by upbringing and social setting. A high work morale is associated with readiness to accept strenuous job demands and unpleasant working conditions, and reluctance to abandon the worker role. When impairments become manifest, workers with a high morale will find it mentally costly to leave employment and claim to be disabled. Departures from their standards, forced by recognized medical and vocational data, create a moral problem which can be resolved, either by correcting the data through rehabilitation, or by modifying one's standards by resigning to unproductivity and dependency. To high (low) morale workers, the second option is assumed to be more (less) painful.

Impaired workers evaluate perceived incongruities between standards and cognitions from the perspective of their current employment situations.[5] Job satisfaction, being the distance between desired and perceived job characteristics, then, may act as a modifying intermediate between innate morale and actual behavior. Even low morale workers will find it painful to part with jobs they experience as being highly satisfactory. High morale workers, on the other hand, may be more inclined to reconsider their standards, if they find their jobs unsatisfactory. If they feel they lack the opportunities to change their employment conditions, they may be willing to resign to disability and accept its inherent stigma costs.

**Summary and Discussion**
Disability behavior is defined as the recognition, by the afflicted individual, of a reduction in the capacity to perform required (work) tasks, followed by the claim to be exempted from (full) performance. Adherence to the disabled role implies that application for DI-benefits is the preferred adaptive strategy. Given the extent of disablement the choice between continuation on the job - with or without rehabilitation - or dependency on DI-benefits is assumed to be determined by employment opportunities and commitment to paid work. Finally, the probability of being found eligible for DI-benefits, or more theoretically, the probability that adherence to the disabled role is judged legitimate, is determined by formal eligibility standards and informal administrative routines.

The hypothesized relations that result from the medical-sociological approach to disability behavior are summarized in scheme 3.2.

**Scheme 3.2  Determinants of Disability Behavior and DI-Enrolment**

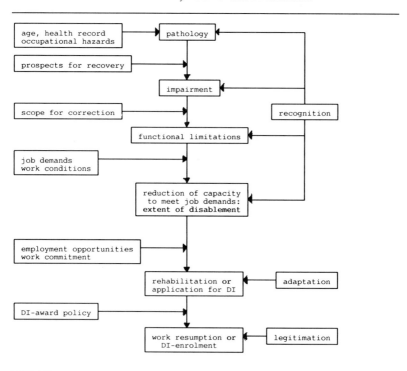

Clearly, the medical-sociological approach to disability behavior adds a number of important non-medical factors to the prime determinants of DI-enrolment, the nature and severity of disablement. The list, however, still is incomplete since, besides formal and informal eligibility standards which define the leniency of the scheme, generosity aspects - benefit size and duration, and the availability of provisions in kind - have been left unconsidered. Such program characteristics determine the opportunity cost of DI-enrolment. They are introduced in the next section where the micro-economic approach is elaborated so as to result in a model that encompasses the full set of determinants of DI-enrolment that evolve from combining the medical-sociological and micro-economic angles.

## 3.3    The Micro-Economics of Disability Behavior

### 3.3.1    Introduction

Utility maximization serves as the paradigmatic, neoclassical, approach in micro-economic models of choice behavior. Such models set out from the premise that people choose according to their preferences. Presumably, they are able to distinguish between, and assign a preference ranking to, heterogeneous states, where each state is defined by a vector of characteristics. A preference ranking over a set of states can be formally represented by a utility function, with the relevant characteristics as its arguments. High rankings, i.e., strong preferences, correspond to high utility values, and vice versa. Budget and time constraints limit the set of feasible states. Within the feasible set, the option yielding the highest utility value will be chosen. In sum, "Economic agents may be taken to reach their decisions in the light of what they want and what they can get" [Arrow and Hahn (1971)].

The utility framework is also used to model individual decisions on labor force participation and the optimal supply of working hours. In that context, utility (U) is usually defined as a function of two characteristics, income per period (Y) and leisure hours per period (L). More specifically, we define Y as after-tax household income, and L as individual leisure consumption. In the absence of borrowing and saving Y equals spending on market goods. Leisure is treated as a consumer good as well, with an implicit price w, the wage rate, as the cost of leisure consumption equals earnings foregone.

The utility values U(Y,L), associated with different combinations of income and leisure, can be graphically represented by indifference curves. Each curve represents (Y,L)-combinations that give the individual the same level of utility. Individuals are assumed to prefer "more" to "less", so indifference curves that lie farther from the origin entail more utility. Finally, indifference curves are assumed to have convex shapes, i.e., bowed away from the origin.

**Health Impacts**

Health, attitudes, and other taste factors determine the shape of the indifference curves. Strong preferences for leisure yield steep curves, strong work commitments imply flat curves. If impairments make market activities painful and, thus, lower the marginal utility of income, the indifference curves of ailing workers get steeper shapes [cf. Zabalza et al. (1980)]. Impairments, however, may also reduce the marginal utility of leisure consumption as leisure activities become less enjoyable and/or the number of freely disposable leisure hours decreases [cf. Bazzoli (1985)]. More formally, the steepness of indifference curves is determined by the marginal rate of substitution between income and leisure defined by

$$\text{MRS} \; = \; -\frac{dY}{dL} \; = \; \frac{\partial U/\partial L}{\partial U/\partial Y} \; .$$

MRS indicates preferences for leisure relative to income (work). A large MRS, i.e., steep curves, implies a relatively large amount of money needed to compensate the utility loss resulting from a one hour reduction of leisure time. From the definition of MRS it may be concluded that if poor health reduces the marginal utilities of both income and leisure, its effect on relative preferences is indeterminate [Berkowitz et al. (1983)]. We can, however, plausibly assume that the overall impact of impairment on work preferences is such that MRS increases. Put more qualitatively, we assume that a persistent impairment reduces the quality of life in general (lower marginal utilities), and, specifically, discourages work (higher MRS).

Total time available per period, T, is fixed, and may either be devoted to market work (H hours), or to other activities denoted as "leisure" (L hours). "Leisure", then, includes time spent on personal care, child care, household chores, sports, entertainment, etc. The inherent scarcity of time is represented by the time constraint

$$T = H + L.$$

The set of feasible (Y,L)-combinations is bordered by a budget line which incorporates the time constraint:

$$Y = w(T-L) + N.$$

The budget line runs from the point defined by maximum leisure, L = T, and non-labor income Y = N, to the point defined by L = 0, and Y = wT + N ("full income"), as depicted in figure 3.1. Since Y is defined at the household level, N contains personal asset income as well as the earnings and asset incomes of other household members.

**Figure 3.1    A Budget-Line Defined by Wage Rate w, Non-Labor Income N, and Time Endowment T**

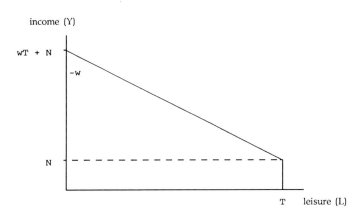

The budget line embodies the essence of the choice problem in determining the individual's optimal supply of working hours - the trade-off between leisure and earnings. The slope of the budget line is determined by the (hourly) wage rate w. Higher wages, producing steeper budget lines, and higher non-labor incomes, increasing the intercept, yield larger sets of feasible options.

If labor markets are perfectly flexible and competitive, the wage rate equals marginal productivity. To the extent that ailing workers are less productive, then, their wage rates are lower than those of their healthy peers. In the absence of any compensatory income system the extreme case of a severely disabled worker whose earning capacity is virtually zero could be represented by a horizontal budget line. Maximum utility would be found in the corner point, where L = T and Y = N. If the household to which the disabled worker belongs would have no other financial means, i.e., N = 0, severe disability would imply equally severe poverty.

Figure 3.2 gives an illustration of the potential impact of health deteriorations on the set of (Y,L)-options.[6] A healthy worker has a budget line given by wage $w_H$, and attains maximum utility at tangent point H of indifference curve $U_{H2}$ = $U(Y_H,L_H)$.

Assume, now, that an ailing colleague, or the same worker after becoming impaired, has the same (flat) preferences but earns a lower wage $w_A$. If he is free to adapt his working hours to his reduced earning capacity, he will choose point A yielding maximum utility $U_{H1}$ = $U(Y_A,L_A)$ with $U_{H1} < U_{H2}$.[7] However, if he were not allowed to accommodate his work effort, he would end up in $A_1$ which, by definition, is a less preferred income-leisure combination.

**Figure 3.2**    Optimal Income-Leisure Combinations for a Healthy Worker (H) and an
            Ailing Worker (A).

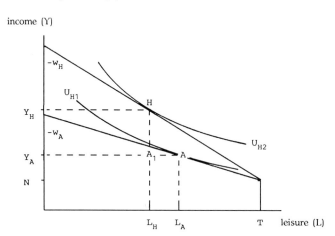

**Figure 3.2**    Optimal Income-Leisure Combinations for a Healthy Worker (H) and an
            Ailing Worker (A).

On top of a wage-reduction, the ailing worker's preferences may change in the
direction of a stronger taste for leisure relative to income. This second impact of
ill health, then, would make his indifference curves run steeper. Such preferences
are depicted in figure 3.3. The highest utility attainable, now, lies at the corner of
the budget set where earnings are zero, and $L_{A*} = T$. Thus, the two impacts of
ill health, together, may result in retirement as the most preferred of all options
available. This illustrates that even in the absence of any transfer program, retirement may be optimal for people in bad health with sufficient non-labor income.

**Figure 3.3**    Optimal Income-Leisure Combination, A*, for an Ailing Worker with a
            Strong Preference for Retirement.

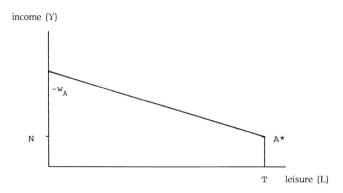

Now suppose a worker with wage $w_H$ who has reached the optimum point H (see figure 3.2) is covered by DI. His insured earnings, then, are equal to $w_H(T-L_H)$. If he would be struck by an impairment that totally incapacitates him, he would be entitled to a DI-benefit B so that

$$B = rw_H(T - L_H),$$

with replacement rate r $(0 < r < 1)$. Hence, as displayed in figure 3.4, DI-eligibility shifts the horizontal budget line of totally disabled workers to the level N + B.

**Figure 3.4**    A Budget-Line for a Worker, Eligible for Full DI-Benefits (B), Based on Insured Earnings Equal to $w_H(T-L_H)$.

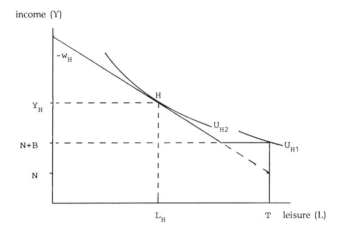

Figure 3.4 may also be used to illustrate the relative adequacy of DI-benefits, by comparison of the highest attainable pre-disability utility level, $U_{H2}$, with the compensated post-disability utility level, $U_{H1}$. The smaller the utility-difference $U_{H2} - U_{H1}$, the more adequately the welfare losses due to disability are covered. Note, however, that such utility comparisons can only be sensibly made if preferences are stable. This is in conflict with the assumption of health-dependent preferences made before.

As documented in the preceding chapter, the Dutch DI-administration often grants partially disabled workers, who are able to earn a post-impairment wage $w_A$, eligibility for full DI-benefits. Would these partially disabled workers nevertheless opt for partial, instead of full, retirement their benefit would be reduced at a 100 percent marginal tax rate so that the combined amount of labor and transfer income would equal the full benefit amount B. Full eligibility, therefore, adds the triangle abc in figure 3.5 to the budget set of partially disabled workers whose residual earning capacity is represented by wage rate $w_A$.

**Figure 3.5**    A Budget-Line Defined by the "Ailing" Wage Rate, $w_A$, for a Worker
Eligible for Full DI-Benefits (B), Based on Insured Earnings Equal to
$w_H(T-L_H)$.

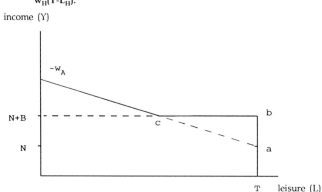

Clearly, on the horizontal stretch (bc) of their kinked budget line, the partially
disabled that are eligible for full benefits reach maximum utility at the angular point
(b). If, as illustrated, most of the ensuing earnings' loss is compensated by the DI-
benefit, the corner solution (b) yields maximum leisure at relatively low cost.

This suggests that partial retirement would always be an inferior option when
eligible for full benefits. If the theoretical case illustrated by figure 3.5 may be
viewed as representative of the Dutch administrative practice, one might be tempted
to conclude that the leniency and generosity of the DI-program are antagonistic to
partial work resumption.

Along the complete budget line, however, flat enough indifference curves may run
through the angular point, and have a tangent point as well. In that case, utility
maximization does not guarantee a unique solution to the time allocation problem.
Still flatter indifference curves of people with strong work commitments, or steeper
sloped budget lines of those with larger residual earning capacities, may result in
a continuation of full labor force participation as the optimal solution.

## A Simple Decision Rule

Simple neoclassical models, as the one illustrated above, portray a static world in
which the economic subjects are fully informed. Upon this information, they choose
according to their preferences from a set of feasible options. The size of this set,
i.e., the room for choice, depends on non-labor income, (residual) earning capacity,
and eligibility for full DI-benefits. The last two elements are related as they both
depend on health status.

Formally, the choice between continued labor force participation and application
for DI-benefits is based on the utility difference between the work option and the

DI-benefit recipiency option. Or, using the notation introduced before

$$U(DI) - U(WORK) = U(B+N, T) - U(wH+N, T-H) \qquad (3.1)$$

Utility maximizing workers with a given health status are inclined to opt out of the labor force by claiming a DI-benefit, if the difference defined by (3.1) is positive. This utility difference may be viewed as measuring the inclination to claim DI-eligibility. It, therefore, may be labeled an **inclination index**.

For groups of similar workers, then, the probability of claiming DI-benefits equals the probability of a positive utility difference:

$$Pr\{CLAIM\} = Pr\{U(DI) - U(WORK) > 0\} \qquad (3.2)$$

Decision rules, like the one implied by eq.(3.2), are a common starting point in micro-economic models of behavioral choice. They represent the micro-economic approach to disability behavior in its simplest form. However simple, they imply a set of hypotheses which, upon elaboration, are empirically testable. These hypotheses can be formulated with respect to the inclination to retire by claiming DI-eligibility.

For a given health status, such inclinations can be shown to be stronger, and the concomitant probability (3.2) higher,

- the smaller the earning capacity, as represented by the wage rate;
- the higher the non-labor income;
- the higher the benefit when eligible;
- the stronger the preferences for leisure relative to income, i.e., the larger the MRS.

Given the assumptions made before, impairment reduces earning capacity and increases the MRS, and, thus, reinforces the inclination to opt out through the DI-route.

These hypotheses show that the micro-economic approach rests on a few key concepts, such as earning capacity and work-leisure preferences, which are closely related to the determinants of disability behavior as proposed by medical sociology. Indeed, one may use the variables derived from the sociological approach to elaborate these micro-economic key concepts. For instance, leisure preferences may be specified as a function of health (clinical) and attitudinal factors, and earning capacity as a function of health and other human capital characteristics (see section 3.3.4). Thus, the micro-economic framework also serves as a device to structure the sociologically based determinants of disability behavior.

Utility based decision rules might suggest that all ailing workers have full liberty to act according to their preferences; that disability could be viewed as a matter of personal choice. Given the dependency, however, of wages on earning capacities, the model is also applicable to cases that virtually have no alternative options. One may plausibly argue that those who are forced to stop working as a result of, say, tragic accidents, terminal diseases, or severe mental illnesses, will be unable to derive any utility from working, even if they would otherwise reluctantly leave the work force. For such severe cases the work option is irrelevant and only the availability of compensatory payments may generate any utility.

On the other hand, decision rule (3.2) should also be applicable to workers in perfect health. Their chance of being found eligible for a DI-benefit is equal or close to zero, irrespective of their preferences for retirement. Consequently, their proclivity to choose the DI-option rather than keep working is likely to be minimal.

### 3.3.2   Elaboration of Pr{CLAIM}: Expected Utility-Streams over Finite Time-Horizons

A number of limitations prevent the decision rule, embodied by eq. (3.2), from being an adequate description of the considerations that underlie disability behavior. Imagine a worker, suffering from a chronic ailment, who finds himself in the grey area between full capacity and full disability. Assume that he perceives the DI-eligibility option as a more or less attractive form of early retirement enforced by ill health. In other words, he views DI-enrolment as an "absorbing state", precluding return to paid work.

In the absence of other alternatives, then, he will weigh the pros and cons of DI-benefit dependency against those of continued labor force participation during the rest of his work-life. Given the potential long-term consequences of DI-applications, he will base his decision on the difference of the **utility-streams** flowing from either option, as opposed to the instantaneous utilities introduced before. What is at stake, therefore, is a once-and-for-all decision on how to spend one's remaining work-life, running from current age $(t=t_0)$ until 65, the age of mandatory retirement, when DI-entitlements run out.

In their evaluation of future utility-streams, individuals are assumed to prefer a given combination of income and leisure now, over the same combination later. Utility derived from future income-leisure combinations, therefore, should be discounted at a subjective rate of time preference $\delta$, $(0 < \delta < 1)$.[8]

Hence, we define the utility-stream flowing from the DI-option as

$$U(DI) = \int_{t_0}^{65} e^{-\delta(s-t_0)} U(DI_0)\ ds = U(DI_0) \int_{t_0}^{65} e^{-\delta(s-t_0)} ds \qquad (3.3)$$

where

$$U(DI_0) = U[B_0 + N_0, T_0],$$  (3.4)

and variables with subscript 0 are evaluated at time $t_0$.

DI-benefits in real terms are taken to be time-invariant, and reflect the award conditions that prevailed before the benefit cuts of 1984 and 1985 were introduced (see section 2.4.1). Moreover, given the limitations of our, basically cross-sectional, data we assume that other household income (N) does not change over time. Time, then, is only represented by the discounting mechanism.

These simplifying assumptions seriously restrict the theoretical model for the evaluation of the utility-stream in the DI-option. First, viewing DI-enrolment as an absorbing state implies the presumption that workers perceive their disablement as unalterable. Our static approach ignores the potential rewards of investments of time and money in medical care and rehabilitation. As a more sophisticated alternative, Grossman's concept of health capital could be used. This approach would require intertemporal utility maximization as its conceptual framework, where utility is derived both from health improvements and leisure, as well as other commodities. Apart from its consumptive aspects, Grossman and Benham (1974) and Berkowitz et al. (1983) stress the human capital returns to health improvements in terms of higher wage rates and better employment opportunities. If appropriately elaborated, then, this investment approach would yield a model in which the time profiles of the optimal stock of health capital, the concomitant wage rates and time endowments, and the optimal supply of working hours, all would be jointly determined [cf. Lee (1982)].

Second, by treating other household income as an exogenously fixed element in the ailing worker's decision function, we ignore the possibility that other household-members may increase their future work effort so as to neutralize the income-loss implied by partial compensation. Joint determination of working hours of all household-members given their health-conditions and wage-rates, would potentially offer a more adequate approach. On the other hand, empirical research regarding labor supply responses of wives to disabling conditions of their husbands does not provide strong evidence of intra-family substitution of market hours or earnings [Parsons (1977), Muller et al. (1979), De Jong et al. (1988)].

Ignoring other options, the utility-stream associated with the DI-option should be confronted with the utility-stream flowing from continued labor force participation

$$U(WORK) = \int_{t_0}^{65} e^{-\delta(s-t_0)} U(WORK_s)\, ds$$  (3.5)

where

$$U(WORK_s) = U[w_s H_0 + N_0 , T_0 - H_0 ]. \tag{3.6}$$

The wage rate $(w_s)$ is allowed to follow an individually determined age-profile, whereas optimal working hours $(H)$ are fixed at their current level. Thus we rigidly assume that, given labor force participation, workers have reached a long-term optimum at $H_0$. Only the possibility of becoming eligible for full DI-benefits would induce them to leave this optimum and choose $H_0 = 0$. Given eligibility, inter-mediate options, in which partial reductions of working hours are combined with partial benefits, are ruled out as being less preferable (see fig. 3.5.). Note that this assumption is corroborated by the Dutch DI-data which shows that recipiency of partial benefits is a relative rarity (see table 2.15).

As a more comprehensive alternative one could posit a dynamic labor supply model that allows for saving and borrowing, in which human capital elements, such as schooling, training, and health; concomitant wages and time endowments; and labor supply, all would be endogenous [Heckman (1976)]. In an even more elaborate version, one might also want to endogenize the stocks of human capital of other household-members, and their ensuing earnings. Such approaches, however, would seem intractable, both theoretically and empirically.

For simplicity's sake, therefore, we postulate a decision framework in which workers are presumed to statically compare utility-streams over finite time-horizons. By fixing hours of work at their observed levels $(H_t = H_0)$, workers are assumed to solve the discrete choice problem of either to stay on the job under current employ-ment conditions or to venture out on the route to DI-application. So, our approach departs from more sophisticated but possibly less realistic ones, which presume static or dynamic utility maximization along a continuous budget line. In these approaches to the retirement decision in general [Bazzoli (1985), Boskin and Hurd (1978), Fields and Mitchell (1984), Gordon and Blinder (1980)], or to DI-application in particular [Hausman (1985)], work force participation involves an unrestricted choice of hours. The zero hours option (retirement or application for full DI-benefits) results as a corner solution if the reservation wage at the zero hours point is larger than the market wage. These approaches use indirect, i.e., maximized, utility as their central concept, where utility is a function of the wage rate and (virtual) non-labor income, as opposed to the direct utility framework used here, and in a number of other discrete choice studies [Fenn and Vlachonikolis (1986), Haveman and Wolfe (1984), Parsons (1980)], Zabalza et al. (1980)].

**Choice under Uncertainty**

Substitution of instantaneous utility by utility-streams may yield a more adequate description of the retirement decision at stake, it leaves the presumption of a riskless world unaltered. Both options, however, entail a variety of risks, potentially affecting utility, that should be taken into consideration.

With respect to the DI-option, claiming DI-eligibility is subject to the risk of being denied a DI-award. Let $p_a$ denote the objective probability of a worker with given medical and vocational characteristics being granted a DI-benefit,

$$p_a = Pr\{AWARD \mid CLAIM\}$$

So, the **expected utility-stream** associated with the DI-option, can be written as a weighted sum of U(DI) and its alternative, EU(work),

$$EU(DI) = p_a U(DI) + (1 - p_a) EU(work), \tag{3.7}$$

where U(DI) is defined by eq.(3.3), and EU(work) is the expected utility-stream in case the application is rejected, and the unsuccessful applicant either returns to the work force, resorts to alternative transfer programs, or is left without income [cf. Treitel (1976), Parsons (1980), Hausman (1985)].

Under Dutch legislation, employers can only dissolve the employment contracts of sick employees after two years of uninterrupted absenteeism, i.e., when the DI-beneficiary status has lasted for at least one year. Formally, therefore, rejected applicants always have the option to resume their jobs.

On the other hand, a benefit denial may jeopardize the financial prospects and employment security of an applicant. Hence,

$$EU(work) \leq EU(WORK)$$

Assuming that work resumption upon a benefit denial, nevertheless, is the alternative most preferred, we will ignore other alternatives. Below, we will elaborate on the differences between EU(work) and EU(WORK).

The utility-stream in the work-option is subject to two kinds of risks. First, there is uncertainty with respect to continuation of current employment, due to disability and unemployment hazards. Second, even if current employment continues smoothly, one's future wage-profile is inherently uncertain [cf. Killingsworth (1983) pp. 261-263)].

Given the fact that less than 20 percent of the Dutch privately employed remain in the labor force until pensionable age, and the others drop out prematurely mainly due to disability, we will represent the "continued work gamble" by concentrating on the disability hazard. For that purpose, we introduce a random variable t, with density function f(t), measuring the duration of the remaining working life of a current labor force participant with age $t_0$ ; $t_{DI} = t_0 + t$, then, is the age of eventual DI-enrolment if one would opt for continued labor force participation now.

Evidently, $t_0 \leq t_{DI} \leq 65$. The parameters of density $f(t)$ should vary according to individual health and vocational characteristics.[9]

Rigorous application of these definitions and assumptions would yield the following specification for the expected utility-stream in the work-option

$$EU(WORK) = \int_0^{65-t_0} f(t) \left[ \int_{t_0}^{t_{DI}} e^{-\delta(s-t_0)} EU(WORK_s)\ ds + EU(DI_{t_{DI}}) \int_{t_{DI}}^{65} e^{-\delta(s-t_0)}\ ds \right] dt \qquad (3.8)$$

The expression within square brackets calculates the expected utility-stream flowing from continued labor force participation for a given draw of $t = t_{DI} - t_0$. The first term is the discounted utility-stream over the remaining working life, running from current age $(t_0)$ until age $t_{DI}$, at which the worker is to become a DI-beneficiary. The second term represents the utility-stream after DI-enrolment with a benefit based on earnings at $t_{DI}$.

Both utility-streams are based on wage-profiles that are subject to randomness. Ideally, the expected values of the instantaneous utilities in (3.8) should be taken over individually varying, time-dependent, density functions of wages[10], $g_s(w)$ so that, using (3.6),

$$EU(WORK_s) = \int_0^\infty g_s(w_s)\ U\ [w_s\ H_0 + N_0\ ,\ T_0 - H_0\ ]\ dw_s \qquad (3.9)$$

Unfortunately, the density functions introduced in (3.8) and (3.9) severely complicate the road to an empirically manageable form. At the expense of theoretical rigor we therefore replace the premise that workers would know these complicated densities by the presumption that they know both their expected age of DI-enrolment, $t^*$, and their expected wage-profile, $Ew_s$. In fact, then, we reimpose perfect knowledge with respect to the future utility-stream in the work-option.

Defining the expected age of DI-enrolment as

$$t^* = Et_{DI} = t_0 + Et = t_0 + \int_0^{65-t_0} t\ f(t)\ dt$$

we may replace the expected utility-stream in the work-option (3.8) by the simpler expression

$$U(WORK) = \int_{t_0}^{t^*} e^{-\delta(s-t_0)} U(WORK_s) \, ds + U(DI_{t^*}) \int_{t^*}^{65} e^{-\delta(s-t_0)} \, ds \qquad (3.10)$$

In this expression the expected age of DI-enrolment, $t^*$, acts as a pivotal variable. In order to obtain a manageable form for $t^*$ we posit a discrete distribution of durations, measured in years. Yearly DI-incidence rates are defined accordingly as the probability of enrolment in the time interval $[t, t+1]$. Specifically, using the variables defined before, the probability that DI-enrolment takes place after at least t but less than $t+1$ years, conditional on uninterrupted labor force participation between age $t_0$ and age $t_0 + t$, equals

$$p_t = \Pr \{ t_0 + t \le t_{DI} < t_0 + t + 1 \mid t_{DI} \ge t_0 + t \} \qquad (t = 1, 2,..., 65\text{-}t_0)$$

The probability of survival as a labor market participant up until $t_0 + t$ is

$$\Pr \{ t_{DI} \ge t_0 + t \} = \prod_{i=1}^{t-1} (1 - p_i) \qquad (t = 2, ..., 65\text{-}t_0)$$

Hence,

$$Et = p_1 + \sum_{t=2}^{65\text{-}t_0} \left[ t p_t \prod_{i=1}^{t-1} (1 - p_i) \right]$$

The expected duration of the remaining working life, Et, is taken over the unconditional probability of DI-enrolment in any year between $t_0 + 1$ and 65.

The expectation is calculated conditional on labor force participation until $t_0 + 1$, excluding the possibility of DI-enrolment during $t_0$. This condition is necessary for a proper definition of the choice under study: Either to apply for DI at $t_0$ or not. Not applying, i.e., continued labor force participation during $t_0$ in combination with the possibility to opt out after $t_0$, rules out the possibility of enrolment during $t_0$. On the other hand, Et does include the probability of uninterrupted labor force participation until 65, when DI-coverage runs out. Since 65 is the mandatory retirement age, we set $p_{65\text{-}t0} = 1$. By this normalization the unconditional DI-probabilities over which Et is calculated add up to one:

$$p_1 + \sum_{t=2}^{65\text{-}t_0} p_t \prod_{i=1}^{t-1} (1 - p_i) = 1$$

Using this equation, we can simplify the expression for Et and obtain

$$Et = 1 + \sum_{t=1}^{64-t_0} \left[ \prod_{i=1}^{t} (1 - p_i) \right] \tag{3.11}$$

The future DI-probabilities $p_t$ ($t>0$) will be positively correlated with the current DI-probability, $p_0 = \Pr\{DI \mid t_0\}$ , or

$$\frac{\partial p_t}{\partial p_0} > 0$$

and therefore, using (3.11),

$$\frac{\partial Et}{\partial p_0} = - \sum_{t=1}^{64-t_0} \left[ \sum_{j=1}^{t} \left[ \frac{\partial p_j}{\partial p_0} \right] \prod_{i=1}^{t} \left[ \frac{1 - p_i}{1 - p_j} \right] \right] < 0.$$

Consequently, the observable and latent factors that determine $p_0$ are likely to affect Et and $t^*$ negatively. The expected age of DI-enrolment, $t^*$, and, the current DI-probability, $p_0$, are mutually dependent, simultaneous, outcomes of the disability process.

Specification (3.10) rests on a number of added, simplifying, assumptions. First, only two states are being distinguished, the WORK and the DI-state. The possibility that workers may be laid off temporarily is ignored. Alternative routes to leave the labor force, such as prolonged spells of unemployment, or voluntary participation in early retirement schemes, are assumed to generate a utility-stream equal to the second term in (3.10). Long-term unemployment and disability hazards, and early retirement options, therefore, are treated as if they were equal although they differ both in terms of benefit amounts and durations as well as in terms of coverage and eligibility standards. Consequently, $p_t$ should be interpreted as the probability of enrolment in a program covering "exit" from the labor force before 65.

Second, both the disability and the long-term unemployment states are assumed to be absorbing. Re-employment upon prolonged unemployment or disability is ignored. The approach, therefore, is strongly "inflow-oriented". Benefit terminations as a result of recovery and/or work resumption are left unconsidered. This simplification may be justified by the Dutch DI-practice with average yearly recovery rates that amount to no more than 4 percent of the beneficiary volume.[11]

**Elaboration of the Inclination Index: Two Extreme Cases**

Using definitions (3.1) and (3.7), the relevant inclination index ($\pi$) can be written as

$$\pi = EU(DI) - U(WORK)$$

$$= p_a [U(DI) - U(WORK)] + (1 - p_a) [U(work) - U(WORK)] \qquad (3.12)$$

where U(WORK) is defined by eq.(3.10) and U(work) will be specified below in (3.19).[12]

From (3.12) it appears that the inclination to apply for DI-benefits ($\pi$) is larger,

- the larger the utility gain upon DI-enrolment; in other words, the larger the rewards to successful application;
- the smaller the difference between the utility-streams of non-applicants and rejected applicants [U(WORK) - U(work)]; in other words, the smaller the penalties of unsuccessful application;
- the larger the probability of being granted an award ($p_a$), provided that U(DI) > U(work).[13]

Both the award probability, $p_a$, and the expected age of eventual DI-enrolment of a non-applicant, $t^*$, are determined by, among others, current health status. One extreme, then, is the occurrence of a disability so severe that it precludes return to paid work. This case can be formally represented by $p_a = 1$, as one can safely assume that under any DI-program the severely disabled will be awarded with probability one, yielding a utility-stream equal to U(DI) as defined by (3.3).

As concerns the work option, the impossibility to perform productive activities could be indicated by zero wages. In the absence of other income maintenance programs than wage-replacement under DI, later DI-application, at $t^*$, would be useless as it would yield no more than zero benefits. In this scenario, then, severely disabled workers can either accept DI-benefits or be left without any labor or transfer income.

For this extreme case the inclination index attains its theoretical upper bound

$$\pi = \left[ U[B_0 + N_0, T_0] - U[N_0, T_0] \right] \int_{t_0}^{65} e^{-\delta(s-t_0)} ds > 0, \qquad (3.13)$$

implying a relatively large value of Pr{CLAIM}, as it should.

The assumptions by which these extreme values for $\pi$ and Pr{CLAIM} are obtained are, of course, unrealistic in that they disregard the actual institutional setting in which the severely disabled make their retirement decisions. Specifically, in defining the alternative to DI-enrolment the presence of alternative transfer programs and statutory minimum wages and benefits is ignored. Accounting for these provisions would reduce the largest possible value of $\pi$ but would still be positive in general.[14]

The other end of the scale for $\pi$ is found when a worker who, at $t_0$, is in perfect health and yet applies for a DI-benefit. His or her chance of being found eligible can realistically be assumed to be zero, i.e., $p_a = 0$. Using (3.12) we then obtain

$$\pi = U(\text{work}) - U(\text{WORK}) \leq 0. \tag{3.14}$$

This value of $\pi$, and the corresponding value of Pr{CLAIM}, are the smallest possible. U(work) represents the utility-stream in case a DI-application is rejected, and the denied applicant returns to the labor force. This calls attention for the potential, financial and vocational consequences of benefit denial [see below, specifically eq.(3.20)].

According to (3.14) $\pi$ equals zero if the career prospects of a rejected applicant would be unscathed, i.e., U(work) = U(WORK). In that case, healthy workers would be indifferent whether or not to apply for DI-benefits, as application would be useless ($p_a = 0$) but costless too [U(work) - U(WORK) = 0].

## The Rejected Applicant

If rejected applicants were not to be penalized [U(work) = U(WORK)], or if all DI-claims were to be awarded ($p_a = 1$), application for DI-benefits would not involve any added costs. In that case, the inclination index (3.12) could simply be written as

$$\pi = U(\text{DI}) - U(\text{WORK}).$$

Or, using (3.3) and (3.10),

$$\pi = \int_{t_0}^{t^*} e^{-\delta(s-t_0)} \pi_s \, ds + [U(\text{DI}_0) - U(\text{DI}_{t^*})] \int_{t^*}^{65} e^{-\delta(s-t_0)} \, ds \tag{3.15}$$

where

$$\pi_s = U(\text{DI}_0) - U(\text{WORK}_s) , \tag{3.16}$$

representing the instantaneous utility-difference at s ($\geq t_0$) when DI-enrolment takes place at $t_0$. In the case defined by (3.15), the only remaining uncertainty pertains to the expected duration of one's remaining working life.

The second term in (3.15) emerges from the fact that wage-related benefit amounts change over time according to the age-profiles of the insured earnings. Utility-streams in the DI-option, therefore, depend on the benefit size that applies at the date of DI-enrolment. If wages were expected to rise (drop) continuously over the remaining working life, the second term represents a penalty (bonus) for premature (before t*) enrolment. However, if earnings-profiles are curved, as they often are, the sign of this term is indefinite.

The assumption that one's current employer, or other potential employers, would not penalize workers after unsuccessful application for DI-benefits and consequential job return, is implausible. More specifically, three factors may cause differences between the expected utility-streams of non-applicants [U(WORK)] and rejected applicants [U(work)]:

(i)     Since application for DI must be preceded by a one-year period of absenteeism covered by Sickness Benefits, denied applicants may be considered productivity risks by their own and other potential employers. Consequently, after work resumption the wage-profiles of rejected applicants may be less favorable than those of similar non-applicants, resulting in a time-dependent difference-term

$$\Phi_s = U(WORK_s) - U(work_s) \geq 0, \tag{3.17}$$

where $U(WORK_s)$ is defined as in (3.6), and $U(work_s)$ is calculated using a "scarred" wage-profile $\tilde{w}_s$. Notice that we maintain the assumption that this potential wage reduction does not affect the number of working hours $H_0$ after return to the job.

(ii)    As a result of their reduced earnings, potential future DI-benefits of rejected applicants are lower than those of successful applicants, yielding a second difference term

$$\Omega_t = [U(DI_t) - U(di_t)] \geq 0, \tag{3.18}$$

where $DI_t$ and $di_t$ are defined by (3.4), and $di_t$ is based on benefit amounts conditional on the reduced earnings of rejected applicants, where t is the date of DI-enrolment.

(iii)   The remaining working life of rejected applicants may be shorter than that of non-applicants. Unsuccessful application now could enhance the likelihood of later DI-enrolment, for instance, if an application would reveal health problems to DI-administrators that warrant future eligibility; if employers would label rejected applicants as productivity risks and henceforth try and promote their DI-enrolment; and, finally, if appeals against benefit denials lead to reversals later on. In such cases the expected date of eventual DI-enrolment for rejected applicants is advanced, say by $\theta$ periods, or

$$\theta = t^* - \tilde{t}^* \geq 0 , \tag{3.19}$$

where $\tilde{t}^*$ is the expected date at which a formerly denied applicant will become eligible.

If, indeed, unsuccessful application increases the probability of future eligibility, $\theta$, unlike the other two difference-terms, is not a penalty but a bonus.

Combining these assumptions with the definition of the utility-stream in the work-option (3.10), we find that the utility-stream of a rejected applicant who returns to his job is

$$U(work) = \int_{t_0}^{t^*-\theta} e^{-\delta(s-t_0)} U(work_s) \, ds \; + \; U(di_{t^*-\theta}) \int_{t^*-\theta}^{65} e^{-\delta(s-t_0)} \, ds .$$

Hence, using the definitions (3.16) through (3.19),

$$U(work) - U(WORK) = \int_{t^*-\theta}^{t^*} e^{-\delta(s-t_0)} \pi_s \, ds - \int_{t_0}^{t^*-\theta} e^{-\delta(s-t_0)} \Phi_s \, ds - \Omega_{t^*-\theta} \int_{t^*-\theta}^{65} e^{-\delta(s-t_0)} \, ds$$

$$+ [U(DI_{t^*-\theta}) - U(DI_{t^*})] \int_{t^*}^{65} e^{-\delta(s-t_0)} \, ds. \tag{3.20}$$

Equation (3.20) contains the potential penalties and bonuses a rejected applicant has to deal with after work resumption. The first term represents the utility-gain (or loss) connected with an advance of future eligibility by $\theta$ periods. The next two terms incorporate the detrimental effects on future earnings ($\Phi$) and awards ($\Omega$) resulting from unsuccessful application. The final term is again related to advanced enrolment. This term is negative if the earnings base on which benefit amounts are calculated steadily increases over the working life.

The utility-difference defined by eq.(3.20) can be interpreted as the smallest attainable value of the inclination index $\pi$ [see eq.(3.14)]. This lower end of the scale for $\pi$ is reached if, at $t=t_0$, a worker would have no chance of meeting the DI-eligibility standards, i.e., $p_a = 0$. This is the case of a healthy worker who would seriously jeopardize his career prospects were he to apply for DI.

This case can now be elaborated by assuming that the financial penalties ($\Phi_s$ and $\Omega_t$) are substantial, whereas the bonus of advanced DI-enrolment is absent ($\theta = 0$). By these assumptions, the only terms in (3.20) that remain, are negative.

**Full Specification of the Inclination Index**

Substitution of (3.15), (3.16), and (3.20) in the inclination index $\pi$, as defined by (3.12), yields

$$\pi = p_a \int_{t_0}^{t^*} e^{-\delta(s-t_0)} \pi_s \; ds \; + \tag{3.21}$$

$$(1 - p_a) \left[ \int_{t^*-\theta}^{t^*} e^{-\delta(s-t_0)} \pi_s \; ds - \int_{t_0}^{t^*-\theta} e^{-\delta(s-t_0)} \Phi_s \; ds - \Omega_{t^*-\theta} \int_{t^*-\theta}^{65} e^{-\delta(s-t_0)} ds \right] +$$

$$\left[ p_a \left[ U(DI_0) - U(DI_{t^*}) \right] + (1 - p_a) \left[ U(DI_{t^*-\theta}) - U(DI_{t^*}) \right] \right] \int_{t^*}^{65} e^{-\delta(s-t_0)} ds$$

This elaboration shows that the inclination index consists of three composite terms. The first term represents the expected utility-gain of successful application relative to non-application. The higher the award probability and/or the larger the utility-stream in the DI-option relative to the WORK-option, the stronger the incentive to participate in the DI-program. The second term incorporates the expected vocational bonuses and penalties of being denied an award, relative to continued labor force participation. For a given denial rate, the proclivity to choose the DI-option is stronger, the larger the advance of future eligibility and the smaller the detrimental financial effects of a benefit denial. The higher the award probability, the smaller the (dis)incentives to program participation exerted by these bonuses and penalties. The third term is the expected value of the benefit differential resulting from premature DI-enrolment.

As can be easily checked, the two extreme values for $\pi$ that correspond with severe disability ($p_a=1$) and perfect health ($p_a= 0$) are as derived before. In case $p_a=1$, we adopt the scenario where $w_s= 0$ (no remaining earning capacity), and substitute $U(WORK_s) = U(DI_{t^*}) = U(N_0, T_0)$. Expression (3.21), then, reduces to eq.(3.13). If $p_a= 0$, we assume that $\theta = 0$ (no advance of DI-enrolment) which by eq.(3.20) obtains eq.(3.14).

Three final remarks about the inclination model.

First, the endogeneity of the expected age of eventual DI-enrolment, $t^* = Et - t_0$, has been ignored so far. Definition (3.11), however, implies that, via $p_0$, Et depends on - the complete set of determinants of - the DI-entry probability. This endogeneity complicates the causal structure of the DI-entry process (see scheme 3.3 below).

Second, the simplifying assumptions on which specification (3.10) of the utility-stream in the work option is based induce perfect foresight regarding the expected duration of the remaining working life Et. This implies that the insured workers are presumed to know their current and future DI-entry and award probabilities, $p_t$ and $p_{a,t}$. Consistency requires, then, that the insured also know the true sizes of their current award rate $(p_a)$ which appears in (3.21).

Finally, note that the utility-streams in the DI-option, introduced in (3.3), and the WORK-option, introduced in (3.5), are defined using one uniform discount rate δ. Time preference rates may, however, be state-dependent. For instance, earnings-conditioned utilities may be discounted at a higher rate than those conditional on, more secure, DI-benefits.

## From $\pi$ to Pr{DI} via the Award Rate $p_a$

The assumptions with regard to perfect foresight can be relaxed by defining the inclination index $\pi$ as a random variable: without specifying the exact causes of its randomness we simply describe $\pi$ by a monotonically increasing distribution function H with $H(-\infty) = 0$ and $H(\infty) = 1$. The transformation of $\pi$ into Pr{CLAIM}, i.e., the probability of claiming DI-eligibility at $t=t_0$, is then made by

$$Pr\{CLAIM\} = H(\pi). \tag{3.22}$$

Next, recalling that the (current) DI-probability, $Pr\{DI\} = p_0 = Pr\{DI|t_0\}$, is the product of the (current) application probability and the (current) probability of an award given application, we get

$$Pr\{DI\} = p_a H(\pi), \tag{3.23}$$

where

$$p_a = Pr\{AWARD \text{ at } t_0|CLAIM \text{ at } t_0\}.$$

The individual award rate, $p_a$, has a direct, administrative, effect on Pr{DI} as well as an indirect, behavioral, effect running via $\pi$. The award rate is determined by a set of policy variables, such as screening rigor, which basically only vary over time,[15] and individually varying clinical and vocational characteristics.

To give a formal example of these effects, assume that screening rigor can be measured by a variable R. Increased scrutiny will lower the award probability $p_a$

of a marginally disabled claimant directly. A smaller award rate, however, may also weaken his or her inclination to claim eligibility, thus lowering the DI-application probability.

These effects can be elaborated by calculation of the elasticity $\varepsilon_R^{Pr\{DI\}}$ of the incidence rate $(Pr\{DI\})$ with respect to screening rigor $(R)$

$$\varepsilon_R^{Pr\{DI\}} = \varepsilon_R^{P_a} + \pi \frac{h(\pi)}{H(\pi)} \varepsilon_R^\pi \, , \qquad \text{where } h = \frac{dH}{d\pi} \, .$$

This equality flows from differentiation of identity (3.23). The negative behavioral response to increased scrutiny appears to reinforce the disincentive administrative impact.[16]

Similar effects can be derived for the savings induced by benefit cuts, where direct price-effects are reinforced by behavioral volume-effects.[17]

**Summary and Discussion of the Micro-Economic Model**

As a summary of this section, in which we have described a micro-economic model for the probability of DI-entry, the implied hypothetical causalities are drawn in scheme 3.3.

**Scheme 3.3  Causal Structure of the DI-Entry Process (Expected Signs in Parentheses)**

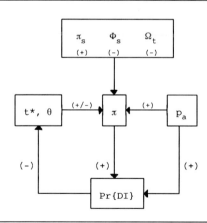

The proclivity to claim eligibility for DI-benefits at time $t_0$ is measured by a theoretical inclination index $\pi$. As defined in (3.21) the index is determined by

- $\pi_s$ ; the utility-gain of DI-enrolment relative to continued labor force participation at time s (s = t, t+1,...), when awarded a benefit at time t, the date of DI-enrolment.
- $p_a$ ; the probability of being found eligible.
- $\Phi_s$ ; the utility-loss from reduced earnings of rejected applicants who return to their job, measured at t = s.
- $\Omega_t$ ; the utility-loss from reduced benefit entitlements for rejected applicants, measured at time t, the date of DI-enrolment.
- $t^*$ ; the expected age of eventual DI-enrolment given continued labor force participation; $t^* - t_0$ is the duration of the remaining working life over which the utility-streams are calculated, and so affects $\pi$ and, through $\pi$, Pr{DI}. On the other hand, by definition (3.11), $t^*$ is inversely related to $p_t$ (t>0). These future DI-entry probabilities are likely to be positively correlated with Pr{DI} (=$p_0$), the current DI-probability. This inverse, reciprocal, influence makes $t^*$ endogenous with respect to Pr{DI}.
- $\theta$; the number of years by which $t^*$ is advanced after a rejected applicant has returned to the labor force.

The simultaneity of the expected exit age, given continued labor force participation, $t^*$, and the current DI-probability, $p_0$ = Pr{DI}, is displayed by their circular relationship, running via the inclination index, $\pi$. The impact of an exogenous variable on Pr{DI}, taking account of this circularity, can be best imagined as an iterative process. Starting with a reduced form specification for Pr{DI}, all exogenous variables, like severity of impairment, that positively affect $p_0$, reduce $t^*$. A reduction of $t^*$ may have a positive or negative effect on $\pi$ depending on, among others, age ($t_0$), earnings profile, and time preference rate, $\delta$ [see (3.21)]. If the direct impact of $t^*$ on $\pi$ is negative (positive) their circular causality will reinforce (dampen) the positive effect of an exogenous factor on Pr{DI}. In a second round the effects on $t^*$ and $\pi$ of a change in Pr{DI} resulting from the first round, could be studied. And so forth. However, when referring to the endogeneity of $t^*$ we will not consider more than one round of this iterative process.[18]
Notice that in a dynamic optimization framework the variable under study would be $t^*$ - the optimal age of exit from the labor force.


### 3.3.3    Specification of the Utility Function

At first glance there seems to be a large distance between the micro-economic approach summarized in the preceding scheme, where the core concepts are theoretical abstractions, and the medical-sociological approach as summarized in scheme 3.2, which uses variables that are, at least in principle, directly measurable.

The final step toward an estimable form of the DI-entry probability model is taken by explicit specification of the utility function, and by defining auxiliary models for the non-observable elements of the theoretical model. These additional specifications will narrow the apparent gap between the medical-sociological and the micro-economic approaches.

Following Fenn and Vlachonikolis (1986), we posit a simple Cobb-Douglas type utility function, which is additively separable after logarithmic transformation. Without loss of generality the degree of homogeneity of this type of utility function can be set at one.[19]
We, therefore, write

$$U(Y,L) = (1-\beta)\ \ln Y + \beta\ \ln L \qquad (0 < \beta < 1)\ . \qquad\qquad (3.24)$$

The parameter $\beta$ varies individually, and indicates preferences for leisure relative to income (work). More specifically, $\beta$ determines the steepness of the indifference curves that result from this utility function, as witnessed by the marginal rate of substitution between income and leisure (MRS)

$$MRS = -\frac{dY}{dL} = \frac{\beta Y}{(1-\beta)L}\ ,$$

hence,

$$-\frac{d\ln Y}{d\ln L} = \frac{\beta}{1-\beta}\ .$$

Thus, the larger $\beta$, the larger the relative income change needed to compensate a given percentage loss of leisure. Being an unobservable preference parameter, $\beta$ will be specified below as a function of health and attitudinal factors.

Using this explicit utility function, the constituent parts of the inclination index can now be expressed as functions of the two utility-generating factors: (leisure) time and money. Applying definitions (3.4), (3.6), and (3.16), the instantaneous utility difference between DI-enrolment at time t and labor force participation at time s (=t,t+1,...), becomes

$$\pi_s = U(DI_t) - U(WORK_s)$$
$$= (1-\beta)\left[\ln(B_t + N_0) - \ln(E_s + N_0)\right] + \beta\left[\ln T_0 - \ln L_0\right]$$

with $E_s = w_s H_0$ (earnings during period s), and variables with subscript 0 are evaluated at time $t_0$.
As can be easily verified $\pi_s$ is larger the larger the amount of other household income ($N_0$), the stronger the relative preference for leisure ($\beta$), and the smaller the wage rate $w_s$, or[20]

$$\frac{\partial \pi_s}{\partial N_0} > 0, \quad \frac{\partial \pi_s}{\partial \beta} > 0, \quad \frac{\partial \pi_s}{\partial w_s} < 0.$$

If $N_0 > 0$, i.e., total household income exceeds worker's earnings $E_0$, we may as well write

$$\pi_s = (1-\beta) \left[ \ln \left[ \frac{B_t}{N_0} + 1 \right] - \ln \left[ \frac{E_s}{N_0} + 1 \right] \right] + \beta \left[ \ln T_0 - \ln L_0 \right]$$

or, by first order approximation,

$$\pi_s \approx \frac{1-\beta}{N_0} \left[ B_t - E_s \right] + \beta \left[ \ln T_0 - \ln L_0 \right] \quad .$$

Similar approximation of the utility-losses of rejected applicants stemming from reduced earnings ($\Phi_s$) and benefit entitlements ($\Omega_t$) yields

$$\Phi_s \approx \frac{1-\beta}{N_0} \left[ E_s - e_s \right] \quad \text{and} \quad \Omega_t \approx \frac{1-\beta}{N_0} \left[ B_t - b_t \right],$$

whereas the utility-differences due to premature enrolment can be approximated by

$$U(DI_t) - U(DI_{t^*}) \approx \frac{1-\beta}{N_0} \left[ B_t - b_{t^*} \right] \qquad (t < t^*) \quad .$$

Substitution of these approximations into the equation for the inclination index (3.21), and multiplication by $N_0/1-\beta$, give the following expression

$$\pi = \frac{\beta}{1-\beta} N_0 \left[ \ln T_0 - \ln L_0 \right] \left[ p_a \int_{t_0}^{t^*} e^{-\delta(s-t_0)} ds + (1-p_a) \int_{t^*-\theta}^{t^*} e^{-\delta(s-t_0)} ds \right] +$$

$$p_a \, B_0 \int_{t_0}^{65} e^{-\delta(s-t_0)} ds + (1-p_a) \left[ \int_{t_0}^{t^*-\theta} e^{-\delta(s-t_0)} e_s \, ds + b_{t^*-\theta} \int_{t^*-\theta}^{65} e^{-\delta(s-t_0)} ds \right] -$$

$$\left[ \int_{t_0}^{t^*} e^{-\delta(s-t_0)} E_s \, ds + B_{t^*} \int_{t^*}^{65} e^{-\delta(s-t_0)} ds \right] \quad .$$

$$(3.25)$$

The resulting approximative form of the inclination index consists of three composite terms that correspond with the lines over which the RHS of (3.21) is divided. The first term measures the expected utility-gain due to increased leisure after DI-enrolment. This utility-from-leisure gain interacts with the marginal rate of substitution between leisure and income (MRS=$\beta/1-\beta$) and the amount of other household income ($N_0 > 0$), to reinforce or weaken the inclination to apply for DI. Given a positive utility-gain due to increased leisure, DI-application is more likely to be the preferred option the larger the "pain costs" of working as indicated by the MRS, and/or the larger the financial means to cushion earnings' losses.

The second term in (3.25) defines the expected income-stream in the DI-option. If an award is granted ($p_a = 1$), the beneficiary receives a yearly transfer income $B_0$ until 65. If, however, the applicant would be confronted with a benefit denial ($p_a$=0) and resume his job, he would follow a less favorable earnings profile ($e_s$) until DI-enrolment at $t^*-\theta$, whereupon he would receive a reduced yearly benefit $b_{t^*-\theta}$ until 65. Clearly, the larger the expected income-stream flowing from DI-application the stronger the inclination to apply.

The final term represents the expected income-stream if a worker would opt not to apply for DI-benefits. The sum in square brackets equals the discounted value of the income-stream a DI-applicant is expected to forego. Until $t^*$ the applicant foregoes earnings $E_s$ , after $t^*$ he suffers a loss of benefits if $B_t^* > B_0$. The total amount of income foregone may be interpreted as the financial damage resulting from the occurrence of total incapacity at $t_0$. This is the damage the DI-program seeks to cover.[21]

Given replacement rates that are smaller than one, potential losses due to premature enrolment, and financial penalties for denied applicants, the balance of expected income-streams in the DI and the work options will generally be negative. And the more so the larger the discounted value of future earnings. Hence, a positive value for the inclination index is only obtained if the utility-gain from increased leisure can compensate the income-losses inherent to DI-application.

We have stated before that $\pi$ attains its maximum when a worker completely loses his/her productive capacities and the only available form of compensation is through DI. This extreme case is represented by $p_a = 1$, $w_s = B_t = 0$ for all $s \geq 0$ and $t > 0$, and $L_0 = T_0$. Substitution of this scenario in (3.25) obtains

$$\pi \approx B_0 \int_{t_0}^{65} e^{-\delta(s-t_0)} \, ds \qquad \text{[cf. (3.13)]}$$

which is, of course, the discounted value of the DI-benefit stream - the only remaining income source.

The smallest value of $\pi$ is defined by the case of a DI-applicant in perfect health. In that case $p_a = \theta = 0$ and so

$$\pi \approx \int_{t_0}^{t^*} e^{-\delta(s-t_0)} [e_s - E_s] \, ds + [b_{t^*} - B_{t^*}] \int_{t^*}^{65} e^{-\delta(s-t_0)} \, ds.$$

Clearly, the value of this lower bound for $\pi$ depends on the severity of the financial penalties a rejected applicant has to face.

In the unlikely case of no penalties, $\pi = 0$. However, in that case $\pi$ could still become negative if $p_a > 0$ and the utility-gain from increased leisure would be insufficient to compensate the income losses related to DI-enrolment. More formally [cf. (3.15)], if

$$\pi \approx \frac{\beta}{1-\beta} N_0 [\ln T_0 - \ln L_0] \int_{t_0}^{t^*} e^{-\delta(s-t_0)} ds + \int_{t_0}^{t^*} e^{-\delta(s-t_0)} [B_0 - E_s] \, ds + [B_0 - B_{t^*}] \int_{t^*}^{65} e^{-\delta(s-t_0)} ds \quad (3.26)$$

would be negative. In other words, even in the absence of financial penalties for rejected applicants DI-application is still relatively unattractive ($\pi < 0$) for those who strongly prefer to stay in the labor force (small $\beta$) and/or have good career prospects (large difference $E_s - B_0$.)

Expression (3.26) also applies if DI-claims would not be screened, i.e., $p_a = 1$. In that case, each worker, regardless of presence and extent of disablement, could retire voluntarily under the DI-program. This retirement scheme would be very attractive as eligibility would not be constrained by age. Moreover benefits would be independent of contributions or retirement age. Under such a generous scheme, workers could choose their retirement age ($t^*$) conditional on career prospects and work preferences.

Note, finally, that all of these approximations and elaborations are based on the assumption that workers have a positive amount of non-labor income ($N_0 > 0$). For workers whose household income solely depends on their earnings $N_0 = 0$. In that case the exact form of the inclination index is obtained from eq.(3.25) by putting $N_0 = 1$ and replacing benefit amounts and earnings by their logs.

This modification does not affect the qualitative conclusions obtained from the preceding theoretical model where $N_0$ was assumed to be positive.

### 3.3.4 The DI-Probability Model; Structural and Reduced Forms

In the preceding section an approximative, structural, form for the inclination index has been derived which may be summarized by

$$\pi = \pi \ (\beta, \ N_0, \ ETG, \ EY_{DI}, \ EY_{WORK}) \tag{3.27}$$

where Expected Time Gain =

$$ETG \ = \ [\ln T_0 - \ln L_0] \left[ p_a \int_{t_0}^{t^*} e^{-\delta(s-t_0)}ds + (1 - p_a) \int_{t^*-\theta}^{t^*} e^{-\delta(s-t_0)}ds \right]$$

Expected (Transfer) Income =

$$EY_{DI} \ = \ p_a \ B_0 \int_{t_0}^{65} e^{-\delta(s-t_0)} \ ds \ + \ (1 - p_a) \left[ \int_{t_0}^{t^*-\theta} e^{-\delta(s-t_0)} \ e_s \ ds + b_{t^*-\theta} \int_{t_0}^{65} e^{-\delta(s-t_0)} \ ds \right]$$

Expected (Labor) Income =

$$EY_{WORK} \ = \left[ \int_{t_0}^{t^*} e^{-\delta(s-t_0)} \ E_s \ ds + B_{t^*} \int_{t^*}^{65} e^{-\delta(s-t_0)} \ ds \right]$$

Next, from definitions (3.22) and (3.23), we obtain a structural version of the DI-probability model

$$\Pr \ \{DI\} \ = \ p_0 = p_a \ . \ H \ [ \ \pi \ (\beta, \ N_0, \ ETG, \ EY_{DI}, \ EY_{WORK})]$$
$$= \ p_0 \ (p_a, \ \beta, \ N_0, \ ETG, \ EY_{DI}, \ EY_{WORK}). \tag{3.28}$$

Ignoring the potential endogeneity of $t^*$, the expected effects of these structural determinants on are such that

$$\frac{\partial p_0}{\partial p_a} \ , \ \frac{\partial p_0}{\partial \beta} \ , \ \frac{\partial p_0}{\partial N_0} \ , \ \frac{\partial p_0}{\partial ETG} \ , \ \frac{\partial p_0}{\partial EY_{DI}} \ > 0, \ \text{and} \quad \frac{\partial p_0}{\partial EY_{WORK}} < 0.$$

Finally, we define a random variable, $I^* = I^* (\pi, p_a)$, underlying the DI-probability process which may be labeled as "proneness to DI-enrolment". To make headway towards an estimable form, we approximate $I^*$ by a linear function of the structural determinants in (3.27) plus a constant and a random term, $\varepsilon$, representing specification and approximation errors,

$$I^* = \gamma'Z + \varepsilon \qquad \text{with } Z = (1, p_a, \beta, N_0, \text{ETG}, \text{EY}_{\text{DI}}, \text{EY}_{\text{WORK}}), \qquad (3.29)$$

where $\gamma$ is a vector of coefficients defined accordingly, and $\varepsilon$ is assumed to follow the standard normal distribution function, F.

Without loss of generality we can normalize $I^*$ so that $I^* > 0$ corresponds to DI-enrolment (DI = 1), or, using the symmetry of the normal distribution function,

$$\text{Pr }\{\text{DI=1}\} = \text{Pr } \{ \varepsilon > -\gamma'Z \} = \text{Pr } \{ \varepsilon < \gamma'Z \} = F(\gamma'Z). \qquad (3.30)$$


## Specifications for $\beta$, $p_a$, and $w_s$

Although expression (3.29) is meant to serve as an empirical version of our structural DI-(probit) model, it still contains a number of unobservable and/or potentially endogenous elements. More importantly, the specifications in (3.28) and (3.29) obscure the causal impacts of core determinants - extent of disablement, employment opportunities, work commitment - as proposed by medical sociology (see scheme 3.2). To be able to reveal these causalities further specification is necessary. In order to make both the inclination model (3.25) and the DI-probability model (3.29) operational, at least the preference parameter $\beta$ and the individual admission probability $p_a$ need further specification. The pecuniary variables, earnings (E), benefits (B), and non-labor income (N), and working hours (H = T-L), all are directly observable although they may be simultaneously, instead of causally, related to DI-enrolment. On the other hand, individually varying time preference rates ($\delta$) and the expected age of DI-enrolment ($t^*$) are unobservable, too. While a measurement model for $t^*$ is given by (3.11), we take $\delta$ to be a model parameter to be estimated.

Following Quinn (1977) we specify $\beta$ as a function of extent of disablement (D), attitudinal or motivational factors (M), and employment opportunities (EO). Extent of disablement has been defined as the interaction of functional limitations and commensurate job demands (see section 3.2.1). Attitudes with respect to work in general (work ethic) and to one's current job (job satisfaction) have been introduced in section 3.2.3. The symbol M, then, indexes strength of work motivation.

Inclusion of health status and motivation as preference parameters is straightforward, and has been argued before (in section 3.3.1). We do not, however, consider the possibility that $\beta$ may contain a number of psychological variables indicating stability of family and personal relations, degrees of social isolation, feelings of stigmatization, etc. Such categories have been associated with disability behavior in medical sociological research.[22] We choose to omit these variables because an attempt to model their interrelations and their relation with the outcome of the disability process would be beyond the level of sophistication attainable with the available database.

Consideration of individual employment opportunities, or labor market conditions in general, as taste factors is less founded. Quinn, Muller (1982), and Zabalza et al. (1980), refer to "discouraged worker" effects in that lack of employment is expected to result in an increased propensity to consider oneself disabled and to accommodate work-leisure preferences accordingly.[23]

In sum,

$$\beta = \beta \, (D, M, EO) \quad \text{with} \quad \frac{\partial \beta}{\partial D} > 0, \quad \frac{\partial \beta}{\partial M} < 0, \quad \frac{\partial \beta}{\partial EO} < 0. \tag{3.31}$$

Often, however, demand side variables are parachuted into micro-economic models of (health-conditioned) retirement behavior without comment or just by pointing at the high correlation between unemployment and disability.[24] In many other studies, especially from the early retirement literature, inclusion of demand side effects is completely omitted, although it may be plausibly argued that ill labor market conditions promote early retirement.[25]

In the context of a DI-participation study the award behavior of the DI-program gatekeepers offers a second path along which employment opportunities may have an impact. Generally speaking, a separate model for $p_a$ may be warranted by the potential simultaneity of award rates and DI-probabilities [cf. Leonard (1986) p.82].

Under the Dutch DI-program, however, there is an added problem. DI-applications, and awards or denials upon these applications, are not separately observable events. One can only observe DI-enrollments as the eventual outcome of - what may be described as - a dynamic process of application and adjudication that takes place during the one year of sickness preceding DI-enrolment. The process may be imagined as starting with a simple sick report (a sickness claim) and a Sickness Benefit award for an initial period. At the end of that period the sickness claim may be extended, and the extension may be granted or denied. This sequence of claims and awards may continue until the mandatory waiting period for DI-eligibility has elapsed. In reality, however, at no point during the DI-enrolment process explicit application for (extension of) Sickness or DI-benefits is required. Eligibility standards are only verified after lapse of the waiting period.

The fact that the Dutch sickness and disability arrangements have no explicit application and adjudication procedures poses a serious measurement problem. For instance, measurement at the start of the waiting period would yield the observation that only about 1 percent of some 8 million yearly sick spells end with DI-enrolment. It would of course be absurd to consider all of these sick reports as potential DI-applications and conclude on a 99 percent unconditional denial rate. On the other hand, at the end of the waiting period for DI-eligibility more than 90 percent are allowed a DI-benefit. This would imply a conditional denial rate of less than 10 percent after one year of sickness. Finally, as an intermediate case, work resumption during the waiting period may result from reluctance to DI-enrolment ("non-application"), Sickness Benefit termination due to recovery ("denial"), or both.

The unobservability of the conditional award rate implies that we need a separate measurement model for $p_a$ [see eq.(3.32) below]. It also means that, for lack of direct observations, neither the claiming behavior of the population at risk nor the award policies of program administrators can be independently analyzed. Therefore, we have to resort to reduced form versions of the structural DI-model.

The individual award rate, $p_a$, measures the probability of being certified as disabled under the prevailing interpretation of the legal standards. According to the law, the extent of disablement should be measured in terms of loss of earning capacity. More accurately, its complement - the residual earning capacity - is defined as the wage an impaired person would be able to earn in suitable work as a percentage of the wage earned by healthy but otherwise similar persons. On the basis of the complement of the resulting percentage, a claimant is assigned to one of seven disability categories (see section 2.3). The minimum degree of disability yielding entitlement to DI-benefits is 15 percent. Fully disabled are those who suffer a loss of more than 80 percent of their earning capacity; they are entitled to full benefits replacing 80, until 1985 and henceforth 70, percent of previous earnings.

Until 1987, the law recognized the difficulties partially disabled workers may have in finding commensurate employment by prescribing that the benefit adjudicators should take account of poor labor market opportunities. The administrative interpretation of this legal provision - the so-called labor market consideration - has been so liberal as to award more than 80 percent of all DI-beneficiaries full benefits (see table 2.15). As will be shown in chapter 5, only part of this volume is fully disabled in terms of the strict definition given above. The remainder - a substantial volume of productive capacity - can be considered as hidden unemployment.

Roughly speaking, then, impaired workers may secure eligibility for full DI-benefits if they lose more than 15 percent of their earning capacity and claim to be unable to find commensurate work. Given the impossibility to accurately verify all of these claims, the DI-administrators are likely to use demographic characteristics, such as age and sex, as screening devices.[26] Whether such forms of statistical discrimination are present is an empirical matter which we, for the moment, choose to ignore.[27] Consequently, the probability of being awarded a full benefit, given completion of the waiting period, will depend both on extent of disablement (D), and employment opportunities (EO),[28]

$$p_a = p_a \ (D, \ EO) \quad \text{with} \quad \frac{\partial p_a}{\partial D} > 0, \quad \frac{\partial p_a}{\partial EO} < 0. \tag{3.32}$$

Besides these two specifications, micro-economic theory offers a third route by which severity of disability (D) and other human capital aspects, like age and education (EDUC), may affect intended and actual DI-enrollments. It runs via the earning capacity, as measured by the wage rate, $w_s$. More specifically, we can posit a separate wage equation:

$$w_s = w_s \ (D, \ AGE, \ EDUC) \quad \text{with} \quad \frac{\partial w_s}{\partial D} < 0, \quad \frac{\partial w_s}{\partial AGE} > 0, \quad \frac{\partial w_s}{\partial EDUC} > 0 \tag{3.33}$$

Positive effects of age (as a proxy for experience) and education are predicted by human capital theory although the age-effect is generally found to be curved, e.g., through a negative effect for $(AGE)^2$.[29] Notice that employment opportunities (EO) are omitted from the specification for the expected wage rate. Unemployment risks, however, do reduce the expected duration of the remaining working life and so affect the sizes of earnings' and other income streams indirectly, via $t^*$ [see eq.(3.25)].[30]

## Reduced Forms

Insertion of the preceding specifications for $\beta$, $p_a$, and $w_s$, into (3.28) yields a "somewhat reduced" form of the DI-participation model defined by eq.(3.29). Specifically, the vector of determinants Z may be written as

$$Z = Z \ (1, \ D, \ M, \ EO, \ N_0, \ -\ln \ [1 - H_0/T_0], \ AGE, \ EDUC), \tag{3.34}$$

using

$H_0 = T_0 - L_0$
$E_s = w_s H_0$
$B_t = r w_t H_0$     (r is the statutory replacement rate)
$t_0 = AGE$
$t^* = t^* \ (Z)$     [by eq.(3.11)]

By further specifying separate submodels for D and EO, a more drastically reduced form model for Pr{DI} is obtained. Estimation of such models yields total effects of exogenous or predetermined variables - age, education, work and medical records, characteristics of the employing firm, labor market conditions - on Pr{DI}. These reduced form estimates are combinations of direct effects and indirect influences that run via intermediary variables such as extent of disablement (D), employment opportunities (EO), work commitment (M), the wage rate (w), or the award probability ($p_a$). Some of these intermediates may be assumed exogenous. Often, however, there are theoretical (joint determination) or data-related (e.g. choice based sampling, self-perceptions) reasons to suspect, and test for, their endogeneity.

## 3.4     Summary, Discussion, and Introduction to the Following Chapters

In this chapter we have tried to integrate the medical-sociological and the micro-economic approaches to disability behavior, in order to build an analytical framework to study the transition from labor force to DI-program participation. Medical sociologists were the first to recognize disability as a behavioral, discretionary, phenomenon. Their studies show that even when the underlying impairment is a random, objectively assessable, misfortune, its disabling consequences may well depend on a number of non-medical factors. As a consequence, similar impairments may prompt diverging behavioral reactions.

From the perspective of medical sociology, work disability emerges from the interaction of functional limitations with the requirements and characteristics of one's normal occupation. The definition of work disability itself, therefore, already combines clinical aspects with non-medical, vocational, attributes. Next, for a given extent of disablement, the employability of one's residual work capacities depends on individual work record, employers' attitudes, and general labor market conditions. On the other hand, the willingness of impaired workers to supply their residual capacities presumably depends on work commitment and availability of acceptable non-labor alternatives. Finally, the probability that self-perceived disability results in a DI-benefit award is determined by the legitimizing behavior of the DI-program administrators.

These sociological assumptions imply a close theoretical relationship between unemployment, disability, and (early) retirement. As a logical next step, then, the micro-economic theory regarding individual labor supply decisions can be applied to construct a more formal model of DI-enrolment. This model describes the pros and cons of DI-application in terms of expected utility evaluations. It starts from the assumption that workers, who are covered by DI, choose to claim a DI-benefit if they prefer to retire rather than continue to work. Their choice is determined by the expected utility-difference resulting from reduced income and increased leisure after DI-enrolment. The implied decision rule, then, works such that an application is filed when the expected difference is positive.

The expected utility-streams flowing from the work and the DI-options take account of the risks inherent to both options. DI-application is subject to the risk of benefit denial, whereas the continued labor force participation option may end prematurely, i.e., before 65, due to voluntary or forced retirement. This second contingency, embodied by the expected duration of the remaining working life, is endogenous with respect to the phenomenon under study - the current DI-probability.

At the end of section 3.3.2, we have drawn a summary scheme representing the causal structure of a theoretical, micro-economic, model of DI-enrolment (scheme 3.3). This model is highly abstract and obscures the causal impacts of core determinants like severity of disability and employment opportunities. Using the specifications proposed in the preceding section, the main elements of a more explicit version of the DI-model are displayed in scheme 3.4.

**Scheme 3.4  A Recursive Version of the Empirical DI-Model[a]**

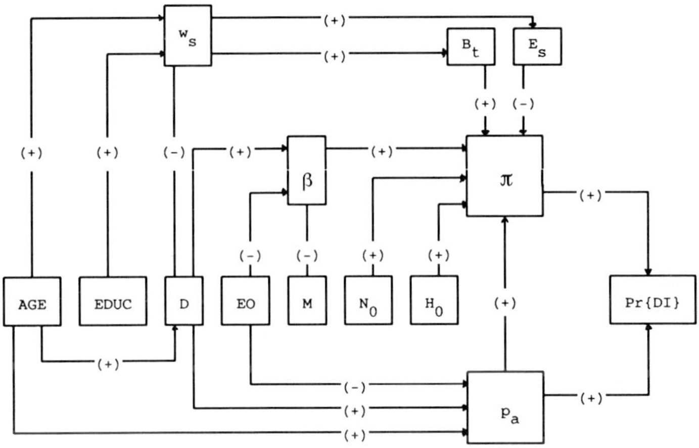

(a) See section 3.3.4 for the meaning of the variables

The (+/-) signs in scheme 3.4 refer to hypothesized effects without accounting for the endogeneity of the expected exit age, $t^*$. In fact, the model as displayed by this scheme ignores all potential endogeneities with respect to DI-enrolment that may result from reciprocal causalities, or causal loops. Hence the label "recursive".
The core determinants, extent of disablement (D) and employment opportunities (EO), are assumed to have a two way impact on the DI-probability both via the inclination index, $\pi$, and via the award probability, $p_a$. Both of these determinants are composed of several empirical factors. The constituent parts of, and potential measurement models for, D are indicated in scheme 3.2 which summarizes the medical-sociological approach. For the sake of simplicity, in scheme 3.4, we have only retained the effect of age, i.e., the wear and tear of a working life, on D.

The extent of disablement (D), or its counterpart, the residual earning capacity, can be regarded as the junction of the medical-sociological and the micro-economic approaches. In chapter 5, the objective prevalence of disability among a sample of Dutch DI-entrants will be described.

Employment opportunities (EO) both refer to the within firm prospects under the current employment contract and one's competitive power in the labor market at large. Two separate chapters are devoted to each of these aspects. In chapter 7 we analyze work histories to develop an instrument for the strength of the external labor market position. Chapter 8 deals with the construction of a variable measuring firm specific disability risks. This instrument encompasses the firm's employment outlook as well as firm related causes and consequences of disability, viz. occupational risks to which the employees are exposed and the firm's policy with regard to impaired employees.

The construction of these instrumental variables serves several purposes. First, they summarize the combined effects of a set of exogenous attributes related to individual labor market records and a set of social and economic characteristics of the employing firms, and so effectively reduce the data to be used in a structural DI-model. More importantly, the submodels from which these instrumentals result reveal the causal pathways along which background variables, such as age, education, or firm size, exert their indirect influences on the DI-probability. And finally, by using instrumentals we can get around the potential endogeneity of direct observations. Some determinants, such as unemployment risks or productivity (wage rates) may not be causally but simultaneously related to the disability risk under study. Such indicators of labor market success may well be jointly determined by unobserved factors like innate abilities and social background. We, therefore, also devote a separate submodel to examine the endogeneity of the wage rate with respect to the DI-probability (see chapter 9). These wage equations will be employed to estimate discounted future earnings' streams.

Another endogeneity problem is more directly related to the cross-sectional nature of the database. Specifically, variables measured by subjective scales may be blurred by preferences or legitimation, which we denote as endogenous measurement errors. In chapter 6 we will test a number of suspicious determinants, such as work ethic and job satisfaction, for the presence of such errors.

After all these preliminary studies we get down to the estimation of structural DI-probability models in chapter 10. For these structural DI-models we will apply the instrumental variables resulting from the preceding auxiliary models.

## Notes

1. The utility concept may also be used to assess the costs and benefits of alternative compensatory systems covering the disability risk, in terms of equity and efficiency. This welfare-theoretic approach was indicated in chapter 1.

2. See Talcott Parsons (1951).

3. Evidence of this proposition can be found in Nagi (1969), pp. 126-136, and Nagi and Hadley (1972).

4. See e.g. Hambor (1975), Lando et al. (1979), who find significant effects of the unemployment rate on the U.S. DI- (applications) volume; Sirén (1976) who obtains similar results for Finland; and Bax et al. (1979) and De Jong (1983a) for the Netherlands.

5. Tazelaar and Sprengers (1984) elaborate such psychological concepts as mental incongruity to study behavioral choices open to the older Dutch male unemployed.

6. People in bad health may need more time for personal care and, hence, may be assumed to suffer exogenous reductions in their net time available for work and "pure leisure" activities. If one would define T in terms of such individually varying net time endowments, this added health impact would further reduce the opportunity sets of ailing workers. [cf. Mushkin (1962), Grossman (1972), Muller et al. (1979)].

7. Here two added assumptions are needed to secure that a wage-reduction will lead to an increase in leisure consumption. Assuming that leisure is a normal good, the resulting income-effect (less income implying a smaller demand for leisure) has to be dominated by the substitution effect (lower opportunity cost of leisure implying a larger demand for leisure).

8. "The parameter $\delta$ (...) is interpreted as reflecting impatience on the part of consumers so that the benefits of future consumption and leisure are more heavily discounted the further into the future they occur." [Deaton and Muellbauer (1983), p. 311].

9. Moreover, $f(t)$ should be calibrated such that

$$\int_0^{65-t_0} f(t) \, dt = 1.$$

10. For instance, one might add a log-normally distributed disturbance term to the expected wage-profile with an over time increasing variance, where the time-path of this variance would depend on work-experience and occupation.

11. See table 11.5.

12. If application for DI were modelled as an "all-or-nothing game", that is, if $U(work) = 0$, then $\pi = p_a \, U(DI) - U(WORK)$. Such an "all-or-nothing" format is used by Leonard (1979) and Parsons (1980) to model US SSDI-applications.

13. In the anomalous case where people would prefer the rejected applicant state over DI-enrolment, i.e., $U(work) > U(DI)$, increasing stringency would trigger DI-applications. Besides common sense, empirical studies rule out this improbable case. Marvel (1982) and Halpern and Hausman (1984) have studied the impact of award rates on applications in the context of the U.S. SSDI-program. Analyzing the American disability policy of the late 70s, Marvel

observes that "the increase in denial stringency had a significant chilling impact on applications" (p. 408). Halpern and Hausman find that "the probability of acceptance has a significant, but not a particularly large, effect on the probability of application".

14. If a severely disabled worker would earn a post-disability wage at the statutory minimum level, he or she would only be entitled to a disability benefit at the minimum level, $B_{min}$. In that case,

$$\pi = \left[ \; U[B_0 + N_0 , T_0] - U[B_{min} + N_0 , T_0] \; \right] \int_{t_0}^{65} e^{-\delta(s-t_0)} ds \; > \; 0$$

A feasible alternative transfer program, like National Assistance, would yield a comparable benefit. National Assistance benefits, however, are means tested, and therefore eq.3.13 would still apply as long as $N_0 > 0$. Only workers covered by an Early Retirement scheme might be better off not choosing DI-enrolment.

15. Formally, all disability determinations are done by the Joint Medical Service (JMS) so as to warrant uniformity. In actual practice, however, independent or groupwise organized insurance boards often make their own disability assessments according to their own standards. This, then, may introduce cross-sectional heterogeneity with respect to screening rigor or other policy variables.

16. Differentiating (3.23) we obtain

$$\frac{\partial Pr\{DI\}}{\partial R} = H(\pi) \frac{\partial p_a}{\partial R} + p_a h(\pi) \frac{\partial \pi}{\partial R} \; \text{ with } \; h(\pi) = \frac{\partial H}{\partial \pi}$$

Hence, using (3.23),

$$\frac{\partial Pr\{DI\}}{\partial R} \; \frac{R}{Pr\{DI\}} = \frac{\partial p_a}{\partial R} \frac{R}{p_a} + \pi \frac{h(\pi)}{H(\pi)} \frac{\partial \pi}{\partial R} \frac{R}{\pi}$$

Notice that

$$\frac{\partial \pi}{\partial R} = \frac{\partial \pi}{\partial p_a} \frac{\partial p_a}{\partial R} + \frac{\partial \pi}{\partial t^*} \frac{\partial t^*}{\partial p_a} \frac{\partial p_a}{\partial R} \; < 0,$$

since

$\dfrac{\partial \pi}{\partial p_a}$ is positive, and $\dfrac{\partial p_a}{\partial R}$, $\dfrac{\partial \pi}{\partial t^*}$, and, $\dfrac{\partial t^*}{\partial p_a}$ are all negative.

17. Let C denote the expected total benefit outlays per year for DI-entrants,

$$C = \sum_{i \in I} B_i P_i,$$

where I is the population at risk, and $B_i$ and $P_i$ are the i-th individual benefit amount and DI-entry probability, respectively.
To simplify, assume that the replacement rate r applies to every insured worker so that

$$B_i = rE_i,$$

where $E_i$ are the earnings covered by DI.
Along the lines of the preceding note, the elasticity of C with respect to r can be written as the sum of an administrative (price) effect with unit elasticity and a behavioral effect with an elasticity depending on the (dis)incentive effect of marginal changes in the statutory replacement rate r on the individual inclination to apply for DI as measured by $\pi$:

$$\varepsilon_r^c = 1 + \sum_i \frac{B_i P_i}{C} \; \pi_i \; \frac{h(\pi_i)}{H(\pi_i)} \; \varepsilon_r^x .$$

18. Let alone that we would dwell upon convergence conditions.

19. If $U^0 = a \ln Y + b \ln L$, then $U^1 = U^0/(a+b)$ has a form which is identical to (3.24) with $ß=b/(a+b)$. While b measures the utility contribution of leisure per se, $ß$ represents the utility contribution of leisure relative to that of income.

20. Notice that the sign of the partial derivative of $\pi_s$ with respect to $w_t$, the wage rate at DI-enrolment, is indefinite as higher wages at t both increase earnings and benefit entitlements. Using the fact that $B_s = rE_s$, with r the replacement rate, we find for $s > t$,

$$\frac{\partial \pi_s}{\partial w_t} < 0 \;\; \text{if} \;\; \left[ 1 - \frac{\partial w_s}{\partial w_t} \frac{w_t}{w_s} \right] B_s < \left[ \frac{\partial w_s}{\partial w_t} - r \right] N_0.$$

To simplify, assume that $N_0 = 0$. Then, the wage effect is negative only if the elasticity of the future wage-profile with respect to the current wage rate is larger than one.

21. The part of this damage that is not covered by DI may be covered by an additional private policy or by litigation against the legal person (e.g., the employer) liable for his disablement [cf. Van Kessel (1985)].

22. Nagi (1969) reports "a consistent association between 'poor' (interpersonal) relations and high (disability) inclination" (p. 133). Merens-Riedstra (1981) stresses the social-psychological consequences of health-conditioned non-participation.

23. Blundell et al. (1987) define a discouraged worker as one who has positive desired hours but yet chooses to stay out of the labor market since search costs (monetary or time) upon labor market entry lead to a utility-loss. If that loss exceeds the expected utility-gain from finding employment a worker is unwilling (discouraged) to engage in job search.

24. Haveman and Wolfe (1984a), Levy and McManus (1978), Marvel (1982), and Parsons (1980, 1982), for instance, implicitly introduce regional unemployment rates or personal unemployment experiences as preference parameters but do not pay any attention to the theoretical validity or empirical significance of these variables.

25. To quote a few, Hausman (1985), in his study on DI-application; Schechter (1981) studying the work effort of the (severely) disabled; and Chirikos and Nestel (1984) examining the economic determinants of self-reported work disability, ignore potential demand side effects. More generally, American studies on participation in the Social Security Early Retirement program do not pay attention to the demand side of the labor market. See e.g., Boskin and Hurd (1978), Burkhauser (1980), Burtless and Moffitt (1984), Haveman et al. (1988).

26. On the influence of demographic factors, especially race, on eligibility for American SSDI benefits see Treitel (1979), Leonard (1979, 1986), Levy (1980), Muller (1982), Hausman (1985).

27. Since age correlates positively with severity of impairment and negatively with re-employment possibilities, we expect a positive effect on the award rate. Whether the gatekeepers of the Dutch DI-program discriminate on the basis of gender is a current topic of research and public debate. So far, the findings have been contradictory. See Bruinsma et al. (1989), Bijlsma and Koopmans (1985, 1986), Hermans (1987), and Ombudsvrouw (1981).

28. Under the Dutch DI-program coverage requirements are negligible and, therefore, do not introduce other variables such as earnings or work record into specification (3.32).

29. In chapter 9 we elaborate, and estimate, the wage equation.

30. Although auxiliary wage equations are frequently estimated in studies regarding the effect of health status on work effort, the use of demand side indicators as explanatory variables for the wage rate is quite uncommon. An exception is Fenn and Vlachonikolis (1986).

Chapter 4

# HISTORY, DATA AND DESIGN OF THE STUDY

## 4.1    Introduction

The study reported in this book is the offspring of a research program on the determinants of growth in disability income support in the Netherlands. The program was initiated by the Dutch Social Security Council in 1975 and carried on until 1987.

In this chapter, we will briefly describe the history of the program and its evolution into what has become known as the *Determinantenonderzoek WAO* (Dutch Disability Study) (section 4.2). We elaborate on the sampling procedures in section 4.3, and present a multivariate analysis of the nonresponse in section 4.4. The limitations of the database are summarized in section 4.5. Some major characteristics of the samples that have been analyzed are depicted in section 4.6. How the limitations of the database have affected the design of this study will become apparent in section 4.7.

## 4.2    Previous History

The DI-program was enacted in 1967. As documented in chapter 2, the number of DI-beneficiaries have been increasing ever since. During the seventies, the annual growth rate was about 10 percent. Program expenditures grew even faster and so did the contributions levied on the wage bill to finance the DI-program.

In 1973, alarmed by these developments, the Dutch Social Security Council[1] installed a committee to study the growth of DI-program expenditures (*Studiecommissie Premieontwikkeling WAO*). From a descriptive analysis of a small sample of files of DI-beneficiaries in 1974, the committee concluded that a large, thorough, and ambitious research program was needed in order to gain insight in the causes of the alarming performance of the DI-program.

The future directors of the Dutch Disability Study, Han Emanuel and Bernard van Praag[2], conceived a research plan and suggested to investigate the determinants of
- entry into the DI-program;
- changes in the degree of disability among DI-beneficiaries;
- exit from the DI-program through re-employment;
- application for provisions in kind;
- and the feasibility of a model to forecast DI-expenditures.

In 1975, the Center for Research in Public Economics at Leiden University was commissioned by the Social Security Council to execute the proposed program in collaboration with staff members of the Council. The Council stressed the particular importance of developing a forecasting model. Moreover, special attention was to be given to policy instruments, such as the DI-benefit replacement rate.

In the same year, a research team of two economists, a sociologist and a data analyst was formed.[3] Legal and medical experts joined the team as consultants. The Council installed a scientific advisory committee to provide the research team with advice, and to evaluate the output of the research.

Since the assignment was stated in fairly broad terms a more specific research strategy had to be developed. The research team preferred to do a survey study, as the analysis of existing aggregate time-series data was expected to produce no more than a description of the surface of problem. It was expected that the analysis of individual disability behavior would reveal major causalities, especially those relevant for the design of effective and equitable policies to contain the number of DI-beneficiaries.

The first decision the team had to take was on the sampling procedure. To survey a sufficient number of DI-entries the basic choice was between two extreme options. The simplest way would be to take a sample of DI-entrants, and confine the project to a study of their characteristics and longitudinal observation of subsequent DI-exits. In that case the selection process preceding DI-entry would be left unobserved. A more ambitious approach would be to take a large sample from the total population at risk which would be followed and reexamined regularly. Given an average yearly DI-incidence of about 2 percent such a sample would either have to be very large, or heavily stratified, or observed for a very long time.

Upon consideration of the costs and benefits of these approaches both were rejected. Instead the team chose to compromise between the two extremes by taking a sample of workers on a long-term (5 months) sick leave. They were to be followed administratively until DI-entry and, possibly, further during their DI-recipiency status. The 5 months sickness point of observation was chosen because half of that group was expected to fulfill the 12 months sickness (waiting) period, whereas the other half would recover. Therefore, this choice would allow for maximal dispersion.

In 1978, a pilot-study was done to explore the feasibility of gathering useful data by taking a sample of workers on prolonged (17 weeks) sick leave from the Sickness Benefit (SB) records and ask them to participate voluntarily in the survey; by reporting those workers who responded positively to a local branch of the Joint Medical Service (JMS) such that they could be medically examined and interviewed by JMS experts and lay-interviewers during the fifth month of their sick leave; by interviewing their employers; and by keeping track of their absence records thereafter.

The pilot, then, served primarily to test the logistics of this elaborate sampling and surveying procedure. An important element was to get an indication of the net response. A target group of long-term sick half-way during their waiting period for permanent disability benefits were likely to produce a large rate of nonresponse. The pilot also served to test the questionnaires which the team had designed with the help of their medical, legal, and vocational consultants.

The pilot-survey yielded a response rate of 47 percent. It resulted in the following conclusions on the required design of the main survey:

- The survey should contain at least 4,000 complete observations.
- Given a 4 week period between sampling and surveying, and a net response rate somewhere between 40 and 50 percent, an initial sample of 10,000 workers in their 17th week of absence had to be taken from the SB administrations. The SB-files of these initial sample persons should contain sufficient data to test and correct for distortions due to nonresponse.
- During the fifth month of their sick leave, these 4,000 SB-beneficiaries should be extensively interviewed on their health, working conditions, work history, job satisfaction and attitudes toward work.
- It turned out to be feasible to include a survey of the sampled persons' employers with information on the firm's financial status, its social policy, and on the work environment of the sampled employee.
- Some seven months after the interviews had taken place, the SB-files were to be consulted to assess whether the sampled persons had resumed work, were admitted to the DI-program, unemployed, or dead.
- The administration of the survey should allow for a subsequent interviews of those who entered the DI-rolls, in order to study DI-exits.
- To be able to control for the selectivity of this SB-sample, a separate sample of at least 1,000 actively working employees should be taken from the total population at risk to serve as a control-group.

The final approval by the Council to start the main survey was only given in December 1979. Two main factors had caused the delay. First, analysis of the pilot-survey took considerably more time than had been anticipated. And second, the administrations that were to be involved in the main survey needed an extended amount of time before they could approve of the data-collection plan. Especially, the safeguarding of the privacy of the sampled SB-recipients appeared to be an issue.


## 4.3     Sampling Procedures

During the first six months of 1980, two samples were surveyed: one taken from the population of Sickness Benefit recipients and the other from the population of *healthy* private sector employees, who are covered under the DI-program. We will refer to these samples as the *SB-sample* and the *(healthy) control-sample* respectively.


### 4.3.1   Sampling Procedure; the SB-Sample

The initial selection of cases was done by the, then, 26 Industrial Associations. They were instructed to select all current SB-recipients whose spell of sick leave had lasted exactly 17 weeks at the time of initial sample selection.

Initially, 9,420 cases were selected (see table 4.1). For all of these cases, a summary questionnaire was completed by the Industrial Associations containing information on age, sex, marital status, residence, occupation, work hours, wage, diagnosis and medical prognosis. This information was gathered from the SB-administration files. Moreover, all of these initial sample cases were followed administratively to record date and reason of SB-termination; recovery, death, or, after the 12 months waiting period had lapsed, DI-entry.

Of the initially selected cases, 2,072 were disregarded either because SB-recipients had resumed work before five months of sick leave (1,674), or because they were in sheltered employment under the WSW (398). The resulting 7,348 cases can be taken to be a representative sample of the population of SB-recipients in the fifth month of their sick leave.

After selection of these initial cases, the Industrial Associations sent a letter to the selected SB-beneficiaries in which the purpose of the research was explained; the letter contained an invitation to participate in the survey. Participation involved a medical examination at one of the 27 offices of the Joint Medical Service by a JMS insurance-physician, an interview by a JMS ergonomist, and an interview by a lay-interviewer hired by the research team. Travel and accommodation expenses were refunded in full. It was stressed that participation was entirely voluntary, and that refusal would neither affect recipiency status nor future eligibility for DI-benefits.

Personal information was considered strictly confidential. The surveys would be handed anonymously to the research team. SB-recipients with a terminal disease and institutionalized psychiatric patients (422) were not invited to participate. Reactions to the call for participation were to be sent to the Industrial Association offices that, in turn, reported those responding positively to the regional JMS offices. These regional offices arranged for the actual interviews and medical examinations.

Table 4.1    The SB-sample; Completion of the Sampling Procedure

| | | |
|---|---|---|
| Initial Selection | | 9,420 |
| Work resumption before 5 months of sick leave | 1,674 | |
| Sheltered employment (WSW) | 398 | |
| | -/- 2,072 | |
| Gross Sample | | 7,348 (100%) |
| Not invited to participate | 422 ( 6%) | |
| Administratively reported to JMS | 169 ( 2%) | |
| | 591 ( 8%) | |
| Invited to participate | | 6,757 (92%) |
| No response | 450 ( 6%) | |
| Negative response | 2,575 (35%) | |
| | -/- 3,025 (41%) | |
| Positive response | | 3,732 (51%) |
| Not reported to JMS | -/- 123 ( 2%) | |
| Administratively reported to JMS | 169 ( 2%) | |
| | +/+ 46 ( 1%) | |
| Reported to JMS | | 3,778 (51%) |
| Not examined/interviewed | -/- 970 (13%) | |
| **Total number examined and interviewed** | | **2,808 (38%)** |

A small number of selected SB-recipients (169) were directly reported to the JMS offices. They were identified by the Industrial Associations as cases that should be reported to the JMS at an early stage ensuing standard administrative procedures. Since these persons were invited to the local JMS offices under standard procedures, they could refuse to cooperate in the survey.

Table 4.1 shows how the sampling procedure has been completed; 6,757 persons actually received a request to participate. To these requests 3,732 SB-beneficiaries (or 55 percent of the invitations) responded positively; 2,575 persons (38 percent of the invitees) responded negatively, whereas 450 (7 percent) did not respond at all.

Of all that responded positively, 123 were not reported to a regional JMS office. In total 3,778 cases were reported to local JMS offices. 2,808 cases were examined and interviewed. Hence, a substantial number of those initially willing to cooperate (970) have not been surveyed. Some of these called off because they had resumed work or because they had reconsidered their initial positive response. Part of the attrition is due to organizational irregularities.

The number of observed cases (2,808) is considerably lower than the intended 4,000 cases. The reason for this is to be found in the size of the initial selection (9,420 instead of the planned 10,000), in the percentage of positive responses (55 percent) which was somewhat lower than expected, and, last but not least, in delays in completion of the sampling procedure at the local JMS offices.[4]

Table 4.2     Available Information in the Gross SB-sample

| | |
|---|---|
| Abstract from SB-file (1) | 1,515  (21%) |
| + Medical examination (2) | |
| + Ergonomic examination respondent (3) | |
| + Lay-interview (4) | |
| + Ergonomic interview employer (5) | |
| + Written employer's questionnaire (6) | |
| (1) + (2) + (3) + (4) + (5) | 2,534  (35%) |
| Minimally completed cases: (1) + (2) + (3) + (4) | 2,808  (38%) |
| Only: (1) + (2), (3) or (4) | 112  ( 2%) |
| Only: (1) | 4,428  (60%) |
| Gross SB-sample | 7,348  (100%) |

A fully completed SB-sample observation consists of the following questionnaires:
1. An abstract from the SB-file of the respondent;
2. A medical examination by a JMS insurance-physician;
3. An interview by a JMS ergonomist;
4. A so-called *lay-interview* by an interviewer hired by the research team;
5. An interview of the respondent's employer by a JMS ergonomist;
6. A written questionnaire sent to the respondent's employer to gather mainly financial and personnel information on the firm.

Information was gathered on a total number of 337 items.

Table 4.2 shows for how many observations these questionnaires were completed. The 2,808 cases for which all information at the employee-level is available are marked as *minimally completed cases*. Among these, 1,515 cases are fully completed, and 2,534 are fully completed with the exception of the written employer's question-naire. Apparently, 1,034 employers who permitted a verbal interview by a JMS-ergonomist did not return the written questionnaire with financial and personnel data. For 4,576 cases information at the employee level is incomplete. This part of the gross sample is considered as *nonresponse*.

A multivariate analysis of the response behavior in the SB-sample is presented in section 4.4.

### 4.3.2  Sampling Procedure; the Control-Sample

The control-sample was designed as a random selection of privately employed persons who are insured under the DI-program.

Table 4.3    The Control-sample; Completion of the Sampling Procedure

| | | |
|---|---|---|
| Initial selection of delivery points | | 4,146 |
| Uninhabited premises | -/-  487 | |
| Inhabited premises | | 3,659 |
| Number of households | | 3,713 |
| Nonsurveyed households | -/-  330 | |
| Surveyed households | | 3,383 |
| Households with no persons 15-65 | -/-  539 | |
| Households with persons 15-65 years | 2,844 | |
| Number of persons 15-65 years | | 6,159 |
| Not covered by the DI-program | -/- 3,911 | |
| Covered by the DI program | | 2,248  (100%) |
| Refusals to participate | -/-  223   (10%) | |
| **Interviewed persons** | | **2,025  (90%)** |
| Unemployed | 71  ( 3%) | |
| No permission for contacting employer | 352  (16%) | |
| | -/-  423   (19%) | |
| Contacted employers | | 1,602  (71%) |
| Employer refusals | -/-  191  ( 8%) | |
| **Interviewed employers** | | **1,417  (63%)** |

Table 4.3 shows how the sampling procedure was completed. A random sample of 4,146 delivery points was taken from the listings of the Dutch Post Office that contain 5 million delivery points (excluding premises with no dwellings). To all selected points a letter of introduction was sent in which the Secretary (Vice-Minister) of Social Affairs called for participation in the research. To a maximum of three per delivery point, all households were visited by an interviewer hired by the research team. All persons within each household, who were insured under the DI-program, were asked to be interviewed. Of the 2,248 persons found to be covered under the DI-program, 90 percent agreed to cooperate. The (employed) respondents were asked for permission to contact their employers; 16 percent of the DI-insured persons did not approve of such contact. Next, 1,602 employers were approached; 12 percent of whom did not cooperate. The result of this procedure is a sample of 1,417 complete observations, i.e., cases in which both employer and employee have been interviewed. In 2,025 cases only the employee has been interviewed.

Information was gathered on a total number of 210 items.


## 4.4     Nonresponse

Although a large part of the nonresponse in the SB-sample is due to organizational defects rather than response behavior of the sampled persons, a 62 percent rate of nonresponse is nevertheless rather high. On the basis of the pilot-study a non-response rate of about 50 percent had been anticipated. At the time, such a high nonresponse rate seemed acceptable only if sufficient information would be available to analyze response behavior and, if necessary, to correct for systematic non-response. The abstracts from the SB-files that are available for all selected cases in the gross sample, contain sufficient information to perform a multivariate analysis of the response behavior by which the possible biases caused by this nonresponse can be assessed.

If response behavior and the predisposition for DI-enrolment are jointly determined by factors such as the nature and severity of impairment, age, etc., or if respondents should behave differently from nonrespondents with regard to disability, the sizeable nonresponse rate would cause serious biases in the disability model when estimated without controlling for sample selectivity. The gravity of this "sample-selection" problem can be analyzed by estimation of a two equation probit model that simultaneously describes the nonresponse and the DI-entry probabilities. The data available in the gross-sample of SB-recipients allow for the estimation of such a model. If response behavior does not affect the predisposition for DI-enrolment, the nonresponse will have no effect on the disability model estimates.

Following (Maddala (1983), pp. 242-247), we define a response variable, $y_{1i}$ and a DI-award variable, $y_{2i}$, for each SB-beneficiary i sampled; $y_{1i}$ is one if i responded

DI-award variable, $y_{2i}$, for each SB-beneficiary i sampled; $y_{1i}$ is one if i responded positively to the call for participation and was interviewed subsequently (i.e., if i belongs to the set of *minimally completed* observations), and zero otherwise. The zeros, therefore, contain both refusals and attrition; $y_{2i}$ is one if i was awarded a DI-benefit and zero otherwise,

$$y_{1i} = 0 \ \text{if} \ y_{1i}^* < 0,$$

$$y_{1i} = 1 \ \text{if} \ y_{1i}^* \geq 0,$$

$$y_{2i} = 1 \ \text{if} \ y_{2i}^* < 0,$$

$$y_{2i} = 1 \ \text{if} \ y_{2i}^* \geq 0,$$

where

$$y_{1i}^* = \gamma_1 \, y_{2i}^* + \beta_1' X_{1i} + u_{1i},$$

$$y_{2i}^* = \gamma_2 \, y_{1i}^* + \beta_2' X_{2i} + u_{2i},$$

(4.1)

with $y_{1i}^*$ and $y_{2i}^*$ being unobserved indices of the propensity to respond and to enter the DI-program, respectively; $\beta_1$ and $\beta_2$ vectors of unknown parameters; $X_1$ and $X_2$ vectors of exogenous variables, and $(u_{1i}, u_{2i}) \sim \text{biv} \, N(0, 0; \sigma_1^2, \sigma_2^2, \varrho)$. The reduced forms of (4.1) are

$$y_{1i}^* = \pi_1' X + v_{1i},$$

$$y_{2i}^* = \pi_2' X + v_{2i},$$

(4.2)

where X is the union of the partly overlapping sets of exogenous variables $X_1$ and $X_2$. If $\text{var}(v_1) = \omega_1^2$ and $\text{var}(v_2) = \omega_2^2$, and assuming $\varrho = 0$, estimation of the reduced forms by probit ML yields consistent, though inefficient, estimates of $\pi_1/\omega_1$ and $\pi_2/\omega_2$.

Writing $\hat{y}_1 = \hat{y}_1^* / \omega_1$ and $\hat{y}_2 = \hat{y}_2^* / \omega_2$ for the predictions from the reduced form probits; and writing $y_1^{**} = y_1^* / \sigma_1$ and $y_2^{**} = y_2^* / \sigma_2$ ; the estimable structural functions are

$$y_{1i}^{**} = \gamma_1 \frac{\omega_2}{\sigma_1} \, \hat{y}_{2i} + \frac{\beta_1'}{\sigma_1} X_{1i} + \frac{u_{1i}}{\sigma_1},$$

$$y_{2i}^{**} = \gamma_2 \frac{\omega_1}{\sigma_2} \, \hat{y}_{1i} + \frac{\beta_2'}{\sigma_2} X_{2i} + \frac{u_{2i}}{\sigma_2}.$$

Table 4.4 presents the estimates of

$$\gamma_1 \frac{\omega_2}{\sigma_1}, \quad \gamma_2 \frac{\omega_1}{\sigma_2}, \quad \frac{\beta_1}{\sigma_1}, \text{ and } \quad \frac{\beta_2}{\sigma_2}.$$

The reduced form estimates are listed in table A.4.1 in the appendix to this chapter.

The results given in the first columns of table 4.4 reveal that the set of minimally completed cases (the response) is a nonrandom selection of the gross-sample of SB-recipients. Compared to a reference group of married males, living in urbanized areas, who are full-time working in the manufacturing industry, whose diagnosis is other than mentioned and who have a favorable prognosis ad sanationem (recovery within two months), the probability of response appears to be significantly higher for: older people, married females, people with a less favorable, although positive prognosis ad sanationem, employees in construction industry and commercial services, people with musculoskeletal diseases, and people who had an accident. Significantly less inclined to respond positively to our call for cooperation were: part-time workers, employees in the noncommercial services, and pregnant women.

The estimated model allows for the assessment of the potentially reciprocal causality that underlies the correlation between the probability of DI-entry and the propensity to respond positively. The significantly positive coefficient of Pr{DI-entry} in table 4.4 implies that people who run a higher risk of DI-entry are also more inclined to participate in the survey.

The estimated provisional model of the disability probability reveals that, compared to the reference group, the probability of DI-program entry appears to be higher for those SB-recipients that are older, single, service workers, that suffer from emotional disorders or cardiovascular diseases, and that have an unfavorable prognosis *ad laborem*. Agricultural workers and pregnant women have significantly lower probabilities of DI-entry.

While the probability of response appears to depend on the (predicted) propensity to enter the DI-program, the reverse is not true. The estimated coefficient of the predicted inclination to respond appears to be insignificant, showing that the probability of DI-entry is not affected by the propensity to respond. Apparently, the mechanism that induced people to participate in the survey has not affected the process leading to DI-entry. This suggests that analyses of the DI-probability are not contaminated by the nonresponse in the SB-sample.

From the significant impact of the exclusion variables in the reduced form probit equations (see table A.4.1 in the appendix to this chapter), we conclude that the model is empirically identified.[5]

**Table 4.4**    **Structural Probit Models Explaining SB-Sample Response and DI-entry**

| Dependent variable: | Pr{response} | | Pr{DI-entry} | |
|---|---|---|---|---|
| Explanatory variables[a] | coefficient | t-value | coefficient | t-value |
| Predicted Pr{DI-entry} | .7747** | 3.721 | | |
| Predicted Pr{Response} | | | .3352 | 1.001 |
| Age | .0063** | 2.970 | .0195** | 9.368 |
| D (Married woman) | .1332* | 2.509 | .0564 | .916 |
| D (Nonmarried) | - .0807 | - 1.732 | .1255* | 2.643 |
| D (Urbanization 50 - 100) | - .0042 | - .007 | | |
| D (Urbanization 20 - 50) | .0245 | .515 | | |
| D (Urbanization < 20) | .0335 | .867 | | |
| D (Part-time worker) | - .2586** | - 4.896 | - .0080 | - .126 |
| D (Fav. Prognosis ad san; >2ms) | .1366* | 2.429 | | |
| D (Uncertain Prognosis ad san) | .0479 | .687 | | |
| D (Unfav. Prognosis ad san) | - .1407 | - 1.391 | | |
| D (Fav. Prognosis ad lab; >2ms) | | | .2126** | 3.500 |
| D (Uncertain Prognosis ad lab) | | | .6712** | 11.290 |
| D (Unfav. Prognosis ad lab) | | | 1.2104** | 15.885 |
| D (Agricultural Worker) | | | - .2169* | - 2.021 |
| D (Construction Worker) | | | .1385* | 2.321 |
| D (Other Industrial Worker) | | | .0410 | .629 |
| D (Commercial Employee) | | | .1106 | 1.446 |
| D (Office Employee) | | | .0653 | .960 |
| D (Medical Employee) | | | - .1191 | - 1.384 |
| D (Domestic Worker) | | | - .0460 | - .529 |
| D (General Service Worker) | | | .0317 | .482 |
| D (Other Service Worker) | | | .1990** | 2.719 |
| D (Agriculture) | .0297 | .304 | | |
| D (Construction) | .1452** | 3.060 | | |
| D (Commercial Services) | .1064* | 2.572 | | |
| D (Noncommercial Services) | - .1777** | - 3.402 | | |
| D (Wage less than $W_{min}$) | | | .0019 | .028 |
| D ($W_{min}$ - 1.25 $W_{min}$) | | | .0611 | 1.398 |
| D (1.50 $W_{min}$ - 1.75 $W_{min}$) | | | - .0718 | - 1.323 |
| D (1.75 $W_{min}$ - 2.00 $W_{min}$) | | | - .0065 | - .087 |
| D (2.00 $W_{min}$ - 2.25 $W_{min}$) | | | .0924 | .975 |
| D (2.25 $W_{min}$ - 2.50 $W_{min}$) | | | - .1526 | - 1.270 |
| D (2.50 $W_{min}$ - $W_{max}$) | | | - .1871 | - 1.388 |
| D (Wage more than $W_{max}$) | | | .0646 | .544 |
| D (Emotional Disorders) | - .0812 | - 1.627 | .1744** | 3.616 |
| D (Cardiovascular Diseases) | .0364 | .593 | .2276** | 3.590 |
| D (Pregnancy) | - .5720** | - 4.371 | - 1.0416** | - 6.267 |
| D (Musculoskeletal System) | .3239** | 7.269 | .1074 | 1.674 |
| D (Accidents) | .2088** | 3.311 | .0557 | .780 |
| Intercept | - 1.0855** | | - 1.5474** | |
| Loglikelihood | 6817.293 | | 6801.417 | |
| Observations | 6,830 | | 6,830 | |

[a]   The reference group contains married males, living in urbanized areas, who are full-time steel workers, working in manufacturing, whose wage is 1.25 to 1.50 times the statutory minimum wage, whose diagnosis is other than mentioned and who have favorable prognoses *ad sanationem* and *ad laborem* (recovery within two months).

*,** Significant at 5 and 1 percent respectively.

Ideally, the above simultaneous probit model should be estimated applying FML
procedures that would produce asymptotically efficient parameter estimates,
including an estimate of $\varrho$. Regarding the limited purpose of this analysis, however,
the simple ML procedure may be acceptable despite the downwardly biased
standard errors that come along with it. Indeed, if the standard errors are biased
downward (and t-values upward), the insignificance of the predicted response
inclination seems even a stronger result.

The nonresponse in the control-sample is much lower than that in the SB-sample.
The estimated percentage is approximately 18 percent. The nonresponse cannot be
calculated exactly since it is not known how many DI-insured people were living
in the 330 households that could not be surveyed.[6]
A comparison of sample and population statistics reveals that the sample of DI-
insured persons is not significantly different from the population of DI-insured
persons with respect to age, sex, and branch of industry.[7]


### 4.5     Limitations of the Database

Before illustrating its richness in the next section, we pay attention to a number
of drawbacks of the database.
- The ideal database to trace all relevant determinants of the disability process,
would be longitudinal. Following an initial survey of DI-insured, periodically
repeated interviews would provide information on the respondents in different
stages of the process. Respondents could be followed all the way through the
process that, for some of them, ends with DI-entry.
For obvious reasons such a design is not very practical. A very large initial sample
would be necessary and the surveys would take several years. The costs of such
a design would be prohibitively high. Instead of taking a large sample of DI-
insured, and observing the absence durations and DI-entry rates all along, we
opted for a more pragmatic approach. First we took two samples separately, one
from the population of SB-beneficiaries, and one from the population at risk. By
merging these two samples, we obtain a database in which the first stage of the
DI-process, that is the transition from healthy worker to long-term absentee due
to sickness, is studied. The second stage, from long-term absentee to DI-entrant, is
studied using the SB-database, which includes information on the actual DI-entry
of the sampled SB-recipients. Although the SB-sample has been interviewed only
once (in the fifth month of sick leave), the addition of administratively collected
records of subsequent DI-entries and other SB-terminations lends the database a
certain longitudinal character. Our approach necessitates application of adequate
statistical procedures to correct for the choice-based character of the sampling
procedure, at least when the first stage is analyzed (in chapters 6 and 10).

- Both the control-sample and the sample of SB-beneficiaries have been questioned about the same topics. The setting of the interviews however, is different. The SB-sample has been interviewed by physicians, ergonomists and *lay-interviewers*. The control-sample is interviewed by *lay-interviewers* only. The objective information on respondents' health status and work capacity that is available for the SB-sample, therefore, has no equivalent in the control-sample. Here, all medical and ergonomic information is self-reported. Furthermore, the medical information in the control-sample is less comprehensive. The SB-sample records contain data on diagnosis, prognosis, etc.; in the control-sample current health status is only indicated by self-reports on functional limitations. Whether these unbalanced measurements of health have invalidated the database is studied in chapter 6.

- The setting of the interviews of SB-beneficiaries may have led to measurement errors due to the fact that the interviews took place after the respondents had been absent from work for five to six months. Especially the subjective information on the period preceding the current spell of sickness may be biased after such a long period of absence. It is conceivable that SB-respondents, consciously or unconsciously, seek to legitimize their current status, for instance, by stressing the strenuosity of their work or exaggerating hazardous conditions. Also their attitudes toward work in general and their jobs in particular may have undergone changes after an extended period of absence. Clearly, such measurement errors would cause serious problems in assessing the causalities underlying the disability process.

Table 4.9, panel 2, for instance, shows that 47 percent of the DI-entrants report that lifting is a regular job activity, as opposed to 22 percent among the DI-insured. Thisdifference suggests that the performance of strenuous work increases the probability of DI-entry. The reverse, however, could also be true: SB-beneficiaries may feel the need to justify their current sickness by exaggerating the strenuousness of their regular job. This type of error, then, would be endogenous to the disability process. In chapter 6, therefore, a statistical model is applied to test and correct for such errors.

- The high level of nonresponse in the sample of SB-beneficiaries has already been mentioned. A multivariate analysis however, has shown, that this nonresponse is unlikely to bias the estimates in the disability probability model, although it may still affect other regression results.

- Apart from the overall nonresponse, there is also a considerable amount of partial nonresponse. The unsystematic partial nonresponse will be dealt with on an ad hoc basis by substitution of sample means or by pairwise deletion of incompletely observed cases. The database contains systematic partial nonresponse as well. For instance, in more than 40 percent of all *minimally completed* SB-cases, the written employer's questionnaire is missing (see table 4.2). In cases where it is present, some of the questions are left unanswered. Especially questions dealing with financial aspects, like total labor costs and annual turnovers, have often not been answered. Apparently, the adjustments in the formulation of these questions that were made after the pilot-study, have not had the intended effects. As a consequence, the impact of the financial status of the firm on the disability process cannot be validly assessed in this study.

- A final limitation of the data regards the project as such. Despite the funding bodies' initial approval of the complete research program, including a study of DI-benefit terminations, the SB-sample persons were never interviewed again because, eventually, the necessary additional means were not supplied. And so, the research reported in this book only deals with entry into the DI-program.


### 4.6     A Preliminary Picture of the Samples[8]

The data generated for this study can be broken down into three categories. It contains information on:
  - the sample of people insured under the DI-program, the *control-sample* (n=2,025);
  - the respondents in the SB-sample who actually entered the DI-program, the *DI-entrants* (n=1,680);
  - the respondents in the SB-sample who have resumed work after five months or more of sick leave, the *resumers* (n=1,128).

As a prelude to the results of multivariate analyses in the following chapters, we will introduce the surveyed (sub-)samples by comparing sample statistics on some major characteristics like age, sex, education, wage, diagnosis, prognosis, work history, work conditions, and firm characteristics. The sample statistics presented in tables 4.6 to 4.13 are corrected for nonresponse bias by applying a weighing procedure in which each observation was assigned a weight according to its sampling probability. These weights, $a_i$, were calculated as follows:

$$a_i = \frac{N_i/N}{n_i/n} ,$$

where $N_i$ denotes the number of observations in cell i in the gross sample, N the total number of observations in the gross sample, $n_i$ the number of observations in cell i in the subsample of complete cases, and n the total number of observations in the subsample of complete cases. The cells i are defined by age, sex, marital status, work hours, degree of urbanization, industry, prognosis, and diagnosis.[9]

Not to our surprise, DI-program entry and the occurrence of prolonged sick spells appear to be linked with age. Table 4.5 shows that only 27 percent of the DI-entrants and 44 percent of the work resumers are younger than 35 years, while among the insured 55 percent are younger than 35. On the other hand, the percentage of people older than 50 is far greater among the DI-entrants (38 percent) than among the work resumers (19 percent) or the insured (12 percent).

Table 4.5    The Age Distributions among DI-Insured, Work Resumers, and DI-Entrants

|  | DI-insured | Work Resumers | DI-entrants |
|---|---|---|---|
| < 20 | 5 | 5 | 2 |
| 20 - 24 | 18 | 12 | 5 |
| 25 - 29 | 16 | 14 | 9 |
| 30 - 34 | 16 | 13 | 11 |
| 35 - 39 | 13 | 13 | 10 |
| 40 - 44 | 11 | 13 | 11 |
| 45 - 49 | 9 | 11 | 14 |
| 50 - 54 | 5 | 9 | 14 |
| 55 - 59 | 5 | 6 | 16 |
| 60 - 64 | 2 | 4 | 8 |
| Total | 100 | 100 | 100 |

Since age is correlated with wage, education, health, work history and other characteristics, it is useful to control for age when comparing the subsamples. We have, therefore, adjusted the distributions in tables 4.6 to 4.13 by reweighing the control-sample and the sample of work resumers according to the age distribution of the DI-entrants.

When age differences are controlled for, the samples appear to be very similar with respect to the percentage of females. In all groups considered about a quarter of the respondents are women. The level of education of the average DI-entrant appears to be significantly lower than that of the average DI-insured. The sample of work resumers ranks somewhere in between, being more similar to the DI-entrants' education level, though. These differences in education are also reflected by the respective income distributions. DI-insured have significantly higher wages than work resumers or DI-entrants. Also the after tax household income of the DI-insured appears to be significantly higher than that of work resumers which, in turn, is significantly higher than the annual household income of DI-entrants.

With regard to health status, the information within the control-sample is restricted to data on duration of complaints if any, sick leave records over the last 12 months before the interview, and to self-reported limitations in the performance of certain activities. This information, and more (see table 4.12), is available for DI-entrants.

**Table 4.6    The Distributions of Sex, Education, After Tax Earnings, After Tax**
**Household Income, among DI-Insured, Work Resumers, and DI-entrants[a]**

|  | DI-insured | Work Resumers | DI-entrants |
|---|---|---|---|
| *1. Sex* | | | |
| Male | 75 | 73 | 75 |
| Female | 25 | 27 | 25 |
| *2. Education* | | | |
| Primary | 39 | 54 | 61 |
| Secondary  vocational | 25 | 25 | 23 |
| Secondary  general | 21 | 14 | 11 |
| College / university | 15 | 13 | 13 |
| *3. Annual net earnings (x Dfl. 1,000)* | | | |
| < 20 | 29 | 39 | 35 |
| 20 - 24 | 30 | 31 | 35 |
| 25 - 29 | 18 | 15 | 18 |
| 30 - 39 | 12 | 9 | 8 |
| > 39 | 11 | 6 | 4 |
| *4. Annual net household income (x Dfl. 1,000)* | | | |
| < 20 | 13 | 12 | 12 |
| 20 - 24 | 19 | 19 | 22 |
| 25 - 29 | 19 | 21 | 23 |
| 30 - 39 | 24 | 28 | 27 |
| > 39 | 25 | 20 | 16 |
| *Total* | 100 | 100 | 100 |

[a]    The distributions in panels 1 to 4 are adjusted for differences in the age distribution
by reweighing according to the age distribution of the DI-entrants.

Table 4.7, shows how these groups compare in this respect. Among the DI-insured
82 percent are without health problems, whereas 27 percent of the DI-entrants never
had any complaints before the onset of their current impairment. Therefore, disabling conditions often have been present for a number of years before the DI-
process starts.
The reported complaints of the DI-insured, on the other hand, appear to have an
even longer past; 8 out of 18 percent ailing persons have been suffering for more
than 10 years. Contrary to the SB-sample, however, we do not have data on the
seriousness of their complaints.
Previous to the current spell of sickness, DI-entrants appear to have been absent
from work more often, and longer, than the DI-insured.

**Table 4.7    Health Record: Duration of Complaints, Sick Leave Record, and Current Functional Limitations[a]**

|  | DI-insured | DI-entrants |
|---|---|---|
| *1. Duration of Complaints* | | |
| never had complaints | 82 | 27 |
| < 5 years | 5 | 40 |
| 5 - 10 years | 5 | 15 |
| > 10 years | 8 | 18 |
| *2. Sick leave incidence during the last year* | | |
| 0 times | 45 | 37 |
| 1 time | 33 | 32 |
| 2 - 3 times | 16 | 23 |
| > 4 times | 6 | 8 |
| *3. Total sickness absenteeism over the last year* | | |
| 0 days | 45 | 37 |
| 1 - 7 days | 20 | 9 |
| 1 - 2 weeks | 12 | 10 |
| 3 - 4 weeks | 8 | 13 |
| 1 - 3 months | 9 | 16 |
| > 3 months | 6 | 15 |
| *4. Functional limitations w.r.t.* *Physical activities* | | |
| Lifting | 7 | 47 |
| Pulling & pushing | 3 | 45 |
| Carrying | 5 | 43 |
| Stooping | 6 | 19 |
| Standing | 7 | 14 |
| Walking | 5 | 12 |
| Sitting | 3 | 3 |
| Humid environment | 4 | 11 |
| *Mental activities* | | |
| Reading | 0 | 4 |
| Writing | 0 | 5 |
| Calculating | 0 | 4 |
| Attending meetings | 2 | 9 |
| Sustained concentration | 5 | 15 |
| Work at high speed | 6 | 21 |
| Work under time pressure | 5 | 18 |
| Noisy environment | 6 | 6 |
| *Total* | 100 | 100 |

[a]  The distributions in panels 1 to 4 are adjusted for differences in the age distribution by reweighing according to the age distribution of the DI-entrants.

As regards physical limitations, the last panel of table 4.7 shows that more than half of the DI-entrants have trouble stooping, standing, and/or walking. These data are based on professional judgments by JMS-insurance doctors. The corresponding data for the DI-insured are self-reported and only recorded in connection with regular performance of the corresponding activities.
Data on mental limitations are collected similarly. Such limitations are less prevalent in both groups, and the difference in prevalence between the two samples is smaller than with regard to physical limitations.

The labor market histories, shown in table 4.8, suggest that the DI-entrants have been comparatively disadvantaged both in terms of type of work and labor market experience. Due to their lower educational attainment their work records are longer and they spent more years in physically strenuous jobs. Despite their longer work experience, their current tenure is shorter than that of the average DI-insured. And the incidence of unemployment among the DI-insured is twice as large.

**Table 4.8    Labor Market Record[a]**

|  | DI-insured | DI-entrants |
|---|---|---|
| **1. Work experience** | | |
| < 10 years | 17 | 13 |
| 11 - 20 years | 19 | 18 |
| 21 - 30 years | 22 | 21 |
| 31 - 40 years | 24 | 27 |
| > 40 years | 18 | 21 |
| **2. Years of physically strenuous work** | | |
| 0     years | 60 | 35 |
| 1 - 10 years | 23 | 29 |
| 11 - 20 years | 7 | 14 |
| 21 - 30 years | 5 | 9 |
| 31 - 40 years | 3 | 8 |
| > 40 years | 2 | 5 |
| **3. Unemployment experience over the last 10 years** | | |
| - never unemployed | 87 | 74 |
| - at least once unemployed | 13 | 26 |
| **4. Duration of current tenure** | | |
| < 1 years | 15 | 16 |
| 2 - 6 years | 26 | 35 |
| 7 - 20 years | 40 | 34 |
| > 20 years | 19 | 15 |
| *Total* | 100 | 100 |

[a]   The distributions in panels 1 to 4 are adjusted for differences in the age distribution by reweighing according to the age distribution of the DI-entrants.

Table 4.9    Characteristics of Current Job[a]

|  | DI-insured | DI-entrants |
|---|---|---|
| **1. Industry** | | |
| Agriculture | 3 | 2 |
| Manufacturing | 36 | 33 |
| Construction | 12 | 23 |
| Commercial Services | 33 | 29 |
| Noncommercial Services | 16 | 13 |
| **2. Required activities** | | |
| *physical* | | |
| Lifting | 22 | 47 |
| Pulling & pushing | 13 | 31 |
| Carrying | 22 | 44 |
| Stooping | 32 | 56 |
| Standing | 48 | 69 |
| Walking | 50 | 65 |
| Sitting | 38 | 24 |
| Work in humid environment | 16 | 26 |
| *mental* | | |
| Reading | 29 | 14 |
| Writing | 36 | 17 |
| Calculating | 31 | 17 |
| Attending meetings | 30 | 15 |
| Sustained concentration | 46 | 41 |
| Work at high speed | 30 | 37 |
| Work under time pressure | 27 | 31 |
| Noisy environment | 23 | 27 |
| **3. Job level** | | |
| Blue collar | | |
| - unskilled | 19 | 33 |
| - skilled | 29 | 34 |
| White collar | | |
| - lower | 20 | 16 |
| - intermediate | 22 | 11 |
| - higher | 10 | 6 |
| **4. Career perspectives** | | |
| None | 66 | 88 |
| Limited | 26 | 10 |
| Ample | 8 | 2 |
| *Total* | 100 | 100 |

[a]  The distributions in panels 1 to 4 are adjusted for differences in the age distribution by reweighing according to the age distribution of the DI-entrants.

Not only the previous jobs of DI-entrants but their current jobs as well, are physically more demanding; their work is reported to be noisier and more stressful, too (table 4.9, panel 2). The mental requirements of their work also reflect that DI-entrants are involved in work at lower job levels with worse career perspectives. They are overrepresented among construction workers.

DI-entrants are affiliated with firms that seem to be smaller. These firms are also less equipped to accommodate impairments by means of institutionalized policies aiming at social guidance during extended periods of sick leave, or the adaptation of jobs to functional limitations (table 4.10).

**Table 4.10   Current Employer Characteristics[a]**

|  | DI-insured | DI-entrants |
|---|---|---|
| *1. Firm Size (no employees)* |  |  |
| <    4 | 7 | 8 |
| 5-   19 | 15 | 22 |
| 20-   99 | 27 | 31 |
| 100-  499 | 28 | 21 |
| 500- 2000 | 16 | 14 |
| >2000 | 7 | 4 |
| *2. Firm policy towards disability* |  |  |
| - Job Adaptation | 68 | 60 |
| - Social Guidance | 86 | 75 |
| *Total* | 100 | 100 |

[a]   The distributions in panels 1 and 2 are adjusted for differences in the age distribution by reweighing according to the age distribution of the DI-entrants.

Not surprisingly, the DI-entrants are less satisfied with their current work than the average DI-insured. Still almost 70 percent report positive attitudes. The percentage of satisfied DI-insured is 82 (table 4.11, panel 2).

As they perceive it, their employment opportunities are less favorable than those of their healthy peers (table 4.11, panel 3).

Despite their relatively unfavorable labor market experiences in the past, their unsatisfactory jobs at present, and their limited future employment opportunities, the DI-entrants have comparatively high morale (table 4.11, panel 1).[10]

For SB-sample respondents extensive information on their present health/disability status and on the outcome of the current sick spell is available for both DI-entrants and those who resume their work after prolonged - at least five months - sickness. In tables 4.12 and 4.13 these two groups are compared.

Table 4.11   Work Attitudes and Employment Perceptions[a]

|  | DI-insured | DI-entrants |
|---|---|---|
| **1. Work Ethic** | | |
| High | 62 | 68 |
| Intermediate | 14 | 12 |
| Low | 24 | 20 |
| **2. Job Satisfaction** | | |
| Respondent likes his job | | |
| - yes | 82 | 69 |
| - nor yes, nor no | 13 | 19 |
| - no | 5 | 12 |
| **3. Labor Market Opportunities** | | |
| Good | 39 | 30 |
| Intermediate | 24 | 27 |
| Bad | 36 | 43 |
| **Total** | 100 | 100 |

[a] The distributions in panels 1 to 3 are adjusted for differences in the age distribution by reweighing according to the age distribution of the DI-entrants.

No significant differences appear to exist with regard to diagnosis, although cardiovascular diseases, and diseases of the musculoskeletal system are found more often among DI-entrants than among work resumers. The opposite holds for accidents, vague symptoms, and other diseases. The latter category contains diseases related to pregnancy and other gynecological diseases.

Some diagnoses are objectively verifiable. That is, they are reducible to organ deviations that can be assessed objectively. Others are more or less subjective.

Among the diagnoses listed in table 4.12, there are at least three categories that contain subjective diseases.[11] If we assume that all emotional disorders and all vague symptoms are of a subjective nature; furthermore, that 80 percent of the diseases of the musculoskeletal system contain subjective elements,[12] we may conclude that approximately 50 percent of all diagnoses are, at least partially, subjective. This figure applies for both groups and seems to confirm the suspicion that eligibility for Sickness- and DI-benefits often is determined solely on the basis of information provided by the applicants themselves.

**Table 4.12**      Diagnosis, Prognosis, and Previous Complaints. Work Resumers and DI-Entrants[a]

|  | Work Resumers | DI-entrants |
|---|---|---|
| **1. Diagnosis** | | |
| Emotional disorders | 18 | 18 |
| Diseases of the nervous system | 4 | 5 |
| Cardiovascular diseases | 10 | 14 |
| Respiratory diseases | 3 | 3 |
| Digestive disorders | 6 | 3 |
| Diseases musculoskeletal system | 33 | 36 |
| Accidents | 10 | 8 |
| Vague symptoms | 7 | 5 |
| Other diseases | 9 | 8 |
| **2. Prognosis ad sanationem** | | |
| Very favorable | 14 | 2 |
| Favorable | 38 | 25 |
| Uncertain | 23 | 29 |
| Chronic condition | 22 | 35 |
| Further deterioration | 3 | 9 |
| **3. History of complaints** | | |
| Never occurred before | 36 | 27 |
| Rarely occurred before | 27 | 27 |
| Often occurred before | 37 | 46 |
| **4. Effect of previous complaints on job performance[b]** | | |
| Not affected | 52 | 38 |
| Somewhat reduced | 31 | 34 |
| Strongly reduced | 17 | 28 |

[a]   The distributions in panels 1 to 4 are adjusted for differences in the age distribution by reweighing according to the age distribution of the DI-entrants.
[b]   Excluding those who never had complaints before.

Extent of disablement depends both on the severity of the resulting functional limitations at one point in time, and on the expected duration of those limitations. In table 4.12, panel 2, expert prognoses with respect to curability of the underlying impairment are compared. Obviously, DI-entrants find themselves in a worse position than those who recover after 5 months sickness.

Note, however, that 25 percent of the work resumers face unfavorable prospects *ad sanationem*. Their condition is expected not to improve; it may even deteriorate. They have nevertheless resumed their job. Although this result may be due to erroneous prognostication,[13] it may also illustrate the fact that functional limita-

tions result in work disability only if they interfere with specific job demands.
Table 4.12, panel 3, shows that the particular health complaints, that caused the
current lengthy period of sickness, have a chronic character. Among DI-entrants,
73 percent report to have had the same complaints previous to the onset of the
current sick spell. Among work resumers this percentage is lower but still 64.
Among DI-entrants with a history of ill health 62 percent report that these previous
complaints have affected their job performance during the two years preceding the
onset of the current sickness. The comparable figure for work resumers is 48
percent. These figures indicate that prolonged spells of sickness often have a
previous history of reduced job performance.

Table 4.13    Contacts between Employers and Employees during Sick Leave. Work
              Resumers and DI-Entrants[a]

|  | Work Resumers | DI-entrants |
|---|---|---|
| **1. *Employer contacted employee during sick leave*** | | |
| never | 36 | 41 |
| sometimes | 40 | 40 |
| often | 24 | 19 |
| **2. *Employee contacted employer during sick leave*** | | |
| never | 25 | 31 |
| sometimes | 49 | 48 |
| often | 26 | 21 |
| **3. *"To the firm, I don't seem to exist anymore"*** | | |
| agree | 22 | 32 |
| nor agree, nor disagree | 9 | 11 |
| disagree | 69 | 57 |

[a]  The distributions in panels 1 to 3 are adjusted for differences in the age distribution
     by reweighing according to the age distribution of the DI-entrants.

A possible determinant of DI-program enrolment may be the relation between
employers and employees. Employers who like to retain an impaired employee, for
instance, because the latter can still be profitably employed may try and keep
contact during extended spells of sick leave. Similarly, employees may express their
commitment to the firm by staying in touch.
Table 4.13 contains some information about these relations. During the sick leave
period, DI-entrants appear to have less intensive contacts with their employers than
work resumers. According to the response on the statement "to the firm, I don't
seem to exist anymore", many long term absentees feel abandoned by the firm. One

out of three DI-entrants expresses this feeling, as opposed to 21 percent of the work resumers. From these figures, one is tempted to conclude that DI-entry is associated with relatively loose ties between employer and employee.

Summarizing the exploratory description of the samples in this study, we conclude: First, that DI-entrants are much older than other workers. And second, that next to age, education discriminates strongly between DI-entrants and others. Their relatively low level of schooling may be (causally?) related to many other apparently typifying attributes of DI-entrants:

- poor education coincides with an early start of one's work life;
- it partly accounts for the fact that a majority (67 percent) of DI-entrants have landed in physically strenuous, blue collar, jobs;
- strenuous work causes impairments while at the same time inhibiting work resumption, even if the resulting functional limitations are mild;
- poor education contributes to the low wages of DI-entrants, and to their lack of career perspectives;
- and finally, poor education weakens their competitiveness on the labor market, where the skills they offer are amply available. As a result, they are confronted with comparatively high unemployment risks, and find themselves employed by relatively indifferent firms.


## 4.7    Design of the study

The core of this book is chapter 10, where the results of multivariate analyses of the disability process are presented. This process will be analyzed by estimating two related models.

First, a probit model describing the transition from worker to DI-entrant will be estimated on the database that results from the merger of the control-sample with the subsample of DI-entrants. This ("somewhat") reduced form model will yield a general picture of the disability process.

Second, we will focus on the last stage of this process by estimating a model describing the transition from long-term absentee to DI-entrant. Here, we hope to provide a more detailed assessment of the extent to which the DI-entry probability is affected by health status, labor market opportunities, admission criteria, and individual preferences.

Before we arrive at these final results, we will present four submodels. These submodels are not only meant to enlighten the causalities that steer the disability process, they should deal with the statistical peculiarities of the (merged) database as well.

First, the general problem of endogenous measurement errors will be analyzed in chapter 6. This part of the study will provide information on the extent to which certain explanatory variables are *contaminated* by the design of the data-collection procedure. For instance, if we are to define extent of disablement as the interaction of job demands with functional limitations, we have to use the data from table 4.7, panel 4, to measure functional limitations, and table 4.9, panel 2, to measure job demands/conditions. The extent to which job demands are physically strenuous and mentally stressful is self-reported. As regards the SB-sample respondents such reports may be contaminated by legitimation. Moreover, while the control-sample contains self-reports of activity restrictions, the assessment of functional limitations in the SB-sample is based on expert examinations. Whether such differentially measured variables may be causally related to the probability of long-term sickness or DI-enrolment is something which requires careful scrutiny.

Second, two separate models are presented: One on the determination of labor market opportunities (in chapter 7), and one on the determination of wage rates (in chapter 9). Wage rates and labor market opportunities are important variables in the disability model as they largely determine the opportunity costs of DI-entry. Moreover, labor market opportunities are explicitly taken into consideration by the gate-keepers of the DI-program when eligibility is to be assessed.

Wage rates and employment opportunities, however, may be endogenous to the disability process: All of these vocational aspects may have unobserved common sources. Appreciating this potential simultaneity, we estimate separate models of wage determination and the determination of labor market opportunities. The results of these analyses will be used to obtain exogenous instruments for the wage-related variables and the indicators for labor market opportunities in the disability models.

Third, we include a separate analysis of the disability process at the firm level in chapter 8. This analysis is also meant to support the estimation of the disability models in chapter 10. The idea behind this strategy is not so much based on statistical arguments as on practical considerations regarding the specification of the firm's influence on the disability process. Presumably, the DI-incidence in a firm depends on various factors, such as the firm's policy towards long term sickness and disability, its economic well-being and, of course, the kind of production it is involved in. Together, these factors contribute to the DI-risk of each individual employee within the firm. Instead of including all these factors separately in the individual disability model, we will specify one single indicator for the firm specific DI-risk. This indicator is obtained from the results of the analysis of the firm specific disability incidence.

This body of research is framed by two related chapters. It is preceded by a detailed description, in chapter 5, of the (residual) work capacity of people who are awarded DI-benefits. This part of the study will be indicative for the relevance of applying standard micro-economic theory of labor market behavior to the analysis of the disability process. To the extent that potential DI-entrants are capable of performing regular jobs, their decision to enter the DI-program is similar to labor market participation decisions in general.

Finally, the analyses of disability behavior in chapter 10 produce the ingredients to forecast the size of the DI-beneficiary population. In chapter 11, then, we will present, among other scenarios, estimates of the potential effects on the future number of beneficiaries of the 1987 social security system reform.

# Appendix to chapter 4

Table A.4.1   Reduced Form Probit Models Explaining SB-sample Response and
DI-entry

| Dependent variable: | Pr{response} | | Pr{DI-entry} | |
|---|---|---|---|---|
| Explanatory variables[a] | coefficient | t-value | coefficient | t-value |
| Age | .0120** | 8.160 | .0207** | 13.769 |
| D (Married woman) | .1920** | 3.423 | .0792 | 1.398 |
| D (Unmarried) | - .0306 | - .654 | .1141* | 2.400 |
| D (Urbanization 50 - 100) | .0060 | .110 | - .0299 | - .534 |
| D (Urbanization 20 - 50) | .0181 | .381 | - .0646 | - 1.320 |
| D (Urbanization < 20) | .0401 | 1.032 | - .0282 | - .707 |
| D (Part-time worker) | - .2360** | - 4.239 | - .0402 | - .718 |
| D (Fav. Prognosis ad san; >2ms) | .1452 | 1.363 | - .0788 | - .733 |
| D (Uncertain Prognosis ad san) | .0689 | .683 | .0208 | .205 |
| D (Unfav. Prognosis ad san) | - .0575 | - .516 | .2110 | 1.840 |
| D (Fav. Prognosis ad lab; >2ms) | .0517 | .470 | .3046** | 2.751 |
| D (Uncertain Prognosis ad lab) | .1749 | 1.710 | .6822** | 6.627 |
| D (Unfav. Prognosis ad lab) | .2836* | 2.577 | 1.1260** | 9.973 |
| D (Agricultural Worker) | - .2001 | - .974 | - .2623 | - 1.213 |
| D (Construction Worker) | - .2202* | - 2.026 | .0735 | .659 |
| D (Other Industrial Worker) | - .1460* | - 2.413 | .0167 | .267 |
| D (Commercial Employee) | - .2010* | - 2.451 | .0372 | .440 |
| D (Office Employee) | - .1316 | - 1.843 | .0107 | .145 |
| D (Medical Employee) | .2050 | 1.936 | - .0701 | - .662 |
| D (Domestic Worker) | .1906 | 1.931 | - .0171 | - .171 |
| D (General Service Worker) | - .0188 | - .271 | .0072 | .108 |
| D (Other Service Worker) | .0774 | 1.011 | .1622* | 2.042 |
| D (Agriculture) | .1026 | .508 | .0500 | .235 |
| D (Construction) | .3074** | 2.927 | .0783 | .728 |
| D (Commercial Services) | .1444** | 2.841 | .0847 | 1.612 |
| D (Noncommercial Services) | - .3338** | - 4.663 | - .0523 | - .734 |
| D (Wage less than $W_{min}$) | - .2333** | - 3.876 | - .0250 | - .413 |
| D ($W_{min}$ - 1.25 $W_{min}$) | - .0231 | - .547 | .0594 | 1.360 |
| D (1.50 $W_{min}$ - 1.75 $W_{min}$) | .0151 | .287 | - .0682 | - 1.256 |
| D (1.75 $W_{min}$ - 2.00 $W_{min}$) | .0478 | .670 | .0017 | .022 |
| D (2.00 $W_{min}$ - 2.25 $W_{min}$) | .0006 | .007 | .0968 | 1.019 |
| D (2.25 $W_{min}$ - 2.50 $W_{min}$) | - .0966 | - .819 | - .1570 | - 1.307 |
| D (2.50 $W_{min}$ - $W_{max}$) | - .0691 | - .518 | - .2023 | - 1.498 |
| D (Wage more than $W_{max}$) | - .2327* | - 2.047 | .0438 | .380 |
| D (Emotional Disorders) | - .0260 | - .538 | .1794** | 3.714 |
| D (Cardiovascular Diseases) | .1196* | 2.048 | .2454** | 3.976 |
| D (Pregnancy) | - .7341** | - 5.969 | - 1.0933** | - 7.053 |
| D (Musculoskeletal System) | .3606** | 8.408 | .1576** | 3.604 |
| D (Accidents) | .2399** | 3.798 | .0964 | 1.505 |
| Intercept | - 1.0253** | | - 1.4781** | |
| Loglikelihood | 6817.486 | | 6812.484 | |
| Observations | 6,830 | | 6,830 | |

[a]   The reference group contains married males, living in urbanized areas, who are full-
time steel workers, working in manufacturing, whose wage is 1.25 to 1.50 times the
statutory minimum wage, whose diagnosis is other than mentioned and who have
favorable prognoses ad sanationem and ad laborem (recovery within two months).
*,**Significant at 5 and 1 percent respectively.

**Notes**

1. The primary functions of the Dutch Social Security Council are to supervise the administration of social security programs and to advise the national government on social security policy (see chapter 2).

2. At the time, Han Emanuel was Secretary to the Social Security Council for Financial and Economic Affairs. Bernard M.S. van Praag, was Professor of Economics and co-director of the Center for Research in Public Economics at Leiden University. He is now Professor of Economics at Erasmus University, Rotterdam.

3. The authors of this book joined the team in 1977 (De Jong) and 1979 (Aarts), respectively.

4. The attrition due to work resumption of the selected SB-recipients is mainly the result of delays in the completion of the procedures at the local JMS offices. The time-interval between date of report by the Industrial Association and the interview was scheduled to be no more than four weeks. In fact, the *average* interval in actually examined cases was 4.15 weeks.

5. Significant exclusion variables are the industry dummies for Pr{response} and the prognosis *ad laborem* dummies for Pr{DI-entry}.

6. Within the 3,383 households that were surveyed, 2,248 DI-insured persons were found. This is an average of .664 insured persons per household. Assuming that, on average, the 330 households that were not surveyed contain the same number of DI-insured persons, we missed approximately 219 DI-insured persons due to the nonresponse of households. While 223 persons, who could be identified to be insured under the DI-program, refused to cooperate, the total number of nonresponding DI-insured amounts to 442. Since 2,025 persons have agreed to cooperate, the total percentage of response will be approximately $[(2,025/(2,025 + 442))\times 100 =]$ 82 percent.

7. Apart from age, sex, and branch of industry no other population statistics are readily accessible.

8. A sample description was presented earlier in Aarts et al. (1982b).

9. This weighing procedure is described in De Jong et al. (1981).

10. Both attitudinal scales - work ethic and job satisfaction - are based on a set of questions. Work ethic is constructed by combining reported (dis)agreement with a number of statements concerning work as social duty, as self-fulfillment, etc. An indicator for job satisfaction is obtained by combining three questions on the extent to which the current job conforms to the respondent's aspirations.

11. Needless to say that subjective diseases can be just as serious as objective diseases.

12. Arthritis and slipped disc are identified as diseases of an objective nature. Together they account for 20 percent of the diseases of the musculoskeletal system. The other diagnoses in this category are assumed to have subjective elements.

13. In chapter 5, where the work capacity of the DI-entrants is discussed, we will further elaborate on this point.

Chapter 5

# RESIDUAL WORK CAPACITY IN THE DI-PROGRAM

## 5.1    Introduction

Unused residual work capacities of DI-beneficiaries became a subject of considerable discussion in the late seventies. With no indications of a decrease in public health, the rising numbers of DI-beneficiaries evoked the issue in several countries. Even in countries where disability assessments are more strictly based on medical standards, the steadily increasing numbers of DI-beneficiaries entailed a discussion on the possible disincentive effects of social disability insurance programs and the resulting productivity losses.[1]

In the Netherlands, the debate was focused on the size of the unemployment component sheltered in the DI-program, and, next, on the question whether DI-beneficiaries who are capable of performing suitable work should be treated like unemployed persons without functional limitations rather than being entitled to (full) DI-benefits. The Dutch debate resulted in a series of amendments, aimed at the elimination of the unemployment component in the DI-program. These amendments were among the major elements of the Social Security System Reform of 1987 (see section 2.5).

The determination of the extent of disablement, or its complement the (residual) work capacity, is a central problem in the equitable provision of social insurances against the risk of income loss due to the occurrence of functional limitations. Within many national DI-programs, only one or two disability categories exist. People either qualify for the full benefit amount or do not qualify at all. Under such programs, little is known about the residual capacities of those who are admitted to the program.

The Dutch DI-program allows for the classification of disability degrees into as many as eight categories, but even here no reliable records of the residual work capacity of DI-beneficiaries are being kept.[2] Nonetheless, several attempts have been made, to define and measure the work, or earning, capacity of Dutch DI-beneficiaries. For lack of adequate data, most of these efforts are of a rather speculative nature.

The issue is not only important because program equity is at stake. Information on the unemployment component is also needed for an effective control of the DI-program. A sizeable unemployment component in the DI-program would imply that the Dutch Disability Insurance serves as an unintended unemployment and/or early retirement scheme. The determinants of the probability of access to such a program are bound to deviate from the set of factors that determine the probability of being awarded disability benefits on strictly medical grounds. The appropriate set of policy instruments to control the program, then, may differ accordingly.

From a researcher's point of view, the early retirement, or unemployment, character of the DI-program may also affect the design of the analysis of the behavioral processes that determine the probability of program eligibility. If the unemployment component within the DI-program is negligible, the analysis of the determinants of the probability of DI-entry may focus on the etiology and epidemiology of disabling health conditions. If, however, the unemployment component is substantial, the scope of the analysis should be broadened so as to include medical sociological concepts and elements of the micro-economic theory of labor market behavior, as we have argued in chapter 3.

In this chapter, we intend to produce an estimate of the amount of work capacity "hidden" among DI-beneficiaries. The availability of 1980 survey data with information on the ability to perform work provided by medical and ergonomic experts should allow us to do so.

We will focus on the extent to which the DI-entrants within the sample of Sickness Benefits recipients are, or will be, capable of performing their current job or another "suitable" job. We will develop two measures of the work capacity of DI-entrants. The classification of DI-entrants according to residual work capacity that results from applying these measures, will be discussed. In the final section, we will speculate on how the 1987 Social Security System Reform might have affected the amount of work capacity sheltered in the DI-program.

The expert ratings of work capacity will be included in the structural model of the disability process in chapter 10.

## 5.2    Disability and Unemployment

In the Netherlands, the legal definition of disability implies that the program adjudicators have to take account of a claimant's education, work history, previous income, region of residence, and other factors, when assessing the extent to which a person is unable to perform suitable work.[3]

"Commensurate" jobs, however, may not be made available to disabled persons either as a result of a general lack of vacancies, or a lack of job opportunities for disabled persons particularly. In the latter case, a disabled person's poor employment opportunities result from discriminatory behavior of employers, and are, indirectly, attributable to the one's mental or physical impairment. Before the 1987 amendments became operative, the law recognized this potential discrepancy between theoretical and actual earning capacity. It stipulated that the program adjudicators, in assessing the degree of disability, should take account of the difficulties partially disabled persons might experience in finding commensurate employment. This legal provision is usually referred to as the "labor market consideration". In daily practice, however, a proper application of this provision turned out to be troublesome, first, because it is difficult to determine a person's degree of disability or its complement, the (residual) theoretical earning capacity, and, second, because it is even more difficult to decide whether the discrepancy between theoretical and actual earning capacities is due to discriminatory behavior of employers, or to ill labor market conditions in general.

As of 1973, this administrative problem was solved by coarsely assuming that poor employment opportunities result from discriminatory behavior, unless the contrary could be proven. As a rule, the ensuing modification was made in an equally coarse fashion; partially disabled applicants were treated as if they were fully disabled.

This liberal interpretation of the law was in defiance of the purpose of the law. Although judgments of the Central Court of Appeal stressed the impropriety of these administrative practices, legislature did not take action and tolerated this *contra legem* interpretation of the provision prescribing consideration of labor market opportunities.[4]

The "labor market consideration", and its interpretation in administrative practice, implied that a substantial number of full DI-beneficiaries were liable to possess residual work capacities. It turned the DI-program into a social insurance that, more or less explicitly, also covered that part of the risk of earnings' loss that is due to unemployment. As a practical consequence of these lenient admission procedures, accurate assessments of theoretical earning capacities became unnecessary. After all, a minimum disability degree of 15 percent would suffice to entitle a person to a full benefit, so that more detailed specifications of the degree of disability would serve no practical purpose.

In the absence of systematic statistical information on theoretical earning capacities of DI-beneficiaries, several attempts have been made to estimate the unemployment component in the DI-program. For instance, Bax et al. (1979) have empirically analyzed the relation between the phenomena of disability and unemployment. They tested the hypothesis that a decrease in the demand for labor increases the number of DI-beneficiaries. Results from their time-series study indicate that the expected relationship exists for large parts of the economy.

Douben & Herweijer (1979) reach similar conclusions. They also find that the positive impact of the unemployment rate on the incidence of DI-entries has increased over the years (they studied the 1968-1976 period).

The aforementioned authors refrained from drawing conclusions on the volume of "hidden" unemployment among the disabled. Such conclusions have been reached by Van den Bosch & Petersen (1980). They assume that disability is caused by economic as well as medical factors and that there is a trade-off between unemployment and disability. Their analysis is based on a comparison of DI-benefits entitlements under the DI-program and the entitlements under the disability pension schemes for civil servants. Assuming that the latter do not include labor market considerations, they interpret variations in the incidence of public sector disability awards as being unrelated to economic conditions. Consequently, they conclude that the positive difference between private and public sector disability incidence rates is accounted for by economic factors. They calculate that 40 percent of the population of DI-beneficiaries in 1980 may be considered to be "hidden" unemployed.

Roodenburg & Wong Meeuw Hing (1985) have produced an estimate of what they denote as the "labor market component" in the DI-program. They have estimated a model explaining intertemporal regional variations in the relative number of DI-admissions by age, sex, industry, a trend variable, and the regional unemployment rate. The coefficient estimate of the unemployment rate is then applied to calculate what part of the annual inflow into the DI-program is due to labor market conditions. The authors conclude that the share of the annual inflow related to labor market conditions has increased from 2 percent in 1971, via circa 20 percent in the mid 1970s, to 35 percent in 1981. The labor market component in the population of DI-beneficiaries is calculated to have increased steadily from less than 1 percent in 1971 to 19 percent in 1981 [Roodenburg & Wong Meeuw Hing (1985), p. 41, 45]. Discussing the interlacement of disability and unemployment, many authors[5] have endorsed the administrative eligibility practices. In their opinion, DI-beneficiaries with residual work capacity should not be treated like "ordinary" unemployed because they do not have equal access to jobs commensurate with their disability, even under favorable labor market conditions. A further argument in favor of a separate treatment would result from the appreciation of the fact that, compared to "ordinary" unemployed, DI-beneficiaries have to put in considerably more effort into finding employment since this would require abandoning a long standing, legitimized, sick-role.

On the other hand, those in favor of disentangling the unemployment and disability components use to stress the iniquities that result from a differential treatment of partially disabled and regular unemployed workers, favoring the partially disabled in terms of benefit amount and benefit duration. A further argument in favor of separation is found in the improvement of the accurateness of national labor market statistics that it would bring about. By allowing substantial parts of the labor force to silently disappear into the DI-program, national unemployment records are biased downward, whereas disability records, containing a sizeable unemployment component, tend to provide ambiguous information on the health status of the labor force and the invalidating character of work conditions. Unambiguous information, however, is needed, for instance for designing policies aimed at rehabilitation of DI-beneficiaries. Such policies will potentially be more effective if its designers appreciate the important impediments for work resumption. To rehabilitate DI-beneficiaries, whose eligibility is strictly based on medical standards, a program granting provisions in order to neutralize functional limitations may be the most appropriate policy. Rehabilitation of disabled workers, whose entitlements are mostly based on poor labor market opportunities, on the other hand, calls for a radically different approach.[6]

Similarly, an effective control of the inflow into the program requires adequate information on the nature of the factors that determine access to the disability status. If indeed employment opportunities are an important factor in this process, control policies will be more effective if this is properly appreciated.

## 5.3    The Administrative Practice of Disability Determination

In administrative practice, eligibility for DI-benefits is determined by the Industrial Associations on the basis of compulsory consultation of the Joint Medical Service (JMS) (see section 2.3). JMS-experts (a physician and an ergonomist) carry out a medical-ergonomic examination to assess the degree of disability and the presence of residual capabilities. The physician determines which activities (as sitting, standing, carrying, working in a noisy environment, collaborating with other people, etc.) are constrained. Subsequently, the ergonomist explores the kind of work that would suit the applicant taking into account these limitations, and the applicant's education, work-history, and income. The degree of disability, and its complement, the residual work capacity, are assessed after the ergonomist has explored the availability of suitable jobs in the applicant's region of residence.

In general, an employee becomes eligible for DI-benefits if the inability to perform one's current job has lasted longer than one year. During that (Sickness Benefit) year, the disability is monitored by physicians of the Industrial Association to which the applicant's employer is affiliated. The Industrial Association provides the Sickness Benefits and verifies their legitimacy. At the end of the SB-year, the Industrial Association submits the case to the JMS.[7]

In the early seventies, the JMS appeared to be unable to handle ever increasing numbers of applicants for DI-benefits. In "clear-cut" cases, therefore, the mandatory consultation procedure was reduced to a formal announcement of applications, omitting compulsory disability examinations by JMS-experts. This condensed procedure was to be applied when a (still) disabled worker was expected to be able to return to his regular job within the near future, or in case the impairments were such that they would preclude any work at all. Whether or not to follow this condensed procedure was at the discretion of the Industrial Association. In practice, approximately 50 percent of all applications were dealt with this way [Van Zaal (1981)].[8] This does not imply that all other DI-entrants are fully examined according to the assessment procedure mentioned above. Emanuel & Vossers (1983) indicate that the annual number of JMS-examinations that include both the assessment of the degree of disability and the assessment of the residual earning capacity, explicitly taking account of the "labor market consideration", is probably less than 4,000 or approximately 5 percent of all DI-entrants. Obviously, the generous interpretation of the "labor market consideration" turned explicit and time-consuming assessments of residual earning capacities into a superfluous activity, since in most cases a minimum disability degree of 15 percent was sufficient for the award of full DI-benefits.

Delegation of disability assessments to the Industrial Associations may have led to erroneous disability assessments. First, the Industrial Associations are not equipped to determine the whole range of jobs that would be commensurate with the functional limitations of a particular DI-beneficiary. Second, Industrial Associations may delegate SB-program administration, and the preparation of DI-eligibility determinations, to groups of affiliated firms, or even to single, large, firms.[9] Such firms may be tempted to develop a disability assessment policy that is subject to private goals rather than in compliance with DI-program regulations. Since the Industrial Associations, and sometimes single firms, decide which cases are handled following the condensed procedure, and which cases are actually submitted to the JMS for a medical-ergonomic examination, there is a real possibility of such non-compliant behavior on the part of some of the larger firms.

## 5.4    The Determination of Work Capacity in the SB-Sample[10]

For the purpose of estimating the amount of (residual) work capacity sheltered in the DI-program, we define work capacity as the ability to perform a job that is suitable in view of one's physical and mental capacities, and in accordance with one's training and former profession. This definition is based on the legal concept of "theoretical earning capacity". It does not incorporate the possibility that a DI-beneficiary with residual work capacities may not find employment because of discrimination, lack of labor market commitment, or lack of job vacancies.

We differentiate between the capacity for one's current job, which by definition is always "suitable", and the capacity for other suitable work. Our concept of work capacity is defined as a dichotomous variable as one is assumed to possess either full capacity or none. By "full capacity", we mean the ability to fully perform a suitable job just like other, healthy, workers do. The complementary category, therefore, includes those partially disabled who may be able to perform their current or other suitable work, but only to a limited extent.

The estimates of the prevalence of work capacity among DI-entrants are derived from the data gathered in the SB-sample containing 2,808 respondents who, at the time of the interviews and examinations, were in their sixth month of sick leave (see section 4.3). All these respondents have been examined and interviewed by JMS-experts. On the basis of medical information, the JMS-physicians completed the questions listed in table 5.1. Subsequently, a JMS-ergonomist completed the questions listed in tables 5.2 and 5.3. The ergonomists were asked to base their evaluations on the information provided by the JMS-physicians, on the information contained in the JMS databases on all prevailing jobs, both vacant and occupied, and on the relevant personal characteristics of the respondent. They were instructed to apply the *legal definition* of "suitable" work (see section 5.2). This procedure departed from the usual assessment routine in two respects. First, the JMS-experts' evaluations would bear no consequences for the eligibility status of the respondents involved; And second, the experts were to make their determinations at an earlier than normal stage in the disability process.

Tables 5.1-5.3 present the experts' opinions. The figures show remarkably high proportions of respondents whose sick leave period develops differently from what the JMS-experts expect. For example, among the 925 respondents whom the physicians expect to be able to resume their current work within seven months after the examination, 39 percent appear to enter the DI-program (table 5.1). On the other hand, approximately 21 percent[11] of those, who according to the JMS-physicians, would never be able to perform their current work, resume work and, therefore, do not complete the twelve months' mandatory waiting period for DI-eligibility.
Among the 246 respondents who, according to the JMS-ergonomists, are able to perform their current work, already at the time of the examination, 19 percent enter the DI-program seven months later (table 5.2). On the other hand, nearly one third of the 1,494 respondents whom the ergonomists regard as being totally or partially incapable to perform their current work or other suitable work at the time of the examinations, resume work before the end of the SB-year (table 5.2, line 3). Even among respondents who are thought never to regain full capacity to perform suitable work, 14 percent appear to have resumed work (table 5.3, line 3).
These figures may raise doubt on the validity and reliability of the experts' opinions. The data, however, do not allow us to draw firm conclusions in this respect. The apparent deviations of the actual outcome of the sick leave period from the experts' evaluations of current and future abilities to perform work will in part result from erroneous judgements on behalf of the experts.

**Table 5.1    Work Resumption Potential According to the JMS Physicians**

| In the future capable of performing: | | Actual outcome: | | | | | | | |
|---|---|---|---|---|---|---|---|---|---|
| current work | other suitable work | work resumers | | | DI-entrants | | | total | |
| | | | %[a] | %[b] | | %[a] | %[b] | | %[a] | %[b] |
| yes, < 7 mths | – | 564 | (50 | 61) | 361 | (29 | 39) | 925 | (33 | 100) |
| yes, > 7 mths | – | 92 | ( 8 | 52) | 85 | ( 5 | 48) | 177 | ( 6 | 100) |
| uncertain | yes | 185 | (17 | 42) | 259 | (16 | 58) | 444 | (16 | 100) |
| no | yes | 107 | (10 | 29) | 267 | (16 | 71) | 374 | (13 | 100) |
| uncertain | uncertain | 114 | (10 | 25) | 335 | (20 | 75) | 449 | (16 | 100) |
| no | uncertain | 26 | ( 2 | 14) | 161 | (10 | 86) | 187 | ( 7 | 100) |
| uncertain | no | 9 | ( 1 | 20) | 36 | ( 2 | 80) | 45 | ( 2 | 100) |
| no | no | 26 | ( 2 | 13) | 170 | (10 | 87) | 196 | ( 7 | 100) |
| unknown | unknown | 5 | ( 0 | 45) | 6 | ( 0 | 55) | 11 | ( 0 | 100) |
| Total | | 1,128 | (100 | 40) | 1,680 | (100 | 60) | 2,808 | (100 | 100) |

[a] Column percentages.
[b] Row percentages.

**Table 5.2    Work Capacity in the Sixth Month of Sickness According to JMS Ergonomists**

| In the sixth month of sickness, capable of performing: | | Actual outcome: | | | | | | | |
|---|---|---|---|---|---|---|---|---|---|
| current work | other suitable work | work resumers | | | DI entrants | | | total | |
| | | | %[a] | %[b] | | %[a] | %[b] | | %[a] | %[b] |
| completely | – | 199 | (18 | 81) | 47 | ( 3 | 19) | 246 | ( 9 | 100) |
| partially/no | yes | 437 | (39 | 42) | 610 | (36 | 58) | 1,047 | (37 | 100) |
| partially/no | no | 485 | (43 | 32) | 1,009 | (60 | 68) | 1,494 | (53 | 100) |
| unknown | unknown | 7 | ( 0 | 33) | 14 | ( 1 | 67) | 21 | ( 1 | 100) |
| Total | | 1,128 | (100 | 40) | 1,680 | (100 | 60) | 2,808 | (100 | 100) |

[a] Column percentages.
[b] Row percentages.

Table 5.3    Expected Future Work Capacity According to JMS Ergonomists

| In the future capable of performing: | | Actual outcome: | | | | | | | |
|---|---|---|---|---|---|---|---|---|---|
| current work | other suitable work | work resumers | | | DI-entrants | | | total | |
| | | $\%^a$ | $\%^b$ | | $\%^a$ | $\%^b$ | | $\%^a$ | $\%^b$ |
| completely | - | 711 | (63 | 61) | 463 | (27 | 39) | 1,174 | (42  100) |
| partially/no | yes | 333 | (30 | 30) | 761 | (45 | 70) | 1,094 | (39  100) |
| partially/no | no | 67 | ( 6 | 14) | 409 | (25 | 86) | 476 | (17  100) |
| unknown | unknown | 17 | ( 1 | 27) | 47 | ( 3 | 73) | 64 | ( 2  100) |
| Total | | 1,128 | (100 | 40) | 1,680 | (100 | 60) | 2,808 | (100  100) |

ª    Column percentages.
ᵇ    Row percentages.

This is especially true with respect to the "false positives", i.e., respondents who erroneously would have been awarded DI-benefits in case the disability assessments would have been based on the experts' opinions in the survey. Here, the experts clearly have been too pessimistic.

On the other hand, the "false negatives", i.e., respondents who erroneously would have been denied entitlement for DI-benefits in case the disability assessments would have been based on the presented experts' evaluations, are not necessarily due to errors in the experts' judgements in our survey. At least part of the apparent "false negatives" may be due to erroneous disability assessments by the Industrial Associations. After all, some 50 percent of all DI-entrants have not been examined by JMS-experts at the time of DI-entry, as they were admitted following the condensed procedure. Furthermore, there is reason to believe that among the remaining DI-entrants that were examined by JMS-officials, some are only marginally screened at the time of DI-entry (see section 5.3). As a consequence, confrontation of experts' expectations with actual DI-entry incidence does not provide a valid test of the quality of the experts' evaluations.

A comparison of the physician's opinions with those of the ergonomists shows that the experts sometimes disagree on future work capacities. Tables A.5.1 and A.5.2 in the appendix to this chapter present detailed information in this respect. For instance, table A.5.I shows that the experts' statements on future abilities are contradictory in about 11 percent of all DI-entrants.[12]

Considering the difficulties in objectively measuring disability, the apparent disagreements should be no surprise. Earlier studies have given evidence of the inherent subjectivity of disability determinations and the divergent ratings of identical cases by doctors or ergonomists not only in the Dutch practice [see Van Zaal (1981)],[13] but also in the administration of the American SSDI-program in which, compared to the Dutch practice, disability assessments are highly standardized [Nagi (1969), (1987), Howards, Brehm and Nagi (1980)].

Uncertainty about the validity of expert ratings calls for a very careful use of the data gathered by JMS-experts in developing a measure of residual work capacity. This is how we proceed:

1. Two estimates of work capacity will be produced. The first predicts the expected eventual work capacity of SB-sample cases, i.e., the expected work capacity after the sickness and remedial processes have reached a stable state. The second estimate indicates whether the sampled cases are predicted to be able to work approximately six months after the time of JMS-examinations, i.e., at the time of (potential) DI-entry.

The estimate of the expected, eventual, work capacity is bound to be more valid because it gets around the problem of reliably estimating the timing of regaining abilities. Both work capacity estimates ignore the possibly beneficial results of rehabilitative efforts.

2. Both estimates are presented as proportions of work-resumers or DI-entrants who are able to perform suitable work. We will estimate the range of these fractions rather than produce a "point-estimate". Thus, we hope to account for inaccuracies in the expert ratings. The lower limit of this range is an estimate based on the principle that the least favorable of the two expert ratings is the criterion for assigning a respondent to a work capacity category. The upper limit is based on a strategy by which respondents are classified as being able to perform suitable work if the expert ratings are compatible.

3. Data on work capacity as perceived by the respondents themselves, are not used in constructing these measures since they tend to give biased information on actual work capacity as defined above.[14]

## 5.5    Expected Future Work Capacity

In this section, we will derive estimates of the expected abilities of the sampled cases to resume work in the future. The available data allow us to classify respondents into one of the work capacity categories listed in table 5.4.

Classification is based on the combination of prognoses by the JMS-physician and the JMS-ergonomist (see tables 5.1 and 5.2). With respect to the incidence of work capacity, the lower limit of the estimated range is a pessimistic measure of expected work capacity (A) and the upper limit constitutes a more optimistic measure (B).

Applying the conservative strategy (A), the least favorable rating is the deciding criterion for classifying a respondent into a work capacity category in case the experts disagree. Applying the more optimistic measure (B), respondents are assigned in the category: "expected work capacity uncertain", in case the experts' opinions are contradictory.

Table 5.4    Expected Future Work Capacity Categories

| Category | Description |
| --- | --- |
| I | In the future able to perform one's current job |
| II | In the future able to perform other suitable work |
| III | Future work capacity uncertain |
| IV | Unable to perform one's current or other suitable work in the future. |

Table A.5.1 shows into which category respondents are classified for each possible combination of expert opinions using the pessimistic measure (A) and the more optimistic measure (B). For example, if the physician regards the possibilities for resumption of one's current job as unfavorable, and is uncertain about the possibilities for resuming other work, while the ergonomist's prognosis for the ability to resume current work is favorable, then measure (A) yields classification into category III: "future work capacity uncertain", whereas measure (B) yields classification into category II: "In the future able to perform other suitable work" (see table A.5.1, line 9).

Classification of the respondents in the SB-sample according to measures (A) and (B) defined by the classification criteria explained in table A.5.1, yields the results presented in table 5.5.

Among all DI-entrants, 53 to 71 percent are expected to be capable of performing suitable work in the future; 20 to 26 percent are expected to be able to perform their current job in the future, and 33 to 45 percent are expected to regain the ability to perform other suitable work. Only 20 to 26 percent of all DI-entrants are expected never to be able to perform suitable work again.

Comparison of the expected, eventual, work capacity of work resumers and DI-entrants yields some information on the number of "false positives"; Only 5 to 7 percent of the resumers were classified in the fourth category: "Unable to perform one's current or another suitable job in the future". Here, the experts clearly have been too pessimistic. As argued before, the table does not reveal any information on possible "false negatives".

**Table 5.5**    Expected Future Work Capacity of Work Resumers and DI-Entrants by
Type of Measure

|                          | measure A (lower limit) | | | measure B (upper limit) | | |
|--------------------------|-----------------|-----------------|-------|-----------------|-----------------|-------|
| In the future able to perform: | work resumers | DI- entrants | all | work resumers | DI- entrants | all |
| I    one's current work   | 51 | 20 | 33 | 60 | 26 | 40 |
| II   other suitable work  | 31 | 33 | 32 | 32 | 45 | 39 |
| I + II suitable work      | 82 | 53 | 65 | 92 | 71 | 79 |
| III  work capacity uncertain | 11 | 21 | 17 | 3 | 9 | 7 |
| IV   no suitable work     | 7 | 26 | 18 | 5 | 20 | 14 |
| Total                    | 100 | 100 | 100 | 100 | 100 | 100 |
| n                        | 1, 128 | 1, 680 | 2, 808 | 1, 128 | 1, 680 | 2, 808 |

Table 5.6 shows how the expected future work capacity varies among groups of
DI-entrants. Expected work capacity rapidly diminishes with age. Among DI-
entrants in the 25-35 age group, an estimated 5 percent will not regain the ability
to resume suitable work in the future, whereas among the oldest DI-entrants 49 to
62 percent are estimated never again to be able to work. However, even in this age
group, 24 to 34 percent of the DI-entrants are expected to be able to resume suitable
work in the future.

While the percentage of entrants with future work capacity is approximately the
same for males and females, at least for those under 45 years (± 70 to 90 percent
are expected to regain work capacity), men are twice as often categorized as being
only capable of other suitable work. Women under the age of 45 tend to be able
to resume their current work more frequently (40 to 53 percent) than men of the
same age (23 to 29 percent). The reason for this may be the fact that female SB-
recipients generally hold less strenuous jobs.[15] This may favor their prospects for
work resumption, even if some of their functional limitations are going to last.

With respect to type of work, we find that blue collar workers tend to be incapable
of resuming their own work, while being capable of resuming other suitable work.
The expected work capacity of higher level white collar workers is frequently unfavorable. The latter finding results in part from the legal definition of work
capacity in which the concept of "suitable" work implies that relatively few jobs
can be regarded to suit their training, wage and former profession.

Table 5.6    Expected Future Work Capacity of 1980 DI-Entrants by Age, Sex, Type of
Work, Diagnosis, Industry, and Type of Measure.

| | one's current work | other suitable work | future ability uncertain | no suitable work |
|---|---|---|---|---|
| In the future able to perform: | | | | |
| | measure A (measure B) | | | |
| **1. Age** | | | | |
| < 25 | 37 (48) | 44 (47) | 18 ( 3) | 1 ( 1) |
| 25 - 34 | 30 (40) | 39 (53) | 26 ( 3) | 5 ( 5) |
| 35 - 44 | 23 (29) | 43 (55) | 23 ( 7) | 5 ( 5) |
| 45 - 54 | 18 (24) | 32 (47) | 25 ( 9) | 26 (20) |
| 55 - 64 | 8 ( 9) | 16 (25) | 14 (17) | 62 (49) |
| **2. Age/sex** | | | | |
| men < 45 | 23 (29) | 47 (60) | 22 ( 5) | 8 ( 6) |
| men ≥ 45 | 12 (16) | 25 (37) | 19 (13) | 44 (34) |
| men total | 17 (22) | 35 (47) | 20 (10) | 28 (34) |
| women < 45 | 40 (53) | 28 (36) | 27 ( 5) | 6 ( 6) |
| women ≥ 45 | 18 (22) | 23 (37) | 22 (11) | 37 (31) |
| women total | 20 (26) | 33 (45) | 21 ( 9) | 26 (20) |
| **3. Type/level of work** | | | | |
| high ⎤ | 21 (23) | 25 (35) | 18 (18) | 37 (24) |
| medium ⎟ white collar | 23 (29) | 23 (32) | 21 (13) | 34 (26) |
| low ⎦ | 29 (39) | 27 (39) | 25 ( 7) | 20 (16) |
| skilled ⎤ blue collar | 16 (22) | 37 (49) | 22 ( 9) | 25 (20) |
| unskilled ⎦ | 19 (25) | 36 (48) | 20 ( 7) | 25 (20) |
| **4. Diagnosis** | | | | |
| mental disorders | 23 (34) | 22 (37) | 30 ( 9) | 24 (20) |
| cardiovascular diseases | 13 (15) | 23 (38) | 21 (12) | 43 (35) |
| diseases of the musculoskeletal system | 14 (19) | 46 (57) | 19 ( 8) | 22 (16) |
| other diseases | 29 (35) | 28 (38) | 19 ( 9) | 24 (19) |
| **5. Industry** | | | | |
| agriculture | 12 (17) | 30 (43) | 20 (10) | 38 (30) |
| construction | 15 (19) | 44 (56) | 20 ( 7) | 22 (18) |
| manufacturing | 18 (25) | 31 (42) | 21 ( 9) | 31 (25) |
| commercial services | 26 (33) | 28 (39) | 22 (11) | 25 (18) |
| noncommercial services | 25 (32) | 29 (43) | 25 ( 9) | 21 (17) |
| **Total** | 20 (26) | 33 (45) | 21 ( 9) | 26 (20) |

Comparatively many DI-entrants with diseases of the musculoskeletal system are expected to be incapable of performing their current job, while being capable of performing other suitable work. These diseases often occur among those who perform strenuous physical labor that apparently prohibits work resumption in their own kind of work. This is probably also the reason why the ability to resume one's current work is relatively rare in agriculture, construction and manufacturing.

More than one third (35 to 43 percent) of DI-entrants with cardiovascular diseases are expected never to regain work capacity. The expected work capacity of mentally impaired DI-entrants is frequently considered to be uncertain, which emphasizes the difficulties in predicting the course of emotional disorders.


### 5.6     Expected Future Work Capacity and Actual Work Resumption

To get an indication of the amount of work capacity sheltered in the DI-program, estimated proportions of DI-entrants that are expected to regain work capacity are not sufficient. Information on actual recovery rates is also needed.

In this section, we will compare the proportion of DI-entrants with future work capacity in our sample with the actual occurrence of recoveries during the 1980-1985 period among the 1980 cohort of DI-entrants. The actual recovery rates in table 5.7 reflect the proportion of DI-entrants whose eligibility for DI-benefits has ended because they recovered. This does not necessarily imply that they actually have resumed work. Moreover, DI-entrants who lost part of their DI-benefits due to partial recovery, are not included in the JMS figures reported in the table.

The discrepancies between expected work capacity and actual work resumption appear to be rather large in the first year after DI-entry. They decrease over time as a result of an increasing cumulative proportion of benefit terminations due to recovery. The incidence of recoveries is concentrated in the first years following DI-entry. Ultimo 1983, 19 percent of the 1980 cohort of DI-entrants have lost eligibility due to recovery. Two years later, ultimo 1985, this fraction has increased by only 1 percentage point. Apparently, after two to three years of eligibility, the probability of benefit termination rapidly decreases to become almost zero after six years.

If indeed 53 to 71 percent of the 1980 cohort of DI-entrants were to regain full capacity to perform suitable work, while the actual percentage of benefit terminations due to recovery is only 20 percent, our conclusion is that 33 to 51 percent[16] of the DI-beneficiaries of the 1980 cohort do not leave the program while being expected to be capable of performing suitable work (see table 5.7, last column). If, with respect to expected work capacity and recovery rates, the 1980 cohort could be viewed as representative of preceding and future cohorts, the structural amount of "hidden unemployment", sheltered in the DI-program, could be estimated to be somewhere between one third and one half of the population of DI-beneficiaries.

If previous or future cohorts would contain less work capacity, then the structural unemployment component would of course be smaller.

Table 5.7 **Incidence of Expected Future Work Capacity and Patterns of Recovery by Age in 1980, Sex and Type of Measure**

| | %[c] | Percentage of DI-entrants with future capacity for suitable work[a] (1) | Cumulative percentage of 1980 DI-entrants who lost eligibility due to recovery[b]: | | | | | | Expected work capacity minus actual recovery |
|---|---|---|---|---|---|---|---|---|---|
| | | | (2) | (3) | (4) | (5) | (6) | (7) | (1) - (7) |
| | | Measure A (B) | 1980 | 1981 | 1982 | 1983 | 1984 | 1985 | |
| *1. men* | | | | | | | | | |
| < 45 | (29) | 70 (89) | 8 | 19 | 24 | 27 | 28 | 29 | 41 (60) |
| 45 - 64 | (43) | 37 (52) | 2 | 4 | 4 | 5 | 5 | 5 | 32 (47) |
| total | (72) | 52 (69) | 4 | 10 | 12 | 14 | 14 | 15 | 37 (54) |
| *2. women* | | | | | | | | | |
| < 45 | (15) | 68 (90) | 13 | 34 | 42 | 47 | 49 | 51 | 17 (39) |
| 45 - 64 | (13) | 41 (59) | 4 | 11 | 13 | 14 | 14 | 14 | 27 (45) |
| total | (28) | 57 (76) | 9 | 23 | 29 | 32 | 33 | 34 | 23 (42) |
| *3. men + women* | | | | | | | | | |
| < 25 | ( 9) | 80 (95) | 14 | 34 | 43 | 48 | 50 | 52 | 28 (43) |
| 25 - 34 | (16) | 69 (93) | 11 | 26 | 33 | 39 | 39 | 40 | 29 (53) |
| 35 - 44 | (19) | 66 (84) | 7 | 19 | 23 | 26 | 27 | 28 | 38 (56) |
| 45 - 54 | (27) | 50 (71) | 4 | 9 | 10 | 11 | 11 | 11 | 39 (60) |
| 55 - 64 | (29) | 24 (34) | 1 | 3 | 3 | 3 | 3 | 3 | 21 (31) |
| total | (100) | 53 (71) | 6 | 14 | 17 | 19 | 20 | 20 | 33 (51) |

[a] Percentages of the DI-entrants in the SB-sample.
[b] Source: GMD (1985, table 54).
[c] Percentages of the 1980-cohort of DI-entrants.

The last column shows that the difference between expected work capacity and benefit termination varies with age and sex. Among female DI-beneficiaries, especially women under 45 years, the difference is relatively small. Since female recovery rates are approximately twice as high as those of men, this is mainly due to sex differences in recovery patterns. We already mentioned that benefit termination due to recovery does not necessarily imply work resumption. This seems to be particularly true for female DI-beneficiaries. Although female recovery rates are higher, work resumption among women is less frequent than among men.[17]

Within the oldest group of DI-entrants, both the proportion of expected recoveries and the actual recovery rate are very low (only 3 percent of the DI-entrants older than 55 years have lost eligibility due to recovery). Therefore, the unemployment component within this age-group is relatively small but still some 20 to 30 percent. The large proportion of expected work capacity contained in the younger age-brackets of DI-entrants, partly vanishes through higher than average benefit termination rates in the years following DI-entry. As a result the volume of "hidden unemployment" among the younger beneficiaries is relatively small.

The percentage of people who keep receiving DI-benefits despite full capacity for suitable work, reaches a maximum of 38 to 60 percent in the age-brackets between 35 and 55 years. Since this particular age-group accounts for almost half of the total number of DI-entrants, the largest share of unemployment in the DI-program is likely to be found among these middle-aged, mainly male, DI-beneficiaries.[18]

## 5.7   Work Capacity at DI-Entry

In the preceding section, estimates of expected future work capacities have been discussed. The data do not permit a precise indication of the time within which the expected work capacity will be regained. Our data, however, allow us to estimate work capacities at the time of DI-entry, that is, after 12 months of sickness. In this section, all SB-sample respondents will be assigned to one of the work capacity categories listed in table 5.8. These categories are analogous to the categories used for the classification of eventual work capacities in table 5.4.

Table 5.8    Work Capacity Categories at DI-Entry

| Category | Description |
| --- | --- |
| I | Able to perform one's current job at time of DI-Entry |
| II | Able to perform other suitable work at time of DI-Entry |
| III | Work capacity uncertain at time of DI-Entry |
| IV | Unable to perform one's current or other suitable work at time of DI-Entry. |

Again, we construct two measures on the basis of JMS-experts' opinions concerning the medical-ergonomic possibilities for work resumption (see tables 5.1 to 5.3). The classification criteria are explained in table A.5.2 in the appendix.

Applying the pessimistic measure (A), respondents are classified into the first category in case both experts agree on the presence of work capacity, that is, if the physician forecasts a restoration of the ability to perform one's current job within seven months and the ergonomist finds that this ability already exists in the sixth month of sick leave. Respondents are classified into the second category in case the ergonomist thinks the ability to perform other suitable work exists in the sixth month and the physician's prognosis for other work is favorable.

Applying the more optimistic measure (B), respondents are classified into one of the first categories in case the experts agree on the restoration of work capacity per se but disagree on its timing. For example, if the physician regards the possibilities for resumption of one's own work as "favorable, within seven months", and the ergonomist thinks the ability to resume one's job is absent at the time of the examination but will be present in the future, measure (B) yields classification into category I: "Able to perform one's current job at time of DI-entry". Using measure (A), this case is classified into category III: "Work capacity uncertain at time of DI-entry" (see table A.5.2, line 14). Both measures yield classification into the category: "Unable to perform one's current or other suitable work at time of DI-entry", if the ergonomist thinks no work capacity exists at the time of the examination and the physician foresees a restoration of abilities only after seven months or no restoration at all.

The results of classifying the sample respondents according to a pessimistic measure (A) and a more optimistic measure (B), are presented in table 5.9.

Table 5.9    Work Capacity at DI-Entry by Type of Measure

| At DI-entry able to perform: | measure A (lower limit) | | | measure B (upper limit) | | |
|---|---|---|---|---|---|---|
| | work resumers | DI-entrants | all | work resumers | DI-entrants | all |
| I    one's current work | 14 | 1 | 6 | 48 | 18 | 30 |
| II    other suitable work | 36 | 28 | 31 | 27 | 30 | 29 |
| I + II suitable work | 50 | 29 | 37 | 75 | 48 | 59 |
| III    work capacity uncertain | 41 | 45 | 44 | 16 | 26 | 22 |
| IV    no suitable work | 9 | 26 | 19 | 9 | 26 | 19 |
| Total | 100 | 100 | 100 | 100 | 100 | 100 |
| n | 1, 128 | 1, 680 | 2, 808 | 1, 128 | 1, 680 | 2, 808 |

Of all respondents who entered the DI-program, 1 to 18 percent have been predicted to be able to perform their current jobs, 28 to 30 percent have been predicted to be able to perform other suitable work, while 26 percent of the newly awarded beneficiaries were thought unable to perform their current or other suitable work at time of DI-entry. The remaining 26 to 45 percent are classified in the category "work capacity uncertain at DI-entry".

Of all respondents who resumed work, 50 to 75 percent appear to have been classified in one of the first two categories. Only 9 percent of the resumers have been classified in the fourth category: "Unable to perform one's own or another suitable job at DI-entry".

A breakdown by age, sex, type of work, diagnosis, and industry shows that the differences in estimated work capacity at time of DI-entry are similar to the distribution of estimated future work capacity (table 5.10); The percentage of DI-entrants who are unable to perform suitable work at the time of entering the DI-program, rapidly increases with age. Among DI-entrants younger than 25, only 5 percent is unable to perform suitable work, whereas among the oldest DI-entrants 57 percent is without work capacity at DI-entry. Applying the less conservative measure B, the youngest age-groups, up to 45 years, show approximately identical percentages of DI-entrants with work capacity. They differ mainly with respect to the percentage of DI-entrants who are able to perform their current work at the time of DI-entry. While over one third of the entrants under the age of 25 is expected to be able to resume their current work, this share is only 20 percent among the 35 to 45 years old. Perhaps these figures reflect an inclination of experts to be too optimistic about the recovery perspectives of younger people.

The percentage of entrants with work capacity is approximately the same for males and females, be it that women under 45 years are relatively often classified into the category "work capacity uncertain". Applying measure B, women tend to be able to resume their current work more frequently (25 percent of all female DI-entrants) than men (15 percent of male entrants).

With respect to type of work, diagnosis, and industry, we find that, also at time of DI-entry, blue collar workers tend to be capable of resuming other suitable work more often than white collar workers, DI-entrants with diseases of the musculoskeletal system are often capable of performing other suitable work, while being incapable of performing their current job, and the ability to resume one's current work is relatively rare in agriculture, construction and manufacturing. Again, a relatively high percentage (40) of DI-entrants with cardiovascular diseases is expected not to be able to work. The work capacity of mentally impaired DI-entrants is frequently considered to be uncertain.

Table 5.10    Expected Work Capacity of DI-Entrants at DI-Entry by Age, Sex, Type of
Work, Diagnosis, Industry, and Type of Measure.

| | At DI-entry able to perform: | | | |
| --- | --- | --- | --- | --- |
| | one's current work | other suitable work | future ability uncertain | no suitable work |
| | measure A (measure B) | | | |
| **1. Age** | | | | |
| < 25 | 1 (34) | 38 (31) | 56 (30) | 5 ( 5) |
| 25 - 34 | 2 (28) | 36 (36) | 54 (28) | 8 ( 8) |
| 35 - 44 | 1 (20) | 33 (38) | 52 (29) | 13 (13) |
| 45 - 54 | 1 (14) | 26 (31) | 48 (29) | 26 (26) |
| 55 - 64 | 1 ( 7) | 15 (19) | 27 (17) | 57 (57) |
| **2. Age/sex** | | | | |
| men < 45 | 1 (21) | 38 (41) | 51 (28) | 10 (10) |
| men ≥ 45 | 1 (10) | 21 (26) | 37 (23) | 41 (41) |
| men total | 1 (15) | 29 (34) | 44 (25) | 26 (26) |
| women < 45 | 2 (35) | 27 (24) | 60 (30) | 11 (11) |
| women ≥ 45 | 0 (15) | 22 (23) | 40 (24) | 38 (38) |
| women total | 1 (25) | 24 (23) | 50 (27) | 24 (24) |
| **3. Type/level of work** | | | | |
| high ⎤ | 2 (20) | 26 (23) | 40 (25) | 32 (32) |
| medium ⎬ white collar | 0 (18) | 21 (20) | 43 (26) | 36 (36) |
| low ⎦ | 1 (26) | 24 (25) | 54 (28) | 21 (21) |
| skilled ⎤ blue collar | 1 (14) | 29 (34) | 45 (27) | 25 (25) |
| unskilled ⎦ | 2 (17) | 30 (35) | 44 (24) | 24 (24) |
| **4. Diagnosis** | | | | |
| mental disorders | 1 (21) | 18 (22) | 55 (31) | 26 (26) |
| cardiovascular diseases | 1 (10) | 22 (27) | 37 (23) | 40 (40) |
| diseases of the musculoskeletal system | 0 (12) | 38 (42) | 40 (24) | 21 (21) |
| other diseases | 3 (25) | 23 (24) | 49 (25) | 25 (25) |
| **5. Industry** | | | | |
| agriculture | 0 (12) | 30 (41) | 36 (12) | 35 (35) |
| construction | 0 (13) | 35 (41) | 42 (24) | 22 (22) |
| manufacturing | 2 (15) | 23 (28) | 45 (26) | 30 (30) |
| commercial services | 2 (23) | 26 (27) | 47 (25) | 25 (25) |
| noncommercial services | 2 (21) | 29 (27) | 48 (31) | 21 (21) |
| *Total* | 1 (18) | 28 (30) | 45 (26) | 26 (26) |

## 5.8     Discussion

Uncertainty with respect to the quality of the judgements of the JMS-experts that were used to estimate work capacities, calls for a careful interpretation of the above results. The quality of the estimates crucially depends on the reliability of the expert-ratings. One may doubt the ability of physicians and ergonomists to accurately forecast the eventual outcome of sickness processes [Van Zaal (1981)].[19] There is some evidence that experts tend to rate conservatively, that is, to give the applicant the benefit of the doubt [Mashaw (1983, p. 45, 85)]. On the other hand, in an experimental setting where judgements would bear no effect on DI-eligibility of the respondents (see section 5.4), JMS-experts may have been inclined to depart from this conservative strategy [Wiersma (1979)].[20] To the extent that the JMS-experts have followed the instructions and applied their usual rating standards, however, our operationalization of work capacity, in which the lower limits of the estimates contain only the cases that are rated equally positive by doctors and ergonomists, would be a "doubly" conservative strategy.

By applying a conservative strategy, we have sought to minimize the proportion of "false negatives", i.e., respondents who erroneously would have been denied entitlement for DI-benefits in case the disability assessments would have been based on our work capacity classifications. Nevertheless, some of the DI-entrants who are assigned in the categories "in the future able to perform one's current or other suitable work", may in fact have no work capacity at all. Our strategy should ensure that the number of this kind of mistakes is smaller than the number of DI-entrants who in fact are able to perform suitable work while being classified into the category "future work capacity uncertain" or "in the future unable to perform any suitable work".

From the confrontation of expected future work capacities with actual recovery rates we have drawn the provisional conclusion that the unemployment component in the DI-program will be somewhere between 33 and 51 percent of the population of DI-beneficiaries.

Using aggregate data, Van den Bosch & Petersen (1980) and Roodenburg & Wong Meeuw Hing (1985) also derive estimates of the "hidden unemployment" volume or the "labor market component". Van den Bosch & Petersen conclude that 40 percent of the 1980 population of DI-beneficiaries may be considered to be "hidden unemployed". From the findings of Roodenburg & Wong Meeuw Hing (1985) we conclude that, under the assumption of identical frequencies of work capacities within all cohorts, their estimate of the labor market component would be about one third of the population. Although these results are not directly comparable to our findings, the fact that the estimates seem to be within the range that we have indicated is worthwhile noting.

**Table 5.11   Expected Future Work Capacity and Work Capacity at DI-Entry of 1980 DI-Entrants.**

### 1. Measure A

| In the future able to perform: | At DI-entry able to perform: | | | | |
|---|---|---|---|---|---|
| | one's current work | other suitable work | work capacity uncertain | no suitable work | total |
| one's current work | 1 | 7 | 10 | 2 | 20 |
| other suitable work | - | 21 | 11 | 1 | 33 |
| work capacity uncertain | - | - | 21 | - | 21 |
| no suitable work | - | - | 3 | 23 | 26 |
| Total | 1 | 28 | 45 | 26 | 100 |

### 2. Measure B

| In the future able to perform: | At DI-entry able to perform: | | | | |
|---|---|---|---|---|---|
| | one's current work | other suitable work | work capacity uncertain | no suitable work | total |
| one's current work | 18 | 2 | 4 | 2 | 26 |
| other suitable work | - | 28 | 16 | 1 | 45 |
| work capacity uncertain | - | - | 6 | 3 | 9 |
| no suitable work | - | - | 0 | 20 | 20 |
| Total | 18 | 30 | 26 | 26 | 100 |

Next to estimating the volume of future work capacity, we have tried to estimate the work capacity existent at DI-entry. We conclude that 1 to 18 percent of DI-entrants is suspected to be admitted to the program while being able to perform their current work. The admittance of people able to perform their current work will largely be the result of the practice of condensed assessment procedures. If our estimates are correct in this respect one may doubt whether the change of procedures introduced in 1985 (see note 8) that implied a more strict definition of "clear-cut" cases will be sufficient to ensure that such marginally disabled applicants are denied DI-benefits.

At program entry, 28 to 30 percent of the DI-entrants are supposed to be able to perform other suitable work. A minority among these people, 2 to 7 percent, are expected to regain capacity for their current job in the future (see table 5.11). The others, 21 to 28 percent, are expected never to be able to resume their current work. With respect to this latter category, rehabilitative efforts could be started right after DI-entry or even sooner since the capacity to perform other suitable work may already exist long before the end of the sick leave year when eligibility for DI-benefits is adjudicated. The introduction, in 1985, of an early announcement of potential DI-entrants to the JMS will certainly contribute to the success of such rehabilitative efforts.

Furthermore, table 5.11 (panel 1) shows that among the 45 percent of DI-entrants whose work capacity at DI-entry is uncertain, some 20 percent are expected to regain work capacity in the future. This seems to be a category of DI-entrants that should be closely monitored in order to ensure that eventual restoration of work capacities, for one's own or other suitable work, is timely noticed and acted upon. Finally, the breakdowns of our estimates in tables 5.6 and 5.10 suggest that large shares of the total volume of work capacity that is "sheltered" in the DI-program are to be found among middle-aged, male beneficiaries, who used to hold blue collar jobs. These are the groups that will be affected most by the 1987 disability amendments aimed at elimination of the unemployment component from the DI-program.

## 5.9     Work Capacity of the Disabled after the 1987 System Reform[21]

### 5.9.1    The System Reform of 1987

One of the main goals of the social security system reform of 1987 has been the elimination of iniquities in benefit entitlements between unemployed and (partially) disabled workers.

Before the reform, the legal status of the partially disabled was considerably more favorable than that of long-term unemployed. Wage-related unemployment benefits terminated after 30 months of unemployment, whereupon those still unemployed could apply for minimum-level, means-tested, UWP-benefits (RWW).[22] The partially disabled, on the other hand, used to be entitled to full disability benefits, replacing 80 percent (1980) of last earnings, due to the so-called labor market consideration. As the preceding sections indicate, the DI-program, therefore, used to cover partial unemployment risks as well.

As part of the system reform, a number of legal steps were taken to eliminate this unequal treatment of the unemployed as compared to the partially disabled. Added motives for revision were the presumed anti-rehabilitative effects of the prevailing disability determination routines, and the fiscal urgency to cut on disability expenditures.

First of all, the labor market consideration has been abolished. Under the new regime, partially disabled persons who are unsuccessful in finding commensurate employment, are entitled to partial DI-benefits supplemented with Unemployment Insurance (WW) benefits. These unemployment benefits, however, have limited durations, depending on age and employment record. To prevent the partially disabled from falling down to means-tested UWP-benefits after elapse of the WW-entitlement period, a special program was introduced to provide social minimum allowances which are tested for household earnings only. This program, the Income Provision for Senior and (partially) Disabled Unemployed Workers (the IOAW program), also covers unemployed workers over 50 years.[23]

Moreover, a regulation was added to the DI-program explicitly prescribing that the availability of commensurate work should not to be taken into account in the assessment of the degree of disability. Furthermore, the stipulation which laid down that commensurate work should be confined to the region in which the employee is living, was dropped.[24]

In its Explanatory Memorandum government indicated a few criteria to determine which jobs may be considered commensurate for disabled employees. With respect to these jobs remaining earning capacities should be measured. The Memorandum cites the following job criteria:

First, the job should be a common one. Rare jobs are to be disregarded. Second, the employer should be able and willing to provide the disabled employee with required facilities. Third, jobs bounded by age limits should be disregarded.[25] And fourth, the limitations of an impaired employee should not burden the firm more than reasonably.

Government may add other standards in the future. As these criteria are not laid down by law, they are not binding upon the administrative bodies. They only serve as a key to the interpretation of the concept of vocational disability.

Apart from the above measures aimed at the elimination of labor market considerations from disability determinations, a number of measures were taken to promote re-employment of partially disabled workers.[26] Among these measures, the introduction of the Handicapped Workers' Employment Act (WAGW) seems to be particularly important. The WAGW obliges employers to accommodate job demands and working conditions to the functional limitations of impaired employees. Furthermore, it opens the possibility to introduce mandatory employment quota for disabled workers.

These amendments of the Social Security Disability Insurance Act should be judged against the purposes they intend to serve. The measures clearly have reduced the generosity of the DI-program, since the partially disabled under the former regime usually were awarded full benefits of unlimited duration by coarse application of the labor market consideration. They also have eliminated entitlement discrepancies between the regular long-term unemployed, and the partially disabled unemployed.[27] Furthermore, arrangements are made to reduce the anti-rehabilitative effects of the former disability provisions, to promote re-employment of the partially disabled, and so to produce a shift from unproductivity and benefit-dependency, to self-reliance through commensurate employment.

The question remains whether, under the new regime, disability assessments will be free from labor market considerations. The answer is not fully affirmative. As mentioned, government has passed down a number of criteria defining the set of commensurate jobs. With respect to this set, one's earning capacity should be established. These job criteria are such that they cannot rule out all labor market considerations.[28] Compared to its pre-reform definition, the main new element in the legal concept of suitable work is the abolition of the restriction to the region of residence.

In view of past experiences, some skepticism about the effects of the reform may be justified. Under the former regime, legislature tolerated a *contra-legem* interpretation of the provision prescribing consideration of labor market opportunities (see section 5.2). Given these facts, administrative bodies may very well stretch the interpretation of the new disability legislation beyond the intentions of legislature. Specifically, the criteria for earning capacity assessments may be liable to such liberal interpretations, as they are neither completely lucid nor binding. In view of the complexity of disability assessments, the insurance administrators may, again, be inclined to give more weight to labor market conditions than the legislator has intended.

Another problem which might come up in practice, is related to the contemplated quota rules in compliance with the WAGW. Most of the WAGW applicants are DI-beneficiaries. Employers might put pressure on employees, whose impairments preclude full performance but who are still able to continue their work, to report themselves sick. After one year of sickness, they may be recognized as disabled and awarded (partial) DI-benefits. If so, they satisfy the definition of "disabled employee" under the WAGW. Subsequently, the employer may offer his employee-turned-DI-beneficiary suitable work, possibly his old job, and then count him for the WAGW-quota. Such adverse reactions may result in increased disability expenditures, instead of savings.

The feasibility of the goals of the system reform crucially depends on the flexibility of the adjudicators of DI-claims to change their coarse assessment practices.

A further reconsideration of the condensed assessment procedures to substantially decrease the proportion of nonexamined DI-entrants may be inevitable.

As the revised DI-program only covers the medical component (where severity of disability is expressed as an earnings' loss percentage), the JMS-experts will have to break up a claimant's unemployability into its medical and labor market components. This entails not only a major increase in the number of disability assessments, but also enhancement of their accuracy, both at program entry and at regular intervals during benefit recipiency, since the unemployment component may increase through (partial) recovery.

The new ruling stresses the importance of rehabilitative efforts to be employed by the JMS. Our estimates of the unemployment component suggest that the rehabilitation potential has not been fully exploited in the past.[29] The fact, however, that JMS has been vested with employment exchange powers which used to be the unique responsibility of the official Employment Exchange Agencies, may contribute to the success of the reform in this respect.

### 5.9.2  Effects of the System Reform on the Amount of Work Capacity

Some indication of the potential effects of the system reform may be derived from the work capacity estimates presented above.

We already mentioned that the concept of "suitable work" has not changed apart from the abolition of the restriction to region of residence. Ignoring this amendment and assuming that the work capacity estimates among DI-entrants in our sample are correct, an indication of the quantitative impact of the system reform can be derived by comparison of future work capacities with work capacities at DI-entry (see table 5.11).

Under the new regime, applicants who, at DI-entry, are expected to regain full capacity to perform their own work at some time in the future, will be admitted to the program and will be entitled to full DI-benefits. Those, whose work capacity at DI-entry is uncertain will also be awarded full DI-benefits. The only category of DI-applicants who are to be denied full benefits after the reform, whereas they would have been awarded full DI-benefits before, are those expected to be unable to do their current work ever again but who, at DI-entry, are capable of performing other suitable work. Applying pessimistic measure (A), this implies that 21 percent of the DI-entrants of 1980 would not have been awarded DI-benefits under the new regime. Applying the more optimistic measure (B), this would be 28 percent of the 1980-entrants.

If, under the new ruling, periodical re-examinations will be carried out, an added number of DI-beneficiaries will lose eligibility in due course upon DI-entry.

In section 5.7 we arrived at an estimate of the structural unemployment component of 33 to 51 percent of the DI-population, under the assumption that pre- and post-1980 cohorts are similar to the surveyed 1980 cohort. Obviously, the maximum effect of the 1987 system reform would be a reduction of the DI-population equal to the size of the unemployment component. The complete separation of the unemployment component can occur only if both admission procedures and periodical re-examination routines are adjusted to the new ruling.

Full compliance with the new ruling at DI-entry alone, could, at most, lead to an approximate halving of the unemployment component: By denying DI-benefits to the claimants who, at DI-entry, would be able to perform other suitable work, while being expected never to be able to perform their current work, the work capacity volume would be reduced by 21 to 28 percentage points, from 33 to 12 percent (A) or from 51 to 23 percent (B). Such a reduction, however, can occur only if none of these claimants would have left the DI-program due to recovery under the pre-reform regime.[30] Since this is not a very realistic assumption, the impact of full compliance with the new ruling at DI-entry is likely to be smaller. A further reduction of the work capacity volume would crucially depend on the administrators' success in revealing the eventual restoration of work capacities through intensified re-examination routines.

So far, preliminary evaluations of the system reform show that, in the first two years after enactment, the effects of the abolition of the labor market consideration have been rather modest. The reductions of the DI-population that occurred during 1987 and 1988, have induced the government to adjust the estimate of the structural reduction of the DI-population to only 10 percent[31] whereas, originally, a structural reduction of 50 percent had been anticipated.[32]

Why has the system reform been seemingly unsuccessful in this respect? There may be various reasons for the discrepancy between the original estimate and the eventual outcome. First, the original estimate of the volume of work capacity within the 1980 cohort may have been too high. If so, this would cause serious doubt on the abilities of JMS-experts to evaluate and predict the outcome of sick leave spells within a reasonable margin.

Second, the sharp decrease in the incidence of DI-awards in the early 1980s (see table 2.15, chapter 2) may have been accompanied by an increasing average degree of disability of DI-entrants. If the pre-reform adjustments of the DI-program (see chapter 2) have reduced the propensity to apply for DI-benefits of people with minor disabilities, the workers that did enter the DI-program in the early 1980s are likely to be more disabled than the 1980 entrants. Consequently, the pre-reform cohorts may contain less work capacity than the 1980 cohort. While the unemployment component may have been correctly estimated with respect to the 1980 cohort, the extrapolation of these estimates for the early 1980s may thus have led to upward biased estimates of the work capacities among DI-awards in the years preceding the system reform. In chapter 10, we will elaborate on the causes of these pre-reform reductions of the DI-incidence.

Third, as we mentioned above, total elimination of the unemployment component requires both strict compliance with the new rulings with respect to the flows into the program and an intensified effort to reveal restored work capacities of those on the DI-rolls. During the first years after the reform, systematic reviews under the new rulings were restricted to DI-beneficiaries younger than 35 years. This restriction implied that only 10 percent of the total DI-population was to be reviewed. This particular group was not only small, but also likely to contain a relatively small amount of residual work capacity (see table 5.7). By thus limiting the review efforts, a substantial part of the work capacities expectedly sheltered in the DI-program were left un-examined. This particular application of the new ruling, a priori, implied that the maximum result of the system reform would, at best, have been a halving of the unemployment component, whatever its actual size.

A fourth reason for the marginal impact of the system reform so far, may be the inability of the gatekeepers to strictly comply with the new ruling when assessing the benefit entitlements of DI-claimants. They may have been unable to change their pre-reform assessment practices as drastically as the new ruling would require. The administrative bodies may need more time to fully adjust, both in terms of attitudes and in terms of equipment, to the amended DI-program.[33]

We will further elaborate on the potential impact of the 1987 Reform in chapter 11, where a forecast of the size of the DI-program in the coming decades is presented.

## 5.10 Conclusions

In this chapter we have tried to estimate the extent to which DI-beneficiaries are able to work. We found that, at DI-entry, 29 to 48 percent of those who entered the program in 1980 may be considered capable of performing a suitable job. Only 1 to 18 percent are able to do their own job. After some time, 53 to 71 percent will have regained the ability to do suitable work; 20 to 26 percent will be able to perform their own work again; and 33 to 45 percent will be able to resume other work which suits their training and work record. Since in fact only 20 percent of the 1980-cohort of DI-entrants have lost eligibility due to recovery, we concluded that the structural share of unemployment hidden in the DI-program amounts to 33 to 51 percent. The unemployment component varies with age, industry, type of work and type of diagnosis. Among middle aged males, working in blue collar jobs, the volume of hidden unemployment is relatively high. This is mainly due to the fact that these people often are unable to resume their current work, while being capable to do other suitable work. It may be worthwhile to concentrate on this particular group when developing or improving policies to stimulate work resumption of DI-beneficiaries.

Our results are consistent with those of Van den Bosch & Petersen (1980) and Roodenburg & Wong Meeuw Hing (1985) with respect to the conclusion that in the process of disability determination, disability and unemployment aspects coincide. Our findings reveal that the DI-program not only covers the risk of losing income due to disability, but also serves as a social insurance for income losses due to unemployment and early retirement. The set of factors determining the probability of DI-entry, therefore, is likely to contain medical and ergonomic variables as well as behavioral indicators derived from sociological and economic theory.

We elaborated on the contents of the Dutch social security reform of 1987 and its implications for the DI-program. Full compliance with the new ruling with respect to initial disability assessments may lead to an approximate halving of the unemployment component. Full elimination, however, will depend on the ability to reveal regained work capacity during the years following DI-entry. Assuming that our estimates of the unemployment component contained in the 1980 cohort are adequate, the fact that the impact of the system reform so far has been only marginal, partly results from the policy to concentrate on the flow into the DI-program. Presumably, the decreasing size of the unemployment component within cohorts that entered the DI-program in the pre-reform years and the administrative inertia in adjusting to new standards have further limited the actual impact of the abolition of the labor market consideration from the DI-program.

# Appendix to chapter 5

Table A.5.1   Classification of DI-Entrants into Work Capacity Categories by Type of Measure.

| | Physician's prognosis *ad laborem* | | Ergonomist's prognosis *ad laborem* | | N=1,680 | work capacity categories[e] | |
|---|---|---|---|---|---|---|---|
| | one's current work[a] | other work[b] | one's current work[c] | other work[d] | perc. | measure A | B |
| 1 | + | + | + | + | 20.21 | I | I |
| 2 | + | + | - | + | 4.47 | II | II |
| 3 | +/- | + | + | + | 2.32 | II | I |
| 4 | +/- | + | - | + | 11.61 | II | II |
| 5 | - | + | + | + | .78 | II | II |
| 6 | - | + | - | + | 13.45 | II | II |
| 7 | +/- | +/- | + | + | 3.64 | III | I |
| 8 | +/- | +/- | - | + | 9.00 | III | II |
| 9 | - | +/- | + | + | .42 | III | II |
| 10 | - | +/- | - | + | 4.83 | III | II |
| 11 | +/- | - | + | + | .12 | III | I |
| 12 | + | + | - | - | 1.14 | IV | III |
| 13 | +/- | + | - | - | 1.38 | IV | III |
| 14 | - | + | - | - | 1.38 | IV | III |
| 15 | +/- | +/- | - | - | 6.10 | IV | IV |
| 16 | - | +/- | - | - | 4.00 | IV | IV |
| 17 | +/- | - | - | + | .60 | IV | III |
| 18 | +/- | - | - | - | 1.26 | IV | IV |
| 19 | - | - | + | + | - | IV | III |
| 20 | - | - | - | + | 1.02 | IV | III |
| 21 | - | - | - | - | 8.94 | IV | IV |
| 22 | unknown | and/or | unknown | | 3.11 | III | III |
| | | | | | Total 99.78 | | |

[a]  +     = Capable of performing one's current work within or after 7 months.
   +/-   = Prognosis uncertain.
   -     = Incapable of performing one's current work (table 5.1).
[b]  +     = Capable of performing other suitable work.
   +/-   = Prognosis uncertain.
   -     = Incapable of performing other suitable work (table 5.1).
[c]  +     = In the future, capable of performing one's current work.
   -     = In the future, (partially) incapable of performing one's current work.
[d]  +     = In the future, capable of performing other suitable work.
   -     = In the future, incapable of performing other suitable work (table 5.3).
[e]  See table 5.4.

Table A.5.2    Classification of DI-Entrants into Work Capacity Categories at DI-Entry by Type of Measure.

| | Physician's prognosis ad laborem | | Ergonomist's prognosis ad laborem | | | | | work capacity categories[g] | |
| | | | in the 6th month of sick leave | | in the future | | N=1,680 | measure | |
| | one's current work[a] | other work[b] | one's current work[c] | other work[d] | one's current work[e] | other work[f] | perc. | A | B |
|---|---|---|---|---|---|---|---|---|---|
| 1 | ++ | + | + | + | + | + | 1.31 | I | I |
| 2 | ++ | + | - | + | + | + | 5.54 | II | I |
| 3 | ++ | + | - | + | - | + | 1.90 | II | II |
| 4 | + | + | + | + | + | + | .30 | II | I |
| 5 | + | + | - | + | + | + | .90 | II | II |
| 6 | + | + | - | + | - | + | .54 | II | II |
| 7 | +/- | + | + | + | + | + | .24 | II | I |
| 8 | +/- | + | - | + | + | + | 1.01 | II | II |
| 9 | +/- | + | - | + | - | + | 6.67 | II | II |
| 10 | - | + | + | + | + | + | .42 | II | II |
| 11 | - | + | - | + | + | + | .30 | II | II |
| 12 | - | + | - | + | - | + | 9.94 | II | II |
| 13 | ++ | + | - | + | - | - | .12 | III | III |
| 14 | ++ | + | - | - | + | + | 9.89 | III | I |
| 15 | ++ | + | - | - | - | + | 1.43 | III | II |
| 16 | ++ | + | - | - | - | - | .72 | III | III |
| 17 | + | + | - | + | - | - | .06 | III | III |
| 18 | +/- | + | - | - | + | + | 1.07 | III | III |
| 19 | +/- | + | - | - | - | + | 4.94 | III | III |
| 20 | +/- | + | - | + | - | - | .30 | III | III |
| 21 | - | + | - | - | + | + | .06 | III | III |
| 22 | - | + | - | - | - | + | 3.51 | III | III |
| 23 | - | + | - | + | - | - | .12 | III | III |
| 24 | +/- | +/- | + | + | + | + | .42 | III | I |
| 25 | +/- | +/- | - | + | + | + | .66 | III | II |
| 26 | +/- | +/- | - | - | + | + | 2.56 | III | III |
| 27 | +/- | +/- | - | + | - | + | 3.88 | III | II |
| 28 | +/- | +/- | - | - | - | + | 5.12 | III | III |
| 29 | +/- | +/- | - | + | - | - | .18 | III | III |
| 30 | - | +/- | + | + | + | + | .06 | III | II |
| 31 | - | +/- | - | + | + | + | .24 | III | II |
| 32 | - | +/- | - | - | + | + | .12 | III | III |
| 33 | - | +/- | - | + | - | + | 2.62 | III | II |
| 34 | - | +/- | - | + | - | - | .18 | III | III |
| 35 | - | +/- | - | - | - | + | 2.21 | III | III |
| 36 | +/- | - | - | + | + | + | .06 | III | III |
| 37 | +/- | - | - | + | - | + | .48 | III | III |
| 38 | +/- | - | - | + | - | - | .06 | III | III |
| 39 | - | - | - | + | - | + | .36 | III | III |
| 40 | - | - | - | + | - | - | .06 | III | III |

(continued)

Table A.5.2    (continued)

| | Physician's prognosis *ad laborem* | | Ergonomist's prognosis *ad laborem* | | | | N=1,680 | work capacity categories[g] | |
| | | | in the 6th month of sick leave | | in the future | | | measure | |
| | one's current work[a] | other work[b] | one's current work[c] | other work[d] | one's current work[e] | other work[f] | perc. | A | B |
|---|---|---|---|---|---|---|---|---|---|
| 41 | +/- | - | - | - | + | + | .06 | IV | IV |
| 42 | + | + | - | - | + | + | 2.27 | IV | IV |
| 43 | + | + | - | - | - | + | .60 | IV | IV |
| 44 | + | + | - | - | - | - | .24 | IV | IV |
| 45 | +/- | + | - | - | - | - | 1.08 | IV | IV |
| 46 | - | + | - | - | - | - | 1.26 | IV | IV |
| 47 | +/- | +/- | - | - | - | - | 5.92 | IV | IV |
| 48 | - | +/- | - | - | - | - | 3.82 | IV | IV |
| 49 | +/- | - | - | - | - | - | 1.20 | IV | IV |
| 50 | - | - | - | - | - | + | .66 | IV | IV |
| 51 | - | - | - | - | - | - | 8.88 | IV | IV |
| 52 | unknown | and/or | unknown | and/or | unknown | | 3.41 | III | III |

Total  99.96

[a]  ++  = Capable of performing one's current work within 7 months.
   +  = Capable of performing one's current work after 7 months.
  +/-  = Prognosis uncertain (table 5.1).
[b]  +  = In the future, capable of performing other suitable work.
  -  = In the future, incapable of performing other suitable work (table 5.1).
[c]  +  = In the 6th month, capable of performing one's current work.
  -  = In the 6th month, (partially) incapable of performing one's current work (table 5.2).
[d]  +  = In the 6th month, capable of performing other suitable work.
  -  = In the 6th month, incapable of performing other suitable work (table 5.2).
[e]  +  = In the future, capable of performing one's current work.
  -  = In the future, (partially) incapable of performing one's current work (table 5.3).
[f]  +  = In the future, capable of performing other suitable work.
  -  = In the future, incapable of performing other suitable work (table 5.3).
[g]  See table 5.8.

**Table A.5.3**   Incidence of Expected Future Work Capacity and of Recovery by Age in 1980, Sex, and Type of Measure. In Terms of DI-beneficiaries and DI-benefit Recipiency Years.

| | Percentage of the 1980 entry-cohort with future capacity for suitable work | | | Cumulative percentage of the 1980 entry-cohort losing eligibility due to recovery[a]: | | | Expected work capacity minus actual recovery | |
|---|---|---|---|---|---|---|---|---|
| | (1)[b] | (2)[c] | (3)[d] | (4)[b] | (5)[e] | (6)[d] | (1) - (4)[b] | (3)-(6)[d] / (2) |
| | A (B) | | A (B) | | | | A (B) | A (B) |
| **1. men** | | | | | | | | |
| < 45 | 70 (89) | .95 | 65 (84) | 29 | .86 | 25 | 41 (60) | 42 (62) |
| 45 - 64 | 37 (52) | .93 | 30 (45) | 5 | .97 | 5 | 32 (47) | 27 (43) |
| total | 52 (69) | .93 | 45 (62) | 15 | .89 | 13 | 37 (54) | 34 (53) |
| **2. women** | | | | | | | | |
| < 45 | 68 (90) | .97 | 65 (87) | 51 | .98 | 50 | 17 (39) | 16 (38) |
| 45 - 64 | 41 (59) | .95 | 36 (54) | 14 | .96 | 13 | 27 (45) | 24 (43) |
| total | 57 (76) | .97 | 54 (73) | 34 | .95 | 32 | 23 (42) | 22 (42) |
| **3. men + women** | | | | | | | | |
| < 24 | 80 (95) | .97 | 77 (92) | 52 | .98 | 51 | 28 (43) | 27 (43) |
| 25 - 34 | 69 (93) | .96 | 65 (89) | 40 | .91 | 36 | 29 (53) | 30 (55) |
| 35 - 44 | 66 (84) | .95 | 61 (79) | 28 | .86 | 24 | 38 (56) | 39 (58) |
| 45 - 54 | 50 (71) | .93 | 43 (64) | 11 | .89 | 10 | 39 (60) | 36 (58) |
| 55 - 64 | 24 (34) | .93 | 17 (27) | 3 | .93 | 3 | 21 (31) | 16 (26) |
| total | 53 (71) | .95 | 48 (66) | 20 | .91 | 18 | 33 (51) | 29 (50) |

[a]  Source: GMD (1985, p. 54).
[b]  Percentages of the 1980 entry-cohort in terms of DI-entrants.
[c]  Conversion coefficient of DI-entry. It is based on the distribution of the degree of disability by age and sex within the population of DI-entrants, cohort 1981 [GMD (1981, p. 96)]. The conversion coefficients are calculated using the following key: a DI-beneficiary in the 15%-25% category of disability is equivalent to .2 recipiency years, a degree of 25%-35% is equivalent to .3 recipiency years, etc., (35%-45% = .4, 45%-55% = .5, 55%-65% = .6, 65%-80% = .7, and 80%-100% = 1.0). For DI-entrants without future work capacity the conversion coefficient is assumed to equal 1.
[d]  Percentages of the 1980 entry-cohort in terms of recipiency years.
[e]  Conversion coefficient of DI-benefit termination. It is derived from the distribution of the degree of disability, before benefit termination, within the population of DI-benefit terminations due to recovery in 1985 [GMD (1985, p. 46)]. Its distribution over the sex-age categories is assumed to be proportional to the distribution of the conversion coefficient within the total population of DI-beneficiaries.

**Notes**

1. See for instance, Copeland (1981), Haveman et al. (1986), Weaver (1986).

2. The statistics on the degree of disability of DI-beneficiaries, annually provided by the Joint Medical Service, do not contain adequate information on the residual capacities of the beneficiaries (see section 5.3).

3. Dutch law defines as disabled "a person who -as a consequence of illness or injury-, fully or partly, is unable to earn -with labor which is commensurate to his force and capabilities and which, with respect to his training and work history, he can reasonably be asked to perform at the place where he works or at a similar place- what physically and mentally healthy persons in otherwise similar circumstances usually earn" (see section 2.3).

4. As early as 1972, the Central Court of Appeal, being the highest jurisdictional body as regards social insurance, judged the administrative interpretation of the labor market consideration to be in defiance with the purpose of the law. According to the Central Court of Appeal, the adjudicators of DI-benefits should check whether reduced employment opportunities were caused by the disability in itself or by other factors, such as prevailing unemployment. Application of the labor market consideration was admissible but the difference with a classification, merely based on loss of earning capacity, should not be higher than one or two disability categories [De Jong et al. (1990)].

5. For example, Bax et al. (1979), Zweekhorst (1981), Hermans et al. (1986).

6. See Haveman, Halberstadt and Burkhauser (1984, pp. 44-52) for a description of the corrective versus the ameliorative response to the disability phenomenon.

7. A small number of cases is submitted to the JMS before the end of the SB-year under standard procedures to initiate rehabilitation activities in an early stage.

8. During the early eighties, approximately 50 percent of applications were handled following this reduced procedure [GMD (1980, 1981, 1982)]. In 1985, the procedures regarding the mandatory consultation of JMS by the Industrial Associations were changed. Since then the "clear-cut cases" are defined more strictly and the (formal) announcement of potential DI-entrants by the Industrial Associations was advanced to the sixth month of the SB-year to increase the probability of successful rehabilitation at an early stage in the disability process. After this change of procedures, less than 40 percent (40% in 1986, 37% in 1987) of all applications were handled following the condensed announcement procedure and therefore not examined by the JMS-experts. These percentages can be calculated from [GMD (1988, Table 2)], by taking the difference of the number of "kennisgevingen" (61,300) and the "meldingen na de zesde maand" (17,000) and expressing the result as a percentage of the sum of "kennisgevingen" (61,300), "spontane meldingen" (10,000), and "zesde maandsmeldingen" (38,200).

9. Within the Industrial Associations, the affiliated firms are divided in separate groups, according to their actual risks in Sickness Insurance. Some groups consist of a few or, in case of very large firms, just one large firm. The largest firms, therefore, bear the total sickness risk themselves. In this respect, they act as if they were an Industrial Association on their own.

10. The determination of work capacity in the SB-sample was presented earlier in Aarts (1987).

11. The average percentage of work resumers in lines 4, 6 and 8 of table 5.1 is 21 percent.

12. The statements are considered to be contradictory if the physician's prognosis is favorable and the ergonomist's prognosis is unfavorable and vice versa; table A.5.1, lines 2, 5, 9, 11, 12-14, 17 and 20.

13. Van Zaal (1981) analyzed the subjective elements in disability assessment procedures. He submitted three DI-benefit application files to a panel of 94 JMS-physicians in order to assess DI-benefit eligibility. He found that 6 percent of the doctors would deny DI-benefits to all three applicants, while 39 percent would deny DI-benefits to none of them. Van Zaal also reports that the annual number of denials by ergonomists vary from 1 to 60. The individual denial rate appeared to be correlated with personal interpretations of the law (p. 30).

14. See for instance Lambrinos (1981) and Parsons (1982), and our results in chapters 6 and 10.

15. Recent research confirms the hypothesis that female DI-beneficiaries indeed used to hold jobs that are less strenuous than the jobs performed by male DI-beneficiaries [Bruinsma et al. (1989)].

16. While 53 to 71 percent of the DI-entrants is expected to regain work capacity, only 20 percent actually recovers and is removed from the DI-roles. Assuming that all recoveries would have been predicted to be able to perform suitable work in the future, 33 percent (53 - 20) to 51 percent (71 - 20) of the 1980 cohort of DI-beneficiaries receive DI-benefits despite their ability to perform suitable work.

17. Bruinsma et al. (1989) show that, among the 1985-cohort of DI-entrants, 28 percent of female beneficiaries and 13 percent of male beneficiaries loose eligibility due to recovery within 2 to 2,5 years (p. 122). The respective percentages of work resumption (including partial resumptions) during the first DI-year are 20 percent for females and 22 percent for males (p. 63).

18. Not all partially disabled receive full DI-pensions. In 1988, 19 percent of all DI-beneficiaries receive partial benefits in accordance with their actual residual earning capacities. Most of these people have partially resumed work. A partially disabled person who appears to be able to earn, say, 50 percent of pre-disability wage by working half the usual hours, will be entitled to partial DI-benefits that supplement the post-disability wage up to 100 percent of pre-disability level. Such a person will of course be registered as a DI-beneficiary, despite his partial work resumption. By expressing the volume of unused, residual work capacities as a proportion of DI-entrants who are registered as DI-beneficiaries, we ignore the possibility that some DI-beneficiaries may be engaged in gainful activities, at least to some extent. The work capacity sheltered in the DI-program would be measured more accurately perhaps, when expressed in terms of DI-benefit recipiency years. In table A.5.3 we calculate the size of the unemployment component in terms of benefit recipiency years. The conversion of beneficiaries into benefit recipiency years leads to only minor adjustments of the estimated size of the unemployment component presented in table 5.7. In terms of benefit recipiency years, the estimated size of the structural unemployment component is 29 to 50 percent. The distribution of hidden unemployment over the categories listed in table 5.7 is hardly affected by the conversion into recipiency years.

19. See note 13.

20. Wiersma (1979) finds that, in an experimental setting, insurance physicians (employed by the Industrial Associations), tend to underestimate the eventual, total, duration of sick leave spells in progress. Particularly the a priori expected durations of spells that appear to result in DI-entry are shorter than the actual realizations (p. 113). In retrospection, however, the physicians appear to stick to their a priori evaluations, since they consider a large proportion of these spells unnecessarily long (p. 125).

21. See [De Jong et al. (1990)] for a detailed description in English of economic backgrounds, legal and policy aspects of the Dutch social security reform of 1987.

22.See section 2.3.

23.The beneficiary status of DI-benefits recipients, who were aged 35 or over at the time of introduction of the disability amendments, has not been revised. The old regulations, including the labor market consideration, therefore, still apply to these beneficiaries.

24."Disability", now, is defined as: "(..) a full or partial incapacity, due to sickness or impairment, to earn an amount equal to the earnings which a healthy employee, with similar education and work history, would normally earn in the same place or region." (art. 5.1 AAW and art. 18.1 WAO)

25.Specifically, jobs that cannot be performed by people over a certain age, in terms of physical and mental job requirements, not in terms of employers' preferences.

26.De Jong et al. (1990) mention the following measures:
  1. A provision to temporarily scale up disability classifications by one category, if partially disabled workers accept jobs paying less than their remaining earning capacities.
  2. The Handicapped Workers' Employment Act (WAGW) obliges employers to accommodate job demands and working conditions to the functional limitations of impaired employees. Employers may be given financial compensation for making such accommodations.
  3. By force of the WAGW, employers may be granted a so-called "wage dispensation" to compensate them for the productivity damages they may incur by employing partially disabled workers.
  4. Government has announced the introduction of mandatory employment quota of 7 percent for disabled workers in the near future, in case trade unions and employers' organizations will not succeed in elaborating quota rules voluntarily.
  5. Since the regional Employment Exchange Agencies, that had the monopoly of job mediation, had been hardly successful in finding employment for the partially disabled, the JMS has been vested with job mediation discretion.
  6. Employment contracts oblige the employer to provide commensurate work to employees who have fallen disabled in current employment. To that end, the employer may even have to change the current division of labor within his company.
  Similarly, a disabled employee may only be dismissed, if continued employment in his current job or in alternative work within the firm, would put a more than reasonable strain upon the employer.

27.The only difference that remains, is the age limit applying to the regular unemployed who are only entitled to IOAW-allowances if they are 50 or older at the start of unemployment.

28.Specifically the criterion implying that the engagement of a disabled employee should not put a more than reasonable strain on the employer, may introduce labor market considerations into disability assessments (see note 26).

29.This suggestion is confirmed by Van Zaal. His study of the 1978 cohort of DI-entrants shows that rehabilitation efforts are initiated for only 12 percent of all DI-entrants [Van Zaal (1981), pp. 29, 31].

30.Before the reform 53% (71% applying measure B) of all DI-entrants is estimated to regain full capacity for suitable work: 20% (B: 26%) one's current work and 33% (B: 45%) other suitable work. The actual recovery rate is 20%, consequently the unemployment component is estimated to be structurally 53% - 20% = 33% (B: 71% - 20% = 51%).
  If the 20% recoveries are all to occur among the 20% (B: 26%) who are estimated to regain the ability to perform their own work, then all entrants who are estimated to regain the ability for other suitable work are part of the unemployment component of 33% (B: 51%). Among this 33% (B: 51%), 21% (B: 28%), would not have been admitted to the program under the new regime, since they were already able to perform other suitable work at DI-entry, while at that time it was already clear that they would not regain the ability to perform their current work (see table 5.11). Strict compliance with the new rulings at the end

of the sick leave year would therefore reduce the unemployment component to 33% - 21% = 12% (B: 51% - 28% = 23%).

31. Source: Tweede Kamer A (1989, pp. 42-46).

32. The original estimate was derived from the estimates provided by Aarts et al. (1982a).

33. There are some indications for such administrative problems. For instance, one would expect the abolition of the labor market consideration to have induced a substantial decrease in the number of DI-entrants with full DI-pensions and an analogous increase in the number of partial DI-benefits awards. Instead, the percentage of DI-entrants who are awarded full DI-pensions has decreased only 7 percentage points, from 88 percent of all DI-entrants in 1986 to 81 percent in 1988. There are no signs of an intensified screening of the DI-population either, since the number of disability re-assessments has been growing at an average rate of 5 percent as of 1984 and has not increased extra as a consequence of the enactment of the 1987 Reform [GMD (various years)]. The system reform neither seems to have had an impact on the outcomes of these re-assessments, since the proportion of re-assessments resulting in a decline of the disability degree remained at its pre-reform level of about 21 percent during 1987 and 1988 [Source: GMD (1985, -86, -87, -88, -89)].

Chapter 6

# ON THE PROBLEM OF ENDOGENOUS MEASUREMENT ERROR

## 6.1   Introduction

The present study aims to explain a discretely observed phenomenon - the transition from labor force participation to DI-enrolment. Part of the explanatory variables represent personal attitudes and appreciations, such as work ethic, job satisfaction, or employers' judgments on the job performance of individual employees. Other potential determinants - job demands, functional limitations, employment opportunities - are measured subjectively for lack of objective assessments.

In the context of a discrete choice model these self-reported attitudes and perceptions may be biased towards the alternative which a respondent prefers to choose or actually has chosen. Such a bias may stem from the need, felt by respondents, to promote or justify desired outcomes or actual choices. In that case, the subjective scales are endogenous - in the sense that they are codetermined by the choice probabilities under study. To the extent that such reverse causalities are unintended and undesirable products of a particular study design, they may be labeled *endogenous errors of measurement*.

Cross-sectional observation of binary choices may aggravate the simultaneity bias engendered by subjective measurement. In a cross-section, part of the respondents are observed *after* they have moved from their usual state (*A*, e.g. WORK) to a new state (*B*, e.g. DI). This disrupts the inherent chronology of cause and effect. In that case, all explanatory variables, even the objectively assessable ones such as income, may become endogenous if they are affected by the transition. Especially attitudes and perceptions are likely to change under so drastic a transition as the one from work to DI-enrolment.

In cross-sectional studies of two state transitions, therefore, the additional problem arises that observed differences between movers and stayers may only be causally interpreted to the extent that they were present already before the movers moved.

The extra differences resulting from the transition itself - which we denote as *post-hoc* effects - will widen the gap between the observed and the "true", causally interpretable, values of the explanatory variables beyond the systematic disturbances created by preferences and justification. The implications are the same, though. Both preferences and *post-hoc* effects may introduce systematic measurement errors which are similarly determined by the transition probabilities under investigation. In general, we trust that the presence of such errors in objective variables has been prevented by careful design of the surveys.[1] We, therefore, focus on subjective variables based on attitudes and perceptions as reported by the respondents.
Statistically, endogenous measurement errors create a problem of simultaneity by the reciprocal influences they introduce. To investigate their presence and size a set of simultaneous equations is needed. This set has at least one equation with a limited dependent variable, namely the original choice probability model, and furthermore one equation for every variable that is under suspicion of being afflicted by endogenous distortions.

In the following section, we propose a model that is fit to examine the presence of endogenous measurement errors. The model also provides a method to correct the afflicted variables. The section concludes with the description of a rough-and-ready estimation procedure. The statistical framework is limited in two respects; it ignores the heteroscedasticity problems inherent in the estimation procedure. And secondly, the estimation model disregards the potential presence of non-zero error covariances between the transition probability and the set of suspicious variables. Sections 6.3 and 6.4 contain the empirical part of the chapter. Our error detection procedure is applied to the subjectively measured determinants of the long-term (5 months) sickness incidence. Both theory and data imply that the probability of a prolonged spell of sickness, possibly resulting in DI-enrolment, is related to a number of subjective attributes such as work commitment and self-perceptions of workload, career prospects, labor market conditions, etc. The presence of endogenous distortions in the observations of these subjective explanatory variables will be scrutinized. In section 6.3, we present a first and preliminary empirical specification of the theoretical model of chapter 3. The core estimation results are presented in section 6.4. Section 6.5 concludes.[2]

## 6.2 Model and Estimation Procedure

### 6.2.1 The Structural Model

Consider a conventional probability model describing the choice between *two* alternatives:

(A)   remaining in the current state, e.g., labor force participation;

(B)   moving to a new state, e.g., DI program participation.

Thus, the dependent variable is a dichotomy $(I_i)$ which takes the value 0 if a person is observed in state A ("stayers"), and 1 if he or she has moved to state B ("movers").

The usual assumption, now, is that a continuous response variable $y_1^*$ underlies the observed dichotomy.[3] This latent variable may be taken to represent the predisposition for moving from A to B. If $y_1^*$ is larger than zero we observe a transition. Hence

$$I_i = 0 \quad \text{iff } y_{1i}^* < 0 \quad \text{(stayers)}$$

$$\quad = 1 \quad \text{iff } y_{1i}^* \geq 0 \quad \text{(movers)}.$$

Consequently the probability of observing a mover - the transition probability - is

$$\Pr\{I_i = 1\} = \Pr\{y_{1i}^* \geq 0\}. \tag{6.1}$$

Assuming that the standard regression model holds for the latent predisposition variable, we write

$$y_{1i}^* = \alpha_1' x_{1i} + \gamma_1' x_{2i}^* + u_{1i} \qquad (i = 1,...,n) \tag{6.2}$$

with

$$Eu_{1i} = 0; \ Eu_{1i}^2 = \sigma_1^2 \ ; \ Eu_{1i}u_{1j} = 0 \text{ for } i \neq j \ ;$$

$x_{1i}$ has $k_1$ elements. This vector contains the values of explanatory variables that presumably are observed without endogenous distortions; the coefficient vector $\alpha_1$ is defined accordingly;

$x_{2i}^*$ is a p x 1-vector containing the *true* values of subjective explanatory variables. Their observed values are potentially afflicted by endogenous errors of measurement. The coefficient vector $\gamma_1$ is defined accordingly;

$u_{1i}$ is a disturbance term with the usual statistical properties; n is the number of observations.

Topic of this chapter is the possibility that the variables $x_{2mi}^{*}$ ($m = 1,...,p$) have been erroneously observed. These errors are assumed to be due to *post hoc* observation or to legitimation of preferred or actual choices. Both of these sources of error would imply that the observations, denoted as $y_{2mi}$, are affected by the transition probability defined in eq.(6.1). As they are not separately identifiable we will henceforth, in our formal treatment, not distinguish between these two kinds of error and act as if they coincide.

First, we presume that the errors $(\delta_{mi}^{*})$ are additive

$$y_{2mi} = x_{2mi}^{*} + \delta_{mi}^{*} . \tag{6.3}$$

Second, the elements of $\delta_m^{*}$ are determined by a function $\delta$ of $y_i^{*}$, up to a random part $\varepsilon_{2m}^{(1)}$,

$$\delta_{mi}^{*} = \gamma_{2m}\delta(y_{1i}^{*}) + \varepsilon_{2mi}^{(1)} ; \tag{6.4}$$

$\delta$ defines some monotonic transformation of $y_1^{*}$ so that the discrepancy between the observed and true values of the subjective variables $y_{2m}$ increases with the transition probability. By (6.4) the presence of endogenous measurement error is tested by the significance of $\gamma_{2m}$.

For ease of exposition, let $\delta(y_{1i}^{*})$ be equal to $y_{1i}^{*}$ for the moment. Combining eqs.(6.3) and (6.4), we get for the true but unobserved values of the suspicious variables

$$x_{2mi}^{*} = y_{2mi} - \gamma_{2m}y_{1i}^{*} - \varepsilon_{2mi}^{(1)}$$

which yields as a reduced form model, using eq.(6.2)

$$y_{1i}^{*} = \frac{\alpha_1' x_{1i}}{1 + \gamma_1' \gamma_2} + \frac{\gamma_1' y_{2i}}{1 + \gamma_1' \gamma_2} + \frac{2u_{1i} - \gamma_1' \varepsilon_{2i}^{(1)}}{1 + \gamma_1' \gamma_2} .$$

Clearly $\alpha_1$ and $\gamma_1$ are not identifiable from this last equation. Moreover, this elaboration shows that estimation of the original model (6.2), using the observed values of the subjective variables $(y_{2i})$, gives biased results for all coefficients if one or more of those variables are erroneously observed. Clearly, the bias would disappear only if all subjective variables were observed correctly - i.e., if $\gamma_2 = 0$.

The identification problem, illustrated by this simple elaboration, can be solved by specification of separate regression equations for the *true part* of each subjective variable[4]

$$x_{2mi}^{*} = \alpha_{2m}' x_{2mi} + \varepsilon_{2mi}^{(2)} . \tag{6.5}$$

The variables contained in each of the $k_{2m}$-dimensional vectors $x_{2mi}$ are assumed exogenous both with respect to $x_{2mi}^*$ and $y_{1i}^*$. The terms $\alpha_{2m}' x_{2mi}$ are instrumental variables to measure the unobservables $x_{2mi}^*$. Specification (6.5) is necessary but not sufficient for the identification of the structural coefficients $\alpha_1$ and $\gamma_1$ in eq.(6.2). Identification is only secured if one or more exogenous variables $x_1$, that enter the original model, are excluded from the instrumentals $x_{2m}$.

Substitution of (6.4) and (6.5) into (6.3) yields a set of p linear equations

$$y_{21i} = \alpha_{21}' x_{21i} + \gamma_{21}\delta(y_{1i}^*) + u_{21i}$$
$$\vdots$$
$$y_{2pi} = \alpha_{2p}' x_{2pi} + \gamma_{2p}\delta(y_{1i}^*) + u_{2pi}$$

where

$$u_{2mi} = \varepsilon_{2mi}^{(1)} + \varepsilon_{2mi}^{(2)}; \quad Eu_{2mi} = 0; \quad Eu_{2mi}^2 = \sigma_{2m}^2 \qquad (m = 1,...,p).$$

This set of p equations, together with the original probability equation (6.2) form the structural model which, in a more concise format, writes as

$$y_{1i}^* = \alpha_1' x_{1i} + \gamma_1' x_{2i}^* + u_{1i}$$
$$y_{2i} = X_{2i}\alpha_2 + \gamma_2\delta(y_{1i}^*) + u_{2i} \quad .$$

$$(6.6)$$

$X_{2i}$ is a (p x $k_2$) matrix where $k_2$ is the number of different exogenous variables used to construct instruments for the true values of the subjective variables; $y_{2i}$, $\gamma_2$ and $u_{2i}$ are (p x 1) vectors, $\alpha_2$ is a ($k_2$ x 1) vector, and $\delta(y_{1i}^*)$ is a scalar.

### 6.2.2 Reduced Form and Estimation Procedure

Given the unobservability of $x_2^*$ we need the p auxiliary measurement models, defined by (6.5), to get an operational form for the probability equation (6.2). Upon substitution

$$y_{1i}^* = \alpha_1' x_{1i} + \gamma_1' X_{2i}\alpha_2 + v_{1i} \qquad (6.7)$$

and

$$v_{1i} = u_{1i} + \gamma_1' \varepsilon_{2i}^{(2)}; \quad Ev_{1i} = 0; \quad Ev_{1i}^2 = \omega_1^2 \quad .$$

Assuming normality throughout, the marginal distribution of $v_{1i}$ is $N(0,\omega_1^2)$ and, hence,

$$P(y_{1i}^* \geq 0) = P(v_{1i}/\omega_1 \leq c_i) = F(c_i) = F_i$$

where $c_i = \omega_1^{-1} (\alpha_1' x_{1i} + \gamma_1' X_{2i} \alpha_2)$ and $F_i$ is the standard normal distribution function, evaluated at $c_i$; $c_i$ is an index function for the unobservable predisposition $y_{1i}^*$. Note that the coefficients that enter $c_i$ can be estimated by ML-probit but only up to an unknown constant $\omega_1^{-1}$.

To derive a reduced form for $y_{2i}$ we first have to specify the error function introduced in eq.(6.4). Our prime hypothesis states that, whatever their source, the measurement errors under scrutiny are governed by the transition probability defined by eq.(6.1). $F_i$ being an instrumental variable for the unobservable transition probability, we choose[5]

$$\delta(y_{1i}^*) = F_i.$$

More specifically, probit estimation of (6.7) will yield consistent estimates $F(\hat{c}_i) = \hat{F}_i$. The resulting form, then, writes

$$y_{2i} = X_{2i} \alpha_2 + \gamma_2 \hat{F}_i + v_{2i}; \quad v_{2i} = u_{2i} + \gamma_2 (F_i - \hat{F}_i) \ . \tag{6.8}$$

The p reduced form equations defined by (6.8) can be separately estimated by ordinary least-squares to give unbiased estimates of $\alpha_2$ and $\gamma_2$. However, the elements of $v_{2i}$ are potentially correlated across equations and correlated with $v_{1i}$, as $v_{2i}$ and $v_{1i}$, both contain $\varepsilon_{2i}^{(2)}$, i.e., the random term introduced in eq.(6.5) to represent errors in the approximation of the true values of the subjective variables. Moreover, since the disturbance terms $v_{2i}$ are obviously heteroscedastic, OLS will produce asymptotically inefficient estimates. OLS, however, is likely to underestimate the true standard errors and, therefore, provides a conservative test for the *in*significance of $\gamma_2$. Given the ordinal character of the subjective scales, estimation of the latent cutoff points by ordered probit would be a more appropriate procedure.[6] Instead we apply the inverted normal transformation to the ordinal variables and then apply OLS.[7]

For each $\gamma_{2m}$ that turns out to be significant, instrumental values for the *true* counterparts $(x_{2m}^*)$ of the erroneously observed variables $(y_{2m})$ can be estimated by $X_{2m} \hat{\alpha}_{2m}$. These instruments, thus purged of measurement error, can be used to consistently estimate $\gamma_{1m}$ in (6.2). If the hypothesis of no error is not rejected, $E y_{2m} = E x_{2m}^*$ [see eq.(6.3)]. Provided that in these cases the covariance of $u_{2m}$ with $u_1$ is zero, the use of the observed values in the estimation of the coefficients of the original model will give consistent results.

## 6.3    Empirical Specifications

The subject of this chapter is the presence of endogenous measurement error in a number of determinants of long-term - 5 months or more - sickness absenteeism.

Crossing the 5 months sickness border is treated as a binary event. As described in chapter 4, this event is observed by merging the so-called control-sample taken from all privately employed, DI-insured, workers with the so-called SB-sample. The SB-sample consists of Sickness Benefit recipients whose sickness spell had lasted 5 months at the time of their interview. Since both samples were taken in 1980 the combined data can be viewed as cross-sectional observations of the transition from the "healthy worker" status to the state of prolonged sickness, potentially leading to DI-enrolment.

As a first approach to model this transition probability - denoted as PSICK - we use a reduced form of the DI-model introduced in chapter 3. For lack of an explicit application procedure for DI-benefits (see subsection 3.3.4) we may interpret such prolonged periods of absence due to sickness as potential DI-claims.

By this interpretation, PSICK and the probability of claiming to be eligible for DI-benefits - Pr{CLAIM} - are identical. So, using the structural specification of the inclination index given by eq.(3.27), we get

$$\text{PSICK} = H\ (\beta,\ N_0,\ \text{ETG},\ \text{EY}_{DI},\ \text{EY}_{WORK}) \qquad (6.9)$$

A reduced form, then, is obtained by insertion of the specifications for $\beta$, (3.31), $p_a$, (3.32), and $w_s$, (3.33), yielding

$$\text{PSICK} = H(D,\ M,\ \text{EO},\ N_0,\ g(H_0),\ \text{AGE},\ \text{AGE}^2,\ \text{EDUC}) \qquad (6.10)$$

where

$$g(H_0)\ =\ -\ln[1 - H_0/T_0].$$

Equation (6.9), now, is the model under scrutiny. This version of the model posits that proneness to long-term absence from work is due to a number of objective characteristics - age, education, number of working hours per week ($H_0$); and three broad concepts - extent of disablement (D), work commitment (M), and employment opportunities (EO). Empirically, the dimensions of these concepts are covered by factual as well as attitudinal information and subjective perceptions.

**Extent of Disablement**
Extent of disablement is measured by four variables. The first two, *physical and mental disabilities*, are interactions of specific job demands and corresponding functional limitations. The extent to which job demands are physically strenuous or mentally stressful is self-reported in both samples used (see table 4.7, panel 4, and table 4.9, panel 2). Those reports may be affected both by legitimation and the effects of *post hoc* observation.

Whether reported impairments prevent standard performance of productive activities is differently observed in the two samples. While the control-sample contains self-reports on required activities that cause health problems, the assessment of functional limitations in the SB-sample is based on examinations by JMS-physicians (see section 4.3.1).[8] Hence, resulting health differences between control-sample persons ("zeros") and SB-sample persons ("ones") may be due to true, causally interpretable, differences as well as divergencies in observation method.

Beside these potentially endogenous measures, two more variables intend to represent health histories. *Absence record* counts the number of weeks missed from work due to sickness in the year preceding the interview (control-sample), or in the year preceding the current sick leave (SB-sample). The relative *duration of complaints* is the number of years of symptom manifestation divided by age. Both of these variables are assumed exogenous since they contain factual information.

### Work Commitment

Two attitudinal scales - *work ethic* and *job satisfaction* - attempt to cover work commitment. Work ethic is based on extent of (dis)agreement with a number of statements concerning work as social duty, as self-fulfillment, etc. An indicator for job satisfaction is obtained by combining three questions on the extent to which the current job conforms to the respondent's aspirations.

### Employment Opportunities

Employment opportunities refer both to the job security and career perspectives offered by the current employer and to external employment possibilities. The internal employment opportunities have been measured at three levels. Employees' perceptions of their within-firm *career prospects* represent one, potentially endogenous, angle. However, as the employers of the SB and control-sample respondents have been surveyed as well, we may also observe internal employment opportunities from the perspective of the firm. Whether employers are inclined to prevent or to accept the occurrence of extended spells of sickness, potentially leading to DI-enrolment, depends on considerations of social policy and economic need (see chapter 8). At the level of individual employees, their productivity and the relative scarcity of their vocational capacities is at stake. Employers' views on *job performance* and *career prospects* may be indicative of their appreciations of individual employees. Moreover, the employer's stated *willingness to adapt job* conditions and demands if the employee under consideration would become impaired may be interpreted as a token of social concern, as an indication of indispensability, or both.

These variables intend to measure employers' appreciations independent of the current health status of their employees. However, other things equal, employers may be less appreciative about a worker-turned-long-term-absentee than they were before the onset of sickness. This would introduce the *post hoc* effect modelled in the preceding section.

External *employment opportunities* are covered by a self-perceived variable measuring respondents' assessments of their chances of finding suitable work would they decide to change jobs. In order to neutralize *post hoc* effects the SB-sample persons were asked to make their assessment as if they had not fallen ill. Whether this setup has worked will be tested below.

As a more general, and more common, variable we use the sex-specific *regional unemployment rate* as well.

**Firm-level Characteristics**

The employers of both healthy and sick respondents have also been interviewed about a number of attributes of the employing firm such as firmsize, size and direction of changes in employment over the past two years, and aspects of social policy.[9] Three of these aspects are used as determinants of PSICK:

- The extent to which, as a rule, firms accommodate job conditions and demands to the limitations of impaired workers (*job adaptation*). By such accommodations firms may monitor the disabling consequences of impairment.
- The extent to which medical services, such as regular check-ups and systematic reviews of work conditions, are available to the firm and its personnel (*medical guidance*).
- Whether, and how, the firm pays attention to workers during an extended period of sickness absence (*social guidance*).

By these policy indicators we attempt to incorporate the firm's efforts - and test their efficacy - to prevent the occurrence of impairment and to correct its disabling effects. These, and other, firm-level characteristics are assumed exogenous with respect to the individual sickness probability.

The ranges and means of the resulting set of 24 structural determinants of PSICK are listed in table 6.1. *Age, sex, marital status, number of dependent children*, and *education*, incorporate non-health related elements of human capital and aspects of health status, time preferences, work-leisure preferences, and employment opportunities, not covered by the specific indicators introduced before.[10] Work hours per week and commuting time measure the potential leisure gain after retirement ($H_0$).

The 9 variables headed under self-perceptions and attitudes of employees and employers' appreciations of their productivity and indispensability all are under suspicion of being affected by endogenous error of measurement.

The means show that the SB-recipients are disadvantaged in many respects: Not surprisingly, their prior health, as indicated by absence record and duration of complaints, has been worse; they, obviously, report more physical and mental ailings; they perceive their career prospects and labor-market opportunities as worse; due to the strong correlation between age (generation) and work ethic, SB-recipients have a higher morale; on the other hand, they are less satisfied with their particular jobs; the firms that employ them have less developed social policies; their employers seem to be less appreciative about their performance and are less willing to provide career possibilities and to adapt their jobs, if needed.

Table 6.1   Ranges, Means, and Probit Coefficients of 24 Structural Determinants of PSICK

| | range[a] | sample means | | PSICK probit results[b] | |
|---|---|---|---|---|---|
| | | controls | SB-recipients | coeffs. | (st.err.) |
| **I. EMPLOYEE-LEVEL** | | | | | |
| *exogenous variables* | | | | | |
| Age | 16-65 | 34.4 | 43.7 | -.0001 | (.0163) |
| Age squared (*10$^{-2}$) | | | | .0121 | (.0204) |
| Female=1 | 0-1 | 0.29 | 0.21 | .0181 | (.0875) |
| Married=1 | 0-1 | 0.72 | 0.85 | .0424 | (.0864) |
| Ndepkids | 0-8 | 1.10 | 1.31 | -.0262 | (.0226) |
| Education[c] | 1-6 | 3.30 | 2.89 | -.0105 | (.0286) |
| g[Working hours][d] | 2-90 | 38.74 | 39.57 | .5398 | (.3567) |
| Commuting time[e] | 0-6 | 2.37 | 2.55 | .0173 | (.0223) |
| Ln(other housch.inc. + 1)[d] | 0-95.2 (*10$^3$) | 7.49 (*10$^3$) | 7.81 (*10$^3$) | .0116 | (.0085) |
| Reg. unempl. rate (*100%) | 2.4-15.0 | 5.30 | 4.95 | -.1632 | (.1326) |
| Absence record | 0-52 | 2.65 | 5.68 | .0096 | (.0044)* |
| Duration of complaints | 0-1 | 0.03 | 0.11 | 1.1560 | (.2359)** |
| *self-perceptions and attitudes* | | | | | |
| Physical disabilities | 1-2 (severe) | 1.04 | 1.38 | 3.0188 | (.1754)** |
| Mental disabilities | 1-2 (severe) | 1.05 | 1.31 | 1.5792 | (.1701)** |
| Career prospects | 1-4 (excellent) | 1.86 | 1.25 | -.1748 | (.0407)** |
| Employment opportunities | 1-3 (excellent) | 2.25 | 1.91 | -.0520 | (.0360) |
| Work ethic | 1-5 (high) | 3.57 | 3.82 | .0861 | (.0272)** |
| Job satisfaction | 1-5 (high) | 4.03 | 3.85 | -.0101 | (.0290) |
| **II. EMPLOYER-LEVEL** | | | | | |
| *policy variables w.r.t.* | | | | | |
| Job adaptation | 1-3 (excellent) | 2.35 | 2.16 | .0619 | (.0374) |
| Medical guidance | 0-3 (excellent) | 0.79 | 0.74 | .0113 | (.0213) |
| Social guidance | 1-3 (excellent) | 2.79 | 2.62 | -.116 | (.0336)** |
| *employers' appreciations* | | | | | |
| Job performance | 1-3 (excellent) | 2.81 | 2.73 | -.1103 | (.0346)** |
| Career prospects | 1-3 (excellent) | 1.56 | 1.14 | -.2959 | (.0429)** |
| Willing to adapt job | 1-3 (excellent) | 2.44 | 1.98 | -.1881 | (.0363)** |

**   Significant at the 1 percent level.

\*   Significant at the 5 percent level.

(a)   For ordinal scales the meaning of the upper end is given; all of these scales have been transformed by the inverted normal; means refer to variables before transformation, probit coefficients are based on variables after transformation. Education and commuting time have been transformed as well.

(b)   See table 6.6 for additional statistics.

(c)   Ordinal scale running from (1), less than primary, to (6), university degree (see Table 4.6, panel 3).

(d)   Range and means are based on straight observations of weekly working hours and household income, respectively; g[Working hours] = $-\ln[1 - H_0/T_0]$.

(e)   Ordinal scale running from (0) to (6), more than 180 minutes per day.

The last two columns of table 6.1 show the results of ML-probit analysis of the long-term sickness probability (PSICK). Since the sick are heavily overrepresented in the dataset used to perform this analysis, the probit likelihood function has been modified to take account of choice-based sampling.[11] While none of the general characteristics, such as age or education, have a significant impact, strong and significant effects are found for the majority of the variables under suspicion. For instance, both variables that measure career prospects, one perceived by the employee, the other from the perspective of the employer, are significant at the 1 percent level. Whether these effects reflect truly unilateral causalities or mere tautologies, will be tested by means of the statistical model proposed in the preceding section.[12]

In order to be able to investigate the presence of endogenous distortions among the 9 variables under suspicion a set of auxiliary regression equations has to be specified following eq.(6.5). Table A.6.1 in the appendix to this chapter, contains the auxiliary specifications in a matrix-format. This matrix is $X_{2i}$, introduced in eq.(6.6). The dotted lines denote zeros. Note that the matrix has full column rank to preclude underidentification.

These specifications have to meet several requirements. They should be theoretically valid; they should be exogenous, both with respect to the 9 variables under scrutiny and PSICK; and, finally, they should be complete enough in order to provide a powerful test for the exogeneity of the suspect variables, and meaningful instrumental variables should they appear to be endogenous.

## 6.4 Further Estimation Results

The specification of the reduced form of the PSICK model is found by combining its assumedly exogenous determinants with the explanatory variables introduced in table A.6.1. The reduced-form probit results are given in table 6.2.

To warrant identification, some of the exogenous variables that have a significant effect in the structural PSICK model are excluded from the auxiliary equations - viz. duration of complaints and the company's policy with respect to social guidance of long-term absentees. According to eq.(6.7), the reduced form coefficients for these variables are consistent estimates of their structural values. Comparison of these estimates with the corresponding ones in table 6.1, shows that the original model tends to underestimate their impacts. Moreover, another, economically relevant, exclusion variable - other household income - was insignificant first but is significant, and twice as large, now. These differences suggest that neglected endogeneities have biased these exogenous effects toward zero.

**Table 6.2   Probit Estimates of Reduced-Form Coefficients on PSICK**

|  | coefficient | (st. error) |
|---|---|---|
| *Employee-level* | | |
| Age | - .0175 | (.0151) |
| Age squared (*$10^{-2}$) | .0542 | (.0199)** |
| Female=1 | .1388 | (.0801) |
| Married=1 | - .0535 | (.0747) |
| Ndepkids | - .0272 | (.0203) |
| Urbanization[a] | .0573 | (.0264)* |
| Education | - .0870 | (.0254)** |
| Strenuous work record[b] | .8863 | (.1734)** |
| Tenure[c] | - .1441 | (.0899) |
| g(Working hours) | .6333 | (.3246) |
| Commuting time | .0172 | (.0191) |
| Ln(other househ.inc. + 1) | .0211 | (.0075)** |
| Regional unempl. rate | - .0353 | (.1083) |
| Previously unemployed=1 | .2029 | (.0633)** |
| Mobility=1 | .0197 | (.0544) |
| Absence record | .0182 | (.0049)** |
| Duration of complaints[b] | 2.4805 | (.3462)** |
| *Employer-level* | | |
| Ln(firmsize) | .0553 | (.0135)** |
| Increasing employment (*$10^{-2}$) | .1570 | (.1000) |
| Decreasing employment (*$10^{-2}$) | - .2340 | (.3000) |
| Perc. fem. employment (*$10^{-2}$) | - .2630 | (.1100)** |
| Workers' consultation=1 | - .1058 | (.0453)* |
| Job adaptation | - .1016 | (.0316)** |
| Medical guidance | - .0483 | (.0209)* |
| Social guidance | - .1584 | (.0310)** |
| Branch of industry | | |
|     Agriculture | .0967 | (.1577) |
|     Steel industry | .0428 | (.0833) |
|     Construction | ref. | |
|     Other industries | .0052 | (.0806) |
|     Wholesale and retail | - .0186 | (.0866) |
|     Other commercial services | .0194 | (.0815) |
|     Health care | - .0940 | (.1295) |
|     Non-commercial services | .0830 | (.1079) |
| Constant | -2.7422 | (.2950) |
| -2 * Loglikelihood ratio | 1311.62** | |
| pseudo-$R^2$ | .260 | |
| # Observations | 3951 | |

| | |
|---|---|
| ** | Significant at the 1 percent level. |
| * | Significant at the 5 percent level. |
| a | For definition of this and other variables, see table A.6.1. |
| b | Divided by age. |
| c | Divided by work experience (years). |

Note that the reduced form effects of age, sex, and education are much more prominent than the structural, but potentially biased, estimates in table 6.1 would suggest.

The reduced form also contains a number of exogenous variables that do not belong to the structural PSICK model but are part of the set of auxiliary equations. A few of those have significant impacts: The more years in physically strenuous work, the larger the employing firm, and the smaller its female employment rate, the higher the probability of an extended sick spell. Workers with previous unemployment experiences also have a higher PSICK.

From the reduced-form results we calculate linear predictions $\hat{c}_i$, and imputed values of PSICK, by evaluation of the standard normal distribution function F at $\hat{c}_i$ . Using eq.(6.8), $\hat{F}_i = F(\hat{c}_i)$ is entered as a separate explanatory variable in the auxiliary OLS regressions on the 9 variables under suspicion. Its coefficient $\gamma_{2m}$ (m = 1,...,9) is the strategic parameter to test for the presence of endogenous distortions. The estimates of $\gamma_2$ are highlighted in table 6.4; the complete estimation results for each of the 9 submodels are reported in table 6.3.

The core results listed in table 6.4 show that, at the 5 percent level, 4 out of 9 suspicious variables are observed with endogenous measurement error - the employees' perceptions of severity of physical disabilities, career prospects, and employment opportunities, and the employer's willingness to adapt job demands and conditions should the employee sampled become impaired. The signs of the effects are as expected: Workers with a strong proclivity for retirement by declaration of incapacity depict their activity restrictions as more severe than a set of objective characteristics would predict.[13] They also report significantly less favorable career prospects and employment opportunities.

Employers appear to be more inclined to accommodate jobs, the smaller the predisposition for long-term sickness of the employee involved. Their reported willingness, therefore, seems to be somewhat gratuitous. To the extent that employers have changed their mind after an employee has shown to remain sick for an extended period of time, this result is typically due to *post hoc* observation.

Relative to their healthy peers, sick employees also tend to report more serious mental disabilities, lower work ethic, and lower job satisfaction. These effects are not significant, though.

The complete auxiliary OLS-results, reported in table 6.3, shed some light on the causal paths along which personal and firm-specific background characteristics affect PSICK. Age appears to be an important predictor of all of the subjective variables under investigation. Other things equal, older workers have more severe disabilities;

Table 6.3   OLS-Regression Results for the 9 Variables under Suspicion

| | self-perceptions and attitudes | | | | | | employers' appreciations | | |
|---|---|---|---|---|---|---|---|---|---|
| | Disabilities: physical | Disabilities: mental | Career prospects | Employment opportun. | Work ethic | Job satisfact. | Job performance | Career prospects | Willing to adapt job |
| **Employee-level** | | | | | | | | | |
| Age | .004 | .007* | -.022** | .012** | -.004 | .020* | .023** | -.015** | -.010 |
| Age squared (*10⁻²) | -.003 | -.001 | | -.039** | .021 | -.027** | -.023** | | .011* |
| Female=1 | .045** | .006 | -.208** | .012 | | .253** | .049** | -.131** | .099** |
| Married Woman=1 | | | | | -.137** | | | | |
| Married Man=1 | | | | | .017 | | | | |
| Urbanization | | | | | -.041** | | | | |
| Education | -.045** | .022** | .130** | .093** | -.096** | .092** | .009 | .063** | .127** |
| Strenuous work record | .334** | | .131** | | | | .162** | .104** | .341** |
| Tenure | | | | | | | | | |
| Reg. unemployment rate | | | | -.474** | | | | | |
| Previously unemployed=1 | | | | -.135** | | | | | |
| Mobility=1 | | | | .164** | | | | | |
| Absence record | .002** | .002** | -.005** | | | | -.006** | -.003** | |
| Work ethic | | | | | | .482** | | | |
| **Employer-level** | | | | | | | | | |
| Branch of industry | | | | | | | | | |
| Agriculture | -.028 | -.024* | | .292** | | | | | -.085 |
| Steel industry | -.016** | .056* | | .052** | | | | | -.088** |
| Construction | .074** | .013 | | .196 | | | | | -.197** |
| Other industries | -.056** | .049* | | -.026 | | | | | -.128** |
| Wholesale and retail | -.030** | .036* | | .045** | | | | | -.043** |
| Other commerc. services | -.050** | .048 | | .140** | | | | | -.161** |
| Health care | -.026 | .014 | | .123 | | | | | -.176** |
| Non-commerc. services | ref. | ref. | | ref. | | | | | ref. |
| Ln(firmsize) | | .006 | .061 | | | -.029 | | .036** | |
| Increasing employment | | .050* | | | | | | | .026** |
| Decreasing employment | | -.029 | | | | | | | .296** |
| Workers' consultation=1 | | -.000** | | | | .111** | | | |
| Job adaptation policy | -.033** | -.022** | | -.284** | | | | | .285** |
| Sickness probability (F̂) | .183** | .085 | -.278* | | -.145 | .007 | -.069 | -.116 | -.350** |
| Constant | 1.039 | .877 | .303 | -.028 | .082 | -.557 | 1.235 | .280 | -.077 |
| R̂² | .221 | .067 | .156 | .155 | .088 | .116 | .048 | .163 | .153 |

*, **   Significant at 5 and 1 percent respectively.

Table 6.4  The Effect of PSICK on the 9 Variables under Suspicion

| | $\gamma_2$ | $[s(\gamma_2)]$ |
|---|---|---|
| *self-perceptions and attitudes* | | |
| physical disabilities | .1832 | (.0440)** |
| mental disabilities | .0848 | (.0478) |
| career prospects | -.2778 | (.1183)* |
| employment opportunities | -.2836 | (.1061)** |
| work ethic | -.1445 | (.0859) |
| job satisfaction | .0067 | (.1887) |
| *employers' appreciations* | | |
| job performance | -.0690 | (.0584) |
| career prospects | -.1156 | (.0723) |
| willing to adapt job | -.3501 | (.1104)** |

** Significant at the 1 percent level.
*  Significant at the 5 percent level.

worse within-firm career prospects and external employment opportunities; higher ethic but lower job satisfaction; employers who, although less satisfied with their productivity, are more willing to suit job demands and conditions to their limitations. While the direct effect of age on PSICK is not significant, the indirect impacts are strong and manifold. With the exception of work ethic and the employer's willingness to adapt the job if needed, these indirect effects reinforce each other. Women report more, and more severe, disabilities but are nevertheless more satisfied with their jobs than men. Although more content with their performance, and more willing to accommodate their jobs, employers do not seem to offer equal opportunities to women and fully exploit their capabilities as they appear to have significantly worse career prospects. Alternatively, women may have lower professional aspirations than men.

The negative reduced form effect of education on PSICK can be attributed to the gamut of advantages better schooling conveys. Higher education leads to jobs that are physically less but mentally more demanding, as witnessed by the coefficients in the first two columns of table 6.3. Educated workers have significantly better internal and external perspectives; lower morale but more satisfactory jobs. Regarding the firm-level characteristics, a structured job adaptation policy appears to be effective in reducing the prevalence and severity of disability. Moreover, workers' consultation procedures significantly reinforce work commitments as indicated by the job satisfaction variable.[14]

The next step is to purge the 4 affected variables of their endogenous distortions by calculating instrumental values on the basis of the OLS results in table 6.3, omitting the error term $\gamma_{2m}\hat{F}_i$.

Table 6.5    **Structural Probit Estimates[a] for PSICK, Before and After Correction for Endogenous Measurement Error**

| | before correction | | after correction | |
|---|---|---|---|---|
| *Employee-level* | | | | |
| *exogenous variables* | | | | |
| Age | - .0001 | (.0163) | - .0089 | (.0161) |
| Age squared (*$10^{-2}$) | .0121 | (.0204) | .0328 | (.0211) |
| Female=1 | .0181 | (.0875) | .1689 | (.0943) |
| Married=1 | .0424 | (.0864) | - .0173 | (.0801) |
| Ndepkids | - .0262 | (.0226) | - .0344 | (.0209) |
| Education | - .0105 | (.0286) | .0288 | (.0545) |
| g(Working hours) | .5398 | (.3567) | .3747 | (.3273) |
| Commuting time | .0173 | (.0223) | .0091 | (.0206) |
| Ln(other househ.inc. + 1) | .0116 | (.0085) | .0239 | (.0080)** |
| Reg. unempl. rate | - .1632 | (.1326) | - .2944 | (.1492)* |
| Absence record | .0096 | (.0044)* | .0150 | (.0048)** |
| Duration of complaints | 1.1560 | (.2359)** | 1.9409 | (.3095)** |
| *self-perceptions and attitudes* | | | | |
| Physical disabilities | 3.0188[b] | (.1754)** | 1.9690[c] | (.3453)** |
| Mental disabilities | 1.5792 | (.1701)** | 1.6351 | (.1830)** |
| Career prospects | - .1748[b] | (.0407)** | .8901[c] | (.2241)** |
| Employment opportunities | - .0520[b] | (.0360) | - .4843[c] | (.1995)* |
| Work ethic | .0861 | (.0272)** | .1194 | (.0248)** |
| Job satisfaction | - .0101 | (.0290) | - .0315 | (.0259) |
| *Employer-level* | | | | |
| *policy variables w.r.t.* | | | | |
| Job adaptation | .0619 | (.0374) | .2665 | (.0755)** |
| Medical guidance | .0113 | (.0213) | - .0322 | (.0224) |
| Social guidance | - .1160 | (.0336)** | - .1454 | (.0317)** |
| *employers' appreciations* | | | | |
| Job performance | - .1103 | (.0346)** | - .1233 | (.0330)** |
| Career prospects | - .2959 | (.0429)** | - .3565 | (.0360)** |
| Willing to adapt job | - .1881[b] | (.0363)** | - .8170[c] | (.2145)** |
| Constant | -7.7982 | (.3802) | -7.1977 | (.8308) |
| -2 * Loglikelihood ratio | 2728.37** | | 1895.28** | |
| Pseudo-$R^2$ | .484 | | .370 | |

** Significant at the 1 percent level.
* Significant at the 5 percent level.
(a) Standard errors are between brackets.
(b) Coefficients are based on observed values of regressors.
(c) Coefficients are based on instrumental values of regressors.

Finally, the original PSICK model is re-estimated, using instrumental instead of observed values for the 4 erroneously measured variables. These corrected probit results are given in the second pair of columns in table 6.5. We add the original results from table 6.1 in the first pair of columns, to facilitate comparison.

The effects of correction are quite drastic. The use of instrumental values for self-perceived career prospects and external employment opportunities, and for the employer's willingness to adapt the job if needed, has unpleasant collinearity effects. Their coefficients and standard errors are being inflated, possibly for lack of potent exclusion variables. For example, the coefficient (and standard error) for career prospects becomes five times as large, and its sign changes. The effect of employment opportunities is 9 times as large and significant after correction. On the other hand, the use of instrumental, instead of observed, values for physical disabilities has a deflatory effect on its coefficient with its standard error being "only" twice as large.

Upon correction, the effects of a number of other regressors increase in absolute value as well. Apparently, the presence of erroneously observed variables in the original probit has led to biased estimation of the effects of those, correctly measured, variables. Such biases are generally found when errors of measurement are correlated with the disturbance term.

After correction, the coefficient for other household income is significant and twice as large. This finding is important as it underscores the usefulness of the micro-economic approach to modelling disability behavior. Moreover, it is in line with a vast body of research on this topic.[15]

Correction yields notably stronger effects for age, duration of complaints, work ethic, and job satisfaction. However, contrary to expectation the effect of work ethic is consistently positive. This may be due to the strong effects of age (positive) and education (negative) on morale (see table 6.3).

Another unexpected result is the positive and significant coefficient on job adaptation policy. Notice that this positive direct effect is more than balanced by the indirect effects that run via the employer's willingness to adapt the respondent's job and the two disability variables. Multicollinearity could, again, be responsible for this unanticipated outcome.

Despite correction the results contained in the second pair of columns in table 6.5 represent only a preliminary, and incomplete, version of the intended structural model for PSICK. Apart from the unsatisfactory results for 3 of the 4 affected variables, the model lacks an indicator for the financial consequences of continuing sickness and eventual DI-enrolment (see chapter 9).

We may nevertheless judge the corrected PSICK probit in terms of the underlying theoretical model summarized by eqs.(6.9) and (6.10). First, PSICK is a combination of health and work status. To the extent that extended sick spells are a major step toward retirement, PSICK indexes potential definite retirement on medical grounds. Consequently, the predominance of the impacts of health indicators on PSICK is hardly surprising - almost tautological. These health factors, therefore, act as powerful controls on the more contentious effects of non-medical aspects.

Nevertheless, a number of non-medical factors suggested by theory have a significant effect. The presence of alternative household means to cushion the financial consequences of transfer dependency has its expected positive effect. On the other hand, background variables like age and education which are potent predictors of prolonged sickness in univariate analyses (tables 4.5 and 4.6) reduce to insignificance in the multivariate framework of table 6.5. The variables measuring the leisure gained by retirement, working hours and commuting time, are insignificant, too. Employers' views on the career prospects and job performance of individual employees, indicating internal employment security, have their expected negative impacts. The implication, here, is that equally disabled workers have differential long-term sickness probabilities depending on employers' appreciations of their pre-impairment productivity.

As concerns work commitment, job satisfaction has its assumed negative influence on absenteeism. Work ethic, however, has a forceful positive direct effect. The auxiliary regression on ethic suggests that this unexpected effect may be due to its correlations with age (generation) and type of work (education). The picture that emerges is that of high-risk workers who do their relatively unpleasant jobs without complaining but have no qualms to opt out after the onset of impairment.

Related to work commitment is the negative impact of the company's policy with respect to social guidance during extended spells of sickness. Apparently, tokens of attention are effective in reducing the long-term sickness risk as they promote commitment to the firm.

The other two policy variables, regarding medical care and job adaptation, have weak or counterintuitive results. In chapter 8 we will try and construct a variable that combines all, social as well as economic, firm characteristics that may affect the disability risks of the employees.

Moreover, as regards employment opportunities we note that the coefficients for regional unemployment rate, self-perceived career prospects and employment opportunities are unsatisfactory. On the other hand, the reduced form effect of previous unemployment experiences is positive as expected. This may point to an issue that has been ignored by the endogeneity tests applied in this chapter - the possibility that disability and unemployment risks are jointly determined. We will, therefore, try and construct more comprehensive indicators for external employment opportunities by analyzing the work histories of our respondents. This is the subject of the following chapter.

## 6.5 Summary and Discussion

In this chapter we have proposed, and applied, a procedure to test and correct for the presence of endogenous measurement errors in subjective variables that are used to describe a binary event - the transition from work to long-term sickness (PSICK). The specification for the PSICK probability model is derived from the theoretical model of chapter 3. Its operational form contains both objectively observable variables, and a number of subjective scales - perceptions and attitudes. Nine subjectively measured variables have been subjected to our error detection procedure. Four of these, employees' perceptions of extent of physical disablement, career prospects and employment opportunities, and the employer's willingness to accommodate the employee's job if needed, are unambiguously affected.

The results show that the presence of such errors, if ignored, leads to biased estimates of the probit coefficients involved. If the 4 erroneously observed variables substituted by instrumental predictions of their true values, the effects of other, correctly observed, variables increase in strength and significance. Due to the lack of forceful exclusion variables, which are necessary for the construction of independent instrumentals, collinearity produces unappealing results for 3 of the 4 affected variables upon substitution by instrumental values.

Hence, both the error detection and the correction procedures crucially depend on the number and quality of exogenous variables available to create instruments. We conclude that our set of exogenous variables is too small to properly cover employment opportunities by the simple auxiliary equations used here.

We, therefore, devote the following three chapters to the creation of adequate instruments by means of more sophisticated modelling.

**Table A.6.1  Specification of Regression Equations for the 9 Variables under Suspicion**

| | self-perceptions and attitudes | | | | | | employers' appreciations | | |
| --- | --- | --- | --- | --- | --- | --- | --- | --- | --- |
| | Disabilities: physical | mental | Career prospects | Employment opportun. | Work ethic | Job satisfact. | Job per-formance | Career prospects | Willing to adapt job |
| *Employee-level* | | | | | | | | | |
| Age | xx | xx | xx | xx | xx | xx | xx | xx | xx |
| Age squared (*10⁻²) | xx | xx | : | xx | xx | xx | xx | : | xx |
| Female=1 | xx | xx | xx | xx | : | xx | xx | : | xx |
| Married Woman=1 | : | : | : | : | xx | : | : | : | : |
| Married Man=1 | : | : | : | : | xx | : | : | : | : |
| Urbanization[a] | : | : | : | : | xx | : | : | : | : |
| Education | xx | xx | xx | xx | xx | xx | xx | xx | xx |
| Strenuous work record[b] | xx | : | : | : | : | : | : | : | : |
| Tenure[c] | : | : | xx | : | : | : | xx | xx | xx |
| Reg. unemployment rate | : | : | : | xx | : | : | : | : | : |
| Previously unemployed=1 | : | : | : | xx | : | : | : | : | : |
| Mobility=1[d] | : | : | : | xx | : | : | : | : | : |
| Absence record | xx | xx | xx | : | : | : | xx | xx | : |
| Work ethic | : | : | : | : | : | xx | : | : | : |
| *Employer-level* | | | | | | | | | |
| Branch of industry[e] | xx | xx | : | xx | : | : | : | : | xx |
| Firmsize[f] | : | xx | xx | : | : | xx | : | xx | : |
| Increasing employment[g] | : | xx | : | : | : | : | : | : | xx |
| Decreasing employment[g] | : | xx | : | : | : | : | : | : | xx |
| Workers' consultation=1 | : | xx | : | : | : | xx | : | : | : |
| Job adaptation policy | xx | xx | : | : | : | : | : | : | xx |

(a)  Ordinal scale running from (1), less than 20,000, to (4), more than 100,000 inhabitants.
(b)  Number of years of physically strenuous work (see table 4.8, panel 2).
(c)  Ordinal scale running from (1), less than 1 year, to (7), more than 30 years with current employer (see Table 4.8, panel 4).
(d)  One or more voluntary changes of employer in past 10 years.
(e)  See table 6.2 for the definition of the 8 industrial branches (dummies) used.
(f)  Number of employees at the employing plant.
(g)  For definitions see section 8.3.2.

## Notes

1. Simultaneity as a result of joint determination, however, cannot be prevented by careful survey design. See the treatment of wage rates in chapter 9.

2. This chapter is a thoroughly revised and re-estimated version of De Jong (1987).

3. The classic reference is Goldberger (1964).

4. In Stern (1989) a similar model is used to investigate the potential simultaneity of self-reported disability and labor force participation.

5. This choice is somewhat arbitrary, as $\hat{c}$, the estimate of the transition propensity, would be another valid candidate for the operationalization of the measurement error under study. We prefer to use $F_i$, so as to reduce multicollinearity.

6. See for the ordered probit model Amemiya (1978), and Lee (1982) or Stern (1989) for applications.

7. This transformation is identical to the so-called quantile method described in section 11.2.6. It presupposes that the distribution function generating the ordinal data is standard normal.

8. See for comparable comprehensive measurements of disability Duchnok (1979) and Chirikos and Nestel (1981, 1984).

9. Chapter 8 contains a more complete description of firm-level characteristics. That chapter deals with a description of the disability process at the firm level.

10. These, and some other, exogenous background variables will be employed in chapter 7 and 9 to construct instrumental variables measuring unemployment and re-employment hazards (chapter 7) and present values of income streams in the WORK and the DI options (chapter 9).

11. See Maddala [1983, p. 91, eq.(4.18)]. This equation defines the log-likelihood that we have maximized. The parameter p equals the ratio of the sampling probabilities of the "ones" (5 months sick) to that of the "zeros" (total population at risk). We have 1980 population and sample statistics to obtain p = (2534/125,355) / (1417/3,470,000) = 49.5.

12. In a critical review of the first publication of the Dutch DI-research project Vrijhof (1981) raises this causality issue.

13. Cf. Anderson and Burkhauser (1985), Lambrinos (1981), Parsons (1982).

14. Cf. Freeman (1978).

15. In addition to the references in note 13, see Bazzoli (1985), Boskin and Hurd (1978), Quinn (1977).

Chapter 7

# LABOR MARKET OPPORTUNITIES

## 7.1    Introduction

Considering the design and history of the DI-program, there are good reasons to believe that a person's labor market position is a particularly important determinant of the probability of entering the DI-program.

A first reason relates to the program admission procedures. In the assessment of DI-benefits entitlements, labor market opportunities are explicitly accounted for. As we explained in the preceding chapters, the degree of disability is measured in terms of (residual) earning capacity. The residual earning capacity is defined as the income, a disabled person would be able to gain in "suitable" or "commensurate" employment, expressed as a percentage of his pre-disability wage. This potential earning capacity is called the "theoretical" earning capacity.

The actual earning capacity, however, will often be smaller than its theoretical counterpart, for instance, because employers prefer to hire healthy workers even in those cases where an impaired person would be perfectly able to perform the particular job. The discriminatory behavior towards impaired individuals reduces their actual earning capacity. Before the 1987 Social Security System Reform, the law acknowledged that such a reduction is attributable to the impairment and that it should be accounted for in the assessment of DI-benefit entitlements. This legal recognition has induced a benefit administration practice by which an impaired person with residual earning capacities is considered to be unable to find gainful employment unless the contrary can be proven. This interpretation of the law practically implies that partially disabled with poor labor market opportunities are nearly always awarded full DI-benefits, as if they were disabled to the highest degree.

The law and its particular interpretation provide a first argument for the hypothesis that labor market opportunities are likely to have a large impact on the probability of being awarded DI-benefits.

A second argument is based on supply side considerations and relates to the concept of utility maximization. The status of DI-beneficiary, and also the process leading to it, involves both tangible and intangible costs to the individual. Nevertheless, the net utility derived from a steady benefit income for the remainder of the working age years may well exceed the net utility resulting from continued labor force participation. Not only because prevailing functional limitations affect the individual's appreciation of leisure, but also because by opting for DI-program enrolment, the individual avoids the risk of unemployment to which he would be exposed if he would decide to continue labor force participation (see chapter 3).

Labor market opportunities are a prominent factor in the disability process. To trace down their effect it seems appropriate to come up with unambiguous indicators. This is particularly important since labor market opportunities as perceived by the sample respondents are not reliable because they appear to be contaminated by information on health or personal tastes (see chapter 6). Although more reliable perhaps, the experts' or the gatekeepers' opinion will neither be free of prejudice and taste. Furthermore, even properly measured labor market opportunities may be endogenous with respect to the disability process when they are jointly determined with the disability probability by some unobserved common source.

To avoid inconsistencies in the estimation of labor market effects, we will construct individually varying labor market indicators that are both informative and exogenous. These constructs will be derived from the estimation of reduced form models that describe individual labor market histories.[1] Given a number of personal and situational characteristics, the parameter estimates resulting from these models can be used to "predict" the theoretical probability of becoming unemployed and the theoretical probability of re-employment upon being unemployed for each individual worker at a particular moment in time. Subsequently, in chapter 10, these predicted labor market opportunities will be included in the models describing the disability probability and the probability of being on sick leave.

The remainder of this chapter deals with the modelling and estimation of individual labor market histories. Section 7.2 summarizes some theoretical aspects. A statistical model is proposed and specified in sections 7.3 and 7.4. In section 7.5, estimation results are discussed. The theoretical labor market opportunities within the healthy control-sample and the sample of DI-entrants will be compared in the last section of this chapter.

## 7.2    Theoretical Modelling of Individual Labor Market Histories

There is no consensus in economic theory on the determinants of labor market opportunities.

A rather rigid picture of the labor market is drawn by dual labor market theory. Here, two labor market segments are being distinguished; a primary and a secondary segment. Jobs belonging to the first segment have all the favorable qualities. They are characterized by attractive fringe benefits and career prospects, by high wages, employment security and agreeable work conditions. The secondary segment is the mirror image of the primary segment. Secondary jobs are characterized by low wages and bad working conditions. Secondary workers lack job security and favorable career prospects.

Dual labor market theory hypothesizes different returns to schooling and hence systematic differences in the wage distributions of the segments. Mobility between the segments is considered to be rare. Particularly, moving from the secondary to the primary segment is almost impossible. The segmentation of the market is enhanced by feedback mechanisms. A crucial element in the theory is the negative feedback between early labor market experience and later labor market behavior. For instance, the experience of unemployment is hypothesized to increase the likelihood of future unemployment. Similarly, employment experiences in the secondary segment will decrease the probability of future employment in the primary sector. Workers who land in the secondary segment contract scars that will prevent them from being engaged in primary segment jobs. Workers in the primary segment, on the other hand, are supposed to get a chance to acquire skills and experience within the firm. These achievements increase their productivity and their wages, and reinforce their job security.

Dual labor market theory, also in its less radically formulated versions, considers a person's labor market opportunities to be primarily determined by the segment in which he finds himself. Theory, however, is less explicit on how people are assigned to a particular segment. Newcomers on the labor market are supposed to be screened on observable characteristics like education, gender, and ethnic-, or family background, i.e., characteristics that employers take to be indicative of their productivity.[2]

A different perspective on the labor market is offered by neoclassical theory. Here, wages are supposed to be determined by the marginal revenue product of labor. Within the framework of the neoclassical paradigm, human capital theory and the theory of job search have been developed. Theory predicts education to increase productivity and, therefore, to lead to higher wages. Employees will be discharged when wages exceed the value of their marginal product. People searching for a job are supposed to be following an optimal strategy that boils down to repeated cost-benefit analyses of accepting successively offered jobs. A particular offer will be accepted, if the expected benefits of accepting the offer exceed the expected benefits of turning it down to continue the search for a better offer. The critical value of the wage that equates the benefits of accepting a particular offer with those of rejecting it, is denoted as the reservation wage.

The expected benefits of continued search, and therefore the value of the reservation wage, depend on the probability of being offered a job and on the distribution of wage offers. The reservation wage may change over time due to changes in either the job offer probability or the wage offer distribution.

Within the framework of the theory of job search, powerful econometric methods have been developed to model and estimate the determinants of individual labor market histories by applying "duration" models, also referred to as "hazard" or "failure-rate" models. This statistical technique was first applied in the field of biology. Although the "hazard rate" technique has also been applied to estimate models describing the duration of employment spells [Burdett (1978), Jovanovich (1979), Flinn and Heckman (1982), Theeuwes (1990)], most empirical research in this area deals with the duration of unemployment spells, in other words, with the probability of re-employment.[3]

Some authors [e.g. Atkinson et al. (1984)] have questioned the value of the theory of search behavior because it is not (yet) sufficiently well developed to provide a more than tenuous link between the theoretical framework and the empirical work. The authors consider the role of the theory as the more circumscribed one of indicating the variables to be included.

The theory of job search may need further specification; the contribution of dual labor market theory is even more limited as it only indicates possibly relevant explanatory variables [Cain (1979)]. Despite their shortcomings in terms of specification, a combination of the two theoretical perspectives may be fruitful, at least when the role of theory is restricted to indicate potentially relevant variables. For instance, within the respective segments, dual labor market theory does not preclude the type of job search behavior that is modelled by search theory. Segmentation of the labor market would then be reflected by different wage offer distributions and job arrival rates within the two segments.

In this chapter, our purpose is to model the probability of becoming unemployed and the probability of subsequent re-employment. We will proceed by applying the statistical apparatus provided by job search theory. First, we sketch the contours of structural models that describe both probabilities. Our data, however, does not allow for the estimation of such structural models. Estimation would require a much more informative database [Narendranathan and Nickell (1985), Lancaster and Chesher (1983)]. Instead, reduced form hazard functions describing the transition from employment into unemployment and vice versa will be estimated.

The following impressionistic theoretical outlines may help to reveal the relevant indicators and their (reduced form) effects on the probabilities of unemployment and re-employment. We will deal with the re-employment probability first.

**Modelling the Probability of Re-employment**

In the theory of job search the re-employment probability of an unemployed person is identified as the product of the probability of getting a job offer and the probability of accepting it. A possible causal structure underlying these probabilities will be discussed below. A graphical illustration is given in scheme 7.1.

Let the c.d.f. $G(w)$ represent the distribution of wage offers. Any job offer received is viewed as a random observation from this distribution. The distribution is assumed to remain constant over time and to be known to the job searcher. Let $r_t$ represent the probability that an unemployed will be made an offer during period $(t, t + dt)$. The elapsed unemployment duration is denoted by $t$. The rate at which job offers arrive may change over the unemployment spell.

If, at time $t$, the unemployed is offered a job with wage $\tilde{w}_t$, the expected marginal return to continued research is

$$r_t \cdot \int_{\tilde{w}_t}^{\infty} [x - \tilde{w}_t] \, dG(x) \,,$$

i.e., the probability of receiving an offer times the expected extra wage amount. The marginal cost of continued search is

$$\tilde{w}_t - b_t + c_t \,,$$

i.e., the wage lost if the offer is turned down minus the amount of unemployment benefits at time $t$ ($b_t$) plus the out of pocket cost of search ($c_t$).

The unemployed person will stop searching when he is offered a wage $\tilde{w}_t \geq w_t^*$, where $w_t^*$ denotes the "reservation" wage, i.e., the wage that equates marginal returns and marginal costs.

$$r_t \cdot \int_{w_t^*}^{\infty} [x - w_t^*] \, d\,G(x) = w_t^* - b_t + c_t \,. \tag{7.1}$$

The instantaneous probability of leaving unemployment at time $t$, $h_t$, is the product of the job arrival rate $r_t$ and the probability that a random offer is acceptable,

$$h_t = r_t \cdot [1 - G(w_t^*)] \,, \tag{7.2}$$

with,

$$\frac{\partial\, h_t}{\partial\, r_t} > 0 \,, \quad \text{and} \quad \frac{\partial\, h_t}{\partial\, w_t^*} < 0 \,.$$

The direct effect of $r_t$ on the probability of re-employment is positive. The impact of $w_t^*$ is of course negative.

The probability of getting a job offer, the job arrival rate $r_t$, may be assumed to depend on personal and labor market characteristics [eq.(7.3)].

$$r_t = r_t \ (AGE, \ ILLHLTH, \ EDUCV, \ EDUCG, \ CHILD, \ UNRATE_t \ , \ t) \qquad (7.3)$$

with

$$\frac{\partial \ r_t}{\partial AGE}, \quad \frac{\partial \ r_t}{\partial ILLHLTH}, \quad \frac{\partial \ r_t}{\partial UNRATE_t}, \quad \frac{\partial \ r_t}{\partial CHILD}, \quad \frac{\partial \ r_t}{\partial \ t} \ < 0, \ \text{and} \ \frac{\partial \ r_t}{\partial EDUCG} \ > 0.$$

Since little empirical information on the determinants of the job arrival rate is available, our hypotheses are partly based on plausibility arguments. We expect AGE to affect the probability of obtaining an offer negatively. Older unemployed are less likely to be offered a job, for instance, because their skills may have become obsolete and because the returns to training investments by the employer will be less for older workers than they are for younger hirees. Although age is often taken to be an indicator of experience, and hence productivity, our hunch would be that for unemployed workers the negative age effects will outweigh this possibly positive impact, since these productivity gains are likely to be firm specific and, therefore, less relevant to a new employer. A monotonously negative age-effect on the job arrival rate has been assessed by Narendranathan and Nickell (1985).

Obviously, ill health (ILLHLTH) is expected to have a negative impact on the probability of obtaining a job offer. Unemployed people with health problems are less likely to be hired since ill health is most likely to be interpreted by employers as a sign of reduced productivity.

The effect of education is not that straightforward. On the one hand, one may expect education to increase productivity and, hence, the probability of being offered a job. On the other hand, to the extent that education leads to specialization, the probability of getting offers commensurate with these specialized skills may be relatively low. We will specify two education variables: EDUCV and EDUCG. EDUCV is dummy variable indicating whether a respondent has basic vocational schooling equivalent to 2 to 4 years of vocational education, following primary school. EDUCG is a dummy variable that indicates the achievement of a general education, equivalent to at least 4 years of secondary or high school. In conformity with the results derived by Narendranathan and Nickell we expect the acquisition of general skills to increase the job arrival rate. With respect to the effect of specialized skills, however, we do not have prior expectations.

In the eyes of employers, also family duties may be indicative of future productivity. Employers may regard females, taking care of dependent children, as less reliable employees because they expect female family responsibilities to conflict with work duties. This traditional line of reasoning may be less relevant in some other modern societies; in the Netherlands, however, the opinion that a woman's primary responsibilities lay with her children is still the popular view. A view that is reflected by the comparatively low labor force participation rates among females with dependent children.[4] Therefore, the variable CHILD, indicating whether the (female) unemployed is taking care of children under the age of twelve, is expected to affect the probability of obtaining job offers negatively.

Narendranathan and Nickell (1985) give empirical support for the demand side of the labor market as an important determinant of the job offer arrival rate. One would expect the probability of obtaining job offers to be low in a depressed, and high in a tight labor market. Hence, the regional unemployment rate (UNRATE) is expected to have a negative impact on the probability of obtaining a job offer. Apart from these personal and labor market characteristics, the probability of obtaining job offers may also be affected by the time elapsed in the current spell of unemployment. The number of weeks spent in unemployment may be interpreted by employers as signs of expected productivity. Lengthy spells are taken to indicate low productivity. This way, the market value of unemployed searchers, and hence the probability of obtaining an offer, gradually diminishes over the spell. Of course one can think of other characteristics that possibly affect the job arrival rate, such as the intensity of search. Here, however, we mention only the potential determinants of the job arrival rate on which our data contains information.

Next, we turn to the probability that the unemployed searcher will accept a job offer, or the probability that the offered wage w exceeds the reservation wage w*. Given the parameters of the wage offer distribution G(w), this probability is determined by w*.

The parameters of G(w) vary across individuals and are assumed to be constant over time. Here we only consider $\mu = E(w)$, the mean of the distribution; $\mu$ may be considered to depend on personal and labor market characteristics [see eq.(7.4)]. Age and education (both general and vocational) are expected to affect the mean of the wage offer distribution positively [Kiefer and Neumann (1979)]. People with health problems and females with dependent children are expected to be confronted with less favorable distributions.

$$\mu = \mu \text{ (AGE, EDUCV, EDUCG, ILLHLTH, CHILD)} \tag{7.4}$$

with,

$$\frac{\partial \mu}{\partial AGE}, \quad \frac{\partial \mu}{\partial EDUCV}, \quad \frac{\partial \mu}{\partial EDUCG} > 0, \quad \text{and} \quad \frac{\partial \mu}{\partial ILLHLTH}, \quad \frac{\partial \mu}{\partial CHILD} < 0,$$

The reservation wage in our model will depend on parameters of the wage distribution G(w), the amount of unemployment benefit at time t $(b_t)$, on the job arrival rate at t $(r_t)$, and on the length of the current spell of unemployment [eq.(7.1), see Mortensen (1986), p. 858-860].

$\mu$ will have a positive effect on $w^*$, be it that the amount of increase of the reservation wage will be smaller than the increase in $\mu$ [Mortensen (1986), p. 864]. The amount of income replacing unemployment benefits will have a positive impact on the reservation wage since high benefits reduce the cost of continued job search. From (7.1) it is clear that the reservation wage is positively affected by the job arrival rate. There is empirical support for a decline of the reservation wage over the spell of unemployment.[5] This decline may be due to an over time decrease in the unemployment benefit income or a decline in the job arrival rate. Mortensen suggests that the decline may also result from the liquidity constraint with which most unemployed are confronted. Since the unemployed will run out of money in due time, they eventually will adjust their reservation wages downward. In summary,

$$w^*_t = w^*_t (r_t, \mu, b_t, t) \tag{7.5}$$

with

$$\frac{\partial w^*_t}{\partial r_t}, \quad \frac{\partial w^*_t}{\partial \mu}, \quad \frac{\partial w^*_t}{\partial b_t} > 0, \quad \text{and} \quad \frac{\partial w^*_t}{\partial t} < 0$$

Combination (7.2) and (7.5) shows that the indirect effect, via the reservation wage, of the job arrival rate on the probability of re-employment, through the reservation wage, is negative; a high job arrival rate increases the reservation wage thereby decreasing the probability to leave unemployment. On the other hand, the direct effect of $r_t$ is positive. Intuitively, one would expect that, on balance, the probability of leaving unemployment will increase as a result of an increase in the probability of obtaining a job offer. Burdett (1981) shows that the sign of the net effect of $r_t$ depends on the functional form of G(w).[6]

Assuming that indeed the indirect, negative, impact of $r_t$ on the hazard rate $h_t$ is smaller than the direct, positive, effect, we are now able to formulate hypotheses with respect to the effects of the explanatory variables in a reduced form model of the probability of leaving unemployment. Scheme 7.1 may prove helpful in tracing down the hypothesized causative relations:

**Scheme 7.1  Structure of a Simple Job Search Model**

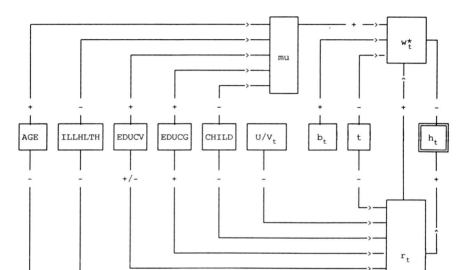

- Age will have a negative impact on the probability of leaving unemployment, both through its positive effect on the reservation wage and its negative effect on the job arrival rate.
- Ill health will have a negative impact on both the reservation wage and on the job arrival rate. Consequently, its effect on the probability of leaving unemployment could be found positive. The intuitively more plausible negative impact will be found only if the health effect on the reservation wage is relatively small.
- Assuming that acquired specialist skills do not increase the job arrival rate, the effect of EDUCV on the probability of leaving unemployment will be negative through its positive impact on the reservation wage.
- A general education will affect $h_t$ negatively through its positive effect on the reservation wage and positively through its positive effect on the job arrival rate. The net effect will depend on the relative weight of the job arrival rate in the hazard function.
- The effect of child care on the probability of leaving unemployment is similarly ambiguous. Via its supposedly negative impact on the reservation wage it will increase the hazard, while through its negative impact on the job arrival rate it will decrease the hazard.

- In our model, the regional unemployment rate will have a negative impact on the probability of re-employment, since it decreases the job arrival rate.
- The amount of income replacing unemployment benefits is expected to have a negative impact via its positive effect on the reservation wage.
- The time elapsed in the current spell of unemployment will affect the hazard both positively, because it is supposed to decrease the reservation wage, and negatively due to its negative impact on the job arrival rate. On balance, the duration time dependence of the hazard may be positive or negative. The structural model therefore does not generate an a priori expectation in this respect.

## Modelling the Probability to Become Unemployed

Job search theory may not be very specific with respect to the impact of possible determinants of the probability of re-employment, at least it has shown to be of some help in unravelling the clew of causal relations. With respect to the determinants of the probability of transition from employment to unemployment, search theory is less informative. Extensions of the job search theory to the analysis of labor turnover deal with the optimal quitting behavior of employees, i.e., with the probability of moving from one job to another without an intervening period of unemployment [see e.g. Jovanovic (1979), Mortensen (1986) presents a review of these extensions]. Transitions from employment to unemployment will typically be initiated by employers and forced upon the employees. To the discharged employee, such transitions are likely to be of an involuntary nature, especially in the Netherlands where the involuntary nature is a necessary condition for unemployment benefit entitlements.

Simple neoclassical theory predicts that employees will be discharged when their wages exceed the value of their marginal product. If for any reason the value of a worker's marginal product becomes less than the minimally required level or the "reservation productivity level", the worker will be discharged. Without any information on either wages or productivity, this theoretical insight is not very helpful for the derivation of hypotheses regarding the determinants of the unemployment probability.

From dual labor market theory we learn that the probability to become unemployed will be relatively high in the secondary segment of the market. This would imply that workers with typical secondary segment characteristics will be particularly prone to unemployment risks. Among others, these typical secondary sector characteristics include:

- Low level of education, since education is supposed to serve as a screening device for primary sector employers;
- Unfavorable working conditions (e.g. strenuous work);
- Frequent unemployment experience;
- Lack of career perspectives.

Consequently, the following prior expectations can be formulated:

- The education indicators, EDUCG and EDUCV, will have a negative impact on the probability of becoming unemployed.
- People with unfavorable working conditions will have an increased unemployment probability.
- Prior experiences of unemployment enhance the unemployment risk.
- Workers who have improved their position during the current spell of employment, for instance by voluntarily switching from one employer to another, are expected to have lower unemployment probabilities.

Apart from these "dual labor market effects", one would expect general conditions on the demand side of the market also to have some impact on the unemployment probability. We expect a rise in the statutory minimum wage to induce a decrease in demand for (cheap) labor, and, as a consequence, an increase of the probability to become unemployed. Recently Van Soest (1989) has provided empirical support for this hypothesis as regards the Dutch labor market. Furthermore, the unemployment probability is expected to be high in a depressed, and low in a tight labor market. Assuming that regional unemployment rates are indicative of the state of the local labor market, we expect the probability of becoming unemployed to increase with the unemployment rate.

Our expectations with regard to the impact of age and health status are largely determined by the particular institutional setting of the Dutch labor market. Without further information one would expect unhealthy or ailing workers to run a higher risk of being discharged, since ill health is bound to decrease a worker's productivity. We can think of at least two reasons why such an effect is not likely to be present. The first relates to the presence and design of the SB- and the DI-program. People with incapacitating health problems have easy access to the Sickness Benefit program and to the DI-program in case of prolonged periods of disability. Compared to the Unemployment program, both these programs are more generous in terms of benefits and less demanding in terms of labor market commitment. Therefore, a worker who is eligible for Sickness or DI-benefits is unlikely to become unemployed and apply for unemployment benefits. The second reason follows from a legal provision that protects employees with health problems, as bad health is not a legitimate ground for dismissal.

Age is expected to have a negative impact on the probability of becoming unemployed. First, because of prevailing seniority rules that are enforced by regional Employment Exchange Agencies, whose approval is needed for a lay-off. A second reason for expecting a negative age effect, are the ample opportunities for elderly workers who are on the verge of non-employability as their productivity has decreased below its reservation value, to qualify for enrolment into the more generous Early Retirement or DI-programs.

## 7.3    A Statistical Model of Individual Labor Market Histories

In modelling individual labor market histories we will more or less follow the
approach used by Flinn and Heckman (1982).

We distinguish two states. Individuals are either employed or unemployed. Consequently, we deal with two kinds of transition probabilities; $\Pr\{E\rightarrow U\}$, the unemployment probability, which is the probability of leaving employment and becoming
unemployed, and $\Pr\{U\rightarrow E\}$, the (re-) employment probability, which is the probability of leaving unemployment to become employed.

In technical terms, the applied model could be referred to as a continuous time,
two-state, multi-episode model for the duration of unemployment and employment
spells [see Flinn and Heckman (1982), p. 45].

The following example may clarify the nature of our model and data.

Over the period 1970-1980, a hypothetical individual may have experienced a labor
market history as is drawn in scheme 7.2.

We start our observations at January 1st, 1970. Ten years later, January 1st, 1980,
the observation period has ended. Time is measured in weeks. Total observation
time (T) equals 520 weeks. The individual is either employed or unemployed.
Therefore,

$$T = \sum_{j=1}^{N_e} t_{je} + \sum_{j=1}^{N_u} t_{ju} + t_{N_{k+1}} \tag{7.6}$$

where $N_e$ and $N_u$ denote the number of completed spells of employment and
unemployment respectively. The last term refers to the $(N_{k+1})$th spell in state k, that
was not yet completed in week 520 when observations stopped. In the hypothetical
case in scheme 7.2 we observe two spells of unemployment and three spells of
employment. The first spell of employment is in progress in the first week of the
observation period.

The hypothetical individual becomes unemployed in week 78 (i.e., the 26th week
of 1971). This first unemployment spell lasts 39 weeks ($t_{1u} = 39$) until the 13th week
of 1972.

Then, he regains employment. This second spell of employment lasts 247 weeks
($t_{2e} = 247$). In the first week of 1977, he becomes unemployed again. This time, he
spends 78 weeks in unemployment ($t_{2u} = 78$). During the 26th week of 1978, he
leaves unemployment to enter the state of employment. This spell of employment
is going on for 78 weeks ($t_{3e} = 78$) at the time the observations are terminated.

Scheme 7.2    A Hypothetical Labor Market History

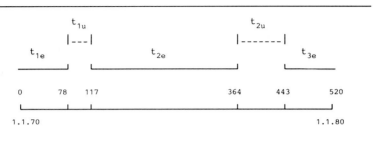

k  = e(employment), u(unemployment)
$t_{jk}$ = weeks spent in state k, during the j-th spell
j   = 1,2,....,$N_k$; the number of completed spells in state k

Now, we turn to the model. The probability of leaving state 1 after exactly t* weeks may be written as

$$h_k (t_k^*) \, dt \tag{7.7}$$

Here $h_k(t_k)dt$ is a conditional probability, namely, the probability of realization of a duration time $t_{jk}^*$, conditional on the probability of realizing a duration time of at least $t_k^*$. The conditional density function, known as the "hazard-function", may be written as

$$h_k (t_k) = \frac{f_k (t_k)}{1 - F_k (t_k)} \tag{7.8}$$

where $f_k(t_k)$ denotes the unconditional density function and $F_k(t_k)$ denotes the corresponding distribution function.
Assuming integrability of $h_k(t_k)$, we may write,

$$\int_0^{t_k} h_k (s) \, ds = \int_0^{t_k} \frac{f_k (s)}{1 - F_k (s)} \, ds$$

$$= -\ln \{1 - F_k (t_k) \}$$

hence,

$$1 - F_k (t_k) = \exp [- \int_0^{t_k} h_k (s) \, ds] \tag{7.9}$$

and,

$$f_k (t_k) = h_k (t_k) \exp [- \int_0^{t_k} h_k (s) \, ds] \qquad (7.10)$$

Since $h_k(t_k)dt$ denotes a probability, $h_k(t_k)$ has to be positive. It is common to choose an exponential function for the hazard function.

The hazard function may be taken to be the reduced form of an underlying, structural model. Here, the employment and unemployment probability models are not fully specified. Theory has only hinted at variables to be included in the analysis.

Our specification of the reduced form hazard function for the j-th episode of state k (k = e,u) is given by:

$$h_k (t_{jk} \mid X_{(\tau_{jk} + t_{jk})}, V_k ; \beta_k , \sigma_k^2 ) = \phi_k (t_{jk} ) \cdot \exp [X_{(\tau_{jk} + t_{jk})} \cdot \beta_k ] \cdot v_k \qquad (7.11)$$

with:

$X_{(\tau_{jk} + t_{jk})}$  (k x 1) vector of (k - 1) observed exogenous variables plus a constant ($X_0$=1); ($\tau_{jk} + t_{jk}$) is an index registering calendar time, $\tau_{jk}$ denotes the week in which the j-th spell in state k began and $t_{jk}$ denotes the weeks elapsed in this particular spell.

$\beta_k$  1 x k vector of coefficients, assumed to be constant over time.

$v_k$  unobserved heterogeneity component, $v_k > 0$. $V_e$ and $V_u$ are assumed to be independent.

$\sigma_k^2$  variance of the gamma-distributed density function $q_k (v)$.

$\phi_k (t_{jk})$  a function describing duration dependence, $\phi_k (t_{jk}) > 0$.

The first term of the rhs reflects the duration time dependence of the hazard. The second term contains all other explanatory variables, $X_{jk}$, suggested by theory.

Similar to the specification of a random error term in linear regression models, a stochastic variable v is specified to control for random disturbance. In the hazard model context, this parameter is often referred to as the "unobserved heterogeneity component". For practical reasons, v is assumed -as often is done- to follow a gamma-distributed density function q(v), with expectation $E(v_k)=1$ and variance $\sigma_k^2$, for $v_k>0$ [see also Flinn and Heckman (1982), Lancaster (1979), Kooreman and Ridder (1983)].[7]

The hazard is a function of time. It may depend on the time elapsed in the j-th spell of state k (duration time dependence). It may also depend on calendar time, that is, the hazard may change over time due to calendar time dependant variations in the exogenous variables. Calendar time is indicated by the index $(\tau_{jk} + t_{jk})$. The duration time dependence is described by $\phi_k(t_{jk})$, which according to eq.(7.11) has to be positive. Our formulation of $\phi_k(t_{jk})$ is equivalent to assuming that duration time is Weibull distributed conditional on $X_{jk}$ and $V_k$. This is a common assumption in the unemployment duration literature [see e.g. Flinn and Heckman (1982), Lancaster (1979), Kooreman and Ridder (1983), Theeuwes et al. (1990)].

$$\phi_k (t_{jk}) = \alpha_k (t_{jk}^{\alpha_k - 1}) \qquad\qquad \text{with } \alpha_k > 0 \qquad\qquad (7.12)$$

If $\alpha_k = 1$, the hazard, or the probability of "escaping" out of state k, does not depend on the amount of time already spent in this state. If $\alpha_k < 1$, the hazard decreases as duration time elapses. This situation is referred to as one of "negative duration dependence". If $\alpha_k > 1$, the hazard increases as duration time elapses. This represents "positive duration dependence".

As both $\phi(t)$ and $q(v)$ are unknown, true duration time dependence and the unobserved heterogeneity component cannot be distinguished empirically [Elbers & Ridder (1982)].[8] Combining (7.10) and (7.11), the probability density function of duration times, $f_k(t_{jk})$, can be written as

$$f_k (t_{jk}) = \int_0^\infty h_k (t_{jk} | v_k) \exp [ -\int_0^{t_k} h_k (s | v_k) \, ds ] \cdot q_k (v) \, dv \qquad (7.13)$$

## 7.4 Data and Further Specification of the Model

The model is estimated on a sample of 1377 male and 584 female persons taken from the 1980 population of employees covered by the DI-program. This is the sample we previously referred to as the healthy control-sample (see chapter 3). This sample has been interviewed in spring 1980. Respondents were asked to give record, in retrospection, of the past ten years of their labor market histories. Besides information on mobility, they provided data on frequency, duration, and year of occurrence of unemployment spells. Under the assumption that the respondents were employed between successive spells of unemployment, we were able to reconstruct individual labor market histories similar to the hypothetical history in scheme 7.2.

The retrospective observations start in the first week of 1970. The histories of those respondents who had not yet entered the labor market at that time, are observed starting from the week they enter.

In the male subsample, we observe 1648 employment spells and 327 unemployment spells. The female subsample contains 649 employment spells and 92 unemployment spells. In total, 2297 employment spells and 419 unemployment spells are observed. The average frequency of unemployment experiences, i.e., the number of unemployment spells per individual, over the ten year period is .21 (.24 among males and .16 among females).

The estimation results are conditional on the prevailing circumstances, that clearly have changed since then. As shown in chapter 2, unemployment started soaring not until the early eighties. While in our database unemployment spells of more than 12 months are a rare phenomenon, they are not in the 1980 decade. We should be careful therefore to generalize our conclusions beyond the first say 12 months of unemployment. Our results do not necessarily apply to the more lengthy spells that can be observed today.

The following variables are specified. For computational convenience, i.e., to facilitate the maximization process, the variables are re-scaled to get similar scaling intervals.

## AGE
Age is specified as a calendar time-dependent variable. $AGE_{\tau jk+tjk}$ denotes a respondent's age in week t of the j-th spell in state k, that began in week $\tau$ of the observation period. The average age in 1980 is 34 years.
AGE is scaled as: (actual age in years - 34)/10.

## EDUCV
EDUCV is a dummy variable that takes on the value 1 in case a respondent has basic vocational schooling. This is equivalent to 2 to 4 years of vocational education, following primary school. EDUCV is constant over time.

## EDUCG
EDUCG is a dummy variable that takes on the value 1 in case a respondent has received a general training, equivalent to at least 4 years of secondary or high school. EDUCG is constant over time.

## STRENWRK
The variable STRENWRK indicates whether a respondent has been involved in strenuous, physical labor. It takes on the value -.5, if respondent has been involved in strenuous physical labor during less than 25 percent of the current spell of employment, the value .5, if this was the case during more than 75 percent of the time, and the value zero in all other cases. For each individual this variable is

constant within a spell of employment. During a spell of unemployment this variable takes on the value of the immediately preceding spell of employment.

## UNRATE

The variable UNRATE, the regional unemployment rate, is specified as a function dependent on calendar time. UNRATE $_{(\tau_{jk} + t_{jk})}$ denotes the sex specific regional unemployment rate in week t of the j-th spell in state k, that began in week $\tau$ of the observation period. It is scaled according to the formula:

$$
\text{UNRATE}_{(\tau_{jk} + t_{jk})} =
\begin{cases}
\dfrac{P_{(\tau_{jk} + t_{jk})} - 3.0}{10} & \text{if } P_{(\tau_{jk} + t_{jk})} > 3.0 \\[2ex]
0 & \text{otherwise,}
\end{cases}
$$

where P $_{(\tau_{jk} + t_{jk})}$ denotes the sex specific regional unemployment percentage. Frictional unemployment is assumed at a constant rate of 3.0 percent. Variation of the unemployment rate below this somewhat arbitrary threshold is assumed not to affect labor market opportunities. The threshold was introduced after preliminary estimates showed strong correlations between the constant term and the coefficient of an unrestrictedly varying UNRATE.[9]

The average national unemployment rates during the seventies are listed in table 7.1.

## MINWAGE

MINWAGE is a variable indicating the deflated, statutory, after-tax minimum wage. It is specified as an index with base year 1975. MINWAGE $_{(\tau_{jk} + t_{jk})}$ denotes the value observed in week t of the j-th spell in state k, that began in week $\tau$ of the observation period. MINWAGE is scaled according to the formula

$$
\text{MINWAGE}_{(\tau_{jk} + t_{jk})} = \frac{I_{(\tau_{jk} + t_{jk})} - 100}{10}
$$

where I $_{(\tau_{jk} + t_{jk})}$ denotes the time specific index value. The net statutory minimum wage is uniform across the country. It is periodically, usually every six months, adjusted by government.

The Minimum Wage Act does not only guarantee a minimum income to wage earners, it also ensures a minimum amount of income replacing benefits to all social security beneficiaries. The variable is included in the analysis to serve as a proxy for the unemployment benefit income, $b_t$, on which no individual information is

available. Since MINWAGE takes on the same value for all respondents at one
particular time $\tau$, all variation in MINWAGE is accounted for by changes in the
real minimum wage during the observation period. From 1970 on, the real statutory
minimum wage has steadily increased [see table 7.1]. Therefore, the estimated effect
of MINWAGE may be expected to contain trend effects, that can not be separated
from the aforementioned hypothesized effects on the respective probabilities.

Table 7.1    Registered Unemployment as a Percentage of All Employees by Year and
Sex; After Tax Minimum Wage Index by Year, 1975 = 100.

|  | '70 | '71 | '72 | '73 | '74 | '75 | '76 | '77 | '78 | '79 |
|---|---|---|---|---|---|---|---|---|---|---|
| **1. UNRATE[a]** | | | | | | | | | | |
| Males | 1.7 | 1.7 | 3.0 | 2.9 | 3.5 | 5.0 | 5.2 | 4.6 | 4.3 | 4.1 |
| Females | 1.3 | 1.3 | 2.0 | 2.5 | 3.3 | 5.0 | 5.9 | 6.6 | 7.5 | 8.2 |
| **2. Min. Wage Index[b]** | | | | | | | | | | |
|  | 83.2 | 86.4 | 86.7 | 88.0 | 93.8 | 100 | 101.5 | 103.7 | 106.9 | 107.4 |

[a]   Source: CBS A (1980).
[b]   Source: CPB (1987).

**ILLHLTH**
ILLHLTH is a dummy variable indicating the presence of more or less persistent
health problems. It takes on the value 1 from the moment of occurrence of any
health complaints.
In the preceding section, we derived hypotheses with respect to the effect of ill
health on the probabilities of entering and leaving unemployment. The coefficient
estimates may however be biased because the risk of ill health may be jointly
determined with the unemployment risk. The risk of ill health may even be
determined by the unemployment risk, as is suggested by many cross section
surveys that show that unemployed are less healthy than employed. To what extent
such differences result from selection mechanisms that increase the unemployment
risk of the less healthy or from possible adverse health effects of unemployment
can only be assessed in longitudinal research. Empirical support of the latter
direction of causality appears to depend on the definition of ill health (mental or
physical), the type of unemployed (old or young, skilled or unskilled) and the
duration of unemployment.[10] Björklund (1985), using Swedish data, concludes that
"the hypothesis of no adverse health effects of unemployment can not be rejected".
Narendranathan, et al. (1985), analyzing the dynamic relationship between spells

of unemployment and spells of sick leave using British paneldata, find no evidence of unemployment leading to sickness. Recent Dutch studies show that the adverse impact of unemployment on health is only weak and seems to occur not until after the first year of unemployment [Schaufeli (1988), Verkleij (1988)]. The latter studies share the common conclusion that personal traits rather than situational character-istics determine the (mental) health risk [see also Spruit (1983)]. In our study, some of the personal traits that may determine both the health risk and the unemploy-ment risk are not observed. As a consequence, our estimates of the impact of ill health on the probability of becoming unemployed may be biased upward and the ill health effect on the re-employment probability may be biased downward.

## UNEXP
The variable UNEXP indicates a respondent's previous unemployment experiences. UNEXP $(\tau_{jk} + t_{jk})$ is a dummy variable that takes on the value 1 if respondent has experienced one or more spells of unemployment prior to the j-th spell in state k, that began in week $\tau$. The variable is specified only in the unemployment proba-bility model. Technically, UNEXP is a predetermined, endogenous, variable. Its coefficient estimate will capture a great deal of the effect of the non-specified determinants of individual labor market histories. To some extent, therefore, a positive impact on the probability of becoming unemployed may partly be viewed as an indication of incomplete specification of the model.

## MOBILITY
MOBILITY is a dummy variable indicating previous labor market experiences. It takes on the value 1 if the respondent has voluntarily switched from one firm to another during the j-th spell of employment that began in week $\tau$.

## CHILD
CHILD is a dummy variable that takes on the value 1 if the respondent has to take care of dependent children under the age of twelve.

### Duration Time Dependence
In the model describing the probability of becoming unemployed, the coefficient $\alpha_e$, that reflects the duration time dependence of the probability to become unem-ployed [see eq.(7.12)], is assumed to equal 1. In other words, the probability to leave employment and become unemployed is assumed to be independent of the amount of time spent in the current spell of employment. This restriction is imposed because the observed labor market histories are "censored to the left". At the beginning of the observation period, January ·1970, all respondents happen to be in the state of employment. We do not know for how long a respondent has already been in this initial state. In other words, the completed length of the

spells, that were in progress at the time when the observation period started, is unknown. As a consequence, the duration time dependence of the probability of
becoming unemployed, can not be validly assessed without further assumptions.
Flinn & Heckman (1982) offer some solutions to this problem. Here, the problem
is coarsely "solved" by assuming that the escape rate from employment is independent of the amount of time spent in employment. As, in reconstruction, all respondents happen to be employed at the start of the observation period, this "left
censoring" problem does not occur in the analysis of unemployment durations,
i.e., the re-employment probability. Therefore, $\alpha_u$ can be estimated.

The analysis of labor market opportunities presented here, has some serious shortcomings. We already mentioned the lack of data to estimate, superior, structural
models. But even in an exploratory study, variables like occupation, earnings,
unemployment benefit income, marital status, etc. can hardly be missed. As it is,
this lack of information is a common problem in unemployment duration studies.
In the empirical literature on the subject, one hardly ever finds a study in which
the ideal of a fully specified model is closely approached. In fact, the analysis is
often restricted to the effects of age, education, and some unemployment indicator.
Our database is comparatively rich in that it allows for repeated spells of employment and unemployment, and the specification of calendar time dependent exogenous variables.[11]

A further limitation of this analysis stems from the already mentioned fact that the
individual labor market histories have been observed in retrospection. This will
have some bearing on the accuracy of the observations. Particularly, the observations
referring to the first years of our 10-year observation period will be less precise
than a panel study would produce.

A third complication relates to the problem of sample selection. As the sample of
labor market histories is derived from a random sample of "healthy" persons who
are insured under the DI-program in 1980, the labor market histories are drawn
conditional upon "survival" up to 1980. Spells of people who, in 1980, were either
self-employed or not in the labor force anymore because of retirement, death or
DI-program enrolment, are not observed. To the extent that the probability of
becoming unemployed or re-employed, and the probability of leaving the labor force
entirely, are determined by similar sets of unobserved variables our estimation
results will be biased. Presumably, the probability of leaving the labor force is
endogenous indeed. The only way to deal with this problem is to estimate a multi-
state model applying information from a panel survey. This procedure would not
only require a much richer database than is available here, it would also lead to
almost unmanageable computational complexity [see Ridder (1987)].

**Estimation Procedure**

Assuming that the individual labor market histories are obtained from a random sample of individuals, the likelihood-function of employment durations and unemployment durations, $t_{jk}$, for the i-th individual, assuming $\alpha_e = 1$, is given by:

$$L_i (\beta_k, \alpha_u, \sigma_k^2) = \int_0^\infty \prod_{j=1}^{N_u} h_u (t_u | v_u) \cdot \exp \left[ - \int_0^{t_{ju}} h_u (s | v_u) \, ds \right] *$$

$$\int_0^\infty \prod_{j=1}^{N_e} h_e (t_e | v_e) \cdot \exp \left[ - \int_0^{t_{je}} h_e (s | v_e) \, ds \right] *$$

$$\exp \left[ - \int_0^{t_{N_{k+1}}} h_k (s | v_k) \, ds \right] * q_k (v) \, dv \qquad (7.14)$$

The last term of (7.14) refers to the state individual i is in, during the last week of the observation period. At that time, i.e., in week number 520, the $(N_{k+1})$-th spell in state k has not yet been completed. The probability that this particular spell has been going on for at least $t_{Nk+1}$ weeks equals:

$$\exp \left[ - \int_0^{t_{N_{k+1}}} h_k (s | v_k) \, ds \right] = 1 - F_k (t_{N_{k+1}})$$

Now, the sample likelihood is:

$$L_k (\beta_k, \alpha_k, \sigma_k^2) = \prod_{i=1}^{M} L_i (\beta_k, \alpha_k, \sigma_k^2) \qquad (7.15)$$

where M denotes the size of the sample.

Maximizing (7.15) with respect to $\beta_e$, $\beta_u$, $\alpha_u$, $\sigma_e^2$, and $\sigma_u^2$, yields consistent and efficient maximum likelihood estimators, which can be shown to be asymptotically normally distributed as the number of event histories becomes large [Flinn and Heckman (1982), p. 47].

For pragmatic reasons, we maximize separate employment and unemployment likelihood functions instead of estimating one single maximum likelihood function containing the likelihood of both employment and unemployment spells. The employment and unemployment probability models are estimated for the male and female subsample separately.[12]

## 7.5    Estimation Results

### 7.5.1    Duration of Employment Spells; The Unemployment Probability

The estimation results for males and females are presented in table 7.2. Maximizing the likelihood function (7.15) under the assumption of a fully specified model yields the estimators that are listed in the first column of the table. The second column refers to the coefficients resulting from the estimation of the model, while allowing for unobserved heterogeneity through a gamma $(1,\sigma^2)$ distributed disturbance factor v.

### Males

Male workers appear to have high probabilities to become unemployed when:
- they are young;
- they did not receive further vocational or general education;
- they are involved in strenuous work;
- regional unemployment is high;
- the minimum wage is high;
- they have been unemployed previously;
- they did not experience voluntary job changes.

All the effects are significant at the 1 percent level. Health problems do not seem to increase the unemployment probability. The results listed in table 7.2 are in accordance with the expectations formulated in section 7.2.

The clearly negative effect of age confirms our hypothesis that prevailing seniority rules together with the presence of easily accessible alternative income replacing programs, outweighs a possibly positive effect of age due to physical and economic obsolescence of a man's productivity during his working life. The same negative effect of age has been found in similar models, estimated on American and British databases [Burdett et al. (1985), Nickell (1979a)]. Theeuwes et al. (1990), find no significant effect of age in a sample of Dutch labor market histories in the early 1980s.

The apparent absence of a positive effect of health problems on the probability to become unemployed is probably due to the particular institutional setting mentioned in section 7.2, in which workers with health complaints are legally protected against lay-offs and have easy access to the financially more attractive SB- and DI-programs. The effects of education appear to be consistent with the expectations derived from dual labor market theory. The significantly negative coefficients of EDUCV and EDUCG indicate that people without education other than primary school appear to run higher risks than those who went through secondary school. Similar results with respect to the effect of education were reported in the Dutch and Anglo-Saxon studies mentioned above.

**Table 7.2**     **ML-estimates; Probability of Becoming Unemployed, Pr{E→U}. Males and Females**

| Duration dependence | $\phi_e(t) \equiv 1$ | | $\phi_e(t) \equiv 1$ | |
|---|---|---|---|---|
| Non-specified heterogeneity | $V \equiv 1$ | | $V \sim \Gamma\ (1,\ \sigma^2)$ | |
| Explanatory variables | coefficient | standard error | coefficient | standard error |
| **1. Males** | | | | |
| Intercept | - 1.059** | - .130 | - .927** | - .162 |
| AGE | - .434** | - .066 | - .466** | - .070 |
| EDUCV (Vocational) | - .573** | - .143 | - .606** | - .164 |
| EDUCG (General) | - .672** | - .145 | - .711** | - .166 |
| STRENWORK | .528** | .139 | .563** | .151 |
| UNRATE | 1.351** | .400 | 1.311** | .439 |
| MINWAGE | 2.817** | .703 | 3.226** | .750 |
| ILLHEALTH | - .196 | - .175 | - .208 | - .190 |
| UNEXP | 1.258** | .131 | .714* | .283 |
| MOBILITY | - .742** | - .180 | - .797** | - .191 |
| $\sigma^2$ | | | .832** | .418 |
| Loglikelihood | - 582.450 | | - 578.110 | |
| Pseudo $R^2$ | .159 | | .163 | |
| No. Spells | 1,648 | | | |
| No. Respondents | 1,377 | | | |
| **2. Females** | | | | |
| Intercept | - 1.620** | - .354 | - 1.608** | - .362 |
| AGE | - .464** | - .135 | - .467** | - .137 |
| EDUCV (Vocational) | .006 | .301 | .003 | .306 |
| EDUCG (General) | - .068 | - .319 | - .069 | - .325 |
| STRENWORK | .874* | .411 | .894* | .425 |
| UNRATE | .588 | .363 | .616 | .375 |
| ILLHEALTH | - .058 | - .364 | - .099 | - .372 |
| UNEXP | .899** | .315 | .774 | .459 |
| MOBILITY | - .438 | - .255 | - .434 | - .259 |
| CHILD | - .306 | - .330 | - .308 | - .335 |
| $\sigma^2$ | | | .198 | .550 |
| Loglikelihood | -189.880 | | -189.790 | |
| Pseudo $R^2$ | .057 | | .057 | |
| No. Spells | 649 | | | |
| No. Respondents | 584 | | | |

\*,\*\* significant at 5 and 1 percent respectively.

Strenuous work appears to be associated with an increased probability of becoming unemployed. Assuming that strenuous work is an unfavorable work condition, typical for the secondary segment, this effect is consistent with dual labor market theory. However, this result may also be a mere artefact of the database, reflecting the high labor turnover in industries characterized by physically demanding production processes (e.g., construction industry), in which case it hardly provides empirical support for dual labor market theory.

The effect of regional labor market conditions is reflected by the coefficient of the unemployment rate. In periods and regions of high unemployment, the probability to become unemployed increases as expected.

The minimum wage appears to be positively correlated with the probability to become unemployed. This result is consistent with neoclassical theory predicting a rising minimum wage to reduce demand for (cheap) labor thereby increasing the probability of becoming unemployed. For reasons mentioned in the preceding section, however, the estimated coefficient may also reflect a possible trend effect. If present at all, this trend effect is likely to be positive. In that case, the pure effect of the minimum wage would be overestimated.

According to the estimated effects of previous unemployment and mobility experiences, a man's work history is an important determinant of his labor market opportunities later on. The probability of becoming unemployed increases when one has experienced spells of unemployment previously and decreases by voluntary mobility. Although dual labor market theory provides a ready explanation for these effects, to some extent the results may also be a consequence of misspecification of the model. Particularly the estimated effect of previous unemployment experience, as a "predetermined" endogenous variable, may be biased. Indicative of such a bias is the presence of unobserved heterogeneity as reflected by the estimated value of the parameter $\sigma^2$. It appears to be significantly (at 1%) positive, implying that indeed the model does not contain all relevant variables.

Comparing the first and the last two columns gives some information on the quality of the estimates. The allowance for unobserved heterogeneity in the model seriously affects some of the estimates reported in the first two columns. The coefficient estimate for previous unemployment decreases by more than 40 percent, while the other coefficients show an increase, in absolute terms, of about 6 percent (except the coefficient for the unemployment rate which decreases by 3 percent). The standard errors of the coefficient estimates also have increased, on average by 9 percent. Again, the coefficient for previous unemployment is the important exception. Its standard error more than doubles.

In our model, the assumption of no unobserved heterogeneity leads to downward biases in the coefficient estimates and their standard errors. The important exception here is the impact of previous unemployment, that would be seriously over-estimated. As expected, the effect of this "predetermined" endogenous variable is particularly vulnerable to misspecification of the model. The reduced, "true", effect of previous unemployment however, still is significantly positive, which provides some empirical support for the "scar-hypothesis" of unemployment. The fact that the ill health coefficient is barely affected by the allowance of unobserved hetero-geneity suggests that ill health as defined here is not jointly determined with the probability of becoming unemployed (see section 7.3). Note that the effect of the minimum wage, that was under suspicion of being time trended, is barely affected by relaxing the heterogeneity assumption.

**Females**
After adding an indicator for the presence of dependent children, the model presented in the first panel of table 7.2 has been estimated in the female subsample. The variable MINWAGE has been excluded after its coefficient appeared to be heavily correlated with the unemployment rate coefficient. Since both the minimum wage and the female unemployment rate have shown a monotonous increase over the 10-year observation period [see table 7.1], the effects of these two variables are not separably estimable.

The results are presented in table 7.2, panel b. They are similar to the results for males. Female workers tend to have high probabilities to become unemployed when:
- they are young;
- they are involved in strenuous work;
- regional unemployment is high;
- they have been unemployed previously;
- they did not experience voluntary job changes.
With only two of these effects (Age and Strenuous Work) significantly different from zero at 5%, the results for the female subsample are far less conclusive. This is also indicated by the rather low value of the pseudo-$R^2$ (.057 compared to .163 for the males). Very different from the male results is the absence of an impact of the education indicators. Among females, education does not seem to affect the probability of becoming unemployed.
The size of the effects of age and previous unemployment on the other hand, is remarkably similar to that of the male coefficients. Although the insignificant estimate of $\sigma^2$ would suggest the absence of unobserved heterogeneity, its inclusion produces a decrease of the coefficient for previous unemployment, suggesting that also the female model is incompletely specified.
The inconclusiveness of the results of the female model may be due to a combina-tion of circumstances. First, the female subsample is a more heterogeneous group, for instance with respect to the number of work hours. Since no previous infor-mation on the number of hours is available, this heterogeneity can not be controlled

for. And second, our assumption that the time intervals between successive spells of unemployment can be treated as spells of employment, probably is a rather heroic one with respect to females. For it is well known that women tend to interrupt their careers for extended periods of time to raise their children.[13] In our model, therefore, we tend to overestimate the length of female employment spells. As a result, female probabilities of leaving employment are likely to be underestimated. Perhaps these particular circumstances also account for the unexpectedly negative, though insignificant, effect of the presence of dependent children.[14]

### 7.5.2    Duration of Unemployment Spells; The Re-employment Probability

The estimation results for males and females are presented in table 7.3. Maximizing the appropriate likelihood, under the assumption of absence of duration time dependence and unobserved heterogeneity, yields the estimators that are listed in the first column of the table. Allowance for duration time dependence of the Weibull-type, results in the estimates given in the third column. The coefficients in the last two columns are the outcomes of a version in which also the unobserved heterogeneity assumption has been relaxed.

**Males**
Unemployed male workers appear to have high probabilities to become re-employed when:
- they are young;
- they have no extended vocational or general education;
- they are involved in strenuous work;
- they do not have health problems.

These four effects are significant at a 5% significance level. There is less certainty about the negative impacts of regional unemployment and the minimum wage.
Age has the expected negative impact on the probability of re-employment. The job search model, outlined in section 7.2, suggests that this negative impact works through a positive age effect on the reservation wage and a negative age effect on the job arrival rate. This result is consistent with other studies [see for instance Kooreman and Ridder (1983), Theeuwes et al. (1990)].
The job search model is inconclusive about the expected impact of EDUCG, general education. Through its positive impact on the reservation wage it would decrease the hazard, while through its positive impact on the job arrival rate it would increase the hazard. On balance, the effect appears to be (insignificantly) negative. Under the assumption that the possession of specialist skills does not increase the job arrival rate, whereas it does increase the reservation wage, the expected effect

of EDUCV is unambiguously negative. The reported significantly negative EDUCV coefficient seems to confirm this "job search" interpretation. Our findings refute the general intuition that schooling improves employment probabilities, because in our model, people without extended secondary education appear to be the most successful job searchers. Our results are consistent with conclusions of some other empirical studies [e.g. Lancaster (1985), Moffitt (1985), Ridder and Gorter (1986), Ridder (1987)], and contradictory to others [e.g. Burdett et al. (1985), Narendranathan and Nickell (1985)]. Sometimes results are inconclusive on this point [e.g. Ashenfelter and Ham (1979), Theeuwes et al. (1990)]. We will return to the effects of education below.

As expected, males who are involved in strenuous work tend to have relatively high probabilities of re-employment. Recall our suggestion, in section 7.5.1, that strenuous work often coincides with labor market volatility.

The negative impact of ILLHEALTH, through the job arrival rate, dominates its presumed positive effect, through the reservation wage. In the preceding section we suggested that the estimated ill health effect might be downwardly biased due to simultaneity of unemployment and ill health. Such a downward bias would partly disappear after the allowance for unobserved heterogeneity. As a consequence the estimated effect of ill health would increase, i.e., it would become "less negative". Inclusion of $\sigma^2$, however, appears to lead to a "more negative" impact of ill health. Assuming that the unobserved heterogeneity component is adequately controlled for, this implies that the risk of ill health is not jointly determined with the probability of re-employment. Consequently, the estimated coefficient in the last column is likely to reflect the "true" negative impact of ill health on the probability of re-employment. Similar effects of ill health on the probability of re-employment have been reported by Schaufeli (1988) and Verkleij (1988), who use Dutch data, and by Nickell (1979a, 1982) and Narendranathan et al. (1985) applying a dynamic analysis on British data. Apparently, men with health problems have more trouble finding employment than healthy men. Although this effect is intuitively plausible, the notion that some stay unemployed because of bad health, has not caught nearly as much public attention as its counterpart - the fact that some people stay on the disability rolls because they are partly unemployed.

Like in most studies, labor market conditions appear to affect the probability of re-employment. Here, they are indicated by the regional unemployment rate which, as expected, has a negative impact. After the introduction of unobserved heterogeneity and duration dependence in the model, however, the standard error of the estimated coefficient increases substantially and the coefficient estimate looses its significance.

**Table 7.3    ML-estimates; Probability of Re-Employment, Pr{U→E}. Males and Females**

| Duration dependence | $\phi(t_e) = 1$ | | $\phi(t) = \alpha_e (t_e)^{\alpha_e - 1}$ | | | |
|---|---|---|---|---|---|---|
| Non-specified heterogeneity | $V = 1$ | | $V = 1$ | | $V \sim \Gamma(1, \sigma^2)$ | |
| Explanatory variables | (1) | (2) | (1) | (2) | (1) | (2) |
| **1. Males** | | | | | | |
| Intercept | 3.706** | -.132 | .837** | .209 | 5.624** | .541 |
| AGE | -.342** | -.064 | -.353** | -.065 | -.483** | -.114 |
| EDUCV (Vocational) | -.504** | -.156 | -.518** | -.157 | -.564* | -.258 |
| EDUCG (General) | -.227 | -.151 | -.233 | -.151 | -.346 | -.253 |
| STRENWORK | .373* | .148 | .391** | .150 | .440* | .229 |
| UNRATE | -.973* | -.436 | -1.016* | -.440 | -.987 | -.669 |
| MINWAGE | -1.086 | -.721 | -1.139 | -.724 | -1.461 | -1.070 |
| ILLHEALTH | -.422* | -.188 | -.436* | -.189 | -.690* | -.295 |
| $\alpha$ | | | 1.038 | .047 | 1.405** | .105 |
| $\sigma^2$ | | | | | .720** | .205 |
| Loglikelihood | 692.16 | | 690.49 | | 702.08 | |
| Pseudo $R^2$ | .192 | | .194 | | .249 | |
| No. Spells | 327 | | | | | |
| No. Respondents | 1,377 | | | | | |
| **2. Females** | | | | | | |
| Intercept | 2.264** | .441 | 2.519** | .492 | 3.593** | 1.050 |
| AGE | -.514** | .180 | -.571** | .188 | -.742** | .273 |
| EDUCV (Vocational) | .595 | .322 | .646* | .326 | .920 | .497 |
| EDUCG (General) | .134 | .348 | .166 | .351 | .187 | .498 |
| STRENWORK | .120 | .545 | .135 | .553 | .004 | .731 |
| UNRATE | -.492 | .466 | -.515 | .475 | -.688 | .631 |
| ILLHEALTH | -.257 | .447 | -.233 | .451 | -.425 | .571 |
| CHILD | .373 | .669 | .434 | .680 | .414 | .814 |
| $\alpha$ | | | 1.118 | .098 | 1.437* | .250 |
| $\sigma^2$ | | | | | .549 | .412 |
| Loglikelihood | 150.50 | | 151.27 | | 152.83 | |
| Pseudo $R^2$ | .171 | | .185 | | .212 | |
| No. Spells | 92 | | | | | |
| No. Respondents | 584 | | | | | |

(1) Coefficient.
(2) Standard error.
**,* significant at 1 and 5 percent respectively.

The effect of the net minimum wage appears to be negative as expected. This negative effect is assumed to reflect part of the negative impact of unemployment benefit income on the duration of unemployment. This effect has often been analyzed. There seems to be consensus on a negative impact of unemployment benefits in this respect [Danziger et al. (1981), Lancaster and Nickell (1980)]. For the Dutch labor market, Ridder and Gorter (1986) report a rather large effect of the replacement rate on the duration of unemployment. As illustrated for instance by Atkinson et al. (1984), however, the size and statistical significance of this effect is highly sensitive to the definition of benefit income and to model specification.

The negative impact reported in table 7.3 is rather large. So is the accompanying estimated standard error. The fact that our indicator only measures the variation in the minimum amount of net benefits, which is equal for all (potentially) unemployed and possibly time trended, will no doubt bear some responsibility for the inconclusiveness of our results at this point.

The simultaneous introduction of unobserved heterogeneity and duration dependence has a major impact on the estimation results. Apart from the coefficient for regional unemployment, all coefficient values -in absolute terms- appear to increase by 10 to 60 percent. The estimated standard errors show an even sharper increase. Apparently, the unobserved heterogeneity allowance accounts for the major part of these changes. Like in the unemployment probability model, the coefficient $\sigma^2$ is significantly positive.

After inclusion of $\sigma^2$ in the model, the duration time dependence parameter $\alpha$ appears to be significantly greater than 1, revealing positive duration dependence of the re-employment probability. As pointed out by Flinn and Heckman (1982), misspecification of the model tends to lead to a downward biased estimate of duration time dependence.[15] Comparison of the estimates of $\alpha$ in the third and fifth column clearly shows that, in our model, the assumption of no unobserved heterogeneity would lead to the apparently false conclusion of absence of duration dependence.[16]

In the model described in the preceding section, the positive duration dependence of the re-employment probability is the net result of the negative effect of duration through its negative influence on the job arrival rate on the one hand, and the positive effect through its negative influence on the reservation wage on the other hand. The reservation wage is assumed to be positively correlated with the unemployment benefit income. Unemployment benefits are decreasing over the spell of unemployment (see chapter 2). Since no individually varying indicator for the unemployment benefit income is available, part of the presumed effect of unemployment benefit income is reflected in the coefficient of duration dependence, thereby causing an upward bias of $\alpha$.

The value of $\alpha$ found in our "best" model implies that the probability of re-employment increases during the unemployment spell. This outcome contradicts popular views which are based on the observation, for instance from labor force statistics, that the long term unemployed have few opportunities to find a job. From this fact one is tempted to conclude that extended durations per se cause re-employment probabilities to decline. Our results indicate that, while such mechanisms may be present, this negative impact is outweighed by positive impacts through the over

time declining reservation wage. This decline may be due to diminishing unemployment entitlements, which increase the opportunity costs of turning down a job
offer, or it may be the result of actual job search experience which may call for
a downward adjustment of the initial reservation wage. Our findings suggest that
the unfavorable labor market position of long term unemployed, relative to that
of short term unemployed, is not caused by the length of the unemployment spell
per se.

**Females**
The estimation results of the re-employment probability model in the female
subsample are presented in table 7.3, panel b.
Unemployed women appear to have a high probability of re-employment when:
- they are young;
- they have extended secondary vocational education.
Except for the effect of vocational education, the results in table 7.4 are qualitatively
similar to the outcomes of the male model. The age effect appears to be stronger
than the age effect in the male subsample (-.742 versus -.483).
After accounting for unobserved heterogeneity by including $\sigma^2$ in the model, the
coefficient for duration dependence reveals a positive relation between the probability of re-employment and the amount of time spent in unemployment. The value
found for $\alpha$ (1.437) is remarkably similar to the one reported in the male model
(1.405).
Although $\sigma^2$ is not found to be significantly greater than zero, its inclusion in the
model certainly affects the estimation results as it leads to an increase of most of
the coefficients - and the accompanying standard errors - and also to an increase
of the pseudo-$R^2$ (from .185 to .212).

While secondary vocational education negatively affects male re-employment
probabilities, it has a positive impact in the female subsample. We can only
speculate on the reason for this difference. In the context of the theoretical model,
this result suggests that the negative impact of education through the reservation
wage is outweighed by a positive impact through the job arrival rate. This implies
that, among females, vocational education would increase, rather than decrease, the
job arrival rate. The negative effect of specialization resulting from secondary
vocational training apparently is smaller among female unemployed. Perhaps this
is due to the fact that young females acquire more generally applicable caretaking
skills, while young males acquire a more specific trade like carpentering, plumbing,
steelwork, etc.[17, 18]
The fact that strenuous work has no effect on the female re-employment probability
may also be due to the particular occupational structure of female employment.
No significantly negative effects are found for the regional unemployment rate and

the prevalence of health problems. Especially, the absence of a significant impact of regional unemployment is remarkable as it is both contrary to expectations and to results from other studies.[19] The insignificance of the negative effects of the unemployment rate and ill health may result from the aforementioned inability to distinguish between spells of employment and spells of non-participation. Particularly within a female subsample such an omission will trouble the analysis. To the extent that the observed transitions out of unemployment are in fact transitions to non-participation, one would expect the unemployment rate and ill health to have a positive, rather than negative, impact. This would imply that by neglecting the difference between employment and non-participation, the estimated impact of these variables will be upward biased. Since the probable impact of child care activities on the transition to non-participation will be positive also, the unexpectedly positive, though insignificant, coefficient of the variable CHILD may also be the result of the failure to differentiate between employment and non-participation.[20]

**Variation of the Unemployment and Re-Employment Probability**
An indication of the sensitivity of the unemployment and re-employment probability to variations in the explanatory variables is given in table 7.4. For different combinations of characteristics we calculate the probability to become unemployed within one year, $Pr\{t_e \leq 1$ year$\}$, and the probability to become re-employed within three months, $Pr\{t_u \leq 3$ months$\}$. The reference, or "typical", person, is defined in note b of the table. The impact of the explanatory variables is reflected by index numbers. The typical person's probability has index value 100. Table 7.4 also gives an impression of the net effect of the explanatory variables on the "unemployment risk", defined as the probability of being unemployed, or rather, the probability of becoming and staying unemployed for at least three months. Here, the unemployment risk is calculated by $Pr\{t_e \leq 1$ year$\} \times (1 - Pr\{t_u \leq 3$ months$\})$. The typical person's unemployment risk has index value 100.

Age comes out as an important factor. The unemployment probability for a fifty year old is only 40 percent of that for a thirty year old. The re-employment probability of a fifty year old male unemployed is only half of that of a thirty year old. For an unemployed woman of fifty years the re-employment probability is even less than one third of that of a thirty year old woman. On balance, the unemployment risk declines with age. A fifty year old has a 42 percent smaller risk than a thirty year old.
Men without extended secondary education who are involved in physically strenuous work, are 2.3 times more likely to become unemployed than men without this combination of characteristics. Their probability of re-employment is (only) 43 percent higher. Their ensuing risk of unemployment is more than two times higher than that of the typical person. This implies that men without extended secondary

**Table 7.4**   Predicted Unemployment and Re-Employment Probabilities, Pr{E→U} and Pr{U→E}[a]; Predicted Unemployment Risk[b]

|  | Males | | | Females | | |
|---|---|---|---|---|---|---|
| Characteristics | Pr{E→U} | Pr{U→E} | Risk | Pr{E→U} | Pr{U→E} | Risk |
| Typical person[c] | 100[d] | 100[e] | 100[f] | 100[g] | 100[h] | 100[i] |
| Age 40 | 63 | 74 | 78 | 63 | 57 | 80 |
| Age 50 | 40 | 50 | 58 | 40 | 30 | 58 |
| General Education | 90 | 113 | 79 | - | 58 | 127 |
| No Vocational Education | 179 | 132 | 128 | - | 49 | 133 |
| No Voc.Educ. + Strenuous work | 227 | 143 | 216 | - | - | - |
| Strenuous work | - | - | - | 149 | - | 149 |
| 1 perc. Unemployment Increase | 113 | 94 | 119 | 106 | 95 | 109 |
| 10 perc. Min. Wage Increase | 136 | 92 | 146 | - | - | - |
| Previously Unemployed | 198 | - | 198 | 214 | - | 214 |
| Voluntarily Mobile | 46 | - | 46 | 65 | - | 65 |
| Ill Health | - | 64 | 132 | - | 73 | 117 |

[a]   For $t_e$=52, $t_u$=13 weeks, the calculated probabilities satisfy:

$$Pr\{t_k < t_k^*\} = 1 - \{1 + \sigma_k^2 (t_k^*)^{\alpha_k}.\exp[X\beta_k]\}^{-1/\sigma_k^2}.$$

[b]   The Unemployment Risk is indicated by: $Pr\{t_e \leq 1 \text{ year}\} \times (1 - Pr\{t_u \leq 3 \text{ months}\})$.
[c]   The typical person is 30 years old and has a low level vocational education. The regional unemployment rate is 5 percent. He or she has no health problems has not been unemployed previously, did not experience voluntary job changes. All other variables take on their average values. The characteristics mentioned in each row are the only ones in which a hypothetical person differs from the typical person.
[d]   $Pr\{t_e <1 \text{ year}\}$ = 3.0 percent.
[e]   $Pr\{t_u <3 \text{ months}\}$ = 47.7 percent.
[f]   (Unemployment)Risk = 1.57 percent.
[g]   $Pr\{t_e <1 \text{ year}\}$ = 1.9 percent.
[h]   $Pr\{t_u <3 \text{ months}\}$ = 39.2 percent.
[i]   (Unemployment)Risk = 1.16 percent.

education, who are involved in strenuous work, are two times more likely to find themselves in unemployment.

Men without extended secondary education with average physical workload are 30 percent more likely to be found among the unemployed. At this point, it seems appropriate to conclude that the overrepresentation, within the population of unemployed, of young people without education, can be explained by their relatively high probability of becoming unemployed, which is only partly balanced by higher than average re-employment probabilities.

We note that the introduction of schooling programs to reduce youth unemployment by improving the employment opportunities of low-educated, young unemployed, may be not as effective as expected since these young people already seem to have re-employment probabilities that are (much) higher than those of the average unemployed.

Compared to the age and education effects, the impact of the regional unemployment rate is rather small. An increase in unemployment from 5 to 6 percent induces an increase in the unemployment probability of 13 percent (females 6 percent), while reducing the re-employment probability by 6 percent. The (male) unemployment risk increases by almost 20 percent as a consequence of a one percentage point rise in the unemployment rate. A 10 percent increase of the minimum wage seems to result in an increase of the (male) unemployment probability of 36 percent. Because of its negative impact on the re-employment probability, this rise of the minimum wage causes the unemployment risk to increase by 46 percent.

The unemployment probability of people who previously experienced unemployment is twice the probability of people without unemployment experiences. Unemployment probabilities of those who voluntarily switched from one firm to another, are 50 percent lower than the unemployment probabilities of those who stick to one firm.

The prevalence of health problems reduces the re-employment probability by 46 percent (males). As health problems appear to have no effect on the probability to become unemployed, the effect on the unemployment risk is an increase of 32 percent. Apparently, the high prevalence of bad health conditions among the unemployed is at least partly due to the fact that ill health tends to lengthen the spell of unemployment.

## 7.6     Unemployment and Re-Employment Probabilities; DI-Insured and DI-Entrants

In the introduction to this chapter we claimed that a person's labor market position will be a particularly important determinant of his probability of entering the DI-program. The empirical assessment of the effects of labor market opportunities requires unambiguous indicators. We concluded that the respondents' or the gatekeepers' perception of labor market opportunities are likely to contain information on health or personal tastes and, therefore, will be endogenous with respect to the disability process (see chapter 6). Instead, we construct alternative measures of individual labor market opportunities that are based on the estimation, using the control-sample of "healthy" respondents, of a reduced form hazard model that describes individual labor market histories. Given a number of personal and situational characteristics, the coefficient estimates resulting from this model can be used to "predict" theoretical unemployment and re-employment probabilities for each individual worker at a particular moment in time.

Although these models are estimated using only the control-sample of "healthy" respondents, individual information on the explanatory variables in these models is also available in the SB-sample. Assuming that both samples behave similarly and that sample-selection effects are adequately controlled for by the set of exogenous variables in the hazard function (by including for instance age, education, ill health and strenuous work), we can calculate theoretical labor market probabilities for respondents in both samples.

Table 7.5 gives the distribution of labor market probabilities among "healthy" DI-insured people and among those who entered the DI-program in 1980. The table clearly shows that the latter, the DI-entrants, have unfavorable labor market opportunities. They appear to have relatively small theoretical probabilities of re-employment and relatively high theoretical probabilities of unemployment. At first glance, the differences with respect to the unemployment probability may seem rather small due to the fact that age is positively related to the probability of DI-entry, while affecting the unemployment probability negatively. When age is controlled for, however, they become very substantial.

Table 7.5    Calculated Unemployment and Re-Employment Probabilities; DI-Insured and DI-Entrants in 1980

|  | DI-Insured | DI-entrants |
|---|---|---|
| **1. Unemployment probability (%)** | | |
| 0.0 - 1.0 | 16.5 | 18.8 |
| 1.0 - 2.0 | 33.1 | 25.1 |
| 2.0 - 3.0 | 21.6 | 18.8 |
| 3.0 - 4.0 | 12.8 | 14.2 |
| 4.0 - 5.0 | 8.1 | 9.1 |
| 5.0 - 6.0 | 4.5 | 9.0 |
| $\geq 6.0$ | 3.4 | 5.1 |
| | 100.0 | 100.0 |
| Average 1980 | 3.2 % | 4.7 % |
| **2. Re-employment probability (%)** | | |
| 0.0 - 10.0 | 6.6 | 15.9 |
| 10.0 - 20.0 | 12.6 | 33.3 |
| 20.0 - 30.0 | 18.5 | 23.5 |
| 30.0 - 40.0 | 20.1 | 13.8 |
| 40.0 - 50.0 | 21.8 | 9.4 |
| $\geq 50$ | 20.4 | 4.1 |
| | 100.0 | 100.0 |
| Average 1980 | 38.2 % | 23.6 % |

The extent to which labor market opportunities determine the probability of DI-entry will be assessed in chapter 10 where we estimate a model describing the probability of entering the DI-program.


## 7.7    Conclusions

With the purpose of developing reliable indicators for individual labor market opportunities, we estimated models describing the labor market histories of a random sample of employees.

Assuming that people are either employed or unemployed, we distinguished two "transition" probabilities; the probability of becoming unemployed and the probability of re-employment.

The specifications of the estimated reduced form models are based on concepts taken from the neoclassical job search theory and the dual labor market theory. The statistical modelling is derived from job search theory. We estimated a continuous time, two-state, multi-episode model for the duration of unemployment and employment spells [see Flinn and Heckman (1982) p. 45].

We find that people have increased probabilities to become unemployed when:
- they are young;
- they have no (extended) secondary vocational or general education;
- they are involved in strenuous work;
- regional unemployment is high;
- the minimum wage is high;
- they have been unemployed previously;
- they are immobile in the sense that they have not changed jobs voluntarily.

People have increased probabilities to become re-employed when:
- they are young;
- they have no (extended) secondary vocational or general education;
- they are involved in strenuous work;
- they do not have any health problems.

*Ceteris paribus*, the probability of re-employment increases during the spell of unemployment. Theoretically, this can be explained by an over time decline in the reservation wage, which dominates an over time decline in job offers.

The unemployment risk, defined as the probability of being unemployed, is found to be high for young, low-educated workers. Their high unemployment risk is caused by a high probability of becoming unemployed, which is only partly balanced by higher than average re-employment probabilities. At this point we noted that the introduction of schooling programs to reduce youth unemployment by improving the employment opportunities of low-educated, young unemployed, may be not as effective as expected, since these young people already have re-employment probabilities that are (much) higher than those of the average unemployed.

Since ill health is not found to increase the probability to become unemployed, we conclude that the overrepresentation of people with health problems among the unemployed is largely due to the fact that ill health tends to decrease re-employment probabilities and thereby lengthen the spell of unemployment.

The results are obtained from a database covering the decade from 1970 to 1980. They are conditional on the prevailing circumstances, that clearly have changed since then. As shown in chapter 2, unemployment started soaring not until the early eighties. While in our database unemployment spells of more than 12 months are a rare phenomenon, they are not in the 1980 decade. We should be careful, therefore, to generalize our conclusions beyond to the first, say, 12 months of unemployment. Our results do not necessarily apply to the more lengthy spells that can be observed today. It is very well possible that a 1980-1990 database would yield different results. For instance, the negative impact of vocational education on the re-employment probability may well become zero or even turn positive when unemployment spells continue beyond 12 months. Similarly, the positive duration time dependence of the re-employment probability may become negative when the unemployment spell becomes very long.[21]

Applying the estimated weights of the determinants of unemployment and re-employment probabilities to calculate the indicators of labor market opportunities, we find that the DI-entrants have less favorable labor market opportunities. Compared to the control-sample of "healthy" workers, DI-entrants run a high risk of becoming unemployed. Their predicted chances to regain employment are low.

# Notes

1. First drafts of these models have been presented in Aarts and Hop (1985).

2. The segmented labor market theory literature is surveyed by Taubman and Wachter (1986) and earlier by Cain (1976). For an empirical confrontation of dual labor market theory with neoclassical theory see e.g. Leigh (1978). The relevance of dual labor market theory for the Dutch labor market was studied by e.g. Valkenburg and Vissers (1979) and Aarts, Paul and De Neubourg (1983).

3. The theory of job search has been surveyed by Mortensen (1986) and earlier by Lippman and McCall (1976). See also Lancaster (1979), Flinn and Heckman (1982). For empirical work see for instance, Narendranathan and Nickell (1985), Lancaster and Chesher (1983), Kiefer and Neumann (1979). Analyses of the Dutch labor market using these particular methods have been published for instance by Kooreman and Ridder (1983), Ridder (1987), Van Opstal and Theeuwes (1986), and Theeuwes, Kerkhofs and Lindeboom (1990).

4. Indicative of the comparatively low labor force participation rates among females with dependent children are the participation rates of married women. In the 25-29 years age bracket only 18 percent of married women is participating. In the 30-34 and the 35-39 brackets participation rates are 16 and 17 percent. These figures refer to 1971. Although the participation rates of married women have increased over the decade (to 35 percent in 1979 in the 25-29 bracket, 28 percent in the 30-34 bracket and 32 in the 34-39 bracket), they are still rather low compared to those of unmarried women in these age brackets where participation rates range from 78 to 65 percent in 1979 [see Hartog & Theeuwes (1985)].

5. Such a decline was assessed by Kasper (1967), Holt (1970), Kiefer & Neumann (1979) and Feldstein & Poterba (1984).

6. A sufficient condition for the net effect of $r_t$ to be positive is the assumption of "log-concavity" of the wage offer probability density function.

7.
$$q(v) = \frac{(1/\sigma^2)^{1/\sigma^2}}{\Gamma(1/\sigma^2)} \cdot v^{1/\sigma^2-1} \cdot e^{v/\sigma^2} \qquad (v > 0)$$

8. Intuitively, this may be clear. Suppose no duration dependence exists in reality ($\alpha = 1$). Furthermore, suppose red-haired unemployed have a higher probability of re-employment while no indicator for hair color has been specified. The red-haired will be the first to leave unemployment, leaving behind the unemployed with a different head of hair, whose re-employment probability is smaller. As time elapses, the average probability will decrease. With no indicator on hair color, the decreasing probabilities will be reflected by an estimate for $\alpha$ that is smaller than 1 and might lead to the false conclusion of negative duration dependence.

9. Since no historical data on region of residence are available, all respondents are assumed to have been living in the province of their residence in 1980, during the entire observation period.

10. For a recent survey of empirical studies of the relation between unemployment and health see Schaufeli (1988).

11. Flinn & Heckman (1982) found that their estimation results are highly sensitive to the allowance of time-dependency in the explanatory variables.

12. The calculations were done using an Algol60 program, developed by J.P. Hop, using numerical procedures from the NAG library for the maximization of the likelihood.

13. Even in the USA or the UK, where female labor force participation is significantly higher than in the Netherlands, two thirds of currently participating women have interrupted their labor force participation at least once [Stewart & Greenhalgh (1984)].

14. Theeuwes et al. (1990), estimate a three state model, distinguishing a separate state "out of the labor force" (N). Among females, the probability of transition from employment (E) to non-participation (N) is positively affected by the presence of dependent children (the probability of transition from non-participation (N) to employment (E) is negatively affected). Therefore, if the transition from E to N is neglected, the effect of the presence of children on the probability of transition from E to U will biased negatively.

15. See note 8.

16. In the literature, negative as well as constant or positive duration dependence is assessed after controlling for unobserved heterogeneity. For instance, re-employment probabilities are found to increase with spell length ($\alpha>1$) by Nickell (1979a) and by Narendranathan, Nickell and Stern (1985), Lynch (1985) reports decreasing probabilities, whereas Lancaster (1979) finds constant re-employment probabilities. Using a Dutch sample, Theeuwes et al. (1990), who do not control for unobserved heterogeneity, arrive at estimates of $\alpha$ very close to the our estimates in the second pair of columns in table 7.3.

17. With 20 percent of the 1979 female labor force working in only two occupations, 29 percent in three, 36 percent in four and over 50 percent in only eight occupations, the Dutch occupational structure is rather strictly segregated. Most of these occupations are in line with "typically feminine" housework and caretaking activities [see e.g., Van Mourik (1988)].

18. Theeuwes et al. (1990) report insignificant impacts of the education variables on the re-employment probabilities of men and significantly positive education effects on the re-employment probabilities of women.

19. E.g., Ridder and Kooreman (1983) report a negative impact of regional unemployment on the female re-employment probability.

20. Theeuwes et al. (1990) find that, among females, the probability of transition from unemployment to non-participation is positively affected by the presence of children.

21. It is reassuring to find, however, that the results of Theeuwes et al. (1990), that are based on a (Dutch) sample of labor market histories from the 1980-1985 period, do not indicate any major shift in the parameters of unemployment and re-employment probabilities in the early 1980s.

Chapter 8

# FIRM SPECIFIC DISABILITY INCIDENCE RATES

## 8.1    Introduction[1]

Formally, the "Industrial Associations" ("bedrijfsverenigingen") decide whether a worker who applies for DI-benefits, will be admitted to the program. The decision to file a claim is made by the worker himself. According to the behavioral model developed in chapter 3, this decision is determined by health status, labor market opportunities, preferences and other factors.

In the process leading to DI-entry, employers play a potentially important role. They determine the level of safety provisions and the production technology, that affect the risk of being injured on the job and, therefore, the probability DI-entry. Employers' reactions to the occurrence of functional limitations, whatever their cause, may be another important factor in the disability process. By accommodating to functional limitations, for instance, employers may reduce the objective need to apply for DI-benefits, thereby also reducing the probability of DI-entry.

The potential influence of employers on the process of DI-enrolment may be especially relevant in the context of the Dutch DI-program where, as has been illustrated in chapter 5, program regulations and administration practices appear to permit private interests to affect the ultimate result of the admission procedure. In this chapter we argue that employers may often have an interest in the award of DI-benefits to their employees. Our focus is on the firm's influence on the process leading to the disability status of its employees. We try to assess to what extent the inter-firm variance in DI-incidence rates, i.e., the relative number of employees enrolling the DI-program, is accounted for by indicators related to the probability of occurrence of functional limitations and by indicators related to the firm's response to these limitations. We will argue that the firm's response depends on the cost-benefit balance of retaining (or replacing) functionally impaired employees.

In section 8.2, the relevance of the DI-program to the firm is elaborated. In section 8.3, a model to examine the determinants of the variation in DI-incidence rates among firms is proposed, estimated, and discussed. From the estimation results, a measure for the firm specific risk of DI-program enrolment will be derived in section 8.4. In the individual disability probability model (chapter 10), this measure will be included as an indicator for the DI-risk to which an individual employee is exposed. Section 8.5 concludes.

## 8.2    The DI-Program and the Firm

By its choice of production technology, the level of safety provisions, and the response to functional limitations, a firm is likely to have an impact on the probability of DI-entry of its employees.

According to standard economic theory, a profit maximizing firm will choose the production technology and level of safety provisions that yield an optimal injury probability. To the firm the risk of injury is optimal if a further reduction would add more to the firm's costs than to its benefits. The optimal response strategy with respect to the occurrence of functional limitations is determined similarly; A firm will increase its efforts to retain employees with functional limitations within the firm as long as the costs of retainment, i.e., the costs of accommodation, do not exceed the benefits.

The optimal injury probability, the optimal level of safety provisions, and the optimal accommodation strategy depend on whether the risks are known to employers and employees, whether disability insurance is provided, whether the insurance is mandatory, whether insurance premiums are experience-rated, to name only a few important factors [see e.g., Worrall and Butler (1986)].[2]

Like in many other countries, in the Netherlands, the risk of income losses due to disability is covered by social insurance: the Sickness Benefit program, that provides income replacing benefits during short spells of disability and the DI-program that covers long term disability. Unlike those in most other Western countries, these programs cover disabilities stemming from vocational diseases and work injuries as well as disabilities originating from injuries and diseases that are not related to job performance.

The firms' contributions to the DI-program are levied as a flat rate payroll tax, uniform across all firms. DI-premiums do not depend on the firm specific disability risk. It is common practice, however, to supplement the statutory Sickness and DI-benefits up to 100% of the previous net wage during the first one or two years of disability.[3] For the firms involved, such provisions add a type of experience rating to the DI-program creating a link between the firms' DI-incidence rates and their disability-related outlays. These supplementary allowances are part of the employees' fringe benefits. In some sectors they are negotiated by trade unions and employers. In the Dutch context, DI-enrolment usually implies a permanent separation of employer and employee. DI-enrolment, then, may be regarded as one way of dissolving a labor contract. Other ways of employer-employee separation are:

- a voluntary quit of the employee;
- mandatory retirement (usually at the age of 65);
- involuntary discharge through enrolment in the unemployment program;
- voluntary retirement through enrolment in an early retirement program.

If the initiative of contract dissolution is partly with the employer, the discharge is likely to be realized through either involuntary enrolment in the unemployment program, early retirement, or enrolment in the DI-program.

In general, firms are inclined to dissolve a labor contract if continued employment is likely to be inefficient, that is, if continuation adds more to the firms costs than to its revenues. Employment may have become unprofitable because the job has turned redundant or because the worker is no longer sufficiently productive and needs to be replaced. In the latter case the worker has become "non-employable" [see Van Praag & Halberstadt (1980), Van Praag & Emanuel (1983)].

Employees and employers will value the alternative discharge routes differently. Taken from the viewpoint of the employee, becoming unemployed under the Unemployment Program is less attractive than entering the DI-program. The employee is likely to prefer the DI-status since the net replacement rate of unemployment benefits will decline in due course and, in case the unemployed is younger than 57.5 years, unemployment benefits will be means tested after 30 months of unemployment. Moreover, unlike the DI-beneficiary, the UP-beneficiary is obliged to search for and accept suitable job offers. The second alternative, entering an Early Retirement program, is still more attractive than DI-entry. The status of Early Retiree involves a minimum of stigma costs and a net income replacement of 85% to 90%. As an "Early Retiree" the employee enjoys entitlement to ER benefits until the age of 65, whereas the status of DI-beneficiary provides no absolute guarantee that the stream of DI-benefits will flow until 65, although actually few beneficiaries loose DI-entitlement.

Taken from the viewpoint of the firm, workers who are not sufficiently productive become "non-employable" unless the employer is able either to reduce the costs of their employment or to increase their productivity. Whether these "non-employable" workers will be labeled as "Unemployed", "Disabled", or "Early Retiree" is only relevant to the extent that it affects the firm's lay-off costs.

To a firm that wishes to lay-off a "non-employable" employee, the feasibility of the first alternative, a lay-off through the Unemployment Program, depends on whether the firm is able to come up with a legitimate ground for dismissal. Dismissals are subject to the approval of regional Employment Exchange Agencies (*Gewestelijke arbeidsbureaus*). In general, permits will not be granted unless the job - not the worker - has become redundant or personal work relations have been seriously damaged. These prerequisites entail limited replacement opportunities. In practice, firms will rarely be allowed to replace a discharged, inefficient worker by a more productive worker within three months, especially if the discharged worker has seniority [Van den Boom (1985)]. The firms' contributions to the Unemployment Program are not experience-rated, although 13 percent of all firms provide extra benefits to supplement the statutory Unemployment income [SoZaWe (1985)].

The firm may find the second alternative, dismissal under an Early Retirement scheme, relatively costly. Particularly the firms that run their own Early Retirement fund, will bear the full costs of every employee who is awarded early retirement benefits. On the other hand, firms that participate in a branch-wise organized ER fund, will be able to pass on part of the costs of early retirement to the other contributors to the fund. Furthermore, the feasibility of the early retirement alternative is restricted. First, the firm has to participate in an Early Retirement fund. This implies that an estimated 60% of the firms (together employing about 30% of all privately employed workers) are excluded from the early retirement option. Then, if the firm is participating, this redundancy option is open only to workers older than 61 who have been with the firm for at least ten years.[4] The latter restriction rules out another 35% of the workers in the relevant age bracket (see section 2.2).

Of course, firms are not free to choose among the alternative "exit" programs. Depending on actual circumstances, the number of redundancy options will often be less than three. Enrolment in the Disability Insurance program is open only if the inefficient worker concerned has some sort of physical or mental limitation that interferes with job performance. Although this essential feature of the DI-program could reduce the relevance of the program as an alternative for early retirement or unemployment, many employees, especially the seniors, are likely to qualify for DI-benefits due to the design of the program and the way it is administrated.

Considering the alternatives we conclude that, the DI-program may often prove to be a feasible and financially attractive way to discharge employees whose employment has become inefficient. It is relatively cheap, as compared to Early Retirement, and, unlike the Unemployment program, it involves no restrictions on the replacement of the discharged employees. Finally, it often is a socially acceptable alternative both for employers and employees.

### Costs and Benefits of DI-enrolment

In this chapter, we study the variation in the firms' inclination to use the exit route of DI-enrolment. Generally, the DI-alternative may become relevant to the firm when functional limitations of any kind or severity occur among one or more of its employees.

Economic theory predicts that the firm's response to the occurrence of functional limitations will depend on the relative cost of DI-enrolment versus the relative cost of retainment of the impaired employee. The costs incurred by DI-enrolment or retainment may vary among firms and among the employees within one firm. In the short run, given the firm's technology and the level of safety provision, the cost-benefit balance of DI-enrolment will depend, for instance, on the efficiency of the job held by the impaired worker. Clearly, the incentive to retain the impaired worker will be very small if his job is redundant. In case the impaired worker's job is considered to be efficient, enrolment into the DI-program will imply the hiring of a replacement. The relative cost of DI-enrolment will then depend on the cost of recruiting and training this replacement. The relative cost of DI-enrolment will further depend on whether the firm is obliged to provide supplemental benefits to their disabled employees. Below, the cost-benefit approach of DI-enrolment is further elaborated.

Consider a firm i with a worker $x_1$ who is assigned to job y. If this worker is so unfortunate as to become functionally impaired, the firm may wish either to retain $x_1$ in employment or to induce $x_1$'s enrolment in the DI-program.

DI-enrolment will be the preferable alternative to the firm if the benefits of enrolment exceed the benefits of retainment, that is, if the following condition holds,

$$\max \{(p.q_2 - w_2) - c_{rec} - c_{DI}, - c_{DI}\} > (p.q_1 - w_1) - c_{adj}$$

with p denoting the market price of the firm's product, $q_1$ and $w_1$ the impaired employee's productivity and wage respectively, $q_2$ and $w_2$ the productivity and wage of a worker $x_2$ who could replace $x_1$, $c_{rec}$ the cost of recruitment of $x_2$ (including the cost of training), $c_{DI}$ the cost of DI-enrolment (e.g., the supplemental DI-benefits) and $c_{adj}$ the cost of adjustments necessary to restore $x_1$'s productivity up to level $q_1$.

If $(p.q_2 - w_2) - c_{rec} < 0$, one could say that the impaired worker's job is redundant since it can not be (re-)occupied profitably. In that case the firm will be inclined to retain the impaired employee only if the net benefit of retainment of the impaired worker, $(p.q_1 - w_1) - c_{adj}$, exceeds the net benefit of DI-enrolment which, in case replacement is not profitable, is negative and equal to $-c_{DI}$.

If job y is not redundant, that is if $(p.q_2 - w_2) - c_{rec} > 0$, the benefits to the firm of DI-enrolment and replacement are equal to the net contribution to the firm's results of worker $x_2$, minus the cost incurred by DI-enrolment, $c_{DI}$. The benefits of retaining the impaired employee are equal to the net contribution of the impaired worker after adjustments to his impairment have been made, denoted by $(p.q_1 - w_1) - c_{adj}$ (the value of his productivity minus his wage, minus the cost of adjustment). If the benefits of replacing the impaired worker exceed the benefits of retainment, the firm will be in favor of DI-enrolment.[5]

The decision rule shows that even if the impaired employee's job is redundant and a replacement would be inefficient, that is if $(p.q_2 - w_2) - c_{rec} < 0$, the firm may still be inclined to retain the impaired employee if the retained employee's net contribution to the firm's proceeds minus the costs of adjustment exceed the costs of DI-enrolment, $- c_{DI}$.

The cost-benefit approach to the determinants of the firm specific DI-incidence rates suggests that the firm's inclination to retain workers who have become functionally impaired depends on:

- p, the firm's proceeds; a rise in p will increase the net contribution of the impaired employee, which, in case the job is redundant, will increase the inclination to retain the impaired employee. If, on the other hand the job is not redundant - and the higher p, the more likely it is not -, a rise in p may reduce the inclination to retain if the productivity of the replacement exceeds the productivity of the impaired employee after adjustment;
- $q_1$ , the impaired employees productivity; the higher the post-adjustment productivity the more inclined the firm will be to retain;
- $w_1$ , labor costs of the impaired employee; by lowering the labor costs of impaired employees, for instance through subsidizing, the firm can be made more inclined to retain them within the firm;
- $c_{adj}$ , the cost of adjustment to the impairments; lowering the costs of adjustments to restore or improve the match of the impaired employee and his job will induce a rise in the firm's inclination to retain the impaired person;
- $q_2$ , the expected productivity of a replacement and $w_2$ , the labor costs of a replacement $x_2$ ; the higher the expected net contribution of a replacing employee, the less inclined the firm will be to retain the impaired worker;
- $c_{rec}$ , the cost of recruiting and training a replacement; the positive effect of $c_{rec}$ implies that the probability that a firm will be inclined to retain its employees after the occurrence of functional impairments will be higher if they have scarce skills. If a replacement would need to go through a long period of job- or firm specific training to acquire the impaired employee's skills, replacement is not a very attractive alternative;
- $c_{DI}$ , the cost of DI-enrolment; the costs incurred to the firm by DI-enrolment of its employees will have a positive impact on the firm's inclination to retain functionally impaired employees.

The cost-benefit framework helps to unravel the determinants of the firm's preferences with respect to DI-enrolment. The extent to which these preferences have an impact on DI-incidence rates depends of course on the behavior of the DI-program gatekeepers and of the impaired employees themselves. Whether or not firms are successful in retaining impaired employees or making them apply, specifically depends on whether the status of DI-beneficiary is attractive to the employee and on the design and administration of the DI-program.

## 8.3    A Model of the Firm Specific Disability Incidence

### 8.3.1    Introduction

In the preceding section, we suggested that the DI-incidence rate in a firm is largely determined by the occurrence of functional limitations among its personnel and by the firm's response to this occurrence depending on cost-benefit considerations. Below, we will estimate a model describing the variation in DI-incidence rate among firms. This exploratory analysis may provide empirical support for the idea that, to some extent, a firm's DI-incidence rate is the outcome of efficiency considerations. In the following subsections we introduce the database, present a formal model and the estimation results.

### 8.3.2    Data and Model

A sample of firms has been derived from the random sample of 2025 persons covered by the DI-program in 1980.[6] All 1954 respondents that were employed at the time of the interviews, were asked permission to contact their employers. In total, 1602 employees granted this permission and gave name and address of their employers. These consents appeared to be uncorrelated with demographic character-istics of the employees.

The 1602 employees represent 1502 different firms. The nonresponse of firms is restricted to 191 cases, randomly distributed among the Industrial Associations. Consequently, the sample of firms contains 1311 observations.

This sample is not a random selection of firms settled in the Netherlands. As it was derived from a random sample of employees, the theoretical probability of firm i to be included in the sample, $Pr_i${sample}, is positively correlated with firm size; The more workers employed by the firm, the higher the probability that one of them is included in the random sample of employees and, therefore, the higher the probability that the firm is included in the sample of firms. By reweighing the original sample cases using weights that are inversely proportional to the theoretical probability of inclusion in the sample, therefore, the resulting sample takes on the properties of a random sample of firms that are settled in the Netherlands.[7]

Comparison with the total population of firms has revealed that, with respect to the firm size distribution, this reweighed sample is not significantly different from the population of firms [Aarts (1984), pp. 16-17)].[8]

A further indication of the accuracy of the database can be found by comparing the actual DI-incidence in the population of insured workers with the DI-incidence rates as estimated using the sample of firms. For each Industrial Association, the actual DI-incidence can be calculated using their annual reports. These incidence

rates can be compared with an estimated DI-incidence based on the DI-entrants reported by the firms in the sample. By taking the sum, over all sampled firms, of
the number of reported DI-entrants and dividing by the sum of the number of employees, we get an estimate of the average DI-incidence rate based on sample
statistics.
In formula:

$$\frac{y_j}{s_j} = \frac{\sum\limits_{i=1}^{m} n_{ij}}{\sum\limits_{i=1}^{m} s_{ij}}$$

where $y_j/s_j$ is the DI-incidence rate within Industrial Association j, and m the
number of sampled firms affiliated with this particular Industrial Association.
Table 8.1 reveals that the estimated DI-incidence rate is quite different from the
actual rate. The reweighed sample of firms generates estimates of the DI-incidence
rate that, on average, are 0.52 percentage points (or more than 20%) below the
actual DI-incidence in the observation period. At the same time, significant differences among the main Industrial Associations become apparent. At the extremes
are Construction Industry, for which we arrive at an estimate of 1.89 DI-awards
per 100 workers insured, while the actual number is 3.40, and Medical Services with
an estimated number of 1.73 and an actual number of 1.29 per 100 workers insured.

Table 8.1    **Mean Incidence of DI-Awards During 1978 and 1979 per Industrial
Association. Population Statistics and Estimates Derived from the
Reweighed Sample of Firms.**

|  | manyears insured (x1000) 1978/79 | | DI-Awards per 100 insured | | | percentage of firms with less than 50 employees |
|---|---|---|---|---|---|---|
|  |  |  | calculated sample statistics | actual[a] population statistics | rel. differ. |  |
|  |  |  | (1) | (2) | [(1)-(2)]/(2) |  |
| Joint Administration Office | 1, 891 | (55) | 1.72 | 2.46 | -0.30 | 36 |
| Construction | 296 | ( 9) | 1.89 | 3.40 | -0.44 | 63 |
| Retail & Wholesale | 365 | (10) | .97 | 1.51 | -0.36 | 56 |
| Medical Services | 602 | (17) | 1.73 | 1.29 | +0.34 | 29 |
| Others | 302 | ( 9) | 1.63 | 2.29 | -0.28 | 45 |
| Total | 3, 456 | (100) | 1.66 | 2.18 | -0.24 | 41 |

[a]  Source: Annual Reports of the Industrial Associations.

Apart from the Medical Services, the ranking of the Industrial Associations in order of estimated DI-incidence rates, appears to be similar to the ranking in order of actual DI-incidence rates. Comparison of the population statistics in column (2) with the deviations in the third column of table 8.1, yields a positive correlation between the actual DI-incidence rate and the level of underreporting; The higher the actual disability risk, the larger the discrepancy between actual and estimated DI-incidence. The obvious conclusion is that, either some sampled firms report less than their actual number of DI-entrants, or firms with a low DI-incidence rate are overrepresented in the sample. Of course, a combination of the two is also possible.

One could think of at least two reasons for the overrepresentation of low-risk firms. First, there is nonresponse. Possibly, those sampled workers (5 percent) who did not grant permission to contact their employers, are employed by firms with a DI-incidence rate higher than average. Potentially more important, may be the nonresponse of firms themselves (13 percent). When asked for information in the context of a study on the determinants of disability, some high risk firms may be unwilling to cooperate in order to preserve the firm's privacy, whereas low risk firms would not mind outsiders to know of their disability records.

A second reason for a more than proportional presence of low risk firms could be a mere artefact of the sampling procedure. While the sample of firms resulted from a random sample of insured, healthy workers (i.e., workers who do not receive Sickness or DI-benefits), there is at least one employee within each sampled firm who did not enter the DI-program in the relevant period. As a consequence, the expected DI-incidence rate in the sampled firms will be lower than the population average. The smaller the firms, the larger this discrepancy will be. Among firms with no more than five employees, for instance, one can expect a discrepancy of on average 20 percent. Among firms with ten employees, this type of error would amount to 10 percent, etc.

The low estimate (1.66) of the overall DI-incidence rate generated by the sample of firms may also be due to a tendency to report less than the actual number of DI-entrants. Many firms, especially smaller ones, will not keep systematic records of their DI-incidence rates. Assuming that firms consider high disability rates to affect their image negatively, there may be a, conscious or subconscious, tendency towards underreporting. Again, this type of error has a more serious impact on the accuracy of the measured DI-incidence rate in smaller firms than it has in large firms. One "omitted" DI-entrant in a firm of five employees, for instance, results in an error of 20 percent, while in a firm of 50 employees the error would only be 2 percent.

The possible causes of the discrepancies between actual and estimated population DI-incidence rates, mentioned above, suggest that the discrepancy is related to firm size. The figures in the last column of table 8.1 seem to confirm this hunch.

Construction, the industry with the largest difference (44 percent), also has the largest share of firms with less than 50 employees (63 percent). On the other hand, Health Services appear to have the smallest share of firms with less than 50 employees (29 percent).

Considering the size of the difference between actual and estimated DI-incidence rates, one may doubt whether the above reasons provide sufficient explanation. However, a further, industry-wise, analysis of the discrepancies between reported and actual DI-incidence rates, has not revealed any systematic pattern in the variance of the level of underreporting beyond the factors mentioned above [see Aarts (1984)]. By restricting the analysis to firms with at least 50 employees, we hope to avoid serious biases in the estimation of the determinants of the firm specific DI-incidence. We should however be careful in interpreting the estimated effects, especially the effects of the industry dummies, that probably will absorb the inter-industry variance in measurement error.

Clearly, our database has some shortcomings. The available data do not allow for an analysis of firm specific DI-incidence rates beyond the exploratory stage. The available information was primarily gathered for the purpose of analyzing the determinants of disability behavior at the micro level, i.e., the level of the DI-insured worker. The analysis of firm specific DI-incidence rates, therefore, is of a secondary nature. Moreover, the partial nonresponse especially on financial issues and on the firm's performance has been rather large (see section 4.4) which has limited the range of possible explanatory variables even further. Compared to other Dutch surveys, however, used for the analysis of firm-wise variation in DI-incidence rates, it does have some advantages as well. With 1311 observations it is relatively large and, unlike other surveys, it contains observations from all branches of industry.[9]

**The Dependent Variable: The Disability Incidence Rate**

Figure 8.1 shows how the DI-incidence rate is distributed in the reweighed sample of firms with at least 50 employees. One fifth of the firms appears to have had zero DI-awards during the years 1978/1979. The highest number observed is 15.2 awards per 100 employees. The average number of DI-awards per 100 employees, taken over the sampled firms, is 1.70. Figure 8.1 suggests that the DI-incidence rate is approximately lognormally distributed.

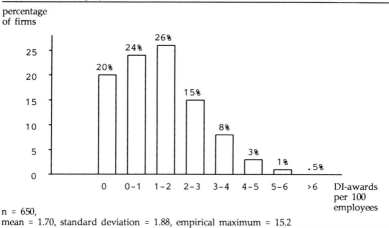

**Figure 8.1**   **Number of DI-Awards per 100 Employees Insured in Firms with at least 50 Employees, 1978-1979.**

n = 650,
mean = 1.70, standard deviation = 1.88, empirical maximum = 15.2

## The explanatory variables
We distinguish two categories of explanatory variables:
- Factors related to the probability of injury within a firm,
- Determinants of the firm's response to the occurrence of functional limitations.

The first category contains the variables that are indicative of the probability that functional limitations will occur. These are the variables related to the firm's production technique, the "vulnerability" of its employees, and the level of safety provisions. The second category contains variables that indicate the firm's policies with respect to retainment of functionally impaired employees and the cost of their replacement.

The available variables are introduced below. First the variables that are meant to control for variation in the DI-incidence rate resulting from variation in the kind of work and work conditions. In this category the **INDUSTRY** dummies are specified. Furthermore, as a proxy for the "vulnerability" of the firm's employees we specify a variable **ln(EMP50PLUS/s)**, indicating the number of employees older than 50 years as a percentage of the total number of employees (s). Since the probability of functional limitations increases with age, we expect that the firm's DI-incidence rate is positively related to the share of elderly employees [Smulders (1984)[10], pp. 236-249].[11]

The percentage of female employees, **ln(EMFEM/s)** is another variable that presumably summarizes a number of firm characteristics that relate to the probability of occurrence of functional limitations. We have reason to expect a negative impact of the share of female employees on the DI-incidence rate. First, because of the relatively low participation rates, especially of elder women, firms with substantial female employment tend to be firms with relatively young employees.[12] As the disability risk tends to be lower for younger workers, it will also appear to be lower in firms with many female workers in case the age structure of the firm's population is not satisfactorily specified otherwise. Second, many working women hold part-time jobs,[13] and part-time jobs appear to be less disabling than full-time jobs, due to the  fact that part-time work implies a smaller amount of exposure time and a larger stock of recuperation time, where the latter has a positive effect on work resumption [Vrijhof (1985), Smulders (1984, p. 198]]. With no indicator of the proportion of part-timers available, the coefficient for the number of female workers is expected to absorb this effect. And third, jobs held by women appear to be less "risky" especially with respect to the work environment. In 1980, for instance, 19 percent of working women reported to be working in a noisy environment, 13 percent reported to be engaged in dirty work, whereas 27 percent of working males were involved in noisy work and 35 percent in dirty work [CBS A (1984) p. 131]. Lacking a firm specific indicator for work conditions, the impact of disabling job demands will be partly revealed by the female workers coefficient. A further indication for the health risks within a firm may be provided by the variable Medical Guidance (**MEDGUID**), that indicates to what extent medical services are available to the firm. These medical services may include the examination of new hirees, periodical personnel check-ups, and systematic reviews of work conditions. By introducing a company medical service and preventive health care measures, probably most firms are aiming at an improvement of the health status of their personnel. In as far as these measures are effective, one should expect the firm's health care efforts to have a negative impact on the number of employees applying for DI-benefits.

On the other hand, the availability of institutionalized medical services within a firm might also induce a relatively large number of DI-applicants. First, because periodical check-ups may lead to the revelation of health problems in an early stage and, thus, to DI-applications that otherwise perhaps would not be filed at all, or would be filed later on. And second, because company boards may be tempted to use the company medical service as an instrument to provide medical support for lay-offs through the DI-program of employees who cannot meet minimal productivity requirements anymore. With respect to the effect of medical guidance on sickness absenteeism, earlier research has yielded ambiguous results. Positive as well as negative effects have been reported [Philipsen (1969), Dijkstra (1977), Smulders (1984b)]. Draaisma (1983) provides empirical support for a negative impact of medical guidance on the firm's DI-incidence rate.

Another indicator of the probability of occurrence of functional limitations in the firm is its policy on workers' consultation. The variable **CONSULT** indicates whether the firm provides its employees -at all functional levels- the institution-alized opportunity to interfere with the planning, organization and evaluation of everyday work activities. Workers' consultation is expected to affect the DI-incidence rate negatively in two ways; First, it is believed to influence the sickness and disability behavior of employees because it presumably enhances their commit-ment to the firm and thereby creates a stimulus not to be absent from work. With regard to short term absenteeism this hypothesis has been empirically confirmed in a number of Dutch studies [Nijhuis and Soeters (1982), Smulders (1984, p. 20)]. Despite the essential differences between (short term) sickness and (long term) disability, the same relation may hold for behavioral responses to the DI-program [Nijhuis and Soeters (1982)]. Second, a process of regular consultation of employ-ees may generate proposals for corrective responses to health problems and hazard-ous work conditions, and thus may lead to a decrease in disability incidence.

Turning to the second category of explanatory variables, we introduce variables that presumably affect the feasibility of retaining (or replacing) individual employees with functional limitations and the balance of benefits and costs of retainment or replacement.

A factor that probably affects the feasibility of retaining employees with functional limitations is the size of the firm (**FIRMSIZE**). Since the probability that an impaired employee can be assigned to a suitable job will be larger if there are many (different) jobs performed within the firm, one might expect the DI-incidence rate in a firm to be negatively correlated with firm size. Firm size, however, is strongly correlated with other firm characteristics that may affect DI-incidence. Therefore, the estimated effect of firm size is very sensitive to the choice of other explanatory variables. The effects of firm size on sickness or disability absenteeism reported in the literature vary accordingly from significantly negative [Kovach (1978), Ruser (1984)] to significantly positive [Nijhuis and Soeters (1982)]. Often an insignificant effect is reported [see Smulders (1984), pp. 110-117].

Next, we introduce two "policy" variables that are also related to the feasibility of retaining impaired employees. The variable Job Adaptation Policy (**JOBADAPT**) indicates whether it is the firm's common policy to adapt job demands to functional limitations that result from sickness or accidents, or from normal degenerative processes. These adaptations may refer to a reduction of working hours, a relaxation of productivity demands, or a transfer to another, more suitable, job. A policy of job adaptation is expected to affect the DI-incidence rate negatively, since it probab-ly increases the possibility of retaining impaired employees.[14]

The second "policy" variable, Social Guidance Policy (**SOCGUID**), refers to the firm's approach to its employees during extended periods of sickness absence. It indicates the firm's effort to stay in touch with the absentees by paying visits or other tokens of attention. Presumably, such contacts enhance the workers' attach-

ment to their work and to the company. By paying attention, the firm may help
to prevent impaired employees to apply for DI-benefits. Social Guidance Policy,
therefore, is expected to have a negative impact on the DI-incidence rate.[15]

Finally, we are able to specify three variables that may be indicative of the cost-
benefit balance of retaining (or replacing) employees with functional limitations.
The dummy variable "Supplementary Benefits" (**SUPBEN**) indicates whether a firm
supplements the statutory Sickness and Disability Benefits to 100% of the net pre-
disability wage. Such a provision adds an element of experience rating to the
financing of the DI-program. It increases the firm's costs of a lay-off through the
DI-program and, therefore, is expected to affect the DI-incidence rate negatively.
On the other hand, the provision of supplementary benefits raises the disability
benefit income of the discharged employees. Other things equal, this may encourage
employees to apply for DI-benefits causing an increase of the firm's DI-incidence
rate. Whether the balance effect of SUPBEN is negative or positive, therefore, is an
empirical matter.[16]
The average level of education (**EDUC**) within the firm is also taken to be indicative
for the firm's costs of DI-entry. As mentioned earlier, economic theory predicts that
firms will put more effort in retaining functionally impaired employees, the more
costly their replacement is going to be. Assuming that a high level of education
is associated with relatively complex production techniques that, in turn, imply
relatively large investments in firm specific human capital, the replacement of highly
educated employees will be relatively expensive. Consequently, firms with specialized personnel have an incentive to retain functionally impaired employees, implying the expectation that the DI-incidence rate within these firms will be low.[17]
A change in the size of the firm may be another indication for the sign of the cost-
benefit balance of retaining functionally impaired employees. A decrease in the size
of employment shows that employees who left the firm have not been replaced.
Employment reductions, therefore, suggest that the benefits of retaining functionally
impaired employees are relatively small. A firm that seeks to reduce employment
may even have an incentive to make its marginally efficient employees apply for
DI-benefits while retaining its most productive employees. Since discharges through
DI-program enrolment may prove to be an attractive and feasible route, considering
the alternatives of discharge through Early Retirement or Unemployment, firms may
be tempted to screen their employees and select those who are likely to be reward-
ed DI-benefits in order to persuade them to apply for the DI-status. This way,
employment can be reduced at a minimum of costs both for the firm and the laid-
off employee. If the observed reductions in employment reflect the firms' preferences with respect to firm size, they are likely to be accompanied by relatively
high DI-incidence rates.
The expected positive impact of a decrease in employment is not necessarily

parallelled by an equally large negative impact of increasing employment. Firms that wish to expand the number of employees may well prefer recruitment on the (external) labor market to retainment of functionally impaired employees. Especially on a slack market, the probability that a firm succeeds in hiring productive replacements will be high. Under these circumstances the net benefit of external recruitment may well exceed the net benefit of retainment. Consequently, we expect the disincentive to retain impaired employees when employment decreases to be larger than the incentive to retain them when employment increases.

We, therefore, introduce a splined specification of the relative change in employment. The variable **ln(DECREASE/s)** indicates the relative reduction in employment, whereas **ln(INCREASE/s)** indicates the relative increase, according to the following definition:

$$\ln(\text{DECREASE}/s) = \begin{cases} 0 & \text{if } s_{79} - s_{77} \geq 0 \\ \ln\left[\dfrac{|s_{79} - s_{77}|}{s}\right] & \text{if } s_{79} - s_{77} < 0 \end{cases}$$

$$\ln(\text{INCREASE}/s) = \begin{cases} 0 & \text{if } s_{79} - s_{77} \leq 0 \\ \ln\left[\dfrac{|s_{79} - s_{77}|}{s}\right] & \text{if } s_{79} - s_{77} > 0 \end{cases}$$

where $s_{77}$ and $s_{79}$ denote the size of the firm ultimo 1977 and ultimo 1979, and s denotes the average firm size over the two-years period.

**Modelling the Firm Specific DI-Incidence Rate**

The dependent variable, representing the average number of DI-awards per 100 workers over the years 1978 and 1979, is censored, as the number of DI-awards is positive or zero. Consequently, application of the Tobit model seems to be appropriate for our purposes [Maddala (1983), pp. 149-156]. Figure 8.1 indicates that the assumption of a lognormal distribution of the DI-incidence, with parameters $\beta$ and $\sigma^2$, is not only convenient but also fairly realistic.

Defining $y_i$ as the number of DI-beneficiaries in firm i, who entered the DI-program during 1978 and 1979, the following model is applied;

$$\ln(y_i + 1) = \begin{cases} 0 & \text{if } y_i^* \leq 0 \\ y_i^* & \text{if } y_i^* > 0 \end{cases} \tag{8.1}$$

where

$$y_i^* = \beta'X_i + \varepsilon_i \qquad \varepsilon_i \sim (N, \sigma^2) \tag{8.2}$$

The index $y^*$ is a latent variable underlying the actual process of generating DI-awards. If $y^* \leq 0$, the observed number of DI-awards is zero. If $y^* > 0$, one ore more employees in firm i have been awarded DI-benefits during the 1978/1979 period. $X_i$ is a vector containing the explanatory variables, $\beta'$ the associated vector of regression coefficients.

If the DI-incidence rate, the number of DI-awards per 100 employees, is assumed to be lognormally distributed, then $\ln(y)$ follows a normal distribution. The Tobit model is estimated with $\ln(y)$ as the dependent variable. The natural logarithm of firm size, taken as an average over the years 1978 and 1979, is an element of vector $X_i$.

In our model, the DI-incidence rate depends on the relative number of employees over 50 years old, the relative number of female employees, and the relative change in the total number of employees, and a number of other variables contained in $A_0$. Hence,

$$\ln y - \ln s = A_0 + \alpha_1 \ln s + \beta_2 \ln(EM50PLUS/s) + \beta_3 \ln(EMFEM/s)$$

$$+ \beta_4 \ln(INCREASE/s) + \beta_5 \ln(DECREASE/s) \qquad (8.3)$$

Instead of (8.3) we have estimated (8.3'),

$$\ln y = A_0 + \beta_1 \ln s + \beta_2 \ln(EM50PLUS) + \beta_3 \ln(EMFEM) + \beta_4 \ln(INCREASE)$$

$$+ \beta_5 \ln(DECREASE) \qquad (8.3')$$

with

$$\beta_1 = (1 + \alpha_1 - \beta_2 - \beta_3 - \beta_4 - \beta_5) ,$$

from which the estimated "pure" firm size-effect, $\alpha_1$, on the DI-incidence rate can be calculated by

$$\alpha_1 = \beta_1 - (1 - \beta_2 - \beta_3 - \beta_4 - \beta_5) . \qquad (8.4)$$

The Tobit likelihood function is,

$$L = \prod_{y=0} \left\{ 1 - F(\beta'X , \sigma^2) \right\} \prod_{y>0} \left\{ \frac{1}{(2\pi\sigma^2)^{1/2}} \exp[- \tfrac{1}{2}\sigma^2(y - \beta'X)^2] \right\} \qquad (8.5)$$

where the first product is over the observations for which $y_i=0$ and the second over the observations $y_i>0$. Maximization of $\ln(L)$ yields consistent estimates of $\beta$ and $\sigma^2$.

Table 8.2 presents the, unweighed, sample statistics of the explanatory variables and the dependent.[18]

**Table 8.2    List of Variables. Sample Statistics**

| Variables | Mean | Standard Deviation | Minimum | Maximum |
|---|---|---|---|---|
| Ln(DI-Awards + 1) | 2.089 | 1.343 | 0 | 6.99 |
| D (Agriculture) | .006 | .078 | 0 | 1 |
| D (Steel Industry) | .178 | .383 | 0 | 1 |
| D (Construction Industry) | .089 | .357 | 0 | 1 |
| D (Other Industry) | .237 | .426 | 0 | 1 |
| D (Retail & Wholesale) | .102 | .302 | 0 | 1 |
| D (Other Commercial Services) | .183 | .387 | 0 | 1 |
| D (Health Services) | .080 | .272 | 0 | 1 |
| D (Other Noncomm. Services) | .125 | .331 | 0 | 1 |
| Ln(EM50PLUS + 1) | 2.868 | 2.013 | 0 | 9.03 |
| ln(EMFEM + 1) | 4.469 | 1.826 | 0 | 9.85 |
| Medical Guidance Policy | 1.126 | 1.394 | 0 | 3 |
| Workers Consultation Policy | 1.667 | .466 | 1 | 2 |
| Ln(Firm size) | 6.267 | 1.209 | 3.4 | 10.74 |
| Job Adaptation Policy | 2.486 | .762 | 1 | 3 |
| Social Guidance Policy | 2.787 | .390 | 1 | 3 |
| D (Supplementary Benefits) | .846 | .361 | 0 | 1 |
| Education level | 3.292 | .815 | 1 | 6 |
| Ln(INCREASE + 1) | 1.934 | 1.867 | 0 | 8.0 |
| Ln(DECREASE + 1) | .872 | 1.581 | 0 | 7.0 |

### 8.3.3    Estimation Results for the Tobit Model

The ML estimation results of the model in eq(8.1) are presented in table 8.3.
First, we consider the variables that are meant to control for variation in the DI-incidence rate resulting from the firm specific kind of work and work conditions. These variables are indicative for the probability that functional limitations will occur.

The INDUSTRY dummies are in this category. We already noted the apparent discrepancies between actual and reported DI-records in Construction Industry (with significant underreporting) and in Health Services (with significant overreporting). This explains why, contrary to expectations based on population statistics, the DI-incidence in Health Services appears to be higher, instead of lower, than in Construction Industry. For the other industries, the estimates reveal a plausible pattern. The DI-incidence rate appears to be low in Agriculture, in Retail & Wholesale, and in Other Commercial Services, while being relatively high in Steel Industry and Other Industries. Apparently, the specification of the industry dummies has served to absorb both the deviant response patterns in Construction and Health Services and the inter-industry variance in the disability risk originating from branch-specific work conditions.

As a proxy for the "vulnerability" of the firm's employees we have introduced variables indicating the number of employees older than 50 years, ln(EMP50PLUS), and the number of female employees, ln(EMFEM). Their effects are as expected.

The DI-incidence rate is high in firms with relatively many older employees, and low in firms that employ relatively many female workers. The positive age-effect is assumedly due to the positive relation between presence of functional limitations and age. The negative coefficient of the share of female employees assumedly summarizes a number of underlying relations; First, an age effect, due to the positive correlation of the proportion of females and the proportion of young employees. Second, a workload effect due to the less disabling character of part-time jobs that are often held by women. And, third, the effect of sex specific differences in work environment which on average is better for women than for men. The variable Medical Guidance (MEDGUID), indicating to what extent medical services are available to the firm, has zero impact on the DI-incidence rate. Apparently, the potential negative effects of the availability of institutionalized medical

Table 8.3    The Firm Specific DI-incidence Rate. Tobit Estimation Results

| Explanatory Variables | coefficients | t-values |
|---|---|---|
| Agriculture | - .4431 | - 1.079 |
| Steel | .2706 | 1.766 |
| Other Industry | .3238* | 2.122 |
| Retail & Wholesale | - .0456 | - .250 |
| Other Commercial Services | .1068 | .689 |
| Health Services | .3668 | 1.818 |
| Other Noncommercial Services | .2302 | 1.217 |
| Ln(Employees over 50) | .0603** | 2.953 |
| Ln(Female Employees) | - .0937* | - 2.624 |
| Medical Guidance Policy | - .0048 | - .163 |
| Workers' Consultation Policy | - .1247** | - 5.056 |
| Ln (Firm size) | .8620** | 15.701 |
| Job Adaptation Policy | - .0166 | - .343 |
| Social Guidance Policy | - .0306 | - .375 |
| D (Supplementary Benefits) | .0946 | .985 |
| Education | - .1805** | - 8.917 |
| Ln (Employment Increase) | .0070 | .295 |
| Ln (Employment Decrease) | .0818** | 2.803 |
| $\sigma^2$ | .8444** | 17.595 |
| Constant[a] | - 2.5463** | - 6.707 |
| Observations | 650 | |
| Log-likelihood | -854.9231 | |
| pseudo-$R^{2b}$ | .461 | |

[a]   The reference group contains firms in Construction Industry that do not provide supple-
      mentary Sickness or DI-benefits.
[b]   Cragg and Uhler (1970)
*,** Significant at 5 and 1 percent, respectively.

services outweigh possible, positive impacts on the DI-incidence rate that we mentioned before.

Finally, we have introduced the firm's policy on workers' consultation as an indicator of the probability of occurrence of functional limitations in the firm. As expected, firms that provide their employees with an institutionalized opportunity to interfere with planning, organization and evaluation of everyday work activities, appear to have smaller DI-incidence rates than other firms. Whether this negative impact is caused by an enhancement of the employees' commitment to the firm or by a timely revelation of health problems and hazardous work conditions, brought about by such policy, is of course difficult to tell. Without being able to precisely indicate how the firm's workers' consultation policy affects the DI-incidence rate, our analysis yields a strong negative effect.

The second category of explanatory variables that we have distinguished contains the variables indicating the firm's response to the occurrence of functional limitations. We have assigned the variable FIRMSIZE to this category because we think that the possibilities of finding commensurate jobs for impaired workers is easier, the larger the firm. The "pure" firm size coefficient can be calculated using eq.(8.4). It is found to be negative, as expected, and equal to -.0826.

The feasibility of retaining (or replacing) individual employees with functional limitations was assumed to depend on the firm's policy towards functionally impaired employees and towards disability in general. We, therefore, expected a negative impact of the variables Job Adaptation Policy (JOBADAPT, indicating whether it is the firm's common policy to adapt job demands to functional limitations), and of Social Guidance Policy (SOCGUID, indicating the firm's effort to keep in touch with its employees during extended periods of sickness). In fact, the respective coefficient estimates appear to be virtually zero.

This does not necessarily imply, however, that these policies are ineffective. We will illustrate this point by referring to branch-wise estimation results presented in table A.8.1 in the appendix to this chapter. For merely technical reasons -to facilitate the calculation of an adequate, individually varying, instrument of the firm-specific Disability Risk- we have estimated the Tobit model for each branch separately. The effects of both policy variables appear to vary among the industries. For instance, Social Guidance Policy leads to lower DI-incidence rates in Steel Industry, Construction and in Other Commercial Services (Transportation, Banking, Insurance etc.), whereas in Other Industry (other than Steel and Construction) and in Retail and Wholesale, Social Guidance has only a small effect or even induces an increase in DI-enrolment.

With respect to the impact of Job Adaptation Policy the results are similar. Such policy seems to induce an increase of DI-incidence rates in Steel Industry and Other Commercial Services, while causing lower than average DI-incidence rates in Other Industry and Other Noncommercial Services. The branch-wise results suggest that these policies may well be effective, be it that the effect may be negative as well as positive. The (unexpected) positive effects may be the outcome of the firms' efforts to "monitor" the process leading to the DI-entry of its employees. These policies, then, particularly Social Guidance Policy, may provide the institutional instruments to enhance the employees' inclination to apply for DI-benefits.[19]

Although the sign of the policy coefficients differ, the combined overall impact of the two policy variables appears to be negative in most branches; the estimated, branch-wise differences in DI-incidence rates between firms with and firms without a policy of job adaptation and social guidance are presented in table 8.4.

The combination of these policies appears to reduce the DI-incidence rate substantially. The reduction varies from 11 percent in Steel Industry and in Other Commercial Services, to 67 percent in Other Noncommercial Services, with the exception of Other Industry, where the overall impact is zero, and of Retail and Wholesale,

**Table 8.4    The Branch-Wise Average DI-Incidence by Job Adaptation, Social Guidance and Medical Guidance**

| DI-Incidence[a] in: | Firms without Disability Policies | Firms with Job Adaptation and Social Guidance Policies | | Firms with Job Adaptation, Social, and Medical Guidance Policies | |
|---|---|---|---|---|---|
| | (1) | (2) | (2)-(1) | (3) | (3)-(1) |
| Steel Industry | 2.30 | 2.05 | ( -.25) | 1.74 | ( -.56) |
| Construction | 3.84 | 2.24 | (-1.60) | 1.24 | (-2.60) |
| Other Industry | 1.82 | 1.81 | ( -.01) | 1.82 | ( .00) |
| Retail & Wholesale | 1.16 | 1.42 | ( .26) | .86 | ( -.30) |
| Other Commercial Services | 1.58 | 1.41 | ( -.17) | 1.65 | ( .07) |
| Health Services | 1.94 | 1.25 | ( -.69) | 1.68 | ( -.26) |
| Other Noncommercial Services | 6.26 | 2.05 | (-4.21) | 2.06 | (-4.20) |

[a]   Calculations are based on the results reported in table A.8.1. The DI-incidence in the first column equals $\exp[A]$ with $A=\ln(\bar{y}/\bar{s}) - (\gamma'z)$, where $z$ and $\gamma$ are (3x1) vectors respectively containing the variables JOBADAPT($z_1$), SOCGUID($z_2$) and MEDGUID($z_3$) and their coefficients. The DI-incidence equals $\exp[A + (\gamma_1 z_1 + \gamma_2 z_2)]$ in the second column, and $\exp[A + (\gamma_1 z_1 + \gamma_2 z_2 + \gamma_3 z_3)]$ in the third column.

where firms with Job Adaptation and Social Guidance Policies have higher DI-incidence rates. A comparison of the overall impact of all three policy indicators, yields a similar picture: a reduction of the DI-incidence rates by 13 to 67 percent in all branches except in Other Industry and Other Commercial Services, where the average DI-incidence rate is virtually unaffected.

The branch-wise variation in the size and sign of the policy coefficients shows that the specified variables lack sufficient accuracy to analyze the effect of job adaptation and social guidance. We have found similar inconsistencies in the effects of job adaptation, social and medical guidance in the literature on DI-incidence. For instance, Nijhuis and Soeters (1982) report a positive effect of their medical guidance indicator and no effect of job adaptation; Draaisma (1983) reports a positive impact of his social guidance indicator and a negative impact of job adaptation possibilities. Apparently, the impact of such policies is difficult to assess. In our analysis the variables JOBADAPT and SOCGUID may be indicating the firms' intentions to do something in these areas rather than the firms' actual efforts. The inconclusive results call for an improved measurement of these policy efforts in order to be able to reveal their full effects on DI-incidence.

Finally, we have introduced four variables related to the cost-benefit balance of retaining (or replacing) employees with functional limitations. The first one, the dummy variable Supplementary Benefits, has no significant effect on the DI-incidence rate. On balance, that is, for the variable presumably has both negative and positive impacts; negative, because the provision of supplemental allowances increases the firm's costs of a lay-off through the DI-program, and positive, because these benefits raise the post-retirement income of the employees and therefore their inclination to retire. The positive sign of the coefficient seems to indicate that the latter impact tends to be dominating.

The average level of education (EDUC) within the firm was introduced because it is taken to be closely related the cost of recruiting replacements. Assuming that high education implies relatively large replacement costs, we expected high education firms to have an incentive to retain functionally impaired employees. Confirming this expectation, the DI-incidence rate appears to be a decreasing function of the education level. The education effect is relatively large and consistent with results from other studies.[20]

We further suggested that firms that reduce their employment have less incentives to retain functionally impaired employees. The significantly positive coefficient of ln(DECREASE) seems to confirm this hypothesis. For instance, according to the estimates listed in table 8.3, a decrease in employment of 10 employees, in the average firm, would induce an increase of 1.1 in the number of DI-awards.[21] Since the DI-incidence rate increases as employment decreases, we conclude that the DI-incidence is at least partly the result of efficiency considerations on behalf of the firm. Furthermore, the results confirm the expected asymmetry in the relation between a change in the size of employment and the DI-incidence rate, as increases in employment do not lead to a reduction in the number of DI-awards at all.

In the next section, the estimation results will be used to construct a measure of the firm specific risk of DI-program enrolment.

## 8.4     Measuring the Firm Specific Disability Risk

According to the model developed in chapter 3, the probability that an individual employee will enter the DI-program is determined by health, work conditions, labor market opportunities, preferences, and other individually varying circumstances. Although workers employed by a single firm may differ individually with respect to these factors, part of the DI-risk they are likely to have in common. This is the part we refer to as the Firm Specific Disability Risk (FIRMRISK). One way of measuring the firm specific DI-risk is based on the results of the analysis presented in the preceding sections. Using the estimated coefficients and the characteristics of the employing firms, we calculate an instrumental indicator of the firm specific DI-risk for all observations in the sample of "healthy" insured employees and in the sample of employees on sick leave.
This instrumental variable will be used in the individual disability probability model in chapter 10.

The branch-wise varying errors (see table 8.1) in the measurement of the dependent variable complicate the calculation of a valid instrument for FIRMRISK. To avoid downward biases for construction workers and upward biases for workers in the Health Services, for instance, a branch specific correction of the predicted values of $\ln(y_{ij}/s_{ij})$ is needed. The correction factor $a_j$ reflects the difference between the true DI-incidence risk in branch j and the predicted risk, calculated using the branch specific coefficient estimates reported in table A.8.1.
The procedure to calculate FIRMRISK runs as follows:

$$FIRMRISK_i = 100 \cdot \exp\left[\ln(\hat{y}_{ij}/s_{ij}) - a_j\right]$$

$$\ln(\hat{y}_{ij}/s_{ij}) = \beta_j' X_{ij} - \ln s_{ij}$$

$$a_j = \ln\left\{\frac{\sum\limits_{i=1}^{n} \hat{y}_{ij}}{\sum\limits_{i=1}^{n} s_{ij}}\right\} - \ln(y_j / s_j)$$

| | | |
|---|---|---|
| $FIRMRISK_i$ | = | the firm specific disability risk in firm i affiliated with Industrial Association j; |
| $\ln(\hat{y}_{ij}/s_{ij})$ | = | the predicted value of the ln of the DI-incidence in firm using the coefficient estimates reported in table A.8.1; |
| $a_j$ | = | the difference of the average predicted value of the ln of the DI-incidence rate in Industrial Association j and the actual value of the ln of the DI-incidence rate; |
| $\ln(y_j/s_j)$ | = | the ln of the actual overall DI-incidence rate in Industrial Association j; |
| $n_j$ | = | the number of firms affiliated with Industrial Association j; |

Table 8.5 presents the mean and standard deviation of the newly constructed variable within the "healthy" control-sample and the SB-sample, the latter broken down into work resumers and DI-entrants.

Table 8.5    The Firm Specific Disability Risk (FIRMRISK) by DI-Status

|  | Mean | Standard Deviation |
|---|---|---|
| Control-sample ("healthy" employees) | 1.961 | .999 |
| Work resumers in SB-sample | 2.325 | .918 |
| SB-sample (employees on extended sick leave) | 2.463 | .928 |
| DI-Entrants in SB-sample | 2.556 | .930 |

The pattern revealed by these figures indicates a correlation between the constructed FIRMRISK and the work status of the respondents, since the "presently employed" status appears to coincide with the smallest, and the DI-beneficiary status with the largest firm specific disability risk.

The risk affecting respondents on sick leave, who are halfway through the process that may lead to the award of DI-benefits, is somewhere in between.
The question whether or not the FIRMRISK is causally related to the disability probability and the probability of being on sick leave will be answered in the context of a multivariate analysis in chapter 10.

## 8.5    Summary and Discussion

Although our database lacks the information that is necessary to draw very specific conclusions, we may summarize the results shown in table 8.3 by concluding that the firm-specific probability of the occurrence of functional limitations (in other words the firm's type of work and type of employee) accounts for only part of the inter-firm variation in DI-incidence rate. Another part is accounted for by variables related to the balance of costs and benefits of retaining, c.q. replacing, functionally impaired or otherwise marginally efficient employees. Policy measures that affect this balance are likely to have an impact on the DI-incidence rate.
The results show that, to a certain extent, the incidence of DI-awards within a firm can be steered by the firm itself. Although the role of individual disability policies has remained somewhat vague, a branch-wise comparison of the combined effect of policies on Job Adaptation, Social Guidance and Medical Guidance has shown that such policies can be effective in monitoring DI-incidence.

As our model is estimated on data referring to firm specific DI-incidence rates during the years 1978 and 1979, these results may depend on the particular circumstances prevailing at that time. For instance, one important aspect of the background against which these results should be evaluated seems to be the attractiveness, to employees, of the DI-program, relative to both continued labor force participation and to the Unemployment Insurance program. Another aspect is the relatively poor state of the national economy during those years.

Since then, major changes have taken place: During the early 1980s the DI-program has lost much of its financial appeal to the (marginally) impaired workers (see chapter 2) and also the 1987 Social Security System Reform may have had a negative impact on the inclination of marginally impaired employees to apply for DI-benefits. The economy has gradually improved and, nowadays, many firms are confronted with labor shortages rather than surpluses. Consequently, firms will be less inclined to persuade their employees to apply for DI-benefits and employees will be less inclined to file the applications.

These changes may have affected the cost-benefit balances of firms (and employees) and may have led to a decrease in DI-incidence rates; they do not imply, however, that the discretion on part of the employer in these matters has been restricted. A replicated analysis on a current database is, therefore, likely to yield conclusions similar to the ones we arrived at here.

## Appendix to chapter 8

Table A.8.1 The Firm Specific DI-Incidence Rate. Branch-Wise Tobit Estimation Results

| Explanatory Variables | Total | Steel | Construc. | Other Industry | Retail & Wholesale | Other Commercial Services | Health Services | Other Noncomm. Services |
|---|---|---|---|---|---|---|---|---|
| Ln(EM50PLUS) | .0603** | .1042° | .1509° | -.0092 | .0682 | .0716 | .0449 | .1354° |
| Ln(EMFEM) | -.0937* | -.1664 | -.0996 | -.0407 | .0016 | -.1538* | .0478 | .2982° |
| Med. Guidance | -.0048 | -.0549 | -.1294 | .0018 | -.1664 | .0530 | .0967 | .0008 |
| Work Consult. | -.1247** | -.1002 | .0880 | -.3579** | .1235 | -.1943° | .0009 | -.2202 |
| Ln(Firm size) | .8620** | .9712** | .8545** | 1.0690** | .7525** | .8037** | .3290 | .3462 |
| Job Adaptation | -.0166 | .1238° | -.0284 | -.0886 | .0885 | .1361 | -.0457 | -.1695 |
| Soc. Guidance | -.0306 | -.1903 | -.2403 | .0855 | .0126 | -.1938 | -.1729 | -.3880° |
| D(Suppl.Ben.) | .0946 | .3905 | -.0230 | -.0175 | -.3285 | .0003 | .6393 | -.0578 |
| Education | -.1805** | -.0605 | -.3025* | -.1664* | .0664 | -.3153** | -.2673° | -.0786 |
| Ln(INCREASE) | .0070 | .0818 | .0664 | -.0234 | .0414 | .1450* | .0165 | .1240 |
| Ln(DECREASE) | .0818** | .1256° | .0092 | -.0057 | .2207* | -.0418 | .0096 | .2571** |
| $\sigma^2$ | .8444** | .8431** | .5287** | .5522** | .7374** | 1.0999** | .3865** | .9894** |
| Constant | -2.5463** | -3.6044** | -1.9779° | -3.1504** | -3.6978** | -.7494 | .5117 | -.6108 |
| Observations | 650 | 116 | 58 | 154 | 66 | 119 | 52 | 81 |
| Log-likelihood | 854.92 | 154.48 | 63.20 | 173.68 | 78.96 | 169.66 | 49.18 | 109.41 |

°, *, ** Significant at 10, 5 and 1 percent respectively.

**Notes**

1. This chapter is a thoroughly revised and re-estimated version of Aarts (1984).

2. For a formal treatment of the optimal level of safety provisions see e.g., Viscusi (1980).

3. In 1984, benefits supplementary to the Sickness Benefits are provided in 95 percent of all firms, while supplementary DI-benefits are provided in 56 percent of all firms [SoZaWe (1985)].

4. The minimum age for early retirement eligibility differs among branches. In most branches the minimum age is 61 or 62 years [Bolhuis et al. (1987)].

5. Rewriting the above decision rule shows that a firm confronted with the occurrence of functional impairments will invest in adjustments of the job requirements in order to retain the impaired employee only if

$$c_{adj} < (p.q_1 - w_1) - (p.q_2 - w_2) + c_{rec} + c_{DI}, \text{ for } (p.q_2 - w_2) - c_{rec} > 0$$

or if

$$c_{adj} < (p.q_1 - w_1) + c_{DI}, \text{ for } (p.q_2 - w_2) - c_{rec} < 0$$

that is, if the costs of adjustment do not exceed the costs of recruiting a replacement plus the cost of DI-enrolment plus the difference in contribution to the firm's results between $x_1$ and his replacement. If the job is redundant, the firm will be in favor of retainment only if the costs of adjustment do not exceed the contribution of $x_1$ to the firm plus the costs of DI-enrolment.

6. See chapter 4 for an account of the database. A more comprehensive description is presented in [Aarts (1984)].

7. The probability that a randomly sampled employee is employed by firm i, with firmsize $n_i$, equals $(n_i/N)$, where N represents the total number of employees in the population. Its complement equals $(1 - n_i/N)$. The probability that none of the 1602 randomly sampled employees, who granted permission to contact their employers, is employed by firm i equals $(1 - n_i/N)^{1602}$. The complement of this latter probability, $[1 - (1 - n_i/N)^{1602}]$, represents the probability that at least one of the 1602 employees is employed by firm i, in other words, the probability of firm i being included in the sample of firms, $Pr_i(sample \mid n_i)$. By reweighing the observed firms by a factor $\{Pr_i(sample \mid n_i)\}^{-1}$, the sample of firms can be made comparable to the population of firms.

8. This conclusion does not hold for the construction industry. Here, smaller firms appear to be overrepresented in the sample of firms.

9. For instance, Nijhuis and Soeters (1982) have only 51 observations available and Draaisma's analysis (1983) is based on a sample of 119 firms.

10. Smulders (1984) presents an international survey of research on sickness absenteeism.

11. Although there is ample empirical support for this positive age-effect, Nijhuis and Soeters (1982) report a negative effect of the percentage of elderly employees on the DI-incidence rate in a sample of 50 firms concentrated in the southern part of the Netherlands (Zuid-Limburg). They suggest that a large share of elderly employees ("survivors") shows that a firm is relatively "healthy".

12. 42 percent of all women covered by the DI-program are younger than 25 years, whereas only 19 percent of the insured males are under 25 [GMD (1980)].

13. In 1979, 45 percent of all working women held a job for less than 35 hours per week; 33 percent were working less than 25 hours per week. Among working men, part-time jobs are rare. In 1979, only 6 percent were working less than 35 hours per week, although the figure has gradually increased since [CBS A (1983), p. 121].

14. Draaisma (1983) reports a negative effect, while Nijhuis and Soeters (1982) report a zero effect of a comparable variable.

15. This expectation is supported Dijkstra (1977) and Ris (1978), who find a negative impact of similar indicators on sickness absenteeism. Draaisma (1983, p. 71), however, provides some empirical evidence of a positive impact of elements of social guidance.

16. Worrall and Butler (1986, pp. 100-106), discussing the lessons from the Workers' Compensation Program in the USA, conclude that there is substantial empirical support for the latter positive impact. Negative impacts of experience rating are reported by Ruser (1984) and Victor (1983, 1985). However, Chelius and Smith (1983) do not find a measurable impact of experience rating on the injury rate in the Workers' Compensation Program.

17. A negative effect of personnel education on the firm's DI-incidence has been assessed by Nijhuis and Soeters (1982).

18. The model is estimated on the original, not reweighed, sample. On the one hand, the positive correlation of firm size with the probability of sample selection would require a reweighing procedure in which each observation is weighed with the inverse of the square root of firm size. On the other hand, the negative correlation of firm size with the measurement error in the dependent variable (see section 8.3.2) calls for a reciprocal reweighing procedure in order to avoid heteroscedasticity. Under these circumstances, it seems appropriate to refrain from reweighing the observations and to use the sample as it is.

19. The insignificance of the effect of SOCGUID on the DI-risk measured at the firm level is in sharp contrast with its prominent effect on PSICK (see table 6.5). The latter effect, however, may be contaminated by the post-hoc effects described in chapter 6. Moreover, the dependent variables and the quality of their measurement differ. While the firm specific DI-incidence rate is blurred by under- and overreports, the binary variables used at the individual level are accurate.

20. E.g. Nijhuis & Soeters (1982).

21. For firm i we may write: $\ln(y_i+1) = A_i + .0818 \ln(DECREASE_i+1)$. For the average firm (see table 8.2), $\ln(y_i+1) = 2.089$ (or $y_i = 7.08$) and $\ln(DECREASE_i+1) = .872$ (or $DECREASE_i = 1.39$). Therefore, $A_i = 2.02$. A ceteris paribus decrease in employment of 10 [$\ln(DECREASE_i'+1) = 2.43$], would result in a total number of DI-awards equal to $\exp(\ln(y_i'+1))-1 = 8.18$; An increase of 1.1 DI-awards.

Chapter 9

# EXPECTED EARNINGS AND DI-BENEFIT STREAMS

## 9.1 Introduction

Micro-economic theory posits that the predisposition to apply for DI-benefits is determined by the balance of expected utility streams associated with two alternatives - continued labor force participation and application for DI-benefits. Utility being a function of income and leisure, the expected utility streams will obviously depend on expectations regarding future income streams in either option.

In chapter 3, where the micro-economic approach to disability behavior was introduced, we distinguished three types of income; individual earnings (denoted by E), the corresponding statutory DI-benefit amount (B), and, finally, other household income $(N_0)$. $N_0$ equals asset income plus earnings or transfers received by other household members. Such alternative income sources are assumed to be independent of the option preferred. Therefore, $N_0$ acts as an exogenous, directly measurable, variable. As such it has been used already in chapter 6. So we will not dwell on it here.

The expected income stream associated with the labor force participation option is the present value of earnings calculated over the remaining work life plus the present value of potential future DI-benefits. The latter term is added because those who decide to continue working are exposed to an over time increasing disability risk. The ensuing future DI-benefit stream runs from the expected age of eventual DI-enrolment, denoted as $t^*$, until 65, when DI-eligibility runs out and earnings related DI-benefits are replaced by old age pensions. Depending on the size and the time profile of the disability risk, $t^*$ may take any value between the current age, $t_0$, and 65.

The expected income stream in the DI-option is determined by the size of the entitlement and the probability that the DI-application will be awarded. Should the award be granted, the beneficiary is assumed to receive an earnings-related transfer income until 65. If the application is denied, the applicant is assumed to return to paid work.

The purpose of this chapter is to determine the expected income streams in either of both options. Given its definition, the expected income stream related to continued labor force participation, $EY_{WORK}$, depends on [see eq.(3.25)]:
- the expected duration of the remaining work life (Et);
- the expected earnings profile over the remaining work years ($E_s = w_s H_0$);
- the expected DI-benefit amount ($B_{t^*}$), associated with DI-enrolment at age $t^*$ ($=t_0+Et$), where $B_{t^*}$ is the benefit size related to insured earnings equal to $E_{t^*}$.

The expected income stream related to the DI-option, $EY_{DI}$, depends on:
- the probability ($p_a$) that the application for a disability transfer benefit will be awarded;
- the amount of transfer income should the award be granted ($B_0$);
- the expected duration of the remaining work life of a rejected applicant $E\tilde{t}$ ($=Et - \theta$) where $\theta$ is the potential number of years the eventual date of DI-eligibility is advanced after an initially failed application;
- the expected earnings profile of a rejected applicant ($e_s = \tilde{w}_s H_0$);
- the expected DI-benefit amount ($b_{t^*-\theta}$), associated with DI-enrolment at age $t^* - \theta$, where $b_{t^*-\theta}$ is the benefit related to earnings $e_{t^*-\theta}$.

Presuming that work hours are predetermined and stay at their current level $H_0$, the only time-varying components of future income streams are the wage rates, $w_s$ and $\tilde{w}_s$. Within our binary choice setting, these wage trajectories determine the earnings' loss due to DI-enrolment. And, given the close relationship between wages and benefits, they also define future benefit entitlements. The estimation of expected wage profiles, therefore, is indispensable for the measurement of income streams and the assessment of their impacts on work status.

In the following section, we start by describing the after-tax hourly wage distributions, and the concomitant DI-replacement rates, for the DI-insured and DI-entrants employing our 1980 sample data and the then prevailing statutory rules. In section 9.3, we describe and estimate the wage equations from which future wage profiles are derived. The estimation model takes account of the potential endogeneity of wages with respect to the probability of an extended spell (5 months or more) of sickness (PSICK).

In section 9.4, we calculate the expected age of eventual DI-enrolment ($t^*$) from a reduced form DI-probit model and, next, the present values of separate earnings and benefit streams. Section 9.5 concludes.

As a final introductory note we want to stress the purpose and limitations of the estimates presented in this chapter, especially those for the sick (SB) sample observations. In order to causally relate the income streams to PSICK (or to the

DI-entry probability) they should reflect the financial options faced by the long-term sick, **before** they reported sick. We, therefore, seek to measure the income streams independent of the current extent of disablement by using pre-sickness earning capacities as their benchmark. Specifically, the income stream related to the continued participation option does not intend to indicate the consequences of disability on lifetime earnings.

Similar limitations apply to the award probability and the expected income stream in case of a benefit denial. Both variables being unobservable, imputed values for these variables should, again, reflect the pre-sickness situation.[1]

## 9.2     Wages and Benefits; A Description

In chapter 2, we have described how statutory DI-benefits are linked with current gross earnings. In 1980, the year from which our sample observations are taken, full DI-benefits replaced 80 percent of gross earnings.[2] Earnings over Dfl. 64,000 per year were not covered.[3] This cap implies a maximum benefit of Dfl. 51,200 per year.[4]

Due to progressive taxation, an 80 percent gross replacement rate translates to approximately 87 percent in after-tax terms. For breadwinners over 23, after-tax benefits were never less than the statutory net minimum wage;[5] minimum wage workers, therefore, are covered by a replacement rate equal to 1. The 1980 net minimum level of hourly wages, and DI-benefits, was Dfl. 8.48.

In 1980, the DI-program covered income losses up to a maximum net wage rate of Dfl. 17.27. Averaging over fiscal groups, the concomitant maximum amount of net DI-benefits equals Dfl. 14.68 per hour of insured work. The ensuing after tax replacement rate at the maximum covered by DI, is 85 percent.

As a result of these institutional constraints, net replacement rates gradually decrease with increasing wage rates. From the net minimum wage up to Dfl. 9.75 the replacement rate goes down from 100 to 87 percent. For wages between Dfl. 9.75 and Dfl. 17.27, replacement rates are constant at approximately 87 percent. For hourly wages above the maximum amount covered, Dfl. 17.27, the net replacement rate gradually decreases to, for instance, 47 percent at an after-tax wage level of Dfl. 40 per hour.

For both the control-sample of DI-insured employees and the sub-sample of DI-entrants, net hourly-wage distributions and the corresponding after-tax replacement rates are given in table 9.1. We employ net wage rates as the prime income concept, first because the sample income observations are in net terms, and, second, because thus earnings are made independent of the number of hours worked. Wage rates for SB-recipients, and DI-entrants in particular, are derived from their pre-sickness earnings.[6]

**Table 9.1**   Distribution of the After-Tax Hourly Wage for DI-Insured and
DI-Entrants, and the Corresponding Replacement Rates, 1980

|  | DI-Insured | DI-Entrants | Replacement Rate |
|---|---|---|---|
|  | | *(percentages)* | |
| *Hourly wage:* | | | |
| < 8.48 (Min. Wage) | 14 | 13 | 100 |
| 8.48 - 9.75 | 22 | 18 | 87 - 100 |
| 9.75 - 13.00 | 37 | 46 | 87 |
| 13.00 - 17.27 | 15 | 16 | 85 - 87 |
| > 17.27 (Max. Insured) | 12 | 7 | 0 - 85 |
| Total | 100 | 100 | |
| straight sample means | Dfl. 12.32 | Dfl. 11.84 | |
| standardized[a] means | Dfl. 12.32 | Dfl. 11.30 | |

[a]   Standardized by age, sex, education, and marital status.

As shown in the table, most of the observations - 52 percent among the DI-insured and 62 percent of the DI-entrants - are in the hourly wage brackets where replacement rates are about constant at 85 to 87 percent. High wage rates, and correspondingly low replacement rates, are relatively rare among DI-entrants. Whether this points to incentive effects can only be concluded from multivariate analysis. After all, high wage earners are expected to possess a greater stock of health capital [Grossman (1972)] and high wage jobs are generally characterized by less disabling conditions (low physical workload, more autonomy, etc.).

The size of the lowest wage bracket - less than the minimum wage - is considerable in both samples. This bracket consists mainly of youths whose statutory minimum is 40 percent of the adult amount for the 15 years old, gradually increasing to 100 percent at the age of 23, and married women who used to be treated less favorably by the tax system.

The straight difference in average wage rates between all DI-insured and DI-entrants is Dfl. 0.48. Hence, on average, high risk workers earn 4 percent less than the complete population at risk. However, after controlling for differences in age, education, sex and marital status, the pre-sickness hourly earnings of DI-entrants appear to be Dfl. 1.02, or 8 percent less than their peers'. This difference suggests that DI-entrants are recruited from a class of workers whose market productivity is lower than average.

## 9.3        The Wage Profiles

### 9.3.1     Specification of the Wage Equation

To predict life-time earnings a functional relation between wage and age, and its interaction with personal characteristics such as sex, marital status, and education, has to be established.

Standard economic theory posits that gross wages reflect the marginal productivities of individual workers. More specifically, human capital theory defines productivity as a function of schooling, training, and experience. Using age as a proxy both for labor market experience in general and on-the-job training in particular, the wage equation should allow for returns to experience that are increasing in early work life and level off later on. Due to obsolescence of professional knowledge, and reductions in workload tolerance that accompany a natural process of aging, marginal returns to experience may even become negative. On the other hand, marginal returns to schooling may relate positively to years of experience.

Assuming a log-normal wage distribution we take the natural log of hourly wages (w) as the dependent variable. Added flexibility is obtained by using the natural logarithm of age.[7] Hence, we obtain

$$\ln w = \alpha_0 + \alpha_1 \ln(AGE) + \alpha_2 \ln^2(AGE) + [\alpha_3 + \alpha_4 \ln(AGE)].EDUC \qquad (9.1)$$

The hypotheses made before imply that $\alpha_1 > 0$, $\alpha_2 < 0$, $\alpha_4 > 0$, and $[\alpha_3 + \alpha_4 \ln(AGE)] > 0$. Three dummy variables are added, one for gender, one for marital status, and one for their combined effect. Using after-tax wage rates, these dummies intend to catch the particularities of a tax system which treats singles, married men (mostly main breadwinners), and married women (mostly secondary breadwinners) differently. The dummies may also pick up other effects to the extent that (married) women have weaker commitments to paid work or are discriminated against by employers. Furthermore, divergent market behavior of, and toward, women may also depress their returns to schooling.[8] We, therefore, enter the interaction between gender and education as well.[9]

This adds the following terms to (9.1)

$$\alpha_5 d(FEMALE) + \alpha_6 d(MARRIED) + \alpha_7 d(MARR.FEM) + \alpha_8 [d(FEMALE)].EDUC \qquad (9.2)$$

For fiscal reasons we expect $\alpha_6$ to be positive and $\alpha_7$ to be negative; $\alpha_5$, $\alpha_7$ and $\alpha_8$ are likely to be negative because of attitudes of, and towards, working women. When using cross-sectional data to predict earnings profiles, the shape of these profiles may be influenced by differences in productivity between the generations sampled. A generation that enters the labor market in an era of economic depression may be less successful than one that starts out when the economy is booming. We, therefore, include a dummy [d(GEN)] indicating whether a person entered the market before 1946. Moreover, as we suspect the detrimental effects of the Great Depression and the Second World War to be stronger for those with more schooling, we also include the product of this dummy and education.[10]

Addition of these two generation-specific terms, and a normally distributed error term $\eta$, to the combined terms in (9.1) and (9.3) yields

$$
\begin{aligned}
\ln w = {} & \alpha_0 + \alpha_1 \ln(\text{AGE}) + \alpha_2 \ln^2(\text{AGE}) + [\alpha_3 + \alpha_4 \ln(\text{AGE})]\text{EDUC} \\
& + \alpha_5 d(\text{FEMALE}) + \alpha_6 d(\text{MARRIED}) + \alpha_7 d(\text{MARR.FEM}) \\
& + \alpha_8 [d(\text{FEMALE})].\text{EDUC} + \alpha_9 d(\text{GEN}) + \alpha_{10}[d(\text{GEN})].\text{EDUC} + \eta
\end{aligned}
\tag{9.3}
$$

where $\alpha_0$ is the constant term, and both $\alpha_9$ and $\alpha_{10}$ are expected to be negative.


### 9.3.2    A Simultaneity Proposition

The average wage differential between DI-entrants and the total population at risk, reported in table 9.1, suggests that low wages, i.e., high replacement rates, induce people to opt for DI-enrolment. However, the causality between earnings and the predisposition for disability may be less straightforward. First, ill health and a lower-than-average productivity may be the joint outcome of a longer history of impairment which cannot be revealed by our cross-sectional data.[11] Alternatively, the joint determination of health and wages may result from a common source of social deprivation [Luft (1978) p. 91].

Second, from a human capital perspective health status and wage rates are mutually dependent. Following Grossman (1972) higher wages increase the rate of return to health investments and, thus, the demand for health. On the other hand, better health raises market productivity and hence wages.[12]

The failure to appreciate the joint determination of health status and productivity leads to biased estimates of the impact of the wage rate and wage-related variables on the probabilities of long-term sickness or permanent disability. We, therefore, propose a simultaneous equation model of the long-term sickness probability (PSICK) and the wage rate. Given the discrete nature of the indicator for PSICK, we use the [Lee (1979)] switching model to allow for a potentially endogenous selection mechanism governing wage determination.[13] Specifically, we want to test whether the pre-disability wage profiles of the long-term sick, i.e., potential DI-entrants, significantly deviate from the profiles of the average DI-insured. Using the structural model for PSICK, introduced in section 6.3, as the switching equation the simultaneous equations system writes

$$\text{PSICK} = F\{\beta, N_0, \text{ETG}, \text{EY}_{\text{DI}}(w_s), \text{EY}_{\text{WORK}}(w_s)\}$$

$$\ln w = \alpha'_z A + \eta_z \quad (z=0,1) \tag{9.4}$$

F is the standard normal distribution function; its arguments have been defined in section 3.3; the matrix A contains the wage determinants summarized in eq.(9.3). The coefficients $\alpha_{zj}$ will be separately estimated for the long-term sick $(z=1)$ and the control-sample taken from all DI-insured employees $(z=0)$. Thus, we can test the neoclassical presumption that, *ceteris paribus*, those who opt out do so because they have less favorable future wage trajectories and, therefore, face lower opportunity costs.

The simultaneity of the two structural equations in (9.4) stems from the possibility that market productivity and health status, or retirement intentions indicated by extended sick spells, are determined by a common set of unobserved socio-medical backgrounds.

This proposition implies that the error terms of the wage rate equations, $\eta_1$ and $\eta_0$, and the error term in the DI-probability model, say $\epsilon$, have non-zero covariances

$$\sigma_{z\epsilon} = \text{cov}(\eta_{zi}, \epsilon_i).$$

Consequently, the equations in (9.4) are not directly estimable.

The wage equations can be estimated, and the simultaneity proposition tested, by treating the disturbances, $\eta_1$ and $\eta_0$, as drawings from a truncated normal distribution where the truncation is determined by PSICK. By including an extra term, $\lambda_z$, representing the conditional expectations of $\eta_1$ and $\eta_0$, the wage equations are directly estimable.[14]

For $z=0,1$ and the i-th sample person, $\lambda_{zi}$ is defined as

$$\lambda_{0i} = \frac{-f(c_i)}{1 - F(c_i)}, \qquad \lambda_{1i} = \frac{f(c_i)}{F(c_i)}$$

where $c_i = \gamma' \Pi_i$, and f and F are the standard normal density and distribution functions, respectively. Given the presumed endogeneity of the wage rate, c is calculated by estimating a reduced form version of the sickness probability model, yielding probit ML-estimates of $\gamma$. Strictly, this reduced form should be obtained by replacing the wage rate in the expressions for $\text{EY}_{\text{DI}}$ and $\text{EY}_{\text{WORK}}$ by its determinants $\exp\{\alpha'_z A\}$ [see eq. (9.4)]. For practical reasons, however, we will use the reduced form probit results presented in table 6.2 to capture the 'switch' - or transition - from the insured to the potential eligibility status.

The wage equations, now, can be written as

$$\ln w_i = \alpha'_0 A_i + \sigma_{0\epsilon} \lambda_{0i} + u_{0i} \qquad \text{for the DI-insured;}$$

$$\ln w_i = \alpha'_1 A_i + \sigma_{1\epsilon} \lambda_{1i} + u_{1i} \qquad \text{for the long-term sick;} \tag{9.5}$$

where $u_0$ and $u_1$ are independently, normally distributed error terms.

Equations (9.5) can be estimated by OLS, yielding consistent, albeit inefficient, estimates of $\alpha_0$, $\alpha_1$, $\sigma_{0\varepsilon}$, and $\sigma_{1\varepsilon}$. The simultaneity hypothesis is confirmed if $\sigma_{0\varepsilon}$ and $\sigma_{1\varepsilon}$ turn out to be significant.[15]

The inclusion of $\sigma_{0\varepsilon}\lambda_0$ and $\sigma_{1\varepsilon}\lambda_1$ in the wage equations serves primarily statistical purposes. However, $\lambda_0$ and $\lambda_1$, both being inverse transformations of the latent predisposition for DI-entry, may be interpreted as behavioral indicators that capture earning capacities as well as retirement preferences. Hence, their effects may be given causal content as well.[16] For lack of a better label, we will refer to the $\lambda$'s as indicators of fitness for market work. Consequently, we expect the estimates of $\sigma_{0\varepsilon}$ and $\sigma_{1\varepsilon}$ to be positive.[17]

## 9.3.3    Estimation Results

The OLS estimation results for the wage equations defined by (9.5), are given in table 9.2. The assumptions that underlie the wage equations are well confirmed by these results. First of all, both $\lambda_0$ and $\lambda_1$ have a significant positive impact. This corroborates the simultaneity proposition: the wage rate itself, and the expected income streams to be derived from the wage rate, appear to be endogenous with respect to PSICK.

Table 9.2    OLS Estimates of Regressions on the Natural Log of Hourly Wages for the DI-Insured and the Long-Term Sick  (Standard Errors between Brackets)

| | DI-Insured | | Long-Term Sick | | t-test for difference |
| --- | --- | --- | --- | --- | --- |
| | $(\alpha_0)$ | | $(\alpha_1)$ | | $(\alpha_1 - \alpha_0)$ |
| ln(AGE) | 3.344 | (.540)* | 3.530 | (.371)* | 1.55 |
| ln²(AGE) | - .417 | (.078)* | - .441 | (.052)* | 1.49 |
| EDUCATION | - .359 | (.098)* | - .463 | (.084)* | -5.39* |
| [ln(AGE).EDUC] | .139 | (.027)* | .154 | (.023)* | .05 |
| d(FEMALE) | - .041 | (.025) | - .020 | (.024) | -3.19* |
| d(MARRIED) | .128 | (.022)* | .129 | (.016)* | -2.34* |
| d(MARFEM) | - .180 | (.032)* | - .317 | (.028)* | - .59 |
| [d(FEMALE).EDUC] | - .062 | (.017)* | - .022 | (.014) | .60 |
| d(GEN) | .005 | (.035) | - .059 | (.017)* | .28 |
| [d(GEN).EDUC] | - .037 | (.028) | - .034 | (.015)* | .59 |
| $\lambda_0$ | .147 | (.055)* | | | |
| | | | | | 3.09* |
| $\lambda_1$ | | | .022 | (.010)* | |
| Constant | -4.164 | (.928)* | -4.659 | (.652)* | |
| adjusted $R^2$ | .48 | | .43 | | |
| #Observations | | 1417 | | 2534 | |

*    Significant at the 5 percent level.

The age profiles have their familiar shape implying decreasing returns to experience. The average worker reaches his or her top at age 55. The positive effect of the age-education interaction, $\alpha_4$, shows that low-schooled workers reach their, lower, top sooner, at the age of 45, while the wages of the best trained keep increasing until 65.

The last column in table 9.2 contains a t-test on the difference of corresponding coefficients.[18] As the results for ln(AGE) and $\ln^2$(AGE) show, the long-term sick do not significantly deviate from their healthy peers as regards the curvature of their profiles. They do differ unfavorably, however, in terms of returns to schooling. Evaluation of the combined effect of $\alpha_3$ and $\alpha_4$ yields the following age-dependent coefficients for education:

|        |    | DI-Insured | Long-Term Sick |
|--------|----|-----------|----------------|
| Age is | 20 | .058      | -.001          |
|        | 30 | .114      | .061           |
|        | 40 | .154      | .105           |
|        | 50 | .184      | .139           |
|        | 60 | .210      | .167           |

The gains to schooling appear to be significantly lower in that part of the labor force from which the long-term sick and, hence, the DI-entrants are recruited.

The negative effects for females, and for married women in particular, may reflect wage-discrimination, different commitments, and less stable work histories. The effect is particularly strong among impaired females. The generation effects are significantly negative among the long-term sick only. Apparently, the difficult conditions that prevailed when the oldest generation entered the labor market have only affected the productivity of individuals with a higher than average disability risk.

### 9.3.4    Wage Rate Predictions

Given our interpretation of $\lambda_0$ and $\lambda_1$ as indicators of fitness, the determinants of the wage rate also have an indirect effect through their impact on the $\lambda$'s. Education, for instance, increases the wage rate directly but also indirectly through its negative reduced form effect on PSICK which translates to a positive effect on $\lambda$. Age, on the other hand, has a positive direct, and a negative indirect, effect on the wage rate, since aging is associated with increasing experience and decreasing fitness. To the extent that, beyond a certain age, marginal returns to experience become negative, as indicated by the coefficient of $\ln^2$(AGE), the decline in the wage rate will be reinforced by the effect of decreasing fitness.

The balance of these direct and indirect effects on the wage rate is shown in table 9.3, where predicted wage rates - conditional on belonging to either of both samples - are reported for various types of individuals. These conditional predictions are based on the estimates listed in tables 9.2 and 6.3. and calculated following[19]

$$\hat{w}_{zs} = \exp\{\phi_{z0} + \phi_{z1} \ln s + \phi_{z2} \ln^2 s + \hat{\sigma}_{z\epsilon}\lambda_z(s)\} \quad (z=0,1; s=age), \tag{9.6}$$

with $\phi_{z1} = \alpha_{z1} + \alpha_{z4}\text{EDUC}$ ; $\phi_{z2} = \alpha_{z2}$ ; $\phi_{z0}$ captures the combined effect of wage determinants that are independent of age; and $\lambda_z(s)$ registers the age-profile of fitness.

The characteristics reported in each row are the ones that differ from the standard set of characteristics. For each combination of attributes the predicted wage rate of DI-entrants is smaller than that of healthy employees. The wage rate differential is large for the well-trained and small for the low-skilled.

Table 9.3    Predicted Net Hourly Wage Rates (Dfl.) for Various Types of DI-Insured (0) and Long-Term Sick (1) Workers. Wage Rate Differentials Between Both Groups

|  |  | DI-Insured | | Long-Term Sick | | |
|---|---|---|---|---|---|---|
|  | k | $w_{0k}$ | $w_{0k}/w_{01}$ | $w_{1k}$ | $w_{1k}/w_{11}$ | $\dfrac{[w_{1k} - w_{0k}]}{w_{0k}}$ |
| Standard employee[a] | 1 | 14.58 | 1.00 | 13.53 | 1.00 | -.07 |
| Age = 25 | 2 | 11.69 | .80 | 10.75 | .79 | -.08 |
| 60 | 3 | 14.97 | 1.03 | 13.97 | 1.04 | -.07 |
| Education = low | 4 | 11.80 | .81 | 11.70 | .86 | -.01 |
| high | 5 | 18.23 | 1.25 | 15.78 | 1.17 | -.13 |
| Age 25, educ = low | 6 | 10.35 | .71 | 10.26 | .76 | -.01 |
| educ = high | 7 | 13.29 | .91 | 11.30 | .84 | -.15 |
| Age 60, educ = low | 8 | 11.19 | .77 | 11.10 | .82 | -.01 |
| educ = high | 9 | 20.37 | 1.40 | 17.83 | 1.32 | -.12 |
| Male, single | 12 | 12.82 | .88 | 11.88 | .88 | -.07 |
| Female, single | 13 | 12.18 | .84 | 11.58 | .86 | -.05 |
| Female, married | 14 | 11.58 | .79 | 9.61 | .71 | -.17 |

[a]    Married man, aged 40, median education level.

This is also illustrated in Figure 9.1, where we draw the earnings profiles for married men with different levels of education. As indicated by the t-tests for differences in table 9.2, the DI-insured and the DI-entrants have comparable returns to experience, as indicated by age. Between age 25 and 40, the expected wage growth rate is about 14 percent for low skilled married men, 25 percent for the median educated, and 37 percent for those with professional training.

**Figure 9.1    Wage Rate Profiles of Healthy Employees and DI-Entrants with High, Medium, and Low Education**

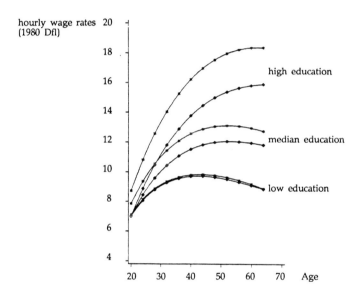

## 9.4        Expected Earnings and DI-Benefit Streams

In chapter 3 we defined the present values of the income streams associated with the two options under study. The present value of the expected income stream in the DI-option is a weighted sum of the DI-benefit stream upon admissal $(EY_{BEN})$ and the potentially "scarred" earnings stream upon rejection of the DI-application $(EY_{RA})$

$$EY_{DI} = p_a\, Y_{BEN} + (1-p_a)\, Y_{RA}$$

$$= p_a B_0 \int_{t_0}^{65} e^{-\delta(s-t_0)}\, ds + (1-p_a)\left[ \int_{t_0}^{t^*-\theta} e^{-\delta(s-t_0)}\, e_s\, ds + b_{t^*-\theta} \int_{t^*-\theta}^{65} e^{-\delta(s-t_0)}\, ds \right] \qquad (9.7)$$

Given this definition, $EY_{DI}$ depends on the award probability, $p_a$, the current benefit size, $B_0$, and the income stream in case the application is rejected, measured by the expression in square brackets which defines $Y_{RA}$ (see subsection 3.3.3). The larger the difference between the income streams for awarded and rejected applicants, the larger the sensitivity of $EY_{DI}$ to changes in $p_a$. Notice that the partial derivative of $EY_{DI}$ with respect to $p_a$ is negative if $Y_{RA} > Y_{BEN}$.

Over the last decade, more than 80 percent of the Dutch privately employed left the labor force before they reached their mandatory retirement age. Such premature terminations of labor force participation are mainly due to disability. Consequently, the present value of the expected income stream related to continued labor force participation now (at $t_0$) is contingent on the risk of later disablement (at $t^*$). Or,

$$EY_{WORK} = \int_{t_0}^{t^*} e^{-\delta(s-t_0)}\, E_s\, ds + B_{t^*} \int_{t^*}^{65} e^{-\delta(s-t_0)}\, ds \qquad (9.8)$$

$EY_{WORK}$, then, writes as the sum of the earnings' stream running from current age, $t_0$, until $t^*$, the expected age of eventual DI-enrolment, and the complementary benefit stream based on earnings at $t^*$, running from $t^*$ till 65.

Under the assumption that hours of work per period $(H_0)$ are predetermined, future after tax earnings' trajectories $E_s$ $(=w_s H_0)$ and $e_s$ $(=\tilde{w}_s H_0)$ and future after tax benefit amounts $B_{t^*}$ $(=\varrho E_{t^*})$ and $b_{t^*-\theta}$ $(=\varrho e_{t^*-\theta})$ can be derived from the estimates in the preceding section, $\varrho$ being the after tax replacement rate (see table 9.1). We cannot, however, calculate the components of $EY_{DI}$ and $EY_{WORK}$ before having imputed values for $t^*$, $\theta$, the subjective discount rate $\delta$, the award rate $p_a$, and $\tilde{w}_s$, the potentially scarred wage-profiles of rejected applicants.

### 9.4.1 The Expected Age of DI-Enrolment (t*)

In section 3.3.2, we have introduced a random variable t, with density function f(t), measuring the duration of the remaining work life of a current labor force participant whose current age is $t_0$ ; $t_{DI}$ (= $t_0$ + t) is the (random) age of eventual retirement by way of DI-enrolment if one would currently opt for continued labor force participation. Since 65 is the mandatory retirement age, $t_0 \leq t_{DI} \leq 65$. The parameters of density f(t) should capture individually varying health and vocational characteristics.

In our model, labor force participants will continue to receive earnings over the remaining work life, running from current age ($t_0$) until age $t_{DI}$, when they are to enter the DI-program. From then on they will receive a DI-benefit income based on the amount of insured earnings at $t_{DI}$. We assume that DI-enrolment is an absorbing state, i.e., that DI-entrants never again return to the labor force.[20]

Our model does not explicitly include f(t). Instead, we replace the premise that workers would know this density by the presumption that they know their expected age of DI-enrolment, t*. Thus we avoid complicated estimation procedures at the expense, of course, of theoretical rigor.

Using the variables defined before, the expected age of DI-enrolment is

$$t^* = Et_{DI} = t_0 + Et = t_0 + \int_0^{65-t_0} t\, f(t)\, dt$$

In order to obtain a manageable form for t* we replace the continuous density function f by a discrete distribution of durations, measured in years. Using the fact that 65 is the mandatory retirement age, we may normalize the resulting duration probabilities so that the expected duration of the remaining work life writes[21]

$$Et = 1 + \sum_{t=1}^{64-t_0} \left[ \prod_{i=1}^{t} (1 - p_i) \right] \quad \text{with } 0 < p_i < 1 \tag{3.11}$$

The future DI-probabilities, $p_t$ (t>0), can be derived from the effect of age on the current probability of DI-enrolment, $p_0$. Formally,

$$\hat{p}_{ti} = F [\, \hat{\gamma}_{0i} + \hat{\gamma}_1 (AGE_i + t) + \hat{\gamma}_2 (AGE_i + t)^2 \,]$$

with

$$\hat{\gamma}_{0i} = \hat{\gamma}_0 + \hat{\gamma}' \tilde{Z}_i$$

As before, we assume F to be the unit normal cdf. Hence, estimates for $\gamma_0$, $\gamma$, $\gamma_1$, and $\gamma_2$, can be obtained by applying the reduced form probit specification for PSICK to Pr{DI}. In this case, the dependent variable equals one for those SB-sample persons who enter the DI-program 7 months after their being interviewed. We, therefore, exclude those SB-sample observations who resume their work before lapse of the DI-waiting period, and DI-benefit denials. The results are listed in an appendix to this chapter (table A.9.1).

We use the ML-probit results in table A.9.1 to predict individually varying DI-risk trajectories, $\hat{p}_{ti}$, for all sample observations including those that were discarded from the DI-probit database.[22] The vector $\check{Z}_i$ contains both time-invariant and unpredictable variables. Substitution of $\hat{p}_{ti}$ for $p_t$ in (3.11) yields expected durations of residual work lifes, $Et_i$, that vary across individuals depending on current age, education, health, etc.

Table 9.4 reports the predicted age at DI-enrolment for various types of individuals. The characteristics reported in each row are the ones that differ from the standard set of characteristics.

Not surprisingly, the pre-sickness characteristics that prevail among the long-term sick are such that they have higher DI-entry probabilities. Hence, if they are to resume their jobs, they are expected to have shorter residual work lifes than the average member of the population at risk. The pre-sickness characteristics of 40 year old SB-sample respondents induce the expected duration of their remaining work lifes to be 6 years shorter than those for average insured workers. This differential is obviously quite sensitive to current age but not to education, sex, or marital status.

**Table 9.4  Expected Age at DI-Enrolment (t\*) for Various Types of DI-Insured and Long-Term Sick Workers**

|  | DI-Insured | Long-Term Sick |
|---|---|---|
| Standard employee[a] | 59 | 53 |
| Age is    25 | 57 | 47 |
|           60 | 64 | 63 |
| Education = low | 58 | 52 |
|           high | 60 | 53 |
| Male, single | 59 | 52 |
| Female, married | 56 | 50 |
| Health record = average DI-insured | 59 | 56 |

[a] See table 9.3.

As appears from the last row in table 9.4, half of the 6 year differential is health related. More precisely, if the workers who are now on a prolonged sick leave would have had the health - i.e., complaints and absence - records of the average member of the population at risk their residual work lifes would be 3 years longer. The other half of the 6 year difference, then, is due to nonmedical - vocational and attitudinal - factors.

### 9.4.2    Other Parameters

Given estimates of future wage trajectories ($w_s$) in table 9.2 and the expected age of eventual retirement through DI-enrolment ($t^*$), we still need values for the discount rate $\delta$ in order to be able to calculate the opportunity cost of DI-enrolment, $EY_{WORK}$. For the assessment of $EY_{DI}$ we also need estimates of the award rate, $p_a$, and predictions on the scarred earnings profiles ($e_s$), and the advance $\theta$ of the eventual age of DI-enrolment, in case of a benefit denial.

#### The Discount Rate, $\delta$
In their evaluation of future utility-streams, individuals are assumed to prefer a given combination of income and leisure now, over the same combination later. Utility derived from future income-leisure combinations, therefore, will be discounted at a subjective rate of time preference $\delta_i$, $(0 < \delta_i < 1)$.
Uncertainty about future income and leisure will be one of the determinants of the time preference rate. Individually varying attitudes towards risk will be another.[23] Obviously, the larger $\delta_i$, the lesser the value of future utility streams. For instance, if $\delta_i = 0.5$ postponement of consumption of a given combination of market goods and leisure hours by one year reduces its utility value by 40 percent. Postponement of consumption by two years reduces its utility value by 63 percent. After five years only 8 percent of the original utility is left. If $\delta_i = 0.1$, the successive percentages of residual utility are 90, 82, and 60, respectively.
Since our data do not allow for measurement of individually varying discount rates, $\delta$ will be regarded as an estimation parameter of the model, indicating average time preference; $\delta$ will be estimated iteratively, that is, the model will be estimated applying different values of $\delta$. The value that yields the best fit of the probability model will be regarded as the best approximation of $\delta$. We will start with $\delta=0$ (see tables 9.5 and 10.2).

#### The Rejected Applicant; $\theta$ and $e_s$
Since our samples do not contain information on benefit denials, we can only calculate income streams for rejected applicants by use of plausible presumptions. For lack of a clue we take $\theta=0$.

The scarred wage profiles of rejected applicants may be represented by the pre-sickness wage profiles found for the long-term sick (see table 9.2). To make these predictions applicable to the general population at risk we can use unconditional wage predictions - i.e., by excluding $\lambda_{1i}$ from the prediction equation (9.6). Given the definition of $\lambda_1$ and its positive coefficient $\sigma_{1\varepsilon}$, the resulting unconditional wage predictions will be lower both for the DI-insured and the long-term sick. The resulting wage "scar" will be larger for the, generally healthy, DI-insured, than for the long-term sick who have less favorable wage expectations anyway.

**The Award Rate, $p_a$**
In our theoretical model the probability of DI-enrolment is defined as the product of the probability of filing a claim and, given a claim, the probability of being found eligible. Such decomposition allows for separation of the two relevant behavioral models; one describing the retirement behavior of the DI-insured; the other describing the eligibility assessment procedures of the program gatekeepers.

However, this theoretical distinction causes empirical problems. As mentioned before in section 3.3.4, DI-applications and subsequent awards or denials cannot be separately observed due to the absence of explicit application and adjudication procedures under the Dutch Sickness and Disability Insurance programs. Claims for DI-benefits are implicitly filed by prolonging a current sick spell.

The observation of an extended sick spell, therefore, does not necessarily reflect preferences for DI-enrolment. At some point during the mandatory one year waiting period, which is covered by Sickness Benefits, employees have to decide whether to opt for the DI-status or its alternative - work resumption. Some SB-recipients may take the decision during the SB-year, or may have chosen to retire before they reported sick, others may postpone this decision until the end or have no room for choice.

As a consequence, individual decisions with respect to DI-application, and the ensuing administrative responses, are unobservable. Ruling out individual measurement these institutional constraints compel us to fix $p_a$ at some reasonable level.


### 9.4.3     Calculation of the Expected Income Streams

Collecting the ingredients elaborated in the preceding sections, the expected income streams associated with the DI-option and its alternative - continued labor force participation - can now be calculated by numerical integration.[24]
Table 9.5 reports, for $\delta=0$ and $p_a=1$, and for various types of individuals, the value of the relevant income streams. To get an impression of the relative cost of DI-enrolment, table 9.5 also contains the replacement rate based on lifetime incomes (RRLT) defined as $EY_{DI}/EY_{WORK}$ .

Table 9.5   Present Value of Income Streams (in thousand Dfls.) for Various Types of DI-Insured (H) and Long-Term Sick (S) Workers for $p_a = 1$ and $\delta = 0$

| | EYWORK | | EYBEN | | EYRA | | EYDI | | RRLT | |
|---|---|---|---|---|---|---|---|---|---|---|
| | H | S | H | S | H | S | H | S | H | S |
| Standard employee[a] | 757 | 679 | 649 | 616 | 668 | 646 | 649 | 616 | .86 | .91 |
| Age is 25 | 1166 | 1036 | 849 | 781 | 1023 | 982 | 849 | 781 | .73 | .75 |
| 60 | 154 | 140 | 137 | 128 | 138 | 134 | 137 | 128 | .89 | .91 |
| Education = low | 584 | 565 | 537 | 532 | 547 | 534 | 537 | 532 | .92 | .94 |
| high | 980 | 824 | 768 | 702 | 824 | 780 | 768 | 702 | .78 | .83 |
| Age 25, educ = low | 932 | 901 | 752 | 746 | 871 | 848 | 752 | 746 | .81 | .83 |
| educ = high | 1458 | 1230 | 966 | 821 | 1214 | 1153 | 966 | 821 | .66 | .67 |
| Age 60, educ = low | 115 | 111 | 104 | 103 | 109 | 106 | 104 | 103 | .91 | .93 |
| educ = high | 212 | 179 | 164 | 159 | 177 | 172 | 164 | 159 | .77 | .89 |
| Male, single | 668 | 598 | 583 | 541 | 587 | 565 | 583 | 541 | .87 | .90 |
| Female, single | 625 | 572 | 554 | 527 | 565 | 541 | 554 | 527 | .89 | .92 |
| Female, married | 594 | 478 | 527 | 443 | 472 | 460 | 527 | 443 | .89 | .93 |
| Health record = average DI-insured | | 695 | | 605 | | 657 | | 605 | | .87 |

[a]  See Table 9.3.

Lower wage-profiles $(w_s)$ combined with earlier retirement ages $(t^*)$ result in lower pre-sickness opportunity costs of DI-enrolment for the long-term sick $(EY_{WORK})$. Their lower expected wages, however, also yield smaller expected benefit streams. Nevertheless, for all types studied the long-term sick appear to face higher lifetime replacement rates.

By its definition the income stream in case the application is rejected $(Y_{RA})$ is larger than the DI-benefit stream $(Y_{BEN})$ and smaller than the continued labor force participation stream $(EY_{WORK})$. However, under the assumption that every claimant would get an award $(p_a=1)$, the relative size of $EY_{RA}$ is irrelevant as it implies that $EY_{DI} = EY_{BEN}$. This assumption underlies the calculations in table 9.5.

Given the unidentifiability of an individually varying award rate, we choose to fix the award rate at $p_a=1$ for the calculation of $EY_{DI}$; not because we find this value to realistically reflect Dutch award policies but because it leaves us with a conservative measure of $EY_{DI}$ which is lower than would be obtained for values of $p_a$ smaller than 1.

In fact, then, $p_a$ drops out of the structural version of the estimation model introduced in section 3.3.4, eq.(3.28). As with the marginal rate of substitution between income and leisure $(\beta)$, $p_a$ can only be sensibly represented by (reduced to) its determinants - extent of disablement and employment opportunities [see eq.(3.32)].

## 9.5    Summary and Conclusions

The topic of this chapter has been the analysis and measurement of the opportunity cost of DI-enrolment.

We have started by reiterating the definitions and theoretical relevance of financial considerations as determinants of the decision to apply for Disability Insurance, elaborated in chapter 3. As a first indication we found, in section 9.2, that the standardized pre-disability wages of DI-entrants are lower than those of the DI-insured. Lower wages entail higher replacement rates and, therefore, may point to incentive effects.

To investigate the potential sources of these wage differentials and their interrelations with health we, next, introduced a simultaneous equations model by which the wage rate was assumed to be endogenous with respect to the probability of long-term sickness. Using an endogenous switching model we were able to confirm the presumed endogeneity: significant effects were found for the covariance of PSICK with the wage rate. This also indicated that part of the wage differentials may be due to health-related differences in productivity.

Differences in returns to schooling, however, appeared to be the main source of healty-sick wage differentials. More specifically, the gains to higher than primary education turned out to be significantly lower in that part of the labor force from which the long-term sick and, hence, the DI-entrants are recruited. Our estimates show that among the well-trained the pre-sickness wages of the sick are about 13 percent below the corresponding population mean.

As a result, the future wage trajectories of the sick, although similarly shaped, lie below those for the general population. The opportunity costs of DI-enrolment measured by earnings foregone, therefore, are significantly lower for the long-term sick than for the average DI-insured.

Using these estimation results we have devoted the last part of this chapter to the definition and measurement of the present values of the expected income streams in the two options at stake: DI-application or continued labor force participation. Since we assume that the labor force option is also subject to a (later) disability risk we first estimated the duration of the remaining work life. Among 40 year olds, the *ex ante* expected age of eventual DI-enrolment is 59 for DI-insured, and 53 for the long-term sick. (Evidently, the *ex post* expectation for long-term absentees is much lower.) Our estimates suggest that half of this 6 years difference is related to health. The other half, then, is due the less favorable vocational characteristics of (potential) DI-entrants.

Combining the estimates obtained in this chapter we were able to construct a measure for the income-stream associated with the labor force participation option. The measurement of the alternative income-stream, however, is plagued by institutional constraints and missing data. Specifically, the award probability and the income-stream for a rejected applicant are unobservable. We, therefore, have to drastically simplify the definition of the income-stream related to the DI-option.

The resulting replacement rate based on life-time incomes (RRTL), is higher for the long-term sick than for average workers. Therefore, the pre-sickness opportunity cost of DI-enrolment appear to be lower for the long-term sick than for the average worker.

# Appendix to chapter 9

**Table A.9.1  Reduced-Form Probit Estimates for Pr(DI)**

|  | coefficient | (st. error) |
|---|---|---|
| ***Employee-level*** | | |
| Age | -.0086 | (.0170) |
| Age squared (* $10^{-2}$) | .0515 | (.0217)* |
| Female=1 | .2475 | (.0933)** |
| Married=1 | -.0303 | (.0839) |
| Ndepkids | -.0364 | (.0217) |
| Urbanization | -.0376 | (.0298) |
| Education | -.0495 | (.0269) |
| Strenuous work record[a] | .9750 | (.1649)** |
| Tenure[b] | -.2938 | (.0999)** |
| g(Working hours) | .9495 | (.3565)** |
| Commuting time | .0241 | (.0210) |
| Ln(other househ.inc. + 1) | .0165 | (.0082)* |
| Reg. unempl. rate | -.0820 | (.1232) |
| Previously unemployed=1 | .2170 | (.0693)** |
| Mobility=1 | .0380 | (.0602) |
| Absence record | .0217 | (.0046)** |
| Duration of complaints[a] | 2.3169 | (.3238)** |
| ***Employer-level*** | | |
| Ln(firmsize) | .0573 | (.0149)** |
| Increasing employment (*$10^{-2}$) | .0002 | (.0010) |
| Decreasing employment (*$10^{-2}$) | -.0039 | (.0034) |
| Perc. fem. employment (*$10^{-2}$) | -.0020 | (.0012) |
| Workers' consultation=1 | -.0783 | (.0501) |
| Job adaptation | -.1228 | (.0352)** |
| Medical guidance | -.0549 | (.0237)* |
| Social guidance | -.1584 | (.0327)** |
| Branch of industry | | |
|     Agriculture | -.1171 | (.1708) |
|     Steel industry | -.0246 | (.0914) |
|     Construction | ref. | ref. |
|     Other industries | -.0785 | (.0884) |
|     Wholesale and retail | -.0632 | (.0957) |
|     Other commercial services | -.0508 | (.0889) |
|     Health care | -.2884 | (.1542) |
|     Non-commercial services | -.0126 | (.1181) |
| Constant | -3.3511 | (.3482) |
| -2 * Loglikelihood ratio | 1393 .10** | |
| pseudo-$R^2$ | .365 | |
| #Observations | 2946 | |

| | |
|---|---|
| ** | Significant at the 1 percent level. |
| * | Significant at the 5 percent level. |
| a | Divided by age. |
| b | Divided by work experience (years). |

## Notes

1. This causality issue is equivalent to the problem of post-hoc observation studied in chapter 6.

2. Within our subsample of DI-entrants only 10 percent get less than the full amount. Moreover, 8 out of 10 of these partial benefits were given to supplement partial earnings reductions due to impairment. In those cases the effective replacement rate is also 80 percent (see chapter 2, pp. 6-7). As a result of the award policy, prevailing in 1980, only 2 percent of the DI-entrants are awarded truly partial benefits.

3. Since 1980, the amount of maximum insured earnings has changed from Dfl. 235.95 to Dfl. 262.28 in 1985 to 265.87 in 1990.

4. Which may be supplemented by private disability pensions.

5. One of the retrenchments preluding the 1987 social security amendments was the abolition of this so-called minimum wage protection.

6. The hourly wage rate is derived from available sample information on net monthly earnings and the individually varying monthly average number of hours worked. In the SB-sample the wage rate information refers to the pre-sickness situation. We have corrected for the possibility that SB-sample respondents mistake monthly Sickness Benefits for monthly earnings by using administrative information on gross wages.

7. This specification for age and education is borrowed from Hagenaars (1985, p. 83). Preliminary estimation showed that it yields the best fit of the wage equations. For education we employ a transformation of the ordinal scale displayed in table 4.6, panel 3. Applying the inverted unit normal distribution function to the cumulative frequencies of the education categories, we obtain a semi-continuous variable with empirically founded class distances.

8. The impediments for women, put up by the Dutch labor market, to realize their professional aspirations is reflected by the participation rates in table 2.5.

9. Ideally, the interaction of sex with experience and other interaction-effects should enter the wage equation, too. Preliminary experiments have shown, however, that such an elaborate specification causes prohibitive multicollinearity. One should bear in mind that ln(AGE) is a poor approximation of the experience of married women since their careers usually are characterized by lengthy interruptions (see chapter 7).

10. The oldest respondents were 20 years old in 1936. Possibly, d(GEN) measures health effects as well, since the oldest generation may have contracted diseases and handicaps, from which the younger generations have remained free. Such generation-specific health problems may be related to the ill effects of World War II, when the oldest sample persons (55-64) were in their twenties.

11. In Chirikos and Nestel (1985) the economic effects of poor health are examined longitudinally. They find that health problems incurred in the past adversely affect current earnings.

12. Empirical evidence for a simultaneous relation of health and wages is found in Grossman and Benham (1974) and, using more appropriate estimation techniques, Lee (1982).

13. Since Heckman (1974, 1979), Hausman & Wise (1976), and Lee (1979) introduced estimation models for simultaneous equations with discrete dependents, the potential endogeneity of earnings (and transfer income) has been a recurrent theme in the labor supply literature. For applications of the endogenous switching model to labor and transfer incomes see, e.g., Haveman & Wolfe (1984a, 1984b), and Fenn & Vlachonikolis (1986).

14. See Lee (1979) and Maddala (1983), section 8.3.

15. Notice that $\sigma_{01}$, the covariance of the two wage equations is not identifiable.

16. The endogenous switching model is usually applied to derive instrumental values for selectively missing observations and not for causal purposes. See for instance, Lee (1978), Lee & Trost (1978), Haveman & Wolfe (1984a). Fenn & Vlachonikolis (1986) compare the stepwise Probit-OLS procedure, applied here, with full ML results. In De Jong et al. (1988) full ML is applied, too.

17. Notice that $\lambda_0$ and $\lambda_1$ are always negative and positive, respectively. Hence, unconditional prediction - i.e., excluding $\lambda_0$ and $\lambda_1$ from the prediction equation (9.6) - of wage rates for the DI-insured requires a positive correction equal to $-\sigma_{0\epsilon}\lambda_0$. Similarly, unconditional prediction of 'sick' wage rates requires a negative correction equal to $\sigma_{1\epsilon}\lambda_1$. In section 9.4.2 we will use unconditional prediction of "sick" wages as indicators for rejected applicants' wages.

18. This test is based on OLS estimation of a modified version of the wage equation using all observations described in Maddala (1983), pp. 227-228.

19. The expected wage rate for the i-th individual is calculated following:

$$w_i = \exp\{\,\mu_i + \tfrac{1}{2}\,\sigma_z^2\,\}\quad \text{with}\quad \mu_i = \alpha_z' A_i + \sigma_{z\epsilon}\,\lambda_{zi} \qquad (z = 0,1)$$

and

$$\sigma_z^2 = \frac{1}{n_z - k}\sum^{n_z}(\mu_i - \mu_z)^2\;;\qquad \mu_z = \frac{1}{n_z}\sum^{n_z}\mu_i$$

$n_0$ is the number of healthy employees, $n_1$ the number of long-term sick, and k the number of explanatory variables (12) for $\ln w_i$. Exp $\{\tfrac{1}{2}\sigma_z^2\}$ serves as a constant correction factor equal to 1.03 for the healthy and 1.02 for the sick.

20. This simplification may be justified by the Dutch DI-practice with yearly recovery rates that amount to no more than 4 percent of the beneficiary volume (see table 2.15).

21. This is eq. (3.11) which has been derived in section 3.3.2. The expected duration of the remaining work life is calculated conditional on continued labor force participation, excluding the possibility of DI-enrolment during $t_0$.

22. Ignoring potential selectivity problems.

23. For an empirical analysis of the determinants of time preference rates, see Van Praag & Van Weeren (1983).

24. In the actual calculation of the DI-benefit stream we have accounted for supplementary benefits, up to after-tax earnings, during the first year after DI-enrolment. These supplements were added depending on employers' reports of such perquisites.

Chapter 10

# DETERMINANTS OF ENTERING THE DI-PROGRAM: UNCONDITIONAL AND CONDITIONAL PROBABILITY MODELS

## 10.1 Introduction

The preceding chapters, 7, 8, and 9, were devoted to the estimation of separate sub-models, each covering one part of the multicausal process governing DI-enrolment. The instrumental variables resulting from these submodels intend to summarize comprehensive sets of socio-medical and economic factors. Moreover, under the untested assumption that these background variables are exogenous the ensuing instrumentals are exogenous too.

In this chapter we will use these instrumentals as building blocks for the definitive version of our structural probability models. The three models under scrutiny are derived from the identity

$$Pr\{DI\} = Pr\{DI \mid 5M.SICK\}.Pr\{5M.SICK\}$$

which links the dependent variables of the probability models. $Pr\{DI\}$ represents the unconditional probability that, within a given period of time - one year - a DI-insured worker reports sick, remains unable to work for 12 months and, subsequently, is awarded a DI-benefit. Analogously, $Pr\{5M.SICK\}$ is the unconditional probability of a DI-insured worker reporting sick and remaining sick for at least 5 months. $Pr\{DI|5M.SICK\}$, then, is the conditional probability of DI-enrolment given 5 months sickness.

The identity also reflects the sampling procedures that have generated our data. Recall that the data stems from two 1980 samples; the SB-sample and the control sample. The first consists of Sickness Benefit (SB) recipients whose sick leave spell had lasted 5 months at the time of their being interviewed. The second is a control sample taken from the complete DI-insured population, i.e., all private sector employees; it has 1417 complete records including employers' information.

The SB-sample (2534 complete observations) was followed administratively to distinguish subsequent work resumers from those who fulfilled the mandatory, 12 months, waiting period for DI-eligibility; 60 percent of the sick sample entered the DI-program. The sample of DI-entrants, therefore, consists of 1529 complete observations.

In section 10.2 we present ML-probit estimates for the unconditional DI-probability model, Pr{DI}, where DI-entrants and DI-insured are the ones and the zeros, respectively.

We also present the results for a companion probit on PSICK (=Pr{5M.SICK}). Here the ones contain all 2534 sick sample persons. A preliminary version of this model was used in chapter 6 where we tested a number of suspicious variables for the presence of endogenous errors of measurement. These tests indicated that the variables used in this preliminary version did not satisfactorily cover a number of aspects, especially those referring to internal and external employment opportunities. Instead we now use the instrumentals flowing from the submodels reported in chapters 7 and 8.

While the probit on Pr{DI} stands on its own as it aims to describe the full transition from work to DI-enrolment, the other two probability models are linked as PSICK and Pr{DI|SICK} represent successive stages in the DI-process. In section 10.3, then, we focus on the last stage of the DI-process by analyzing the DI-probability conditional on 5 months sickness. In comparison to the general population at risk a sample consisting of long-term absentees is obviously much more homogeneous and may, therefore, be poorer in terms of explanatory variation. On the other hand, contrary to the control sample of DI-insured all sick sample persons have been medically and ergonomically examined. This unusually rich data allows for a confrontation of self-perceptions with expert - i.e., gatekeepers'- opinions on work limitations and residual capacities. Employing this dataset we try to assess the relative impacts of self-perceptions, and gatekeepers' and employers' views, on the conditional DI-probability. Given the potential endogeneity of the self-perceived work capacity with respect to the conditional DI-probability, we use a simultaneous equations system to describe the last stage in the process of DI-enrolment.

In section 10.4 we return to the unconditional DI-probit and use its estimated version to simulate the effects on Pr{DI} of two drastic changes that occurred between 1980 and 85, viz., a surge in unemployment and a series of cuts in real DI-benefits (see chapter 2).

Section 10.5 concludes.

## 10.2 Unconditional Probability Models

### 10.2.1 Introduction

In chapter 3, we have built an analytical framework to study the transition from labor force to DI-program participation, integrating the medical-sociological and the micro-economic approaches to disability behavior.

In eq.(3.28), we arrived at the following specification for the individual DI-risk

$$\Pr\{DI\} = H_0 (p_a, \beta, N_0, ETG, EY_{DI}, EY_{WORK})  \qquad (3.28)$$

with

$$\beta = \beta(D, M, EO)  \qquad (3.31)$$

and

$$p_a = p_a(D, EO)  \qquad (3.32)$$

Recall that

$H_0$ = the standard normal cdf implying the standard probit ML-model; all probit models reported in this section, however, have been modified so as to take account of endogenous stratification;[1]

$p_a$ = the probability of being awarded a DI-benefit given a claim;

$\beta$ = a parameter reflecting relative preferences for retirement;

$N_0$ = other household income (OTHHINC);

ETG = expected leisure gain after DI-enrolment;

$EY_{DI}$ = the present value of the expected income stream in the DI-option;

$EY_{WORK}$ = the present value of the expected income stream in the work option;

D = extent of disablement;

M = commitment to paid work;

EO = internal (within firm) and external employment opportunities.

Substitution of (3.31) and (3.32) in (3.28) yields an empirical version of the structural DI-probit model[2]

$$\Pr\{DI\} = H_0 (D, M, EO, N_0, ETG, LnLOSSLT)  \qquad (10.1)$$

LnLOSSLT is a logarithmic transformation of the lifetime income loss associated with DI-entry, $EY_{WORK} - EY_{DI}$.[3] Or rather LnLOSSLT = -ln [RRLT] where RRLT is the lifetime replacement rate documented in the previous chapter (table 9.5). Although RRLT and LnLOSSLT give the same qualitative results we prefer to use the latter variable because it has a larger coefficient of variation.[4]

As argued in section 6.3, we use an empirical specification of the unconditional probability of extended sick leave (PSICK) which is analogous to eq.(10.1).

Earlier, in chapter 3, we derived hypotheses with respect to the sign of the effects of the theoretical concepts listed above (see scheme 3.4). Then, in chapters 6 through 9, we reported how we chose to operationalize the dimensions of these concepts. The resulting explanatory variables and their hypothesized effects are summarized below. Their means and standard deviations are listed in an appendix to this chapter (table A.10.1).

- D, the extent of disablement is measured by four variables; two reflecting one's health record, two representing current health status. COMPLREC counts the duration of the existence of the current health complaints in years, divided by age, and ABSNREC counts the number of weeks lost from work due to sickness during the last year before the current sickness spell started (SB-sample) or the last year before the interview (control sample).

  PHYSDIS (physical disabilities) and MENTDIS (mental disabilities) are inter-actions of current job demands and corresponding functional limitations. More specifically, these two disability indicators are weighed sums of activity restric-tions, where the weights correspond to the importance of these activities for performance on the current job.

  Previously, in chapter 6, these health indicators appeared to have their expected positive impacts. PHYSDIS, however, turned out to be endogenous with respect to PSICK. Hence we use predicted instead of observed values for PHYSDIS, stemming from the regression reported in table 6.4.

- M, the commitment to paid work, is specified by two indicators: JOBSAT (job satisfaction) and WETHIC (work ethic). Upon testing, in chapter 6, these attitu-dinal scales appeared to be exogenous with respect to PSICK. Unexpectedly, the effect of WETHIC on PSICK turned out to be positive.

- EO, employment opportunities has two dimensions - the first refers to the labor market in general; the second, by focusing on the internal market, indicates the security of one's current job. The first dimension is measured by $Pr\{E \rightarrow U\}$, the individual risk of becoming unemployed, and $Pr\{U \rightarrow E\}$, the reemployment probability. Both probabilities are derived from the hazard models described in chapter 7; their impacts on $Pr\{DI\}$ are expected to be positive and negative, respectively.

  As regards the internal dimension, employers' views on career prospects, PROSPEC, and job performance, JBPRFORM, are included as indicators of the internal labor market opportunities for the individual worker. In chapter 6, both variables have been shown to be exogenous with respect to PSICK, and to have the expected negative effects.

- Information on both the unemployment and the disability risk is contained in the variable FIRMRISK, the firm-specific DI-incidence rate. FIRMRISK is an instrumental variable representing medical and socioeconomic aspects of the work environment. It is based on the model described in chapter 8. Given its definition it is expected to affect Pr{DI} positively.
- LnLOSSLT, the size of the financial penalty related to DI-enrolment is likely to affect the DI-probability negatively.
- OTHHINC, the log of other household income is expected to have a positive effect on Pr{DI}.
- ETG, the potential leisure gain from DI-enrolment seeks to capture the effect of time preferences. Since ETG is based on formal working hours, we also include a variable COMTIME, measuring the commuting time related to one's current job. Other things equal such gains are hypothesized to promote retirement.
- Finally, AGE, $AGE^2$, and dummy variables for gender and marital status, D(FEM=1) and D(MAR=1), are included in the DI-probability model as well.

### 10.2.2 The Unconditional Disability Probability

The probit estimation results for the structural DI-probability model are presented in table 10.1. We have estimated versions with and without age. Given the insignificance and the theoretical redundancy of the age effects (see below), the second version is the preferred one.

The third column contains standardized impacts of the explanatory variables omitting age. The estimated effects are corrected for differences in scaling by multiplying the estimated probit coefficients with the sample standard deviation of the explanatory variables ($\hat{\beta}s_x$). Under the presumption that the latent inclination underlying the binary dependent variable is standard normal, the standardized coefficients measure the effect on Pr{DI} of a one sample standard deviation change in a explanatory variable. By thus making the probit effects unit free we get an impression of the relative impact of the explanatory variables.

### Extent of Disablement

All four indicators of the extent of disablement appear to have the expected impact on the DI-entry probability. Current work disabilities as well as previous health status, as measured by duration of health complaints and worktime lost due to sickness, all increase the DI-entry probability. This is of course hardly surprising. On the contrary, it is rather the relatively modest discriminatory power of these health effects which is remarkable. After all, the binary dependent discriminates between the working and the long-term sick, and although there are mildly impaired persons among the working, the dependent is by definition a strong

Table 10.1    Probit Coefficients and Standardized Effects of the Determinants of
              Pr(DI)[a]  (Standard Errors between Brackets)

| explanatory variables | $\hat{\beta}$ | $(s_\beta)$ | $\hat{\beta}$ | $(s_\beta)$ | $\hat{\beta}.s_x$ |
|---|---|---|---|---|---|
| | | | dependent variable: Pr(DI) | | |
| AGE | - .0108 | (.0193) | | | |
| AGESQ (x10$^{-2}$) | .0209 | (.0234) | | | |
| D(FEM=1) | - .6928 | (.1285)** | - .7449 | (.1264)** | -.3383 |
| D(MAR=1) | - .0429 | (.0941) | - .0363 | (.0919) | -.0163 |
| COMPLREC | 1.2494 | (.2847)** | 1.1456 | (.2764)** | .1343 |
| ABSNREC | .0136 | (.0048)** | .0126 | (.0047)** | .0669 |
| PHYSDIS[b] | 1.3520 | (.3101)** | 1.4131 | (.2874)** | .1484 |
| MENTDIS | 1.5474 | (.1669)** | 1.5734 | (.1672)** | .2565 |
| WETHIC | .0895 | (.0293)** | .0969 | (.0291)** | .0943 |
| JOBSAT | - .0348 | (.0305) | - .0356 | (.0304) | -.0320 |
| D(MALE=1).Pr{E→U}[c] | .3671 | (.1250)** | .3490 | (.1250)** | .1070 |
| D(FEM=1) .Pr{E→U}[c] | .3826 | (.3161) | .2947 | (.3036) | .0423 |
| D(MALE=1).Pr{U→E}[c] | - .0040 | (.0007)** | - .0046 | (.0006)** | -.4222 |
| D(FEM=1) .Pr{U→E}[c] | - .0033 | (.0012)** | - .0038 | (.0011)** | -.2416 |
| FIRMRISK[d] | .2390 | (.0566)** | .2345 | (.0556)** | .1297 |
| PROSPECTS | - .3404 | (.0466)** | - .3508 | (.0462)** | -.2677 |
| JOBPERF | - .1005 | (.0376)** | - .1001 | (.0376)** | -.0725 |
| LnLOSSLT[e,f] | - .6142 | (.0743)** | - .6276 | (.0729)** | -.3752 |
| OTHHINC | .0115 | (.0090) | .0077 | (.0086) | .0332 |
| ETG[f] | .7655 | (.1465)** | .6961 | (.1421)** | .1838 |
| COMTIME | .0698 | (.0242)** | .0689 | (.0242)** | .0786 |
| Constant | - .7946 | (.7868) | - .6866 | (.7759) | |
| -2loglik.ratio | 1977.68** | | 1972.28** | | |
| Pseudo-R$^2$ | .4976 | | .4956 | | |
| #Observations | 2946 | | | | |

| | |
|---|---|
| a | All ordinal variables are rescaled by the inverted normal transformation. |
| b | Predicted values of PHYSDIS are based on the estimates in section 6.4. |
| c | Predicted values of the regressors are based on the estimates in chapter 7. |
| d | Predicted values of FIRMRISK are based on the estimates in chapter 8. |
| e | Predicted values of LnLOSSLT are based on the estimates in chapter 9. |
| f | Discount rate is 30 percent. |
| * | Significant at the 5 percent level. |
| ** | Significant at the 1 percent level. |

correlate of health status. The two disability indicators, therefore, should act as severe controls on the effects of the other, non-medical, factors.

## Commitment to Paid Work

A worker's commitment to paid work does not seem to be a particularly strong predictor of the DI-entry probability. The direct impact of job satisfaction is all but absent. Again, we find that people who adhere to traditional values with respect to work appear to face a significantly higher DI-risk. Older workers being the stronger supporters of traditional values, the positive impact of WETHIC may reflect a generation effect. After having done one's share for 40 years or more, often in menial, physically strenuous jobs, the older generation may feel entitled to paid rest. Under these circumstances the mental incongruity between a traditional morale and transfer dependency may dissolve.

The positive effect of WETHIC appears to be very stable. Its estimated value is insensitive to variations in model specification. Comparison of the WETHIC-coefficient estimates in the column 1 and 3, for instance, shows that the estimate is not affected by the exclusion of age from the DI-model, despite the fact that WETHIC and age are strongly correlated.

Below, in section 10.3, we will reiterate the role of work commitment in the disability process.

### Employment Opportunities

We have included two variables to assess the impact of external employment opportunities on the probability of DI-program enrolment; these two variables, $Pr\{E \rightarrow U\}$ and $Pr\{U \rightarrow E\}$, the predicted probabilities of becoming unemployed and re-employed, respectively, summarize the vocational characteristics and unemployment experiences that are likely to distinguish high from low DI-risk workers.[5] To account for their differential work patterns, the hazard models by which these probabilities are predicted have been separately estimated for men and women. Hence, we obtain gender-specific labor market impacts. The other two indicators, PROSPECTS and JOBPERF, reflect employers' evaluations of the employee's performance and career prospects.

All effects are as expected. With a given health status a high probability to become unemployed raises the probability of DI-entry. And a high probability of re-employment decreases the risk of DI-entry. Notice that the standardized effect on the male re-employment probability is the largest - larger than the effects of the health variables.

The DI-risk reducing impact of internal career prospects (PROSPECTS) is large too. Employers' appreciations of their employees' job performance (JOBPERF) has a smaller effect but is still significant at the 1 percent level. These two effects seem to provide further support for the popular belief that employers use the DI-route to dismiss unproductive or easily replaceable workers.

### Firm Specific Disability Risks

In chapter 8 we have estimated a model to describe the inter-firm variation in DI-incidence rates. As explanatory variables we used firm specific conditions such as the firm's personnel policy, its policy towards the occurrence of disabilities, changes in employment, and general characteristics of the firm. The variable FIRMRISK, therefore, stands for the firm specific "disability environment" to which the workers sampled are exposed. Its coefficient appears to be positive as expected. As we have argued in chapter 8 that at least part of its variation can be attributed to firm specific cost-benefit considerations, the impact of FIRMRISK seems to underscore the suspicion that the DI-program is effectively used as an instrument of personnel management.

**Life Time Income Loss, Other Household Income, and Life Time Leisure Gain**
In chapter 3 we straightforwardly derived standard neoclassical hypotheses with respect to the expected lifetime utility difference between the DI-option and its alternative - continued labor force participation. More specifically, the expected income loss and the expected leisure gain associated with DI-entry are believed to affect the probability of DI-application and, thus, the DI-entry probability.
The financial, lifetime, consequences of DI-entry appear to be a prominent factor in the disability process. When expected DI-benefits rise relative to expected earnings, the probability of DI-enrolment increases. Similarly, the less one expects to be able to earn, the more likely one is to enter the DI-program.
Qualitatively, this outcome is supported by a number of related American studies.[6] To make quantitative comparisons as well we transform our coefficient on LnLOSSLT by

$$[\partial y/\partial EY_{DI}].EY_{DI} = 0.6276 \ EY_{DI} \ .[EY_{WORK} - EY_{DI}]^{-1} \approx 3.85$$

The resulting parameter is the partial derivative of the standard normal ordinate underlying the probit model $(y)$ with respect to the expected income-stream in the DI-option $(EY_{DI})$, multiplied by $EY_{DI}$ to make the parameter free of scaling.[7] It is calculated at the sample means of $EY_{DI}$ and $EY_{WORK}$.
Applying the same transformation to the probit effects found in two representative US studies, viz., Parsons (1980) and Haveman & Wolfe (1984a), yields - 0.30 and -2.55 respectively, for the effect of disability transfer income on male labor force participation.[8] These negative impacts on work effort can be compared with our estimate of 3.85 for the positive effect of disability transfer income on DI-program participation.
Since the effect in Parsons (1980) is more in line with those reported in other US studies, we conclude that the Dutch DI-program exerts a much stronger disincentive effect on work effort than comparable US provisions. Given the considerable differences in generosity and leniency between the Dutch and the US DI-program these divergent results are not completely unexpected.[9]
The log of other household income appears to have a positive but insignificant impact on the DI-probability. The significantly positive impact of ETG (expected time gain) confirms our initial expectation. ETG - a function of current formal working hours - appears to be among the relatively powerful predictors of the DI-

probability. The effect of COMTIME, i.e., commuting time, which adds to the leisure gain effect of ETG, is less prominent but still significantly positive.

### The Discount Rate

The effects of LnLOSSLT and ETG are conditional on the discount rate chosen for the calculation of present values of the future income and leisure streams. In chapter 3, the rate at which future income is depreciated by the potential DI-applicants, was defined as a fixed parameter in the DI-application model. The table below shows the results of an iterative search procedure for the best fitting - most likely - value of the discount rate.

Table 10.2    The DI-Probit Likelihood and the Estimated Coefficients of LnLOSSLT and ETG for Different Values of the Discount Rate ($\delta$)

| discount rate | -loglikelihood | $\beta_{LnLOSSLT}$[a] | $\beta_{ETG}$[a] |
|---|---|---|---|
| .00 | 1085 | -.1633 | .0038[n.s.] |
| .10 | 1067 | -.2765 | .0440 |
| .20 | 1056 | -.3477 | .1118 |
| .30 | 1054 | -.3752 | .1838 |
| .40 | 1056 | -.3840 | .2532 |
| .50 | 1059 | -.3869 | .3224 |
| .60 | 1063 | -.3884 | .3914 |

a. standardized probit coefficients;  n.s.: not significant.

The highest value of the likelihood function, i.e., the smallest absolute value of the loglikelihood, is obtained when $\delta$ equals 0.30. A 30 percent discount rate - six to seven times the real market rate in 1980 - implies that the average worker has a strong preference for present income.[10] The table also reveals the sensitivity of the standardized effects of present values to changes in the discount rate, by which these values are calculated. This may be due to the fact that lower discount rates produce a stronger (negative) correlation between age and the income loss and time gain variables (as illustrated by the calculations in table 9.5).

### Sex and Marital Status

Apart from its indirect, positive, effects running via PHYSDIS and LnLOSSLT, and its interaction with the unemployment and reemployment hazard variables, being a woman as such seems to reduce the probability of DI-enrolment. Although its mere size suggests that women are less likely to be found eligible for DI-benefits, the estimated effect of D(FEM=1) may well contain inadequately specified, or omitted, interactions with gender. In labor market studies women are generally found to be more sensitive to financial incentives.[11] Such results may be seen as a confirmation of differential work-leisure preferences of men and women. Interactions of sex with variables like LnLOSSLT and ETG, then, would be justified. Collinearity problems, however, preclude the estimation of such interaction effects.[12]

Note also that the reduced form effect of D(FEM=1) is significantly positive (see table A.9.1).

Marital status turns out to be irrelevant to the outcome of the disability process.

**Age-Effects**

In the analysis of disability behavior, age, sex, marital status, and education, often emerge as prominent determinants of the disability probability. In a structural model, the causal impact of such exogenous background variables is assumed to run via "intermediate" concepts. Their direct effects are more difficult to interpret. For instance, as hypothesized in chapter 3, the reduced form effect of age can be attributed to the structural effects of determinants like extent of disablement, expected lifetime earnings, and employment opportunities. In a structural model, then, the causal meaning of a direct age effect is limited to its interpretation as a screening device employed by the program gatekeepers - comparable to the only remaining causal interpretation of the estimated direct effect of D(FEM=1). Surely, a direct age effect may also contain elements of unobserved or inaccurately specified factors that are correlated with age.

While the reduced form effect of age is significant (see chapter 9, table A.9.1), its structural effect appears to reduce to insignificance. Comparison of the two probit specifications in table 10.1 shows that age can be dropped from the structural Pr{DI}-model without loss of performance both in terms of goodness-of-fit and robustness of the estimates.

### 10.2.3   Predicted DI-Probabilities

Although exclusion of age from the structural model is legitimate, its indirect impact on the DI-probability still is sizeable as shown by the standardized probability predictions reported in table 10.3. These are calculated by combining the structural probit estimates excluding age, with the age effects contained in the instrumental variables.

The first column contains probability predictions for the DI-insured relative to a fictitious standard employee, evaluated at the corresponding (control) sample means if not mentioned otherwise. The characteristics reported in each row are the ones that differ from the standard employee. The second column shows the *ex ante* predictions for those workers who turn out to be DI-entrants later. These are evaluated at the relevant part of the SB-sample. The probability prediction for the standard DI-insured employee is set equal to one; hence, all other values are relative to the standard DI-insured.

The resulting predictions show that, other things equal, a 60 year old married man runs an 11 times larger DI-risk than his 25 year old peer. Table 10.3 also reveals the strong indirect impact of education which mainly runs via the income variables that underlie LnLOSSLT, and via PHYSDIS. Low educated married men run a more than 6 times larger DI-risk than well trained but otherwise similar workers. As witnessed by its relatively weak discriminatory power, marital status is an unimportant factor in the DI-process.

Table 10.3  Standardized DI-Probability Predictions for Various Types of DI-Insured Employees and DI-Entrants

| | DI-Insured | DI-Entrants |
|---|---|---|
| **1. males** | | |
| Standard employee[a] | 1.00 (=0.0296) | 10.89 |
| Age = 25 | 0.28 | 6.77 |
| 60 | 3.15 | 17.33 |
| Education = low | 2.20 | 12.83 |
| high | 0.34 | 6.10 |
| Single | 1.52 | 12.35 |
| Health record = | | |
| average DI-entrant | 5.49 | |
| and age is 25 | 3.10 | |
| and age is 60 | 11.37 | |
| **2. females** | | |
| Standard employee[a] | 1.00 (=0.0430) | 8.60 |
| Age = 25 | 0.34 | 8.40 |
| 60 | 2.54 | 13.21 |
| Education = low | 1.65 | 17.32 |
| high | 0.57 | 4.00 |
| Single | 1.01 | 5.83 |
| Health record = | | |
| average DI-entrant | 3.32 | |
| and age is 25 | 1.80 | |
| and age is 60 | 6.94 | |

a   see table 9.3.

If the standard DI-insured would have the ill health status of an average DI-entrant, his DI-risk would be 5.5 times as large. The *ex ante* DI-risk of a standard DI-entrant, however, is 10.9 times as large since the entrants differ from the general population at risk in a variety of non-medical aspects too. The implication, here, is that about half (4.49/9.89) of the difference in DI-risks between insured and awarded men can be accounted for by health status, the rest being determined by attitudinal and vocational factors.

The corresponding probability differentials for married women are less pronounced than those for married men. This may suggest that women are more homogeneous with respect to their disability behavior. It may also be that the estimated DI-model is better equipped to describe male than female retirement behavior.

### 10.2.4   The Probability of Extended Sick Leave, PSICK

The estimation results for the probit on PSICK - the probability of being on sick leave for more than 5 months - are contained in table 10.4. This model is estimated using the control-sample observations as "zeros" and all SB-sample observations who have been interviewed after 5 months sickness as "ones". Hence, the data for the PSICK-model differs from the DI-probit data as it has 1,005 added "ones". These additional observations did not fulfill the 12 months mandatory waiting period for DI-benefit entitlement, mostly because of job resumption. They did, however, complete the first stage in the DI-enrolment process which, given the fact that 60 percent of the 5 months sick fully complete the DI-waiting period, may be denoted as crucial.

The same dependant has been used before in chapter 6, where we estimated the reduced form (see table 6.2) and preliminary versions of the structural PSICK probit-model (table 6.5). These versions that were preliminary because they contained endogenous, or unsatisfactorily operationalized, variables, nevertheless confirmed the presence of non-medical elements in the determination of PSICK. Specifically, career prospects, other household income, and the firm's social policy with regard to absentees, appeared to be significant.

The specification for the final structural form of the PSICK-model is the same as the DI-probit model reported before. This warrants a direct comparison between both models. Age being insignificant again, the version excluding age is the preferred one. The last column contains the standardized coefficients corresponding to this version. Considering the fact that the "ones" for the DI-model in table 10.1, who actually entered the DI-program, are a select subsample of the "ones" for the PSICK-model in table 10.4, the (standardized) coefficients of both probits are remarkably similar, both in terms of size and significance. Comparison of the standardized effects yet shows marginal differences with regard to the impact of employment opportunities and the income variables. While expected income losses and leisure gains weigh less, re-employment opportunities and FIRMRISK have a considerably larger impact on Pr{DI} than on PSICK. These differences suggest that within firm, and general, employment opportunities affect the transition from 5 months sickness to DI-enrolment.

Notice that the standardized effects of the four health indicators show less pronounced differences. Whether these combined results imply that the DI-probability conditional on 5 months sickness would be determined by employment conditions rather than impairment will be more fully scrutinized in the next section. At any rate, from these probit results we may conclude that in the first, and crucial, stage of the DI-process - the transition from work to prolonged sickness - financial and labor market considerations are as important as health.

Note also that the effect of gender is negative again, and as strongly so as in the DI-probit. To the extent that this effect is due to discriminatory behavior of program administrators, the combined results in tables 10.1 and 10.3 suggest that selection on gender takes place in the first half of the sickness benefit year, and not when judging DI-eligibility at the end of the waiting period.

Table 10.4     Probit Coefficients and Standardized Effects of the Determinants of PSICK[a] (Standard Errors between Brackets)

| *explanatory variables* | dependent variable: Pr{SICK} | | | | |
|---|---|---|---|---|---|
| | $\hat{\beta}$ | $(s_\beta)$ | $\hat{\beta}$ | $(s_\beta)$ | $\hat{\beta}.s_x$ |
| AGE | - .0210 | (.0172) | | | |
| AGESQ $(\times 10^{-2})$ | .0265 | (.0208) | | | |
| D(FEM=1) | - .7746 | (.1158)** | - .8040 | (.1134)** | -.3653 |
| D(MAR=1) | - .0531 | (.0827) | - .0614 | (.0816)** | -.0277 |
| COMPLREC | 1.3472 | (.3019)** | 1.3369 | (.2987)** | .1566 |
| ABSNREC | .0097 | (.0047) | .0097 | (.0047)* | .0515 |
| PHYSDIS[b] | 1.2027 | (.2871)** | 1.1382 | (.2654)** | .1193 |
| MENTDIS | 1.6282 | (.1697)** | 1.6336 | (.1697)** | .2664 |
| WETHIC | .0848 | (.0255)** | .0863 | (.0253)** | .0839 |
| JOBSAT | - .0362 | (.0265) | - .0360 | (.0264) | -.0323 |
| D(MALE=1).Pr{E→U}[c] | .2939 | (.1114)** | .2994 | (.1105)** | .0924 |
| D(FEM=1) .Pr{E→U}[c] | .2086 | (.2799) | .2614 | (.2640) | .0386 |
| D(MALE=1).Pr{U→E}[c] | - .0034 | (.0005)** | - .0033 | (.0005)** | -.3070 |
| D(FEM=1) .Pr{U→E}[c] | - .0026 | (.0008)** | - .0024 | (.0007)** | -.1488 |
| FIRMRISK[d] | .1530 | (.0479)** | .1577 | (.0473)** | .0876 |
| PROSPECTS | - .3048 | (.0365)** | - .3045 | (.0360)** | -.2319 |
| JOBPERF | - .1281 | (.0336)** | - .1307 | (.0335)** | -.0947 |
| LnLOSSLT[e,f] | - .6994 | (.0664)** | - .7177 | (.0650)** | -.4282 |
| OTHHINC | .0170 | (.0081)* | .0143 | (.0079) | .0618 |
| ETG[f] | .8575 | (.1381)** | .8323 | (.1347)** | .2189 |
| COMTIME | .0542 | (.0213)* | .0539 | (.0212)* | .0614 |
| Constant | - .7079 | (.7177) | .6043 | (.7065) | |
| -2loglik.ratio | 2110.36** | | 2107.74** | | |
| Pseudo-R² | .4065 | | .4062 | | |
| #Observations | 3951 | | | | |

a   All ordinal variables are rescaled by the inverted normal transformation.
b   Predicted values of PHYSDIS are based on the estimates in section 6.4.
c   Predicted values of the regressors are based on the estimates in chapter 7.
d   Predicted values of FIRMRISK are based on the estimates in chapter 8.
e   Predicted values of LnLOSSLT are based on the estimates in chapter 9.
f   Discount rate is 30 percent.
*,** Significant at 5 and 1 percent respectively.

## 10.3    The Conditional DI-Probability

### 10.3.1   Introduction

In this section we shift the perspective from broadly modelled unconditional probability models that describe the relatively large transition from work to DI-entry (or to prolonged sickness), to a more detailed analysis of the last stage in the disability process, the transition from prolonged (5 months) sickness to DI-enrolment - i.e., the formal recognition of the disability status.

The database for this analysis is the sample of 2534 Sickness Benefit recipients. This sample has been both interviewed and medically and ergonomically examined at the moment when their sickness absence had lasted 5 months. After these examinations the sick sample has been followed administratively to record Sickness Benefit terminations due to recovery before elapse of the mandatory - 12 months - waiting period for DI-eligibility. The majority of those who fulfilled the waiting period were admitted to the DI-rolls. In a binary context these DI-awards are the "ones", as they were before in the estimation of the unconditional DI-probit model. The "zeros" consist of recoveries as well as DI-refusals - those who have been found to be less than 15 percent disabled at the end of the DI waiting period.

The resulting dataset is not only richer in terms of medical and ergonomical information than the control sample, it is also more adequate statistically than the merger of the control and the SB-sample used so far. Specifically, the fact that the dependent variable - DI-entry - has been generated longitudinally within the SB-sample solves some statistical problems inherent in the merged data. First, the relation between the binary event under study and its, predetermined, explanatory factors is not affected by the kind of endogenous measurement error studied in chapter 6. Second, the SB-sample is a random sample taken from all 1980 SB-recipients that crossed the 5 months sickness border, whereas the merged sample is choice based.

### 10.3.2   Modelling Disability Behavior

In chapter 3 we introduced the DI-probability as the product of the application probability and the probability of being awarded a DI-benefit given application. By this decomposition we were able to structure the determinants of the DI-probability around the behavioral options open to potential claimants and to the program gatekeepers. Unfortunately, this decomposition has only theoretical value since, due to the design of the Dutch DI-program, applications are unobservable. Our SB-data, however, do contain measurements of (impaired) workers' and gatekeepers' perceptions of the extent of disablement. What we denote here as gatekeepers' perceptions are in fact the combined expert ratings by JMS-physicians and ergonomists of respondents' work capacity at DI-entry. Two versions of these ratings - one more favorable than the other - have been described in section 5.7. Both versions are scaled by distinguishing four categories (see table 5.8). The self-perceptions are scaled conformally, except that they do not refer to a specific period of time.[13]

Using these perceptions we may rearrange the unconditional DI-probability model (10.1) so as to obtain a more truly structural model in which self-perceived work disability (DISresp) acts as the pivotal, potentially endogenous, variable. As an approximation to the theoretical model we specify the conditional DI-probability as a function of DISresp and the gatekeepers' rating of the respondents' extent of disablement (DISgate).

Formally, then, the structural model writes

$$\text{DISresp} \quad = H_2 \ (D, M, EO, N_0, ETG, LnLOSSLT, \hat{p}_{DI}) \qquad (10.2)$$

$$\text{DISgate} \quad = H_3 \ (D) \qquad (10.3)$$

$$\text{Pr}\{DI|SICK\} = H_4 \ (\text{DISresp, DISgate, EO}) \qquad (10.4)$$

Eq.(10.2) describes the formation of respondents' perceptions. This equation may act as an empirical counterpart of the theoretical specification for Pr{CLAIM} in eq.(3.27). It contains all elements of the unconditional DI-model (10.1). By adding the predicted conditional DI-probability we aim to test, and control, for the endogeneity of self-reported health with respect to DI-enrolment. The argument, here, is that those who prefer to leave the labor market have an incentive to declare themselves in poor health.[14] The instrumental variable $\hat{p}_{DI}$ is calculated by application of the reduced form specification in table 6.2 to Pr{DI|SICK} (see table A.10.2 in the appendix to this chapter).

The expert ratings (DISgate) correspond to the conceptualization of disability as described in sections 3.2 and 5.3; The JMS-physicians base their assessments on type and extent of functional limitations; The ergonomists confront these limitations with the requirements in suitable jobs disregarding the actual availability of such jobs. Hence, we specify DISgate as a function of the extent of disablement (D) proper. Notice that, given its strictly medical operationalization, DISgate is an incomplete measure for the actual award behavior which, by the so-called labor market consideration, takes account of employment opportunities too.

The third equation is what we may denote as a truly structural model of DI-enrolment. The DI-probability is written as a weighted sum of self-perceptions, expert ratings, and employment opportunities (EO). EO is added for two reasons. First, the admission probability should account for labor market considerations.

Second, to the extent that EO reflects the opportunities offered by the current employer it seeks to represent the employer as a third agent influencing the transition from prolonged sickness to DI-enrolment.

### 10.3.3   Self-Perceived Work Disability: OLS Results

Table 10.5 contains the OLS results for DISresp. As argued before, the set of explanatory variables in eq.(10.2) is equal to the one used for the specification of the unconditional probabilities, Pr{DI} and PSICK, adding $\hat{p}_{DI}$ to test for simultaneity due to mutual dependency of DISresp and Pr{DI|SICK}.

**Extent of Disablement**

The medical data contained in the SB-sample allows for more consistent, and additional, indicators of the extent of disablement. The JMS-physicians assessed the current severity, i.e., at 5 months sickness, and the expected duration of three types of limitations - energetical, locomotive, and mental (including emotional). From these assessments three severity scales have been derived. The first, ENERLIM, indicates the severity of energetical limitations, e.g., due to malfunctioning of cardiovascular or respiratory organs. The second, measuring the extent of locomotive limitations, refers to the capacity of the musculo-skeletal and nervous systems to endure physical strain. Confrontation of this variable with the presence of physically strenuous aspects of the current job, as rated by JMS ergonomists, has yielded the variable PHYSDIS, used before. MENTDIS is defined similarly, by interaction of mental limitations with intellectual as well as stressful job demands. Contrary to PHYSDIS and MENTDIS energetical limitations are supposed to impair performance in general. Therefore, they are not interacted (i.e., weighed) with corresponding job demands.[15]

As expected, all three, expert based, disability indicators contribute significantly to self-assessments of one's work disability. Physical disabilities, indicated by PHYSDIS and ENERDIS, have a stronger impact than MENTDIS, possibly because of larger incongruities between patients and doctors when judging mental impairments.

The health status during the years prior to the current sick spell, as measured by duration of health complaints (COMPLREC) and weeks lost due to sickness (ABSNREC), do not significantly affect respondents' perceptions of work disability. The sixth health indicator, DIScurat, represents the disability prognoses of the treating general and specialized practitioners, as reported by the respondents. Its relatively large effect indicates that the views of the curative sector exert a strong independent influence on their patients' perceptions of work capacity. Assuming that its potential endogeneity is adequately controlled for by the inclusion of $\hat{p}_{DI}$,[16]

Table 10.5   OLS Coefficients and Standardized Effects of the Determinants of Self-Perceived Work Disability (DISresp)[a]  (Standard Errors between Brackets)

| explanatory variables | | dependent variable: *DISresp* | | |
|---|---|---|---|---|
| | | $\hat{\beta}$ | $(s_\beta)$ | $\hat{\beta}[s_x/s_y]$ |
| AGE | | - .0730 | (.0113)** | - .9934 |
| AGESQ (x10⁻²) | | .0932 | (.0125)** | 1.0560 |
| D(FEM=1) | | .0124 | (.0810) | .0057 |
| D(MAR=1) | | - .0500 | (.0521) | - .0200 |
| COMPLREC | | .1575 | (.1174) | .0272 |
| ABSNREC | | .0031 | (.0018) | .0310 |
| ENERLIM | | .1199 | (.0215)** | .0964 |
| PHYSDIS[b] | | .1531 | (.0200)** | .1304 |
| MENTDIS | | .0736 | (.0224)** | .0562 |
| DIScurat | | .3371 | (.0175)** | .3327 |
| WETHIC | | - .0340 | (.0157)* | - .0395 |
| JOBSAT | | - .0630 | (.0146)** | - .0763 |
| D(MALE=1) .Pr{E→U}[b] | | .1139 | (.0630) | .0406 |
| D(FEM=1) .Pr{E→U}[b] | | .2178 | (.2108) | .0262 |
| D(MALE=1) .Pr{U→E}[b] | | - .0012 | (.0004)** | - .0873 |
| D(FEM=1) .Pr{U→E}[b] | | - .0018 | (.0009)* | - .0520 |
| FIRMRISK[b] | | .0560 | (.0329) | .0293 |
| PROSPECTS | | - .0024 | (.0345) | - .0012 |
| JOBPERF | | .0126 | (.0198) | .0109 |
| LnLOSSLT[b] | | - .0147 | (.0246) | - .0168 |
| OTHHINC | | .0101 | (.0049)* | .0455 |
| ETG[b] | | - .0557 | (.0752) | - .0182 |
| COMTIME | | - .0109 | (.0124) | - .0149 |
| $\hat{p}_{DI}$[c] | | .8111 | (.1793)** | .1447 |
| Constant | | .9225 | (.3275)** | |
| Adjusted $R^2$ | | .3268 | | |
| #Observations | | 2534 | | |

a   All ordinal variables (including the dependent) are rescaled by the inverted normal transformation.
b   See notes under table 10.1.
c   Reduced form prediction of Pr{DI I SICK} from probit estimates in table A.10.2.
*,**   Significant at 5 and 1 percent respectively.

the size of the coefficient of DIScurat in comparison with the weights of the JMS-expert ratings suggests divergent opinions, or angles, regarding (future) work capacity.

## Commitment to Paid Work

While a worker's commitment to paid work did not seem to reduce the unconditional DI-probability, it does affect the respondent's evaluation of his or her ability to perform suitable work in the near future.

We find that the more satisfaction workers derive from their employment, the more optimistic they are about their residual work capacities. Similarly, people who strongly adhere to traditional values with respect to work tend to rate their future work capacity more favorably.

### Employment Opportunities
Unemployment and reemployment hazards, $Pr\{E{\to}U\}$ and $Pr\{U{\to}E\}$, have their expected positive and negative impacts. Specifically, poor reemployment opportunities significantly increase the inclination to declare oneself in poor health.
The effects of the three variables indicating disability hazards (FIRMRISK) and employment opportunities (PROSPECTS, JOBPERF) related to the current job are insignificant. Hence, employers' views do not seem to affect the work capacity perceptions of their impaired employees.

### Other Household Income, and LifeTime Income Losses and Leisure Gains
To the extent that self-assessments of incapacity reflect individual preferences for retirement, we expect income and leisure considerations to affect the perception of disability. As regards financial considerations, the expected income loss due to DI-enrolment has its expected negative impact but it is small and insignificant. The presence of household income sources, other than the respondent's labor or DI-benefit income, appears to induce more pessimistic disability perceptions. Expected leisure gains (ETG and COMTIME) have no interpretable effect on the self-perception of disability.

### Demographic Variables
While sex and marital status appear to be of no relevance to the perception of disability, age has a significant, U-shaped, impact. Reaching its minimum at the age of nearly 40 years, self-ratings of the extent of disablement become increasingly more pessimistic beyond 40. Age being a strong predictor of capacity reductions, the estimated age coefficients may partly reflect the impact of health status. However, with the inclusion of six health indicators, representing diverse angles and dimensions, and the predicted conditional DI-probability, we think that the increasing age effect merely reflects feelings of obsolescence and entitlement to paid rest after having done one's share for many years.

### The Conditional DI-Probability, $\hat{p}_{DI}$
The significance of the reduced form prediction of the conditional DI-probability confirms the endogeneity of the disability perception. Like others have found before, the predisposition for DI-enrolment and self-reported incapacity to work are strongly interrelated.[17] However, whether this outcome points to incomplete specification of the self-perception of disability or to a truly mutual relationship remains unclear.

### 10.3.4  Expert Rating of Work Disability: OLS Results

Although, by eq.(10.3), we have specified the gatekeepers' rating of disability (DISgate) as a function of the extent of disablement in a strict medical-ergonomic sense only, we apply the full specification for the self-perception of disability (DISresp) here too. This puts a severe test on the validity of both the expert ratings and the set of explanatory variables. If indeed the expert opinions are based on medical facts alone all variables, other than the six health indicators and possibly age as a screening device, should be insignificant. Significance of any of the non-medical factors either implies that it contains medical information or that DISgate is contaminated by non-medical elements. Moreover, inclusion of $\hat{p}_{DI}$ allows for an exogeneity test.

As appears from the OLS results reported in table 10.6, four of the six health indicators as well as age are strongly significant. ENERLIM, PHYSDIS, and MENTDIS, represent more detailed assessments by the same experts that have provided the broad ratings on which DISgate is based. Their significance, therefore, is nothing more than a confirmation of internal consistency. As such they act as powerful controls on the presence of other, medical and non-medical, effects.

Nevertheless, DIScurat, representing the work capacity rating of the curative sector as understood by the respondents, has an effect which is equal in size and significance to the other three health measures. This is remarkable as the respondents were interviewed after their examination by the JMS-experts. We may, therefore, assume that the respondents' understanding of the views of their doctors was unknown to the experts. Consequently, DIScurat seems to contain essential medical data which is left uncovered by the other health variables.

The age effect is U-shaped again with, according to the experts, increasing severity of disability beyond age 32. In comparison with respondents' perceptions the increasing part of the age-effect is stronger in that it starts at an earlier age and increases more steeply.[18] This prominent age-effect may represent both medical and vocational aspects of the experts' judgments. To the extent that it picks up such non-medical data, the validity of DISgate as a pure health variable is questionable. But even then, it may still validly reflect the determination of the views of the gatekeepers.

The sole, marginally significant, nuisance effect is that of job satisfaction. This may either mean that impaired workers are less satisfied because of their health problems, or that the gatekeepers take account of work attitudes when assessing the extent of disablement. Given its size, however, the effect of JOBSAT does not seriously jeopardize the validity of DISgate.

Finally, the insignificance of $\hat{p}_{DI}$ warrants the exogeneity of the expert ratings with respect to the conditional DI-probability.

Table 10.6   OLS Coefficients and Standardized Effects of the Determinants of Expert Ratings of Work Disability (DISgate)[a]  (Standard Errors between Brackets)

| explanatory variables | | dependent variable: DISgate | | |
|---|---|---|---|---|
| | | $\hat{\beta}$ | $(s_\beta)$ | $\hat{\beta}[s_x/s_y]$ |
| AGE | | - .0361 | (.0107)** | - .5127 |
| AGESQ (x10⁻²) | | .0571 | (.0119)** | .6831 |
| D(FEM=1) | | - .0177 | (.0772) | - .0085 |
| D(MAR=1) | | .0157 | (.0496) | .0066 |
| COMPLREC | | .1099 | (.1118) | .0200 |
| ABSNREC | | - .0010 | (.0017) | - .0055 |
| ENERLIM | | .2455 | (.0205)** | .2080 |
| PHYSDIS | | .2345 | (.0191)** | .2106 |
| MENTDIS | | .2275 | (.0214)** | .1831 |
| DIScurat | | .2149 | (.0167)** | .2237 |
| WETHIC | | - .0045 | (.0149) | - .0055 |
| JOBSAT | | - .0281 | (.0139)* | - .0358 |
| D(MALE=1) | .Pr{E→U}[b] | - .0372 | (.0600) | .0140 |
| D(FEM=1) | .Pr{E→U}[b] | .2078 | (.2007) | .0263 |
| D(MALE=1) | .Pr{U→E}[b] | .0003 | (.0004) | .0263 |
| D(FEM=1) | .Pr{U→E}[b] | .0004 | (.0009) | .0120 |
| FIRMRISK[b] | | .0191 | (.0314) | .0106 |
| PROSPECTS | | - .0061 | (.0329) | - .0032 |
| JOBPERF | | .0364 | (.0189) | .0332 |
| LnLOSSLT[b] | | - .0007 | (.0235) | - .0009 |
| OTHHINC | | - .0044 | (.0047) | - .0205 |
| ETG[b] | | .0087 | (.0716) | .0030 |
| COMTIME | | .0093 | (.0118) | .0133 |
| $\hat{P}_{DI}{}^c$ | | .2406 | (.1707) | .0453 |
| Constant | | .2091 | (.3119) | |
| Adjusted R² | | .3210 | | |
| #Observations | | 2534 | | |

a   All ordinal variables (including the dependent) are rescaled by the inverted normal transformation.
b   See notes under table 10.1
c   Reduced form prediction of Pr{DI I SICK} from probit estimates in table A.10.2.
*,**   Significant at 5 and 1 percent respectively.

Summarizing, we note that while self-reports appear to be influenced by a number of motivational and economic factors, the experts' ratings are mainly determined by health data and age. The picture of the disability determination process emerging from the estimates in table 10.6, may be described as a stepwise procedure. First, the gatekeepers - JMS-physicians and ergonomists - translate health complaints in terms of functional limitations, and confront these with the demands in commensurate jobs, to assess the nature and extent of disablement. Next, these first assessments are modified by incorporating data from the medical files as reflected by DIScurat. And, finally, age is taken into account such that similar health data lead to more pessimistic ratings of (future) work capacity the older the patient.

### 10.3.5 The Conditional DI-Probability: Probit Results

Table 10.7 presents the probit estimates of the structural conditional DI-probability model. After a sick leave period of five months, the DI-entry probability appears to depend on impaired workers' self-perception of disability (DISresp), on expert ratings of work disability (DISgate), and on employers' behavior as reflected by the firm specific DI-risk (FIRMRISK). Hence, all three agents in the process leading to DI-enrolment exert a significant influence. This confirms the notion that the program gatekeepers leave enough room for the insured workers and their employers to steer the outcome of the DI-process in the preferred direction.

The standardized effects of DISgate and of DISresp are remarkably similar. It implies that, after five months sickness, self-ratings are as important as gate-keepers' assessments in determining the probability of DI-entry. In other words, these two agents seem to have equal latitude.[19]

### Age and Sex
While employment opportunities, sex, and marital status have no impact on the conditional DI-probability the under 45 age spline is quite prominent. The insignificance of predicted unemployment and reemployment hazards is unexpected. After all, under the regime prevailing in 1980, employees with minor disabilities were presumed to be incapable of finding suitable employment as a result of discrimination against partially disabled, unless the contrary could be proven. As a result, partially disabled workers were awarded full DI-benefits, as if they were disabled to the highest degree. Thus (re-) employment opportunities were explicitly accounted for in DI-eligibility determinations. One would, therefore, expect the predicted unemployment and re-employment probabilities to play a significant role in the process of awarding DI-benefits.

An explanation for the absence of labor market effects may be found in the apparent age effect. For workers under 45 the conditional DI-probability increases with age; beyond 45 the direct effect of age vanishes. Assuming that, by the subjective and objective measurements employed, the extent of disablement is adequately controlled for, this kinked age-effect may be seen as a reflection of the labor market component in DI-eligibility. More specifically, given the zero impact of the variables representing labor market opportunities on the one hand, and the

**Table 10.7**   **Probit Coefficients and Standardized Effects of the Determinants of the DI-Probability Conditional on Five Months Sickness[a] (Standard Errors between Brackets)**

| explanatory variables | dependent variable: Pr(DI\|5M.SICK) | | |
|---|---|---|---|
| | $\hat{\beta}$ | $(s_\beta)$ | $\hat{\beta}.s_x$ |
| AGEspline <45 | .0266 | (.0058)** | .2105 |
| AGEspline ≥45 | .0065 | (.0069) | .0364 |
| D(FEM=1) | - .0398 | (.1028) | -.0163 |
| D(MAR=1) | - .0253 | (.0790) | -.0091 |
| Disresp[b] | .6450 | (.0812)** | .2903 |
| Disgate | .3692 | (.0370)** | .3138 |
| ABSLEGIT | - .0318 | (.0184) | -.0471 |
| D(MALE=1) .Pr{E→U}[c] | .0700 | (.1108) | .0128 |
| D(FEM=1)   .Pr{E→U}[c] | .3290 | (.3712) | .0362 |
| D(MALE=1) .Pr{U→E}[c] | .0003 | (.0007) | .0222 |
| D(FEM=1)   .Pr{U→E}[c] | - .0007 | (.0016) | -.0176 |
| FIRMRISK[c] | .1944 | (.0597)** | .0913 |
| PROSPECTS | - .0111 | (.0618) | -.0050 |
| JOBPERF | - .0237 | (.0352) | -.0183 |
| Constant | - .3333 | (.3996) | |
| -2loglik.ratio | 465.00** | | |
| Pseudo-$R^2$ | .1654 | | |
| #Observations | 2534 | | |

a   All ordinal variables are rescaled by the inverted normal transformation.
b   Predicted values of DISresp are based on the estimates in table 10.5.
c   Predicted values, see notes under table 10.1.
*,**   Significant at 5 and 1 percent respectively.

undisputed presence of labor market considerations in DI-eligibility assessments on the other, the resulting age-effect is probably due to the administrative routine to use age as a screening device. Acknowledging the correlation between age and labor market opportunities, gatekeepers seem to assume that the labor market position worsens with increasing age up until 45. Beyond that age partially disabled workers are generally presumed to be unable to find suitable, gainful, employment.[20]

Consequently, to the gatekeepers age seems to serve a dual purpose in the determination of DI-eligibility. First, in its effect on the extent of disablement as measured by DISgate age is taken to contain health information not accounted for by the specific disability indicators (see table 10.5). And second, given the extent of disablement, age is likely to measure the ability to find suitable, gainful, employment.

Contrary to the unconditional probit results reported in tables 10.1 and 10.3 the sex-dummy is insignificant. This confirms what the previous results suggested, namely, the absence of indications of direct sex discrimination in DI-eligibility assessments.[21]

**Controlling the Legitimacy of the Sick Leave (ABSLEGIT)**
Next to the two crucial standards for DI-eligibility - viz., extent of disablement and labor market considerations - the conditional DI-probit model contains an indicator for the rigor by which DI-eligibility is scrutinized. ABSLEGIT counts the number of checks by SB-insurance doctors that the SB-beneficiaries have had during the 5 months of their sick leave. Intensity of control during the first months of the DI-waiting period intends to serve as a proxy for the rigor by which fulfilment of the complete waiting period - the prime DI-eligibility standard - is verified. Its coefficient has the expected negative sign but it is small and insignificant.

**10.4   Simulation of the 1980-85 Changes**

The preceding estimation results are all based on 1980 data applied to basically static models. Although in qualitative terms these results may be interpreted as a general description of the DI-enrolment process, their predictive value outside the period of observation is unknown. Given the spectacular changes that have occurred after 1980, we will use this section to test the predictive potential of the unconditional DI-model.
Between 1979 and 1985, the overall probabilities of entering the DI-program declined from an average of 22.4 entries per 1,000 workers insured to the pre-1970 level of 14 entries per 1,000 insured. Since 1985, the DI-incidence rate more or less stabilized at this relatively low level (see chapter 2, table 2.15). This remarkable decline has been observed for all age-categories, both for men and women.[22]
This drop in DI-enrolment was accompanied by a series of cuts by which DI-beneficiaries lost 25 percent of their purchasing power.[23] In 1985 these retrenchments were concluded by lowering the statutory DI-replacement rate from 80 to 70 percent. During the same years real wages declined by 10 percent, implying a drastic reduction of the after-tax benefit-wage ratio.
While DI-program participation decreased in the early 1980s unemployment soared: Between 1980 and 1984 the overall unemployment rate increased from 6 to 14 percent. The rise in unemployment was largely due to increased supply by youths and women. At the same time, the overall probability of re-employment decreased, which led to longer unemployment durations. In 1985, when the DI-incidence stabilized, unemployment started to decline gradually.

According to the unconditional DI-probit estimates in table 10.1 both labor market conditions, represented by (re)employment probabilities, and the financial consequences of DI-enrolment measured by LnLOSSLT are powerful predictors of the DI-probability. To investigate the predictive potential of the estimated DI-model we may, therefore, apply the actual 1980-85 changes to these variables and see how these changes, which have opposite influences, affect the average DI-incidence rate.

### 10.4.1  Benefit Cuts

The data in table 2.15 show the severity of the successive 1980-85 DI-benefit cuts: By a series of marginal changes the after-tax benefit-wage ratio for a modal worker first drops from 0.87 in 1980 to 0.78 in 1984. Then, by lowering the before-tax statutory replacement rates from 80 to 70 percent in 1985, the after tax benefit-wage ratio reduces to 0.72.

The consequences of these cuts for the lifetime income variables are illustrated by the distributions in table 10.8, where we use the lifetime, after-tax, replacement rate $RRLT=EY_{DI}/EY_{WORK}$ as our yardstick. While only 1 percent of the population at risk faced a lifetime replacement rate of less than 0.75 in 1980, after the benefit cuts 69 percent would have less than 0.75 of their earnings replaced. On average the lifetime replacement rate dropped from 86 to 73 percent. Due to these retrenchments the loss in lifetime income that a DI-entrant would suffer increased by 7 percent after logarithmic transformation.[24] This increase in LnLOSSLT would induce a *ceteris paribus* reduction in the DI-incidence of 54 percent as implied by the mean change in predicted DI-probabilities given in the bottom row of table 10.8.

Table 10.8  **Distributions and Means of LifeTime Replacement Rates (RRLT) for DI-Insured in 1980 and 1985; Resulting Mean Changes in LnLOSSLT and the Predicted DI-Incidence Rate, Pr{DI}**

| RRLT | 1980 | 1985 |
|---|---|---|
| | | *(percentages)* |
| < 0.70 | 0 | 42 |
| 0.70 - 0.75 | 1 | 27 |
| 0.75 - 0.80 | 2 | 14 |
| 0.80 - 0.85 | 35 | 15 |
| 0.85 - 0.90 | 55 | 1 |
| > 0.90 | 7 | 1 |
| total | 100 | 100 |
| mean of RRLT | 0.860 | 0.726 |
| mean of LnLOSSLT | 9.191 | 9.850 |
| mean of pred. Pr{DI} | 0.024 | 0.011 |

Consequently, if between 1980 and 1985 except for the benefit cuts and the ensuing increase in LnLOSSLT no other changes would have occurred our estimated DI-probability model would predict a reduction in the average DI-probability from 0.024 to 0.011. This overshoots the actual drop in the average DI-incidence rate that went from 0.0224 to 0.014.[25]

### 10.4.2   The Rise in Unemployment

Next to retrenchments, the 1980-85 period has also been plagued by a tripling of the unemployment rate. In terms of the variables representing labor market conditions, this surge leads to the multiplication factors reported in table 10.9. These factors result from higher unemployment rates and lower real minimum wages (see tables 7.2, 7.3, and 7.4). According to the unconditional DI-probability model, soaring unemployment alone would have led to a doubling of the average predicted DI-incidence between 1980 and 1985.

Table 10.9   Multiplication Factors Representing the 1980-85 Rise in Unemployment; Induced Average DI-Incidence for 1985

|  | males | females |
|---|---|---|
| Unemployment probability | 2.607 | 1.436 |
| Reemployment probability | 0.486 | 0.668 |
| Induced 1985 value of Pr{DI} | 0.048 | |

### 10.4.3   The Combined Effects of Benefit Cuts and Increased Unemployment on Pr{DI}

If we implement the 1980-85 increases in income loss and unemployment in the unconditional DI-probability model, these combined effects appear to cancel. That is, the simulated average DI-incidence for 1985 remains at its 1980 sample mean of 24 per 1,000 insured. On average, therefore, the estimated DI-model is unable to reproduce the 38 percent drop in the DI-incidence.

There may be several causes for this poor prediction result. First, the variables used as causal factors to simulate the DI-drop may be inadequate or incomplete. Parallel to its rise the character of unemployment has changed as the average duration of unemployment spells grew much faster than the frequency of spells. The variables representing labor market conditions which are derived from hazard models estimated on data from the 1970s may be unfit to capture the 1980s type of "hard core" unemployment.

Moreover, the increase in unemployment durations suggests a trade-off between long-term unemployment and disability. More specifically, among the long-term unemployed of the 1980s one may expect to find may persons that would have entered the DI-rolls under the circumstances prevailing in the 1970s. Such aggregate dynamic relationships are of course ignored by the static micro-models used here.

Finally, other changes not covered by our specifications have taken place. For instance, the early 80s witnessed the surge of early retirement arrangements providing entitlements for older workers that are comparable to DI-benefits but less stigmatizing.

To further scrutinize the predictive power of the DI-model, and to locate its apparent predictive failures, we apply the 1985 values of the unemployment and reemployment probabilities and LnLOSSLT to obtain type-specific simulations of the 1980-85 change in the DI-probability. The simulated changes in table 10.10 shed new light on the predictive potential of the DI-model. The separate changes in unemployment and expected income loss after DI-enrolment generally confirm the findings in the two previous tables. For female standard employees, however, the DI-risk enhancing effect of soaring unemployment is predicted to be considerably smaller than that for their male counterparts.

**Table 10.10**  Predicted 1980-85 Changes[a] in DI-Probabilities for Male and Female DI-Insured Resulting from Changes in Unemployment and Income Loss

|  | males | | females | |
|---|---|---|---|---|
|  | predicted | actual[b] | predicted | actual[b] |
|  | *(percentages)* | | | |
| Changes in Pr{E→U} | | | | |
| and Pr{U→E} | + 278 | - | +123 | - |
| Change in LnLOSSLT | - 70 | - | - 72 | - |
| Combined changes and | | | | |
| age is 25 | + 171 | - 42 | - 3 | - 43 |
| age is 40 | - 17 | - 35 | - 65 | - 55 |
| age is 60 | - 53 | - 53 | - 69 | - 54 |

a  With reference to the 1980 DI-probability predictions for standard a employee (see table 10.2).
b  Derived from the Statistical Appendices of the JMS, Annual Reports, 1983, 1988.

In the lower part of the table the combined effects of the simulated changes are compared with the actual, age and sex specific, reductions in DI-incidence rates. Such comparison allows us to identify the predictive failures of the model. The predictive quality appears to strongly increase with age. For 25 year old male standard employees the model predicts a 171 percent rise in the DI-risk whereas the actual change for the corresponding category was a 42 percent drop. The result

for young women is somewhat better in that the predicted change has the right sign but grossly underestimates the actual reductions of the DI-inflow rates.
For 40-year old men the unemployment effect is still too large but its discrepancy with the actual change is significantly smaller. The predicted DI-drop for males aged 60 is faultless. The predictions for 40 and 60 year old women are reasonable approximations of the real changes.

From these simulations we may conclude that, using the combined effects of benefit cuts and soaring unemployment, the unconditional DI-probability model is reasonably capable to track the 1980-85 drop in DI-enrolment, especially for older workers. For workers under 40, however, the model fails to predict the reduction in DI-entries appropriately. This is possibly due to the changed character of unemployment, specifically for youths, and to the coarse, uniform, way by which the 1985 employment opportunities have been generated.[26]

## 10.5    Summary and Conclusions

In this chapter we have reported on the core results of our study of the determinants of DI-enrolment. Two approaches have been employed: First, using the structural probit model derived in chapter 3, we described the unconditional DI-probability (Pr{DI}) without taking explicit account of the 12 months waiting period that lies between work and DI-enrolment. As a second approach we cut the waiting period in two parts. Thus we were able to distinguish between the transition from work to 5 months sickness and the final stage in the DI-process, the transition from 5 months sickness to DI-enrolment. This enabled us to investigate the mechanism determining the outcome of a prolonged spell of sickness.

In the specifications for these probability models we have used the instrumental variables that flow from the submodels discussed in the chapters 6 through 9. These submodels have revealed the multiple causal pathways along which background variables, such as age, education, or firm size, exert their indirect influences on the DI-probability. Only by the use of instrumentals we were able to structure the intricate causalities that govern the DI-process and, more specifically, to get around the potential or proven endogeneity of direct observations.

### Pr{DI}

The probit results on the transition from work to DI-enrolment, reported in table 10.1, convincingly confirm the notion that the unconditional DI-probability is determined both by medical and a diversity of non-medical factors. The disability indicators reflect the medical-sociological definition of disablement and, therefore, incorporate the influence of both the nature and severity of impairment and the strenuousness of job requirements.

Having controlled for these prime determinants, employment opportunities as well as income and leisure considerations have remarkably powerful impacts on the individual DI-risk. Specifically, employees with vocational characteristics that induce poor reemployment possibilities when unemployed, appear to face strongly increased DI-probabilities. This finding is supported by the significant effects of the firm-specific variables FIRMRISK and JOBPERF which contain firm-level and individual dimensions of internal employment security.

The size and significance of the variables reflecting income and leisure considerations (LnLOSSLT, ETG, COMTIME) which are core elements in the micro-economic approach, confirm the validity of that approach to disability behavior. Their combined effects, supported by the prominent impact of career perspectives (PROSPECTS), stress the individual choice, or voluntary retirement, aspects of disability behavior. These results are qualitatively similar to findings in comparable US studies, but quantitatively more significant.

The picture emerging from these results is that socio-economic "traumas" - i.e., lack of labor market success as witnessed by unemployment experiences and inferior career prospects - are as important as the extent of disablement proper for the distinction between the recognized disabled and the general population at risk.

The absence of a significant direct age-effect seems to underscore the validity of our approach to structure the underlying causalities. Its indirect (reduced form) effect, however, turns out to be sizeable. For instance, summation of the indirect effects that run via the instrumental, structural, variables, reveals that married men, aged 60, run a risk 11 times larger than that of their 25 years old peers.

The DI-probit estimates also contain a number of unexpected results. Work ethic appears to be positively related with Pr{DI} whereas the effect of job satisfaction is negative but insignificant. Given the insignificance of age and the strong correlation of age with work morale, ethic may stand for generation and length of work life.

Being a woman appears to strongly reduce the probability of DI-entry. To the extent that other factors are adequately controlled for the negative impact of the sex dummy would point to a discriminatory attitude by the administrators of the Sickness Benefit scheme. More likely, however, the models used lack the flexibility to fully incorporate the effects of gender differences in social roles.

In section 10.4 we have tested the predictive power of the estimated DI-probit model by studying its capacity to reproduce the drastic 1980-85 drop in the average DI-incidence. We assumed that this drop was the combined result of two opposite forces; rising unemployment and a series of benefit cuts. By implementing these changes the DI-model proved to be capable to track the 1980-85 drop for workers over 40. Due, probably, to the changed character of unemployment after 1980, the model failed to predict the actual fall in DI-incidence rates for younger workers.

## PSICK and Pr{DI | 5M.SICK}

As a potentially more accurate and informative approach we have also investigated the DI-process by dividing the 12 months waiting period in two parts: The transition from work to prolonged - 5 months - sickness, and from 5 months sickness to DI-enrolment.

The probability of being on sick leave for more than 5 months is analyzed using a probit model which has the same specification as the unconditional DI-model. The results appeared to be remarkably similar, both in terms of size and significance. This implies that the occurrence of prolonged spells of sickness is governed by the same set of medical and socio-economic factors as those that determine DI-entry. It might also suggest that the second stage in the DI-process is random and has no meaningful structure.

However, analysis of the transition from 5 months sickness to DI-enrolment, using the sick (SB) sample data only, adds significantly to our knowledge of the DI-mechanism. Evidently, the SB-sample is select in ways described by the PSICK probit model. Hence, it consists of workers that, apart from their health status, differ from the average insured by lack of labor market success.

Given this selection, then, the outcome of the DI-waiting period appears to depend on the views and preferences of the three agents involved - the impaired employee, his or her employer, and the gatekeepers of the DI-program. First, we found that self-perceptions of the extent of disablement are formed, again, by a combination of medical and non-medical factors. Among the health indicators the views of the treating physicians are very influential. This finding emphasizes their decisive role in legitimizing disability behavior. Next to the impacts of the nature and severity of disablement we found a strong U-shaped age-effect, indicating that self-ratings become increasingly more pessimistic beyond 40. This may reflect feelings of obsolescence. Moreover, people have shown to feel more disabled the less satisfaction they derive from their job and the less they adhere to a traditional work morale. Unfavorable employment opportunities and the presence of other household income also tend to bias the self-perceived extent of disablement upward. However, the influence of these non-medical factors is much weaker than found for the unconditional probabilities.

Finally, the reduced form prediction of Pr{DI | 5M.SICK} appeared to be strongly significant, underlining the endogeneity of self-reported health with respect to retirement. Apparently, those with a strong predisposition for DI-enrolment are more inclined to declare themselves in poor health.

In a separate regression the expert - i.e., the program gatekeepers' - ratings of the respondents' extent of disablement have been analyzed. Although these judgments were assumed to be solely based on medical data and age, we applied the more comprehensive specification that was used for the description of self-perceptions. The ratings appear to depend mainly on medical data, including the reports from the curative sector, and on age. In comparison with the self-perceptions the age-effect is stronger. Apparently, similar health data lead to more pessimistic work capacity ratings the older the patient.

The estimation of a structural conditional DI-probit model has revealed the relative impacts of self-perceptions and gate-keepers' ratings of disability on the outcome of the DI-entry process. We have found equally important contributions of both these parties. This finding stresses the discretion of the insured workers to obtain DI-eligibility and, indirectly, the legitimizing role played by their medical attendants. In their DI-determinations the gatekeepers seem to add age to their medical data represented by their ratings of extent of disablement. The age-spline for under 45 year olds is strong and significant; the complementary spline has a small and insignificant effect. Given the policy of explicit labor market consideration in DI-assessments on the one hand, and the insignificance of the variables measuring employment opportunities on the other, the gatekeepers seem to use age as a proxy for labor market opportunities.

The predicted DI-incidence rate in the employing firm is also found to be a moderately important determinant of the conditional DI-probability. To some extent, this effect represents the influence of the employer which adds to the much stronger impacts exerted by employers in the first stage of the DI-process.

# Appendix to chapter 10

Table A.10.1    Means and Standard Deviations of Explanatory Variables[a]

| | DI-insured | | 5m.sick | | DI-entrants | |
|---|---|---|---|---|---|---|
| | mean | st.dev. | mean | st.dev. | mean | st.dev. |
| AGE | 34.41 | 11.54 | 43.68 | 12.06 | 46.11 | 11.47 |
| AGESQ $(\times 10^{-2})$ | 13.18 | 8.76 | 20.53 | 10.15 | 22.58 | 9.93 |
| D(FEM=1) | 0.29 | 0.45 | 0.21 | 0.41 | 0.20 | 0.40 |
| D(MAR=1) | 0.72 | 0.45 | 0.85 | 0.36 | 0.86 | 0.35 |
| | | | | | | |
| COMPLREC | 0.03 | 0.12 | 0.11 | 0.15 | 0.11 | 0.16 |
| ABSNREC | 2.65 | 5.30 | 5.68 | 9.07 | 6.16 | 9.54 |
| ENERLIM | | | 0.10 | 0.72 | 0.19 | 0.77 |
| PHYSDIS[b] | 1.18 | 0.11 | 1.28 | 0.13 | 1.30 | 0.14 |
| MENTDIS | 1.05 | 0.16 | 1.31 | 0.37 | 1.33 | 0.37 |
| | | | | | | |
| DISresp | | | 0.05 | 0.90 | 0.29 | 0.86 |
| DISgate | | | 0.07 | 0.85 | 0.31 | 0.80 |
| DIScurat | | | 0.01 | 0.88 | 0.21 | 0.87 |
| | | | | | | |
| ABSLEGIT | | | 2.74 | 1.48 | 2.69 | 1.46 |
| | | | | | | |
| WETHIC | 0.00 | 1.00 | 0.38 | 1.04 | 0.43 | 1.03 |
| JOBSAT | 0.00 | 1.00 | -0.15 | 1.08 | -0.17 | 1.10 |
| | | | | | | |
| D(MALE=1).Pr{E→U}[c] | 0.23 | 0.31 | 0.24 | 0.32 | 0.22 | 0.29 |
| D(FEM=1) .Pr{E→U}[c] | 0.07 | 0.14 | 0.04 | 0.11 | 0.03 | 0.10 |
| D(MALE=1).Pr{U→E}[c] | 97.54 | 92.59 | 62.00 | 67.27 | 55.52 | 58.98 |
| D(FEM=1) .Pr{U→E}[c] | 27.03 | 63.24 | 8.33 | 25.84 | 6.30 | 19.99 |
| | | | | | | |
| FIRMRISK[d] | 1.09 | 0.55 | 1.24 | 0.47 | 1.27 | 0.46 |
| PROSPECTS | 0.00 | 1.00 | -0.43 | 0.45 | -0.46 | 0.40 |
| JOBPERF | 0.00 | 1.00 | -0.28 | 0.77 | -0.28 | 0.77 |
| | | | | | | |
| LnLOSSLT [e,f] | 9.19 | 0.60 | 8.70 | 1.02 | 8.66 | 1.02 |
| OTHHINC | 5.77 | 4.29 | 6.33 | 4.02 | 6.08 | 4.10 |
| ETG[f] | 0.84 | 0.26 | 0.74 | 0.29 | 0.71 | 0.30 |
| COMTIME | 2.37 | 1.14 | 2.55 | 1.22 | 2.58 | 1.23 |
| | | | | | | |
| #Observations | 1417 | | 2534 | | 1529 | |

[a]   All ordinal variables are rescaled by the invated normal transformation.
[b]   Predicted values of PHYSDIS are based on the estimates in section 6.4.
[c]   Predicted values of the regressors are based on the estimates in section 7.5.
[d]   Predicted values of FIRMRISK are based on the estimates in section 8.3.3.
[e]   Predicted values of LnLOSSLT are based on the estimates in section 9.3.3.
[f]   Discount rate is 30 percent.

Table A.10.2    Reduced-Form Probit Estimates for Pr{DI|5M.SICK}

|                                       | coefficient | (st. error) |
|---------------------------------------|-------------|-------------|
| **I.  EMPLOYEE-LEVEL**                |             |             |
| AGEspline <45                         | .0227       | (.0048)**   |
| AGEspline ≥45                         | .0325       | (.0069)**   |
| Female=1                              | .3371       | (.1116)**   |
| Married=1                             | .0243       | (.0927)     |
| Ndepkids                              | - .0362     | (.0240)     |
| Urbanization                          | - .0014     | (.0221)     |
| Education                             | - .0034     | (.0330)     |
| Strenuous work record[a]              | .3357       | (.1167)**   |
| Tenure[b]                             | - .3348     | (.1161)**   |
| g(Working hours)                      | .8620       | (.3862)*    |
| Commuting time                        | - .0094     | (.0230)     |
| Ln(other househ.inc. + 1)             | - .0123     | (.0091)     |
| Reg. unempl. rate                     | - .2615     | (.1487)     |
| Previously unemployed=1               | - .0481     | (.0745)     |
| Mobility=1                            | - .0099     | (.0708)     |
| Absence record                        | .0090       | (.0031)**   |
| Duration of complaints[a]             | .6729       | (.1794)**   |
| **II. EMPLOYER-LEVEL**                |             |             |
| Ln(firmsize)                          | .0127       | (.0170)     |
| Increasing employment ($*10^{-2}$)    | - .0035     | (.0012)**   |
| Decreasing employment ($*10^{-2}$)    | - .0040     | (.0036)     |
| Perc. fem. employment ($*10^{-2}$)    | - .0001     | (.0015)     |
| Workers' consultation=1               | .0564       | (.0547)     |
| Job adaptation                        | - .0030     | (.0330)     |
| Medical guidance                      | - .0160     | (.0266)     |
| Social guidance                       | - .0382     | (.0548)     |
| Branch of industry                    |             |             |
|    Agriculture         | - .3583     | (.1682)*    |
|    Steel industry      | - .4293     | (.0935)**   |
|    Construction        | ref.        |             |
|    Other industries    | - .3609     | (.0922)**   |
|    Wholesale and retail| - .2496     | (.1090)*    |
|    Other commercial services | - .3546 | (.0971)**  |
|    Health care         | - .5749     | (.2000)**   |
|    Non-commercial services | - .4483 | (.1387)**    |
| Constant                              | -2.0217     | (.3823)     |
| -2 * Loglikelihood ratio              | 285.12**    |             |
| pseudo-$R^2$                          | .094        |             |
| #Observations                         | 2534        |             |

| | |
|---|---|
| ** | Significant at the 1 percent level. |
| * | Significant at the 5 percent level. |
| a | Divided by age. |
| b | Divided by work experience (years). |

**Notes**

1. See section 6. footnote . The ratio of sampling probabilities (p) varies of cours with the specific subsample used for the construction of the dependent variable.

2. Theoretically, this DI-model still is a reduced form emerging from the underlying structural equations for Pr{CLAIM} and Pr{AWARD|CLAIM}. As noted before, however, claims and awards can not be separately observed under the Dutch DI-program. We, therefore, denote the version in eq.10.1 as (empirically) structural to distinguish this final specification from previous ones used in chapters 6 and 9.

3. In order to account for negative differences between $EY_{WORK}$ and $EY_{DI}$ the loss has been defined as sg(LOSS).ln{abs[LOSS+sg(LOSS)]} where sg stands for "sign of" and abs for absolute value. However, sg(LOSS) appeared to be -1 in only 2 out of 3951 cases.

4. RRLT has been used in Aarts and De Jong (1987).

5. See chapter 7, table 7.5.

6. An overview of such studies is provided by Leonard (1986).

7. For two reasons we do not complete this transformation to obtain probit elasticities. First, the dependent variable is always a binary choice variable, either measuring labor force participation [see e.g. Parsons (1980), Slade (1982), Haveman and Wolfe (1984a), or Haveman et al. (1991)] or DI-program participation [Leonard (1979) or this study]. Moreover, given the non-linearity of the probit model the proper calculation method is somewhat ambiguous. For instance, the Haveman-Wolfe (1984a) study shows implausibly small elasticities when calculated at sample means as compared with the mean elasticity of individuals on the margin of some hypothetical policy change [cf. Leonard (1986)].

8. Calculated from Parsons (1980), table 5, p. 127, and table A1, p. 131; and Haveman and Wolfe (1984a), table 4, p. 60.

9. Cf. Wolfe et al. (1984, p. 627) who conclude "that the 1970s increase in the leniency of gaining access to transfers and in the generosity of transfers (...) has reduced work hours about 0.65 per year in the U.S. and about 2.7 percent per year in the Netherlands."

10. The estimated value of the discount rate is remarkably similar to the one empirically estimated by Van Praag & Van Weeren (1983).

11. See M.R. Killingsworth and J.J. Heckman (1986) and for the Netherlands J.J.M. Theeuwes (1988).

12. Separate estimation of the DI-probit model for males is published in Aarts and De Jong (1992). These estimates closely resemble the results for the complete sample in table 10.1.

13. The scale for self-perceived disability is based on two questions:
"In due course, do you think you will be able to resume your old job?"
"In due course, do you think you will be able to perform other suitable work?"
Possible answers were "sure", "think so", "don't know", "don't think so", "surely not".

14. Cited from Parsons (1982, p. 81). In a footnote, Parsons adds "One might expect that relatively few of those induced to leave the market practice wilful deceit. Most are likely to make marginal adjustments in their own perception of their health status."

15. See Aarts et al. (1983) on the construction, reliability, and validity of the limitation scales, and their relation with 18 possible job activities. The dimensions "energetical", "locomotive", and "mental", are supported by a principal components analysis.

16. That is, if self-reports on physicians' views and self-perceived disability are similarly colored by latent preferences, and if these latent preferences are adequately covered by $\hat{p}_{DI}$.

17. See chapter 6, and the references given there.

18. As witnessed by the partial derivatives of DISgate and DISresp with respect to age, evaluated in the mean of age (=43.7); 0.0138 for DISgate, and 0.0084 for DISresp.

19. We have also estimated a conditional DI-probit including the interaction between DISresp and DISgate. Although this version showed the expected negative sign for the interaction variable DISresp*DISgate, implying smaller latitude for impaired workers as the severity of disability increases, its effect was insignificant (t=1.57).

20. See Van der Veen (1990).

21. Among Dutch sociologists there is a yet unfinished discussion on whether (married) women are being discriminated against by the Dutch DI-administration. See Bijlsma and Koopmans (1986), Hermans (1986, 1987), and Bruinsma et al. (1989).

22. See JMS annual reports 1980-1988.

23. These successive retrenchments have been described in section 2.5.

24. Before log transformation the loss in lifetime income ($EY_{WORK}$-$EY_{DI}$) increased by 94%!

25. Despite correction for choice based sampling, the sample mean of Pr{DI}, as predicted from the unconditional DI-probit, is not exactly equal to the population mean of 0.0224, probably due to rounding errors.

26. To the extent that the growth in long-term - more than one year - unemployment is indicative of its changed character the unemployment statistics show differential age-specific trends as witnessed by

**percent share of long-term in total unemployment, by age, 1980, 1985, and 1980-1985**

| age-group | 1980 | 1985 | 1980-85 change |
|-----------|------|------|----------------|
| < 25 | 15 | 42 | 180 |
| 25  - 39 | 24 | 61 | 154 |
| 40  - 57.5 | 32 | 68 | 113 |
| 57.5 - 64 | 42 | 79 | 88 |
| total | 23 | 55 | 139 |

source: Min.SoZaWe (various years).

Chapter 11

# FORECASTING THE SIZE OF THE DISABLED POPULATION

## 11.1    Introduction

In 1967, when the Dutch Disability Social Insurance (DI) program for private sector employees was introduced, the number of beneficiaries was predicted to reach 200,000 in 1972, and to remain stable thereafter. From its inception, however, the DI-beneficiary volume showed sustained growth, from 200,000 in 1970, via 250,000 in 1972, 500,000 in 1980, to 630,000 in 1990.

Between 1970 and 1980, the number of civil servants receiving an invalidity pension grew at a slower pace but soared after 1980. Moreover, in 1976 the National Disability Program (AAW) was introduced covering others than employees, particularly the self-employed and those who are handicapped congenitally or in early childhood - the so-called early handicapped (see chapter 2). The total number of disability beneficiaries flowing from the labor force, which we denote as the DIS population, then, consists of DI-beneficiaries - i.e., private sector employees - *plus* AAW-receiving civil servants and self-employed persons. It excludes the early handicapped.

**Figure 11.1  The DIS-Population, 1968-1990**

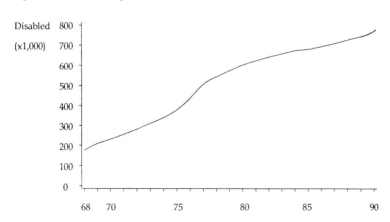

In figure 11.1 we have drawn the growth of the DIS-population. Until 1976, the DIS and the DI graphs almost coincide, the difference being a, then, modest number of disabled civil servants; after 1976, the DIS graph also contains the disabled self-employed.

In this chapter we report on a number of alternative extrapolations of the DIS-graph until 2050. If nothing else would change, the growth of the DIS-population can be predicted to accelerate for demographic reasons alone. Given the strong age-dependency of the disability incidence, greying of the insured population implies an enhanced influx of new disability recipients. This demographic effect adds to the systematic imbalance between entries and exits which has caused the DIS-volume to grow incessantly right from the start of the DI-program in 1967.

To be able to predict these demographic and systematic effects we have built a mechanistic forecasting model which uses the 1990-2050 population forecasts by the Dutch Central Bureau of Statistics (CBS) as its input data. The model is centered around two flow models describing the flows in and out of the labor force and the DIS-population, respectively. The element that links these two flow models is of course the disability incidence, as it defines the numbers that flow out of the labor force into the disabled population.

The results obtained with our calculation model, therefore, hinge upon assumptions with respect to the development of the disability incidence rate. For instance, we may apply the unconditional DI-probit model of the preceding chapter to design behavioral scenarios represented by alternative time-paths for the disability incidence. Or, we may use the expert ratings on the work capacity of DI-entrants of chapter 5, to estimate what the effect would be if DI-claimants would be scrutinized more rigorously. Such simulations may indicate what behavioral or administrative changes could bend the upward trend in the disability volume.

This chapter has 5 sections. In the following section we present the calculation model which is designed to simultaneously generate forecasts of the labor force and the DIS-population. In section 11.3 we describe the input data - viz. the 1988 CBS population forecast and the 1990 starting values for the two specific populations to be extrapolated, and the transition probabilities in and out of these two subpopulations. The resulting forecasts for the DIS-population are given in section 11.4. Besides a central variant, in which we presume constant labor market and disability behaviors, we offer a number of alternatives by staging modifications in disability policy, disability behavior, and labor market conditions. Section 11.5 concludes.

## 11.2    The Calculation Model

### 11.2.1   Two Flow Models

The age and sex-specific sizes of the labor force (L) and DIS-populations (DD) are calculated using simple models that describe the flows in and out of these populations.

Year-to-year changes in the age-specific size of the labor force can be written (suppressing the subscript for gender) as

$$L_{j+1,t+1} = L_{j,t} + I_{j,t} - O_{j,t} \quad (j = 15,...,64) \tag{11.1}$$

$L_{j,t}$ is the size of the labor force, aged j at the start of year t;

$I_{j,t}$ is the size of the inflow into the labor force of j years olds during year t;

$O_{j,t}$ is the size of the flow out of the labor force of j years olds during year t.

Notice that $I_{j,t}$ may consist of new entrants, e.g. school-leavers, as well as re-entrants, e.g. married women having reduced their child care activities.

The flow out of the labor force can be broken down into three components,

$$O_{j,t} = D_{j,t} + M_{j,t} + P_{j,t} \tag{11.2}$$

$D_{j,t}$ is the number of new disability beneficiaries, age j, during year t;

$M_{j,t}$ is the number of persons, age j, who die during year t;

$P_{j,t}$ is the number of persons, age j, who, during year t, leave the labor
   force for other reasons than death or disablement (i.e., old age, early
   retirement, child care, emigration, etc.).

Since the number of workers that, in year t, have to retire from the labor force due to disability equals the inflow into the disability population, $D_{j,t}$ links the flow models of the labor force and the DI-populations.

Analogously to (11.1) we may define the age-specific size of the DIS-population by

$$DD_{j+1,t+1} = DD_{j,t} + D_{j,t} - Z_{j,t} \tag{11.3}$$

$DD_{j,t}$ is the size of the DIS-population, aged j at the start of year t;

$Z_{j,t}$ is the size of the flow out of DIS-population of j years olds during year t.

$Z_{j,t}$, the number of disability benefit terminations, also has three components; recoveries, deaths, and old age - becoming 65,

$$Z_{j,t} = R_{j,t} + DM_{j,t} + DP_{64,t} \tag{11.4}$$

$R_{j,t}$ is the number of disability beneficiaries, age j, who recover during year t;

$DM_{j,t}$ is the number of disability beneficiaries, age j, who die during year t;

DP$_{64,t}$ is the number of disability beneficiaries, age 64, who leave the DIS
    population during year t, as they turn 65.
A separate assumption has to be made on the recoveries' fate. It may be realistically
assumed that recoveries return to the labor force. In that case the inflow into the
labor force ($I_{j,t}$) should be defined so as to include $R_{j,t}$. Implicitly, therefore, recovered disability beneficiaries provide a second link between the labor force and
the DIS populations.

### 11.2.2   The Parameters of the Forecasting Model

If it were possible to predict the future course of the 7 flow variables, I, D, M, P,
R, DM, and DP, by age and sex, the system (11.1)-(11.4) would yield a feasible,
albeit purely mechanistic, device to forecast the number of disability beneficiaries
given starting values for both the labor force and the DIS-populations.
The model, however, will gain in terms of reliability, transparency, and practical
value, by adding a number of identities that link the flow variables to the stock
variables. Such links can be realized by introducing (relative) frequencies which
reflect the conditional probability that a person of certain age and sex will move
from one population to the other. Some of these transitions - labor market entry,
early retirement, and to some extent, entry into the DIS-population - may be
regarded as being largely determined by choice, based on individual preferences
and circumstances. These frequencies, therefore, contain behavioral elements. They
are, however, also contingent on legal definitions, policies, and administrative
routines, and therefore may be used as instrumental variables to demonstrate the
effects of changes in labor market, disability, or retirement policies. Finally, the
mortality probabilities are of course "pure" risks in the sense of being uncontrollable.
They are a demographic datum.
The output of the calculation model hinges on the assumptions made about the
future values of these relative frequencies. If all frequencies retain their current
value, the generated forecasts are conditional upon the assumption that policies at
the macro level and behaviors at the micro level will remain unaltered. The
potential effects of political or behavioral changes can be simulated through adjustments of the transition frequencies. Thus, the impact of policy changes on the
disability volume can be evaluated.

### 11.2.3   The Relative Frequencies of Entering and Leaving the Labor Force

The relative frequencies that link flow to stock quantities are introduced in the
model by adding a number of identities. The first identity links the inflow into the

labor force to the non-participating part of the total population

$$I_{j,t} = \iota_{j,t} \, [N_{j,t} - L_{j,t}] \tag{11.5}$$

$N_{j,t}$    is the size of the Dutch population, aged j at the start of year t;

$\iota_{j,t}$    is the relative frequency of inflow into the labor force of j years olds during year t.

The relative inflow frequency $\iota_{j,t}$, reflects the probability that a man or woman of age j who did not belong to the labor force at the beginning of year t will enter the labor force during t. A current labor force entrant, however, may have been a labor force participant somewhere in the past.

Identity (11.5) links the calculation model with the size and composition of the population at large. Exogenous forecasts of the size and composition of the total population up to 2050 are provided by the Dutch Central Bureau of Statistics [see CBS (1989)]. These demographic prognoses are used as input data for our forecasting model. Therefore, our prognoses are based on the CBS population forecasts and their assumptions with respect to fertility, migration, and mortality.

The inflow into the DIS-population, being a component of the outflow out of the labor force, is linked with the labor force through the relative disability frequencies,

$$D_{j,t} = \delta_{j,t} \, L_{j,t} \tag{11.6}$$

$\delta_{j,t}$    is the disability incidence rate of labor force participants, aged j at the start of year t.

The disability incidence $\delta$, is the central parameter of our model. To prognosticate its age-specific values one may either assume that these values remain constant over time, implying an increasing average incidence rate as a result of aging of the population at risk, or a constant average incidence rate implying that the age-specific incidence rates decrease to accommodate aging. To be able to implement this last assumption we have constructed a separate sub-model that will be discussed in section 11.2.5.

Under the presumption that the total labor force, including civil servants and the self-employed, is comparable in its disability behavior to the private sector employees analyzed in the preceding chapters, $\delta$ may be interpreted as the unconditional DI-probability which we studied in section 10.2.

The mortality component of the outflow out of the labor force is determined by sex- and age-specific death probabilities published in CBS (1982),[1]

$$M_{j,t} = \mu_j \, L_{j,t} \tag{11.7}$$

$\mu_j$    is the probability that a person of age j dies before he or she turns j+1.

The mortality rates pertain to the population at large as separate rates for the labor force alone are not available. Hence, we are forced to heroically assume that the population statistics on mortality apply to the labor force too. Moreover, since they underlie the population forecasts that are used as input data, we have to keep these death rates constant over time.

The third component of the outflow out of the labor force, $P_{j,t}$, is defined by

$$P_{j,t} = \pi_{j,t}\, L_{j,t} \tag{11.8}$$

$\pi_{j,t}$   is the probability that a person of age j leaves the labor force for reasons other than disability or death during year t.

$\pi_{j,t}$ denotes the probability that a person of age j more or less voluntarily leaves the labor force because of early retirement, childbirth, or other reasons. This retreat may be only temporary.

## 11.2.4   Relative Frequencies of Leaving the Disability Population

The outflow out of the disability population has three components: recovery, death, and becoming 65. These components correspond to the reasons for losing entitlement for disability benefits.

The recovery incidence rate is defined by linking the number of recoveries to the size of the DIS-population,

$$R_{j,t} = \varrho_{j,t}\, DD_{j,t} \tag{11.9}$$

$\varrho_{j,t}$   is the recovery rate of disability beneficiaries of age j, during year t.

Analogously, the mortality rate among disability beneficiaries is defined by

$$DM_{j,t} = \delta\mu_j\, DD_{j,t} \tag{11.10}$$

$\delta\mu_j$   is the probability that a disability beneficiary of age j will die before he or she turns j+1.

The mortality rates that pertain to the DIS-population are assumed to be constant over time. Clearly, they differ from the death rates among the complete population. The disability outflow due to statutory benefit termination at the age of 65 is of course completely determined by $\varrho_{j,t}$ and $\delta\mu_j$

$$DP_{64,t} = DD_{64,t} - R_{64,t} - DM_{64,t} = [1 - \varrho_{64,t} - \delta\mu_{64}]\, DD_{j,t} \tag{11.11}$$

$$= \delta\pi_{64,t}\, DD_{64,t}$$

where

$$\delta\pi_{64,t} = 1 - \varrho_{64,t} - \delta\mu_{64}\,.$$

### 11.2.5  The Forecasting Scheme

Except for the disability incidence $\delta_{j,t}$ the relative frequencies introduced in the preceding two sections will be used as fixed, i.e., time invariant, model parameters. As regards the labor force, the outflow is related to its size and composition, whereas the inflow is linked to the population at large. Given the CBS population projections, and estimates of the parameters $\iota_j$, $\delta_{j,t}$, $\mu_j$ and $\pi_j$, and given the sex and age-specific composition of the labor force and the DIS-population in the base year 1990, we can generate forecasts of $L_{j,t}$, $I_{j,t}$, $D_{j,t}$, $M_{j,t}$, and $P_{j,t}$ for the 1990-2050 period, through the recursive relation

$$L_{j+1,t+1} = [1 - \iota_j - \delta_{j,t} - \mu_j - \pi_j]\, L_{j,t} + \iota_j\, N_{j,t} \tag{11.1'}$$

Given the relative frequencies which act as the model parameters, the size and composition of the labor force is solely determined by demographics.
A similar recursivity for the DIS population writes

$$DD_{j+1,t+1} = [1 - \varrho_j - \delta\mu_j - \delta\pi_{64}]\, DD_{j,t} + \delta_{j,t}\, L_{j,t} \tag{11.3'}$$

The outflow contingencies (recovery, old age, and death) are assumed fixed. Given these parameters, the DIS-population only depends on the size and composition of the labor force which, in turn, is completely determined by demographics.
This implies that, given the parameters, the prognoses of the size and composition of both the labor force and DIS-populations are derived from the CBS prognoses of the population at large.


### 11.2.6  A Submodel for the Disability Incidence Rate

Regarding the future values of the disability incidence rate, we have two options. The first is to treat $\delta_{j,t}$ equally to the other parameters, assuming that the age-specific disability probabilities have fixed values. A changing age-composition of the labor force will cause the average DI-incidence to change over time. Specifically, greying will cause the mean incidence to rise.
As a second option the average disability incidence may be assumed to be constant. In that case the age-specific incidence rates will have to adapt to a changing age-composition of the labor force in order to keep its mean value constant. Specifically, greying will require the age-specific incidence rates to fall.
Keeping the mean disability rate constant is a way to control for the effect of aging on the course of the DIS-volume. In the framework of the proposed calculation scheme any program growth that remains after controlling for aging is due to the persistence of a positive difference between entries and exits - an imbalance that has been endemic to the program from its inception.

Apart from its technical merit as a method to isolate the demographic causes of future program growth from its systematic causes, a constant average disability rate can also be argued by interpreting age in terms of productivity and, hence, competitive power. After all, increasing age enhances the disability risk directly, by more or less natural processes of physiological and psychological obsolescence, but also indirectly, to the extent that employers associate increasing age with reduced strength and obsolete skills. Consequently, the relative competitive power that an age-cohort j commands in the labor market, may be presumed to be determined by its relative position within the age distribution of the labor force. If, through greying, the number of labor force participants under j decreases, and the number of more than j years olds increases, age j gains in competitive strength. And, as shown in the preceding chapter, enhanced competitive power reduces the disability risk, *ceteris paribus*. As a result of greying, therefore, the disability incidence of age-cohort j can be assumed to decrease.

**The Quantile Method**
To allow for a constant, or exogenously chosen, average disability incidence rate we assume that the individual disability risk (studied in the preceding chapter) is determined by *the relative position of an age-cohort within the age-distribution of the labor force.*
The relative position of age j in a given age distribution is determined by the proportion of labor force participants under age j.
Formally,

$$l_{j,t} = \sum_{k=15}^{j} L_{k,t} / L_t ; \quad L_t = \sum_{j=15}^{64} L_{j,t} \quad (j=15,...,64) \tag{11.12}$$

$l_{j,t}$ is the cumulative age distribution function of the labor force in year t.

Transforming the empirical distribution function $l_{j,t}$ by the standard normal, we can assign a value $x_{j,t}$ to each proportion $l_{j,t}$ that satisfies the condition

$$l_{j,t} = F(x_{j,t}) = \int_{-\infty}^{x_{j,t}} f(s)ds \tag{11.13}$$

F and f are the standard normal distribution and density function, respectively; $x_{j,t}$ will be referred to as the *quantile value* of age j.[2]
Alternatively, $x_{j,t}$ can be written as a function of the cumulative proportion $l_{j,t}$ by means of the inverted normal transformation,

$$x_{j,t} = F^{-1}(l_{j,t}) \tag{11.14}$$

Instead of age j we use the quantile value $x_{j,t}$ as the predictor of the age-specific disability incidence $\delta_{j,t}$. To that purpose we introduce a monotonically increasing function $g(x_{j,t})$ such that

$$\delta_{j,t} = g(x_{j,t}) = g[F^{-1}(l_{j,t})]$$  (11.15)

Thus defined, the mean disability incidence, $\mu_\delta$, writes

$$\mu_\delta = \int_{-\infty}^{\infty} g(x) \cdot f(x) \, dx = E\{g(x)\}$$  (11.16)

By Taylor expansion of $g(x)$ around $\mu_x = 0$, $\mu_\delta$ can be shown to be independent of time.[3]

The quantile method, therefore, serves our purposes. Aging implies that the proportion of younger labor force participants decreases. Hence, the cumulative proportions $l_{j,t}$ in (11.12) decrease. According to (11.13), then, the quantile value $x_j$ associated with age j reduces too. As a final result, the age-specific disability incidence rates, calculated by (11.15), drop in order to keep the mean incidence rate defined by (11.16) constant.

By keeping the average disability risk at a constant level, then, the quantile method presumes that greying of the labor force will have such a beneficial market effect on the age-specific disability risks that it neutralizes the demographic effect on program growth. It therefore presents a scenario which is optimistic relative to the constant age-specific, i.e., unaltered disability behavior, option.

The quantile method has an additional practical advantage as it allows to exogenously manipulate the mean disability incidence rate. Specifically, we may link the unconditional disability probability model with $\mu_\delta$ so as to construct "causal" scenarios.

### 11.2.7  Summary

The forecasting scheme that we employ to simulate the effects of population aging on the number of disability beneficiaries basically consists of two recursive relations; one to forecast the labor force population, viz. the population at risk; the other to forecast the DIS-population. The transition probabilities in and out of these two populations are exogenously determined and, therefore, act as model parameters. The core parameter, of course, is the disability incidence rate as it explicitly links the two flow models.

In the base model the age-specific in and outflow incidence rates are taken to be constant, reflecting unaltered labor market and disability behavior. As an alternative we fix the mean disability rate using the so-called quantile method in order to control for the effects of aging. Thus, we stage a variant that optimistically deviates from the base model in that it reflects improved employment opportunities for older labor market participants thanks to greying.

Clearly, the model as such is a purely mechanistic calculation scheme. By exogenous manipulation of the transition parameters, however, we may introduce alternative behavioral scenarios.

## 11.3    Definitions and Input Data

### 11.3.1   Definitions

**Labor Force**
We apply the definition used by the Central Planning Bureau for its labor force predictions [CPB (1989)]. The labor force includes privately and self-employed persons, and their collaborating family members, civil servants, and unemployed persons who are currently engaged in job search activities and readily available for paid work. Persons older than 65 years are excluded.

Thus defined, the labor force equals total labor supply.

**DIS-population**
The DIS-population includes all impaired persons who are entitled to at least the base disability benefit (AAW-benefits, see chapter 2), and who were labor force participants at the onset of their incapacity. We therefore exclude the early handicapped and other groups out of the labor force, such as students - who are covered by the AAW-program as well.

Although the labor force appears in the denominator of the disability incidence rate, it does not coincide with the population at risk. For instance, unemployed persons without a work record who receive a benefit under the National Assistance scheme for the unemployed (RWW) belong to the labor force but are not covered for income loss under the disability program.

For the starting year of our calculations, 1990, the age- and sex-specific numbers that result from these definitions are shown in table 11.1 below. In the table we also present the *dependency rate* which is the DIS-population divided by the sum of the labor force and the DIS-populations (see also chapter 2, table 2.15).[4] The early-retirement character of the disability program is clearly mirrored by the dependency rates of the oldest age-groups. These data also highlight the impact of the age-distributions within the two populations on the average dependency rate. Other things equal, greying therefore will increase the dependency rate.

**Table 11.1   Labor Force and DIS-Populations, by Age and Sex, 1990, *thousands***

| Age-group | Labor Force Participants | | | Disability Beneficiaries | | | dependency rate |
|---|---|---|---|---|---|---|---|
| | men | women | total | men | women | total | |
| 15 - 19 | 120 | 128 | 248 | (a) | (a) | (a) | .001 |
| 20 - 24 | 465 | 435 | 900 | 3 | 3 | 6 | .007 |
| 25 - 29 | 609 | 399 | 1008 | 10 | 10 | 20 | .019 |
| 30 - 34 | 587 | 303 | 890 | 22 | 15 | 37 | .040 |
| 35 - 39 | 556 | 276 | 832 | 39 | 18 | 57 | .064 |
| 40 - 44 | 572 | 299 | 871 | 54 | 24 | 78 | .082 |
| 45 - 49 | 416 | 193 | 609 | 67 | 28 | 95 | .135 |
| 50 - 54 | 316 | 124 | 440 | 89 | 35 | 124 | .220 |
| 55 - 59 | 219 | 72 | 291 | 117 | 44 | 161 | .356 |
| 60 - 64 | 51 | 22 | 83 | 129 | 45 | 174 | .677 |
| Total | 3910 | 2250 | 6160 | 531 | 222 | 753 | .109 |

a  Less than 500 persons.
Sources:  CPB (1991); AAf (1989); SVr (1991); own calculations.

Notice that we do not make an allowance - neither in our forecasting model nor in the definition and measurement of our input data - to translate the population sizes which are counted in persons into man-years.

This implies two limitations:

• Changes in the prevalence of part-time work among labor force participants are not accounted for. Hence, the part-time work rate, that is average actual working hours per week divided by its full-time equivalent, is implicitly kept at its current level.

• More importantly, changes in the prevalence of partial disability benefits are ignored. In other words, the partial benefit rate (*de herleidingsfactor*), that is the weighted average degree of disability where the weights represent the relative frequencies of the disability categories among the DIS-population, is assumed to stay put.[5]

The last restriction makes it difficult to determine the budgetary consequences of DIS-population forecasts in persons if the underlying partial benefit rate would change.

## 11.3.2   CBS Population Prognoses 1990-2050

Our forecasts of the size and composition of the DIS-population are based on the medium variant of the 1988 CBS population prognoses. Like other welfare states, the Netherlands have entered a period of accelerating population aging. The aging is primarily caused by the 1945-1955 baby boom, that waves through the population pyramid. Moreover, steadily increasing life expectancies have been obtained by improvements in the general level of education and health care.

**Table 11.2   Age-Composition and Size of the Dutch Population, 1950 - 2050**

| Year | 0 - 19 | 20 - 64 *(percentages)* | over 65 | size (x1000) |
|------|--------|----------|---------|--------------|
| 1950 | 37.6 | 54.6 | 7.8 | 10,027 |
| 1960 | 38.2 | 52.7 | 9.1 | 11,417 |
| 1970 | 36.0 | 53.8 | 10.2 | 12,958 |
| 1980 | 31.5 | 57.0 | 11.5 | 14,091 |
| 1990 | 25.6 | 61.6 | 12.8 | 14,894 |
| 2000 | 24.2 | 62.0 | 13.8 | 15,717 |
| 2010 | 23.2 | 61.6 | 15.2 | 16,143 |
| 2020 | 21.0 | 60.0 | 18.9 | 16,218 |
| 2030 | 20.9 | 56.9 | 22.3 | 16,092 |
| 2040 | 21.1 | 54.8 | 24.1 | 15,565 |
| 2050 | 20.7 | 56.9 | 22.5 | 14,857 |

Source: CBS (1989).

Table 11.2 illustrates these demographic developments. The youngest age-group in 1990 is born after the baby boom and since fertility is not expected to increase in the future, the size of this group will gradually decline. The size of the potential labor force, the age-group 20-64, is expected to increase at a modest rate of 0.7 percent per year until 2010 when the first baby boomers reach 65. Between 2010 and 2040 the size of the middle age-group will decrease, both in absolute and in relative terms. The baby boomers will enter the oldest age-group after 2010 as shown by its relative size. The grey wave is expected to reach its top in 2040 when almost 1 of 4 is over 65.

## 11.3.3   Incidence Rates of Labor Force Entries and Exits

Age and sex-specific labor force entries are derived from a 1985 CBS sample (*Arbeidskrachtentelling 1985*). Since the entry rates $(\iota_j)$ are defined by eq.(11.5) conditional on being out of the labor force, these absolute numbers have to be divided by the difference between the total and the labor force populations in order to obtain the required relative frequencies.

We, therefore, combine the CBS survey data with the population forecasts and labor force population forecasts for 1995 and 2000 by the Central Planning Bureau (CPB). Entry rates for males can be directly calculated from these two sources.

Female entry profiles, however, are less stable because they reflect the changing patterns in their lifetime labor force participation. These incidence rates are calibrated such that they, combined with the other model parameters, reproduce the CPB female labor force forecasts for 1995 and 2000.

Table 11.3 Relative Frequencies of Entry[a] ($\iota_j$) into and Voluntary Exit ($\pi_j$) out of the Labor Force, by Age and Sex

| Age-group | Males | | Females | |
|---|---|---|---|---|
| | $\iota_j$ | $\pi_j$ | $\iota_j$ | $\pi_j$ |
| 15 - 19 | .106 | .038 | .155 | .064 |
| 20 - 24 | .292 | .017 | .222 | .061 |
| 25 - 29 | .532 | .007 | .140 | .089 |
| 30 - 34 | .508 | .004 | .095 | .071 |
| 35 - 39 | .354 | .002 | .085 | .067 |
| 40 - 44 | .248 | .001 | .085 | .053 |
| 45 - 49 | .117 | .001 | .033 | .042 |
| 50 - 54 | .079 | .004 | .017 | .056 |
| 55 - 59 | .023 | .042 | .009 | .102 |
| 60 - 64 | .005 | .159 | .004 | .335 |
| Total | .137 | .010 | .082 | .068 |

a Conditional on being out of the labor force.
Sources: CBS (1989), CPB (1989), own calculations

The relative frequencies of outflow out of the labor force, for other reasons than death or disability, are directly calculated from the two sources mentioned above. For the oldest age-groups these exit rates should appropriately reflect early retirement behavior.

The resulting labor force entry and voluntary exit rates for men and women are contained in table 11.3. The incidence rates reflect the stereotyped labor market behavior of men and women: Under the age of 55, male voluntary exit rates are virtually zero. Beyond this age the exit rate sharply increases due to early retirement. Among females, the exit rate first peaks in the 25-29 bracket, then starts to increase again from 50 onwards. The first peak reflects the conventional pattern as women retreat from the labor force to take on childcare and housekeeping duties. Sex-specific patterns are also revealed by the inflow rates. In the youngest age-group the proportion of women entering the labor force exceeds its male counterpart. The female inflow rate gradually declines after 24. Male inflow rates reach much higher levels and start declining later, after the age of 29. The inflow of males older than 40 mainly originates from recoveries among disability beneficiaries.

Lacking adequate data, we assume that the entry and exit rates keep the values listed in table 11.2. Consequently, our prognoses are conditional on the assumption of unaltered labor market behavior. The assumption of constant labor market behavior, however, does not imply that age- and sex-specific participation rates $p_{j,t}$ = $L_{j,t}/N_{j,t}$ are time invariant too.

## 11.3.4   The Disability Incidence

In section 11.2.6 we introduced a function g which relates the quantile-value of age $(x_{j,t})$ to the age-specific DI-incidence rate $(\delta_{j,t})$. Given the definition of $\delta_{j,t}$ it seems appropriate to specify g as a probability function. For its analytical convenience we choose the logistic probability function

$$\delta_{j,t} = [1 + \exp\{-d_{0,t} - d_1\, x_{j,t}\}]^{-1};  \tag{11.17}$$

$d_1$, the sex-specific logit coefficient on the age-quantile, is assumed to be time invariant. It is estimated using our 1980 samples;[6] $d_0$ includes a time parameter since it may vary over time depending on additional, exogenous, assumptions.

Although defined on a somewhat larger insured population, the age-specific disability incidence $\delta_{j,t}$ may be regarded identical to the unconditional DI-probability analyzed in section 10.2. We may, therefore, interpret the logit coefficients $d_0$ and $d_1$ with reference to the structural DI-probit model in table 10.1. Since the direct age-effect in table 10.1 appeared to be insignificant, the coefficient $d_1$ assembles the age-effects that run via the structural determinants of the DI-probability. In the same vein $d_0$ represents the age-independent elements of those determinants. For instance, the wear of physical abilities due to aging is caught by $d_1$, whereas improvements thanks to better job conditions are covered by $d_0$.

Keeping $d_0$ constant, then, implies the hypothesis of unaltering disability behavior. Simulated modifications in the age-independent parts of one, or more, of the explanatory variables, on the other hand, induce $d_0$ to change as well.

Substitution of the logit function into the general formula for the mean DI-incidence rate (11.16) and approximation by the first three terms of a Taylor series, yields after some elaboration[7]

$$\mu_\delta = (1 + 0.5\, d_1^2)\,(1 + \exp\{-d_0\})^{-1}.  \tag{11.18}$$

Evidently, $\mu_\delta$ is a constant if $d_0$ and $d_1$ are fixed. On the other hand, the mean incidence rate, $\mu_\delta$, and the concomitant age-specific rates, $\delta_{j,t}$, can be manipulated by varying $d_0$. Using the 1989 values for $\mu_\delta$, being 0.016 for men, and 0.017 for women, as inputs we can express $d_0$ in terms of the estimates for $d_1$.[8] We choose that value for $d_0$ which yields the highest correlation with the observed 1989 distribution given in table 11.4 below.

If the 1989 averages are compared with their 1969-88 values, the mean disability incidence rate appears to be increasing again. This may be partly due to ageing of the insured population, increasing labor force participation of women over 30, and increases in age-specific incidence rates which point to a revival of interest in the disability benefit option.

Notice also that, for the first time since the introduction of a comprehensive Social Security Disability program in 1967, the mean disability rate for women is larger than that for males. This is probably due to growing labor force participation rates among women aged 30-55.

Table 11.4   Disability Incidence Rates by Age and Sex, 1989

| Age-group | Males | Females |
|---|---|---|
| 15 - 24 | .005 | .006 |
| 25 - 34 | .010 | .015 |
| 35 - 44 | .017 | .019 |
| 45 - 54 | .031 | .038 |
| 55 - 64 | .046 | .057 |
| Total | .016 | .017 |

Sources:  GMD (1990); SVr (1990); own calculations. (See also table A.11.2 in the appendix)

## 11.3.5   Recovery and Mortality Rates

To be able to calculate the outflows out of the DIS and the labor force populations we need age and sex-specific recovery and mortality rates for the DIS-population as well as mortality rates for the labor force.

Recovery rates for the disabled are given in table 11.5.

Table 11.5   Recovery Rates by Age and Sex, 1989, *percentages*

| Age-group | Males | Females |
|---|---|---|
| 15 - 19 | 62.1 | 55.7 |
| 20 - 24 | 47.3 | 43.0 |
| 25 - 29 | 23.1 | 20.2 |
| 30 - 34 | 11.6 | 12.7 |
| 35 - 39 | 8.4 | 9.1 |
| 40 - 44 | 5.4 | 6.1 |
| 45 - 49 | 3.2 | 3.9 |
| 50 - 54 | 1.9 | 2.2 |
| 55 - 59 | 0.8 | 0.9 |
| 60 - 64 | 0.1 | 0.1 |
| Total | 3.3 | 4.8 |

Sources:  AAf (1989); SVr (1990); own calculations.

Due to the preponderance of older persons among disability beneficiaries and their extremely small recovery rates, the overall rates are modest - less than 5 percent. The average rate is almost 50 percent higher for women than for men. This is mainly due to the differential age-distribution of the male and female disabled. When the age differential is controlled for, the female average recovery rate drops to 3.56 percent.

**Table 11.6**    **Mortality Rates of the Labor Force and DIS-Populations, by Age and Sex,**
**1989,** *per thousand*

|  | Labor Force Participants | | Disability Beneficiaries | |
| --- | --- | --- | --- | --- |
| Age-group | men | women | men | women |
| 15 - 19 | 0.8 | 0.4 | 64.7 | 34.6 |
| 20 - 24 | 0.9 | 0.4 | 33.8 | 17.9 |
| 25 - 29 | 0.8 | 0.4 | 9.4 | 7.9 |
| 30 - 34 | 0.9 | 0.6 | 8.1 | 6.9 |
| 35 - 39 | 1.2 | 0.9 | 7.4 | 6.5 |
| 40 - 44 | 2.6 | 1.4 | 7.5 | 6.6 |
| 45 - 49 | 4.1 | 2.4 | 9.4 | 8.2 |
| 50 - 54 | 7.0 | 3.6 | 13.9 | 9.2 |
| 55 - 59 | 11.9 | 5.3 | 19.3 | 10.4 |
| 60 - 64 | 17.8 | 8.0 | 24.0 | 13.6 |
| Total | 2.8 | 1.2 | 15.6 | 9.6 |

Sources: AAf (1989); CBS (1982, 1989); own calculations.

In each age-group male mortality is higher. While among the relatively healthy
population of labor force participants death rates monotonically rise with age,
mortality among the disabled is U-shaped. With growing age the death rates of the
disability beneficiaries approach those of the general population.

In sum, these recovery and mortality data underscore the picture of leniency of the
program gatekeepers increasing with age and, hence, the early retirement character
of the disability program.

## 11.4    DIS-Population Forecasts

In this section we present the forecasts obtained by applying the input data
described in the preceding section to the calculation scheme of section 11.2.[9] We
start in 11.4.1 by focussing on the assumption of unaltered disability behavior, by
keeping the age-specific disability incidence rates at their 1989 levels. This *central
variant* purports to estimate the effects of population aging on the volume of
disability beneficiaries. As it is based on the presumption that the volume-effects
of greying will not evoke any countervailing forces, the central variant represents
a maximum estimate of the DIS-population.

Other variants stage a variety of offsetting scenarios. The first is the so-called
*quantile variant* introduced in 11.2.6. By this variant the mean disability incidence
rate is kept constant. This variant, then, presumes that the demographic effect is
fully off-set by the enhanced competitive power of older workers in a greying labor
force.

Next, in subsection 11.4.2, we try to simulate the course of the DIS-volume if the
*policy changes* implied by the 1987 Social Security system reform would be rigorously
effectuated as of 1990. As far as disability insurance legislation is concerned, the

major modification was the elimination of labor market considerations from disability assessments. To simulate the potential DIS-volume-effects of this amendment we employ the work capacity estimates discussed in chapter 5.

Finally, in subsection 11.4.3 we shift our focus from the gatekeepers of the disability provisions to the other agents affecting the volume of disability transfer dependency. These *behavioral scenarios* are based on the unconditional DI-probit model in table 10.1. We simulate the effects of employers' efforts to reduce the extent of physical disablement through the adaptation of jobs or working conditions; the effects of better employment opportunities for impaired workers; and the effects of a somewhat larger income loss in the disability transfer option due to benefit reductions, wage rises, or both.

### 11.4.1 Central and Quantile Variants

In the first panel of table 11.7 we show the course of the male, female, and total, DIS-populations assuming constant labor market and disability behavior.

The total DIS-population will grow from the 1990 volume of 753,000 to 1,374,000 in 2020. This 82.5 percent growth implies an average rate of 2.75 percent per annum which is comparable to the average 1980-90 growth rate of almost 3 percent.

Women are anticipated to follow a much steeper time-path than men.[10] The 1990-2020 female annual growth rate is 4.7 percent whereas male disability beneficiaries grow by a modest annual percentage of 0.6. A number of causes may be held responsible for this outcome. First, as a result of the conventional work patterns of Dutch (married) women in the past the female labor force is relatively young, and so is the corresponding DIS-population. Therefore, while recovery rates are low anyway, the outflow out of the female DIS-population due to death or, more importantly, pensioning is relatively small, too.

The female incidence rates, on the other hand, parallel those of males, reaching equal equilibrium levels of 2.1 percent in 2010. As a consequence, the female DIS-volume is much farther away from its saturation point where inflow equals outflow than its male counterpart. Currently, inflow into the female DIS-population is 1.8 as large as the outflow whereas the male inflow/outflow rate is 1.2. In the central variant both rates are expected to decline until they reach 1 in 2020. Notice that these inflow/outflow rates of the DIS-population are larger than those of the labor force. This inflow surplus will cause the DIS-volume to grow further, independent of greying.

The calculation scheme discussed in section 11.2 generates forecasts of two inter-related populations - the labor force and the DIS-population. Evidently, the emphasis here is on the DIS-population forecasts.

**Table 11.7**   1990-2050 Forecasts of the DIS-Population (DDx10⁻³) and the Disability
Incidence (δ) by Sex; the Reduction Rate[a] and the Dependency Rate:
*Central and Quantile Variants*

| | men | | women | | total | | |
|---|---|---|---|---|---|---|---|
| | DD | δ | DD | δ | DD | reduction rate(x100) | dependency rate(x100) |
| **1. Central Variant** | | | | | | | |
| 1990 | 531 | .016 | 222 | .017 | 753 | 0 | 10.9 |
| 1995 | 606 | .018 | 305 | .018 | 911 | 0 | 12.3 |
| 2000 | 685 | .019 | 382 | .020 | 1,067 | 0 | 13.9 |
| 2005 | 766 | .020 | 454 | .021 | 1,220 | 0 | 15.6 |
| 2010 | 829 | .021 | 511 | .021 | 1,340 | 0 | 17.1 |
| 2020 | 839 | .021 | 535 | .021 | 1,374 | 0 | 18.0 |
| 2030 | 779 | .021 | 501 | .021 | 1,280 | 0 | 18.0 |
| 2040 | 685 | .020 | 447 | .021 | 1,132 | 0 | 16.9 |
| 2050 | 699 | .021 | 457 | .021 | 1,156 | 0 | 17.5 |
| **2. Quantile Variant** | | | | | | | |
| 1990 | 531 | .016 | 222 | .017 | 753 | 0 | 10.9 |
| 1995 | 593 | . | 300 | . | 893 | - 2 | 12.1 |
| 2000 | 642 | . | 362 | . | 1,004 | - 6 | 13.1 |
| 2005 | 682 | . | 412 | . | 1,094 | - 10 | 14.1 |
| 2010 | 701 | . | 444 | . | 1,145 | - 15 | 14.7 |
| 2020 | 661 | . | 440 | . | 1,101 | - 20 | 14.6 |
| 2030 | 598 | . | 404 | . | 1,002 | - 22 | 14.3 |
| 2040 | 545 | . | 369 | . | 914 | - 19 | 13.8 |
| 2050 | 557 | .016 | 377 | .017 | 934 | - 19 | 14.3 |

a   Percentage reduction of the number of disability transfer beneficiaries as compared
with the central variant.

The DIS-forecasts, however, crucially depend on the labor force projections. For
the central variant these are contained in table A.11.1, in the appendix to this
chapter. By keeping the inflow and voluntary outflow rates in and out of the labor
force constant, the resulting participation rates are more or less stable too: about
.75 for men and .45 for women. Evidently, constant female participation is an
unrealistic assumption which is likely to lead to underestimation of the population
at risk and, hence, the DIS-population. The dependency rate shows an increase of
7.1 percentage points, or 65 percent, between 1990 and 2020. The difference between
this increase and the DIS-volume growth of 82.5 percent can be attributed to a
growing labor force. After all, the increase in the dependency rate reflects the
prediction result that, in the central variant, the DIS-population is growing faster
than the labor force. This is the result of aging and the positive correlation of age
and disability risks on the one hand, and the positive difference between entries
and exits in and out of the DIS-population on the other hand. After 2020 the
dependency rate becomes stable because, by then, aging will result in a dominance
of exits over entries.

The results for the quantile variant, contained in the second panel of table 11.7, present a more moderate alternative in which the demographic effects are neutralized. By keeping the mean disability incidence rate at its, historically low, 1990 level the age-specific incidence rates have to drop to accommodate population aging. As a result, the time trajectory for the DIS-population levels off sooner and has a lower top.

This variant purports to simulate the attenuating effect on the DIS-volume of an increased demand for older workers for lack of younger ones, as a countervailing force induced by aging. If this mechanically obtained labor market scenario would come true, the eventual reduction with respect to the central variant would be about 20 percent. The resulting growth of the DIS-volume is 52 percent over the 1990-2010 period, and 46 percent over the 1990-2020 period. The comparable 1990-2020 growth according to the central variant, which takes full account of the disability enhancing effect of an aging population at risk, is 82.5 percent. Consequently, 36.5 percentage points, or 44 percent of total program growth over the coming 30 years, are attributable to greying.

Before, we estimated that 17.5 percentage points, or 21 percent of total program growth, are due to labor force growth. Hence, the residual 28.5 percentage points, or 35 percent of total program growth, are due to the persistence of an inflow surplus that, according to the central variant, will only disappear after 2020.

### 11.4.2 The Potential Effects of the 1987 Disability Amendments

Among other things, the 1987 social security system reform aimed at two goals; the abolition of iniquities in benefit entitlements between older unemployed and partially disabled workers, and cost containment by reducing the unemployment and disability volumes.

By an amendment of the Disability Insurance Acts (WAO and AAW), the legal provision that, by lenient interpretation, allowed the administrators to award full benefits to the partially disabled who were unable to find commensurate employment, was abolished. This amendment, then, intended to effect the elimination of the controversial "labor market consideration" which we described in chapters 2 and 5.

Through elimination of labor market considerations from disability determinations, legislature hoped to serve both the equity and the budgetary goals. In fact, a major part of the projected savings resulting from the reform program, was related to this particular amendment. As documented in section 5.9 these government projections were, among others, based on our 1980 work capacity estimates, which were first published in 1982. As documented in section 5.7 the structural unemployment component has been estimated to be 33 to 51 percent of the population of DI-beneficiaries. The maximum effect of the abolition of the labor market consideration, therefore, would be a reduction of the DI-population equal to the size of the unemployment component.

In reality, however, the reduction rates in the three years after enactment of the disability amendments have been so modest that government felt compelled to adjust its estimate of the eventual structural reduction of the DI-volume from 50 to 10 percent. In subsection 5.9.2 we list a number of potential explanations for this disappointing policy outcome. For one thing, total elimination of the unemployment component requires full compliance with the new rulings. Full compliance means disentanglement of the medical and unemployment components of disability. This requires more rigorous disability assessments both at program entry and, at regular intervals, during benefit recipiency. *At program entry* the adjudicators of disability claims should be able to separate the unemployment from the medical part, and award only the latter part by granting a partial benefit corresponding to the earnings' loss caused by impairment proper. However, as witnessed by the annual statistics and our 1980 survey data, the program administrators have great difficulties to apply such refined definitions of disablement.

As an alternative, therefore, we may employ our estimates of work capacity at DI-enrolment - in section 5.7 - and catch the spirit of the reform by assuming that those who are able to fully perform commensurate work are not allowed to the DI-rolls.[11] By this definition we ignore the seven statutory disability categories and reduce disability determinations to a dichotomy.

*During benefit recipiency* DI-beneficiaries should be regularly re-examined to assess improvements in health status and corresponding reductions of the extent of disablement. If we apply the simplified, dichotomous, definition of disability here too, those who have regained the capacity to fully perform commensurate work will lose their eligibility in due course upon program entry. If they are unable to find such work they are henceforth unemployed, and not disabled anymore.

In short, in order to identify and separate the unemployment component from the disability beneficiary population, we apply a coarse definition of disability - the incapacity to fully perform commensurate work. This definition, then, allows us to use the work capacity estimates of chapter 5 for the simulation of the potential volume-effects of full compliance with the disability amendments that were enacted as part of the 1987 social security system reform.

### Additional Assumptions

First, we assume throughout that the work capacity estimates of chapter 5, that pertain to the (sample of) DI-entrants, are also applicable to the - somewhat larger - DIS-population which includes civil servants and the self-employed. As regards civil servants this assumption is not very heroic given the picture emerging from their disability statistics.[12] The self-employed are only insured for minimum (base) benefits and have a different market position. This group is relatively small, and their disability behavior has not been studied yet.

Second, the work capacity estimates are based on our 1980 sample of DI-entrants and, therefore, may be outdated. More importantly, they may overstate the unemployment component among later DI-cohorts. The early 1980s witnessed sharply decreasing DI-incidence rates, for both sexes in all age-groups.[13] These decreases are likely to have been accompanied by an increasing share of "medical disability" at the expense of "social disability" - viz. the unemployment component. We will, therefore, only use the lower variant of the work capacity estimates, i.e. measure A in chapter 5.

**Policy Scenario I: Enhanced Rigor at Program Entry**
In this scenario we implement only the first step towards elimination of the unemployment component from the DIS-population by assuming that disability benefit determinations at program entry are based on whether claimants are capable to perform commensurate work. In this scenario workers who are judged capable to perform commensurate work will be denied a disability benefit.

According to table 5.11 this would imply that 29 percent of those who are granted benefits now, would be facing a denial under the more rigorous regime. Equally, it would imply that the average disability incidence rate would decrease by a factor of 0.71. Using the conservative variant of our 1980 work capacity estimates we can derive reduction factors for each age-sex cell. Application of these factors to the 1990 age and sex-specific disability incidence rates obtains the reduced award rates that would prevail under the stricter ruling. These reduction factors and the resulting lowered disability incidence rates, by age and sex, are shown in table A.11.2 in the appendix.

On the other hand, application of a stricter definition of disability at program entry implies that those awarded are more seriously impaired and, therefore, are likely to have lower recovery and higher mortality rates. Using additional sample data on recoveries during the first 18 months after DI-enrolment, we observe that among those without capacity for commensurate work at DI-entry, the male recovery rate is 22 percent lower than the male sample mean of 0.133, whereas the female recovery rate is 16 percent less than the female sample mean of 0.324.[14] In our first policy scenario where we ignore periodical re-examinations upon enrolment, we use the implied reduced recovery rates.

For lack of reliable estimates of mortality among those without capacity for commensurate work we put the mortality rates at their upper limit by assuming that the *number* of deaths among disability beneficiaries, observed in the central variant, also applies in the current, stricter, assessment variant. Since the number of DI-beneficiaries decreases the resulting mortality *rate* increases.

The DIS-forecasts obtained by reduced disability incidence and recovery rates, and increased mortality rates, are given in the first panel of table 11.8. These forecasts show that elimination of labor market considerations from disability awards, implemented as of 1990, substantially reduces the DIS-volume relative to the central variant which is based on unaltered award policies.

Table 11.8    1990-2050 Forecasts of the DIS-Population ($DD \times 10^{-3}$) and the Disability Incidence ($\delta$) by Sex; the Reduction Rate[a] and the Dependency Rate, According to Two Policy Scenarios: More Rigorous Disability Assessment at Program Entry; More Rigorous Disability Assessment at Entry and during Benefit Recipiency

| | men | | women | | total | | |
|---|---|---|---|---|---|---|---|
| | DD | $\delta$ | DD | $\delta$ | DD | reduction rate(x100) | dependency rate(x100) |
| **1. At Program Entry** | | | | | | | |
| 1990 | 531 | .011 | 222 | .013 | 753 | 0 | 10.9 |
| 1995 | 521 | .013 | 269 | .014 | 790 | -13 | 10.7 |
| 2000 | 539 | .014 | 320 | .015 | 859 | -19 | 11.3 |
| 2005 | 577 | .015 | 375 | .016 | 952 | -22 | 12.4 |
| 2010 | 611 | .016 | 421 | .017 | 1032 | -23 | 13.4 |
| 2020 | 608 | .016 | 440 | .017 | 1048 | -24 | 14.0 |
| 2030 | 566 | .016 | 411 | .016 | 977 | -24 | 14.0 |
| 2040 | 493 | .015 | 367 | .016 | 860 | -24 | 13.0 |
| 2050 | 505 | .016 | 375 | .016 | 880 | -24 | 13.5 |
| **2. At Entry and during Benefit Recipiency** | | | | | | | |
| 1990 | 531 | .011 | 222 | .013 | 753 | 0 | 10.9 |
| 1995 | 509 | .013 | 258 | .014 | 767 | -16 | 10.4 |
| 2000 | 498 | .014 | 288 | .015 | 786 | -26 | 10.4 |
| 2005 | 504 | .015 | 317 | .016 | 821 | -33 | 10.8 |
| 2010 | 514 | .016 | 339 | .017 | 853 | -36 | 11.3 |
| 2020 | 491 | .016 | 338 | .017 | 829 | -40 | 11.4 |
| 2030 | 456 | .016 | 313 | .016 | 769 | -40 | 11.3 |
| 2040 | 396 | .015 | 281 | .016 | 677 | -40 | 10.6 |
| 2050 | 405 | .016 | 286 | .016 | 691 | -40 | 11.0 · |

a    See table 11.7.

In due course, rigorous application of the disability amendments concerning awards would lead to 24 percent less disability beneficiaries. It does not, however, stop the absolute numbers nor the dependency rate from growing. Despite the reduction in the inflow rates, eventually, greying will cause the average rate to converge at a level equal to the current disability incidence. Therefore, the outcomes in this policy scenario are similar to those obtained by the quantile variant.

## Policy Scenario II: Enhanced Rigor both at Program Entry and During Benefit Recipiency

In this scenario we stage a complete separation of the unemployment component from the disability rolls. To the stricter award policy implemented in the preceding scenario by lowering the age and sex-specific incidence rates we add increased recovery rates resulting from periodical re-examinations of disability beneficiaries. These increases can be derived from cross-tabulation of the work capacity estimates at program entry against those in due course upon enrolment. Such breakdowns are given in panel 1 of table 5.11. These indicate that among those 71 percent who are unable to fully perform commensurate work at entry, and hence, under the stricter ruling, would still be granted an award, 24 percent are expected to recover in the future. These percentages imply an average yearly recovery rate of 24/71 = 0.34 among those who meet the more rigorous eligibility standards. This estimate is in sharp contrast with the actual recovery rates observed among all beneficiaries. Five years after program entry the 1980 cohort of disability beneficiaries is observed to have a cumulative recovery rate of 20 percent (see table 5.7). Consequently, under the stricter regime the average recovery rate would rise by a factor of 34/20 = 1.7 despite the more rigorous award policy.

Making the same cross-tabulation for each age-sex cell we obtain age and sex-specific recovery increase factors. These increased recovery rates are given in table A.11.3 in the appendix. They are applied to the 1990 and later cohorts of DIS-entrants only. In doing so, we assume that the stock of disability beneficiaries, present at the beginning of 1990, are not made subject to systematic reviews.

Summing up, the only difference between the two policy variants is that the second variant, which purports to simulate complete elimination of the labor market component from the DIS-population, assumes increased instead of reduced recovery rates.[15] The disability and mortality rates are the same in both policy variants.

The lower panel of table 11.8 displays the forecasts obtained under full compliance with the 1987 disability amendments, as of 1990. Assuming that the work capacity estimates used to implement this scenario still apply, full compliance would turn the demographic wave. Due to higher benefit termination rates the inflow surplus would vanish and the DIS-population would stop growing, and so would the dependency rate. Upon convergence, the reduction relative to continuation of the current award and termination policies is 40 percent. This reduction rate suggests that the structural gain from full elimination of the unemployment component would, in terms of the DIS-volume, amount to 40 percent.

Comparison of the two policy options indicates that the structural gain from regular reviews using the stricter, dichotomous, definition of disability, is an added reduction of the DIS-volume of 16 percentage points, over the 24 percent reduction under a more rigorous award policy alone. Implementation of a more rigorous award policy alone, therefore, would eliminate 60 percent of the total unemployment component - somewhat more than the 50 percent found by cross-sectional estimation in chapter 5.

Notice, however, that the increase factors in table A.11.3 indicate that the largest stock of unused work capacity is estimated to be found among the older bene-ficiaries, up to 60. Hence, the major returns to regular, and more stringent, reconsiderations should be realized by terminating the benefits of older workers who have been treated relatively leniently in the past.

The monetary savings from these two policy options may well be lower than these volume-effects suggest. In section 11.3.1 we noted that we implicitly keep the partial benefit rate, which indicates the actual relative number of partial beneficiaries, at its current level. Under the amendments staged here, however, those found ineligible will strongly overlap with the current recipients of partial benefits. If we, then, conservatively assume that under the stricter regime all partial, and an additional number of full, beneficiaries will lose their entitlements, the budgetary savings in terms of recipiency years will be in the order of 35 percent.


### 11.4.3    Three Behavioral Scenarios

As a final exercise we investigate what changes, other than the policy modifications studied in the previous subsection, would be necessary to counter the structural inflow surplus and the wave of baby boomers. We propose three scenarios by implementing changes in alternative sets of determinants of the unconditional DI-probability which we studied in section 10.2. To that end, we have to make the assumption that the structural model found for the privately employed also applies to civil servants and the self-employed.

The first scenario stages a reduction of the average degree of physical disablement by one standard deviation. By table A.10.1, first pair of columns, this boils down to a 9 percent decrease. Since PHYSDIS is based on a confrontation of job demands and conditions with limitations to endure physical strain, such a change can be brought about by numerous causes. One may think of increased efforts by employers to adapt job demands or working conditions to prevent impaired employees from being forced to retire.[16] Or, to the extent that physical limitations have job-related causes, employers may intensify their efforts to reduce the occurrence of physical impairment by preventive measures.

The second scenario stages improved employment opportunities for the (partially) disabled, e.g., by job creation or introduction of quota. In this variant we let individual unemployment probabilities $(\Pr\{E \rightarrow U\})$ decrease by one half, and re-employment probabilities $(\Pr\{U \rightarrow E\})$ increase by 100 percent. If such improvements were effectuated by general increases in labor demand this scenario may also be viewed as an alternative for the quantile variant.

In the third scenario we stage an increase in the opportunity cost of disability program participation by a $\frac{1}{2}\sigma$ increase of LnLOSSLT, which is equivalent to a 3 percent increase in the income loss due to disability benefit dependency. Such an increase can be brought about by keeping benefits at their current level while earnings rise.

Using the probit results in table 10.1 we calculate the effects of these changes on the DI-probability for each sample observation. For reasons of model consistency, however, these "structural" changes must be accompanied by a comparable change in FIRMRISK. For if all individual disability risks are assumed to drop, so does the population average, and hence the average firm-specific disability incidence rate.

Table 11.9  Average Male and Female Disability Incidence Rates before and after Occurrence of Three Types of Structural Changes: *Less Physical Disablement; Better Employment Opportunities; Larger Income Loss*

|  |  | Less Physical Disablement[a] | | Better Employment Opportunities[b] | | Larger Income Loss[c] | |
|---|---|---|---|---|---|---|---|
|  |  | men | women | men | women | men | women |
| "before" | (1990) | .016 | .017 | .016 | .017 | .016 | .017 |
| "after" | (2000) | .009 | .011 | .008 | .012 | .011 | .011 |

[a]  PHYSDIS - σ ; and FIRMRISK - σ.
[b]  Pr{E→U} × 0.5 ; Pr{U→E} × 2; and FIRMRISK - σ.
[c]  LnLOSSLT + ½σ ; and FIRMRISK - ½σ.

As indicated in table 11.9, the average disability incidence rates are gradually decreased from their current level to the level implied by each scenario, using eq.(11.17), over a period of 10 years. Given exogenous manipulation of the average disability incidence, the forecasts are necessarily generated by the quantile mechanism. Next, we calculate the relative deviations of these quantile results from the quantile results in table 11.7, and apply these to the central variant. The results for the total DIS-population, thus obtained, are given in table 11.10.

The resulting forecasts show that the implemented changes present three alternative ways to stop further growth of the DIS-volume, despite aging of the population at risk. The proceeds from the implemented changes are comparable, both in terms of the dependency rate and the percentile reduction relative to the central variant of constant behavior.

The largest reduction is obtained by a decrease in the prevalence, and average extent, of physical disablement. This suggests that increases in rehabilitative or preventive efforts are as effective as full compliance with the disability amendments (see table 11.8).

The second scenario gives better results than the comparable, but more mechanistic, quantile variant. In so far as the staged improvements result from enhanced rehabilitative efforts this scenario resembles the policy option of stricter disability assessments and reviews. For instance, the improved employment opportunities scenario may be based on stricter compliance with the already existing ruling that commensurate job offers must be accepted on penalty of benefit termination.

Table 11.10  1990-2050 Forecasts of the DIS-Population (DDx10$^{-3}$), the Reduction Rate[a] and the Dependency Rate, According to Three Behavioral Scenarios: *Less Physical Disablement; Better Employment Opportunities; Larger Income Loss*

|      | Less Physical Disablement[b] | | | Better Employment Opportunities[b] | | | Larger Income Loss[b] | | |
|------|------|------|------|------|------|------|------|------|------|
|      | DD | red.rate (x100) | dep.rate (x100) | DD | red.rate (x100) | dep.rate (x100) | DD | red.rate (x100) | dep.rate (x100) |
| 1990 | 753 | 0   | 10.9 | 753 | 0   | 10.9 | 753 | 0   | 10.9 |
| 1995 | 864 | - 5 | 11.5 | 867 | - 5 | 11.7 | 875 | - 4 | 11.8 |
| 2000 | 891 | -16 | 11.6 | 900 | -16 | 11.7 | 925 | -13 | 12.1 |
| 2005 | 898 | -26 | 11.5 | 913 | -25 | 11.7 | 957 | -22 | 12.3 |
| 2010 | 910 | -32 | 11.6 | 932 | -30 | 11.9 | 987 | -26 | 12.6 |
| 2020 | 859 | -37 | 11.3 | 885 | -36 | 11.6 | 947 | -31 | 12.4 |
| 2030 | 782 | -39 | 11.0 | 809 | -37 | 11.4 | 867 | -32 | 12.2 |
| 2040 | 690 | -39 | 10.3 | 713 | -37 | 10.6 | 765 | -32 | 11.4 |
| 2050 | 705 | -39 | 10.7 | 730 | -37 | 11.0 | 783 | -32 | 11.8 |

[a]   See table 11.7.
[b]   See table 11.9.

As indicated by the third scenario a somewhat larger rise in (real) wages than in (real) benefits may induce the DIS-population to reach a level which is 32 percent below that of the central variant. Such a change can be easily realized by refraining from automatic full indexation of benefits. This scenario suggests that a policy of controlled cost of living adjustments would suffice to realize considerable reductions in the disability beneficiary volume.

Notice that the proviso made before with respect to the budgetary savings implied by reductions of the number of beneficiaries applies here too. To the extent that the reductions are realized by rehabilitation of current recipients of partial benefits the savings are correspondingly smaller.

## 11.5   Summary and Conclusions

In this chapter we have concluded the analytical part of our study by extrapolating the number of disability beneficiaries - the so-called DIS-population - until 2050. These forecasts are based on a simple calculation scheme which basically consists of two recursive relations; one to forecast the labor force population including civil servants and the self-employed; the other to forecast the DIS-population, i.e., the number of labor force participants turned disability beneficiaries. The transition probabilities in and out of these two populations are exogenously determined, and act as the parameters of our calculation model. The core parameter is the disability incidence which links the two flow models. As input data we have used the CBS 1990-2050 population forecasts, and the current (1990) values of the two populations to be predicted and their transition probabilities. All of these input data and starting values are broken down by age and sex.

The resulting predictions are measured in terms of persons, not man-years. Specifically, we do not account for changes in the partial benefit rate, i.e., the average adjudicated degree of disability. It should be kept in mind, therefore, that there is a less than perfect correspondence between our DIS-population forecasts and their budgetary consequences.

The forecasts are given in several variants. We have begun by assuming that all age and sex-specific incidence rates keep their current values. Due to population greying and a structural inflow surplus, this *central variant* predicts 82.5 percent increase of the DIS-population from its current size of 753.000 to 1.374.000 in 2020 (see figure 11.2). This corresponds to a 65 percent increase in the disability dependency rate from 0.109 to 0.180 which is partly due to greying of the population at risk and partly to the persistence of an inflow surplus until 2010.

Since an 18 percent dependency rate may well turn out to be unbearable, both for financial and social reasons, we present 6 alternative scenarios by which the demographic wave, induced by the market mechanism or by conscious policy measures, may be prevented from flooding across the DIS-population. First, if due to aging the demand for older workers, for lack of younger ones, increases the average disability incidence may remain at its current level. Such a scenario is implemented by the so-called quantile mechanism. Apart from its labor market interpretation keeping the average disability rate constant is a way to control for the effect of aging on the DIS-volume. The resulting forecasts following the *quantile variant* anticipate the DIS-population to grow by 46 percent between 1990 and 2020. From these two forecasts, then, we may conclude that the 82.5 percent growth predicted by the central variant can be broken down into three components:

36.5 percentage points (44 percent) are due to greying of the population at risk; 28.5 percentage points (35 percent) are due to the persistence of an inflow surplus; and the last 17.5 percentage points (21 percent) are on account of labor force growth.

Next, we have simulated the effects of strict compliance with the 1987 disability amendments that were aimed at the elimination of labor market considerations from the assessment of disability. We implemented these modifications by introducing a stricter, and simpler, eligibility standard that would deny a benefit to those who are fully capable to perform commensurate work. Using the work capacity estimates discussed in chapter 5, we first lowered both the award and the recovery rates in order to simulate an award policy based on this definition of disability. Figure 11.2 displays that by this policy the number of disability beneficiaries will be 24 percent less than in the central variant, after the demographic wave has flooded across the disability schemes. With a dependency rate reaching 14 percent the results are comparable to those of the quantile-variant.

In a second policy variant we simulated the volume-effects of complete separation of the unemployment component from the DIS-population. This would entail a stricter benefit termination policy on top of enhanced rigor at program entry. In this variant the dependency rate appears to stay at its current level, suggesting that full compliance with the disability amendments as of 1990, would redress the inflow surplus despite greying of the labor force (see figure 11.2). Upon convergence the DIS-population would be 40 percent smaller than if award and termination policies would not change. This suggest an equally large - 40 percent - unemployment component.

**Figure 11.2   1990-2050 Forecasts of the Dutch Disabled Population, According to the Central Variant (I); and Two Policy Variants: Compliance with the 1987 Amendments at DI-Entry (II), and Full Compliance with the 1987 Amendments (III).**

Disabled (x1,000)

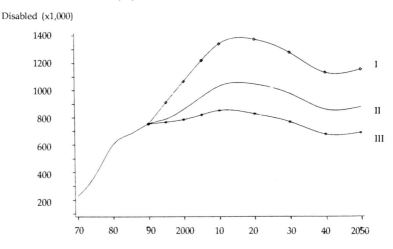

Given the Dutch disability experience full compliance with a strict definition of disability may be too grand a task. As a final exercise we, therefore, presented three scenarios whose outcomes are similar to the second, more rigorous, policy option. These scenarios are based on the behavioral DI-enrolment model presented in table 10.1. The first staged a reduction of the prevalence, and extent, of physical disablement by one standard error. The second was based on the assumption that employment opportunities for (mildly) impaired workers might improve considerably. As an alternative to narrowing the gates of the disability insurance programs, such changes may be induced by promoting rehabilitation.

The last scenario staged a modest increase of the income loss due to disability benefit dependency. At the expense of benefit adequacy this option might prove to be the easiest to implement.

## Appendix to chapter 11

Table A.11.1    1990-2050 Forecasts of the Labor Force ($L \times 10^{-3}$) and the Labor Force Participation Rates (pr), by Sex

|      | men |      | women |      | total |      |
|------|-----|------|-------|------|-------|------|
|      | L   | pr   | L     | pr   | L     | pr   |
| 1990 | 3909 | .750 | 2250 | .445 | 6159 | .600 |
| 1995 | 4117 | .775 | 2378 | .461 | 6496 | .620 |
| 2000 | 4194 | .778 | 2406 | .458 | 6600 | .620 |
| 2005 | 4184 | .765 | 2396 | .447 | 6579 | .608 |
| 2010 | 4119 | .747 | 2369 | .436 | 6488 | .593 |
| 2020 | 3966 | .739 | 2291 | .433 | 6256 | .585 |
| 2030 | 3701 | .741 | 2140 | .430 | 5841 | .585 |
| 2040 | 3518 | .747 | 2062 | .439 | 5580 | .594 |
| 2050 | 3448 | .743 | 2016 | .435 | 5464 | .589 |

Table A.11.2    Disability Incidence Rates before ($\iota_0$) and after ($\iota_1$) the Introduction of a More Rigorous Award Policy, and the Reduction Factors (rf) Implied by the Work Capacity Estimates in Chapter 5

|           | Males |     |          | Females |     |          |
|-----------|-------|-----|----------|---------|-----|----------|
| Age-group | $\iota_0$ | rf  | $\iota_1$ | $\iota_0$ | rf  | $\iota_1$ |
| 15 - 19   | .003  | .62 | .002     | .004    | .67 | .002     |
| 20 - 24   | .005  | .63 | .003     | .007    | .63 | .004     |
| 25 - 29   | .008  | .49 | .004     | .010    | .63 | .006     |
| 30 - 34   | .010  | .60 | .006     | .014    | .71 | .010     |
| 35 - 39   | .013  | .60 | .008     | .017    | .80 | .014     |
| 40 - 44   | .018  | .60 | .011     | .022    | .79 | .017     |
| 45 - 49   | .023  | .69 | .016     | .029    | .81 | .023     |
| 50 - 54   | .030  | .74 | .022     | .038    | .77 | .029     |
| 55 - 59   | .043  | .82 | .036     | .053    | .71 | .037     |
| 60 - 64   | .074  | .89 | .066     | .084    | .88 | .074     |
| Total     | .016  | .69 | .011     | .017    | .76 | .013     |

Table A.11.3    Recovery Rates before ($\varrho_0$) and after ($\varrho_1$) the Introduction of a More Rigorous Benefit Termination Policy, and the Recovery Increase Factors (if) Implied by the Work Capacity Estimates in Chapter 5

|           | Males |      |          | Females |      |          |
|-----------|-------|------|----------|---------|------|----------|
| Age-group | $\varrho_0$ | if   | $\varrho_1$ | $\varrho_0$ | if   | $\varrho_1$ |
| 15 - 19   | .621  | .57  | .354     | .557    | .57  | .317     |
| 20 - 24   | .473  | .94  | .445     | .430    | .94  | .404     |
| 25 - 29   | .231  | 1.00 | .231     | .202    | 1.00 | .202     |
| 30 - 34   | .116  | 1.11 | .129     | .127    | 1.11 | .141     |
| 35 - 39   | .084  | 1.42 | .119     | .091    | 1.42 | .129     |
| 40 - 44   | .054  | 1.68 | .091     | .061    | 1.68 | .102     |
| 45 - 49   | .032  | 1.81 | .058     | .039    | 1.81 | .071     |
| 50 - 54   | .019  | 2.76 | .052     | .022    | 2.76 | .061     |
| 55 - 59   | .008  | 3.02 | .024     | .009    | 3.02 | .027     |
| 60 - 64   | .001  | 1.40 | .001     | .001    | 1.40 | .001     |
| Total     | .033  | 2.04 | .011     | .048    | 1.94 | .013     |

Sources:  CBS (1989), CPB (1989); own calculations.

## Notes

1. The CBS mortality tables concern the total population not just the labor force.

2. We have applied the same transformation to rescale all of the ordinal variables used in our study (cf. section 6.2).

3.

$$g(x) = \sum_{k=0}^{\infty} \frac{x^k}{k!} \, g^{(k)}(0) \quad \text{where } g^{(k)}(0) = \left[ \frac{d^k \, g(x)}{dx^k} \right]_{x=0}$$

therefore,

$$\mu_{\delta} = E\{g(x)\} = \sum_{k=0}^{\infty} \frac{E\{x^k\}}{k!} \, g^{(k)}(0) = \sum_{m=0}^{\infty} \frac{g^{(2m)}(0)}{m! \, 2^m} \quad \text{with } 2m = k.$$

Hence, $\mu_{\delta}$ can be expressed as a sum of constants and, consequently, is independent of variables that change over time.

4. The discrepancy with the DI-dependency rate shown in table 2.15 is due to divergent definitions of the population at risk. More specifically, the dependency rates of both added groups (self-employed and civil servants) are lower.

5. Currently the partial benefit rate is 0.88.

6. The logit estimates for $d_1$ are .738 (.078) for men, and .707 (.124).

7. Actually $\mu_{\delta}$ is approximated using the Taylor expansion in note 2; fourth and higher order terms are neglected.

8. $d_0 = - \ln [1/\mu_{\delta} (1 + 0.5 \, d_1^2) - 1]$.

9. The calculations are based on an ALGOL-60 computer program, named VERZPOPL, specially designed by Peter Boot and J.Peter Hop that is described in Boot (1984).

10. Past average annual growth rates show that, in the 1970-80 decade, female (male) disability grew by 14.9 (13.4) percent per year (!) and in the 1980-90 decade by 6.8 (1.9) percent. Consequently, the share of women in the DIS-population grew from 22 percent in 1970 to 30 percent in 1990. According to our central variant it will further increase to 39 percent in 2020.

11. "Full performance" has been defined in section 5.4 as being able to perform like other, healthy, workers do.

12. Especially since 1980 when public sector employment was gradually reduced, the public sector disability incidence has reached proportions that are comparable with the market sector.

13. See JMS, Annual Reports, 1984-88.

14. See De Jong (1984), p. 12. Through the disability insurance administration we have recorded how our 1980 cohort of DI-entrants fared 18 months after their enrolment. These added data are used in Hermans (1986).

15. Strictly, increased recovery rates should raise the rate of inflow into the labor force, especially among older recoverees. We have omitted this feedback effect.

16.As part of the social security system reform the WAGW is enacted to stimulate employers to take such rehabilitative actions (see section 5.9). As yet there is little proof of the efficacy of this ruling. Currently, more drastic measures are being proposed. Government has proposed to reward firms if they re-employ partially disabled workers, and to penalize firms that allow such workers to enter the disability rolls.

Chapter 12

# ECONOMIC ASPECTS OF DISABILITY BEHAVIOR; SUMMARY AND CONCLUSIONS

## 12.1    Introduction

Although the Netherlands have not been plagued by epidemics or wars, the number of recipients of Social Disability Insurance (DI) benefits has been growing steadily over the past two decades. Ever since, by 1975, the trend in DI-program participation had proved to be uncontrollable, there has been a widespread feeling that the main causes of sustained growth of the disability volume are to be found in the operation of the program and the ways in which it is used by employees and their employers, rather than in deteriorations of the state of health among the insured population.

Our study has endeavoured to analyze the potential determinants of DI-program enrolment and to assess their relative impacts. Combining the medical-sociological and the micro-economic perspectives we described how distortions in the balance of functional abilities and job requirements lead to DI-program entry, taking explicit account of the roles played by employers, program gatekeepers, curative medicine, and, most importantly, the DI-insured workers themselves. We have been able to demonstrate that the process leading to DI-benefit eligibility is a multi-dimensional phenomenon governed by medical as well as a variety of non-medical factors. As a general conclusion this finding is not new. Others have reached similar conclusions for other countries, and called attention for the complexity of the disability risk. The novelty of our outcomes, however, is that they are based on an unusually rich dataset containing observations of impaired and able-bodied workers that are covered by an unusually generous and lenient disability insurance scheme. Besides information reported by the sampled employees, our data contain objectively measured disability indicators and information provided by the respondents' employers. We have, therefore, been able to properly control for differences in the extent and nature of disablement, and thence to assess the relative weights of self-perceived health, employment opportunities, commitment to paid work, job performance and income-leisure preferences, as determinants of DI-enrolment.

Below, we summarize the main findings of our study. In a final section we draw some conclusions with respect to public policy towards disability.

## 12.2    Summary of the Main Findings by Chapter

### The Dutch DI-program in National and International Perspective (chapter 2)

A cross national survey of social security systems shows that during the seventies and early eighties real social security expenditures increased in all major capitalist economies. The level of spending appears to be substantially higher in Europe than in the USA and Japan, and among the European countries the Netherlands rank first, both in terms of spending and transfer recipiency.

The Dutch Social Security System grew in many directions. Between 1965 and 1976, coverage, both in terms of risk and people, was extended, while benefits rose faster than wages. The behavioral effects prompted by this growth, exacerbated by exogenous factors such as the economic recessions of 1975 and 1981-83, have induced a massive increase of transfer recipiency.

A major part of this growth is accounted for by the DI-program. During the 1970 decade, disability income support became an instrument to encourage early retirement. As a reaction the 1980s witnessed a series of amendments and retrenchments inducing small decreases in the level of social security spending, not only in the Netherlands but also in other EC member states. In the Netherlands these policy changes culminated in the 1987 Social Security System Reform whose main feature is the elimination of labor market considerations from DI-eligibility assessments. Notwithstanding these changes the Dutch DI-benefit dependency rate of 139 beneficiaries per 1,000 labor force participants was, by the start of the 1990 decade, substantially higher than that in Sweden (78), Germany (55), or the United States (43).

The comparatively exuberant growth of the Dutch disability programs is considered to be partly the result of specific program principles, such as the absence of a distinction between job related and other impairments in disability assessment, and the very low minimum requirement for benefit eligibility. However, the administrative practice to award full DI-benefits to the partially disabled on the assumption of poor labor market opportunities may be regarded as the major source of the substantial growth in DI-expenditures.

The financial burden of the Dutch Social Security System weighs heavily on the wage bill, more so than in most other countries. The Dutch minimum benefit level is comparatively high, causing an upward pressure from the bottom of the wage distribution. Transfers to and from the government flatten out the overall income distribution further to become one of the flattest in the modern capitalist world. The assumedly adverse impacts of a relatively large wedge between gross labor cost and net earnings and the relative generosity of the DI-programs have contributed to the relatively low Dutch labor force participation rates. Despite the fact that female participation has been growing steadily and the decline in male participation had stopped by the end of the 1980 decade, both male and female rates are still among the lowest to be observed internationally.

### Residual Work Capacity among DI-Entrants (chapter 5)

Given its generosity and its lenient administration the Dutch DI-program is liable to shelter a considerable amount of residual work capacity. Based on the ratings of insurance physicians and ergonomists we have estimated the extent to which DI-beneficiaries are able to work. Having derived two measures, one more and one less conservative, we found that, at DI-entry, 29 to 48 percent of those who entered the program in 1980 may be considered capable of performing a suitable job. Only 1 to 18 percent are able to do their own job. After some time, 53 to 71 percent will have regained the ability to do suitable work; 20 to 26 percent are expected to be able to perform their own work again; 33 to 45 percent will be able to resume other work which suits their training and work record.

Since in fact only 20 percent of the 1980-cohort of DI-awards were terminated due to recovery, we concluded that the structural share of unemployment hidden in the DI-program amounts to 33 to 51 percent. The unemployment component varies with age, industry, type of work and diagnosis. Among a major group of beneficiaries - middle aged males working in blue collar jobs - the volume of hidden unemployment is relatively high. Although unfit to resume their old job, these people are often capable to do other suitable work but claim to be unable to find it. It may be worthwhile to concentrate on this particular group when developing or improving policies to stimulate work resumption of DI-beneficiaries.

Our results are consistent with those reported by other Dutch authors as regards the conclusion that the DI-program not only covers the risk of income loss due to disability but also serves as a social insurance for unemployment and early retirement.

### Sample Design and Endogenous Measurement Error (chapters 4 and 6)

Our database consists of two samples. The first, labeled the "control" or "healthy" sample, has been taken from the population at risk - viz. all private sector employees. The second, labeled the SB-sample, is composed of employees on an extended sick leave.

Under the Dutch system, DI-entry is preceded by a 12 months spell of sickness covered by Sickness Benefits (SB). Among the SB-sample respondents who were examined and interviewed in the sixth month of their sick leave, 60 percent appeared to have entered the DI-program after lapse of the 12 months waiting period. The remaining 40 percent had resumed their work.

By merging these two samples we were able to either compare 2534 complete (including employers' data) observations on long-term (5 months) sick, or 1529 observations on DI-entrants, with 1417 complete observations on members of the population at risk. Multivariate analyses were made applying the probit model to either the probability of long-term sickness (PSICK) or the probability of DI-enrolment - the unconditional DI-probability Pr{DI}. Since these probit datasets are endogenously stratified the probit likelihood has been modified accordingly.

Within the SB-sample the 1529 DI-entrants have been compared with the 1005 long-term absentees who resumed their work before lapse of the 12 months DI-waiting period. This sample was used for the description of the DI-probability given 5 months sickness, Pr{DI|5M.SICK}. Hence the distinction between conditional and unconditional DI-probability models.

Straight comparison of the two samples suggested that the SB-recipients are disadvantaged in many respects. After correction for age-differences, the long-term sick, and the DI-entrants in particular, appear to have lower education and more unemployment experiences; their prior health as indicated by prevalence and duration of complaints has been worse; and they perceive their career prospects and labor market opportunities as less favorable. Moreover, their employers have less developed policies regarding job adaptation and social guidance for the functionally impaired.

Acknowledging the possibility that, in the context of a binary choice model, the explanatory variables that represent attitudes and perceptions may be biased towards the alternative which a respondent prefers to choose or actually has chosen, we have tested for endogeneity in the measurement of such subjective scales. Using a preliminary probit model for PSICK, we found that among 9 variables under suspicion four were significantly affected by endogenous error of measurement: physical disabilities, career prospects, and employment opportunities (measured at the employee level) and the willingness to adapt job requirements or conditions (measured at the employer level). On the other hand, the observations on mental disabilities, work ethic, and job satisfaction (at the employee level) and job performance and career prospects (at the level of the employer) turned out to be unbiased.

The results have shown that the presence of these errors, if ignored, lead to severely biased results in multivariate analysis. If the 4 erroneously observed variables are substituted by instrumental estimates of their true values, the effects of other, correctly observed, variables increase in size and significance. Due to a shortage of powerful exclusion variables, necessary to warrant identification, collinearity produces unappealing results for all error-ridden variables except physical disabilities.

The analysis led to the conclusion that while the coefficient on physical disabilities was sufficiently identified by an instrumental variable, alternative, exogenous, indicators for employment opportunities and job adaptation were to be derived from separate submodels describing individual labor market histories and firm specific DI-incidence rates.

**Labor Market Opportunities (chapter 7)**
With the purpose of developing reliable indicators for individual labor market opportunities, we estimated models describing the labor market histories of a random sample of private sector employees - our control-sample. Assuming that people are either employed or unemployed, we distinguished two "transition" probabilities; the probability of becoming unemployed and the probability of re-employment upon unemployment.
The specifications of the estimated reduced form models are based on concepts taken from the neoclassical job search theory and the dual labor market theory. The statistical modelling is derived from job search theory. Specifically, we estimated a continuous time, two-state, multi-episode model for the duration of spells of unemployment and employment.
We found that the probability to become unemployed is higher for those who are young; who have no (extended) secondary vocational or general education; who are involved in strenuous work; who had been unemployed previously; who are immobile in the sense that they have not changed jobs voluntarily. Moreover, the unemployment risk appears to be higher when and where the regional unemployment is high; and when the minimum wage is relatively high.
Re-employment probabilities turned out to be comparatively high for the young; those without (extended) secondary vocational or general education; those involved in strenuous work; those without health problems. Since ill health is not found to increase the probability to become unemployed, we conclude that the overrepresentation of people with health problems among the unemployed is largely due to the fact that ill health tends to decrease re-employment probabilities and thereby prolong the duration of unemployment.
*Ceteris paribus*, the probability of re-employment appears to increase during a spell of unemployment. Theoretically, this can be explained by an over time declining reservation wage which dominates the over time decline in job offers.
These results are obtained from a database covering the 1970-80 decade. Therefore, they are conditional on then prevailing circumstances that clearly have changed since. As documented in chapter 2, unemployment started soaring after 1980. While in our database unemployment spells of more than 12 months are a rare phenomenon, they are quite common since. Our results, therefore, do not necessarily apply to the type of hard-core unemployment that still exists today.
The estimated weights of the determinants of unemployment and re-employment probabilities were used to calculate instrumental variables that represent labor

market opportunities. Using these indicators we found that the work histories of those workers that have been observed to enter the DI-program are less favorable as compared to the labor market experiences of similar "healthy" workers. Before they became disabled the vocational attributes of the DI-entrants were such that their probability of becoming unemployed was relatively high and their re-employment probability relatively low.

**Firm Specific Disability Insurance Risks (chapter 8)**
We found that the firm specific DI-incidence rate is partly determined by variables whose impact can be readily interpreted within a cost-benefit framework. This provides some empirical support for the hypothesis that the DI-incidence rate is dependant on firm specific cost-benefit considerations. Although our database lacks the information that is necessary to draw very specific conclusions, we may conclude that the firm-specific probability of the occurrence of functional limitations, as determined by the firm's type of work and type of manpower, accounts for only part of the inter-firm variation in DI-incidence rate. Another part is accounted for by variables related to the balance of costs and benefits of retaining, c.q. replacing, functionally impaired or otherwise marginally efficient employees. Policy measures that affect this balance are likely to have an impact on the DI-incidence rate.
The results show that, to a certain extent, the incidence of DI-awards within a firm can be steered by the firm itself. Although the role of firm-specific disability policies has remained somewhat vague a branch-wise comparison of the combined effect of policies on Job Adaptation, Social Guidance and Medical Guidance has shown that such policies can be effective in monitoring the DI-incidence.
Using the tobit coefficients explaining the inter-firm variance in DI-incidence we calculated instrumental values for the firm specific DI-risk for all respondents in our samples. Comparison of the control sample, the subsample of SB-recipients who recover before lapse of the DI-waiting period, and the subsample of DI-entrants, revealed a positive correlation between the constructed FIRMRISK variable and the work/health status of the respondents. On average, the firm specific DI-risk is small among control-sample respondents, intermediate among work resuming SB-recipients, and high among those SB-sample respondents that enter the DI-program.

**Expected Earnings and DI-Benefit Streams (chapter 9)**
As micro-economic theory posits that the predisposition to apply for DI-benefits depends on expectations regarding future income, a separate chapter has been devoted to the measurement of the expected income streams associated with the two options at stake: DI-program enrolment or continued labor force participation.
The main ingredients for the calculation of expected income streams are: the expected wage profile, other household income, the DI-benefit replacement rate, the

discount rate, and the expected duration of the remaining work life in the labor option.

Wage profiles have been obtained from an estimation model taking account of the potential simultaneity of wages and health. The amount of other household income was assumed to be exogenous. The expected residual duration of the remaining work life was derived from a reduced form DI-probit model.

The age profiles appeared to have their familiar shape suggesting decreasing returns to experience. The average worker reaches his or her top at age 55. Low-schooled workers reach their - lower - top sooner, at the age of 45, while the wages of the best trained keep increasing until 65. The returns to schooling appeared to be significantly lower in that part of the labor force from which the long-term sick and, hence, the DI-entrants are recruited. Among the SB-recipients we also found a negative generation effect, suggesting that the difficult conditions prevailing when the oldest generation entered the labor market have only affected the productivity of individuals with a higher than average disability risk.

Moreover, the pre-sickness characteristics of the SB-recipients predict a shorter remaining work life than the average insured, were the SB-recipients to opt for continued labor force participation. The type of workers from which the long-term sick appear to stem have vocational characteristics that both enhance their disability risks and damage their earnings prospects. As a consequence these employees are expected to drop from their lower wage trajectories at a younger age. We may, therefore, conclude that the pre-sickness opportunity costs of DI-enrolment for the long-term sick are lower than those for average healthy workers.

**Determinants of the Disability Process (chapter 10)**

In chapter 10 we reported on the core results of our study of the determinants of DI-enrolment. Two approaches were employed: First, using the structural probit model derived in chapter 3, we described the unconditional DI-probability (Pr{DI}) without taking explicit account of the 12 months waiting period that lies between an initial sick report and DI-enrolment.

As a second approach we cut the waiting period in two parts. Hence, we were able to distinguish between the transition from work to 5 months sickness and the final stage in the DI-process, the move from 5 months sickness to DI-enrolment. This enabled us to investigate the mechanism determining the outcome of a prolonged spell of sickness.

In the specifications for these probability models we used the instrumental variables that flow from the submodels discussed in the chapters 6 through 9. These submodels revealed the multiple causal pathways along which background variables, such as age, education, or firm size, exert their indirect influences on the DI-probability. Only by the use of instrumentals we were able to structure the intricate causalities that govern the DI-process and, more specifically, to get around the potential or proven endogeneity of direct observations. We have, therefore, dared to label the resulting probability models as structural.

*The First Approach: The Unconditional DI-probability, Pr{DI}*
As expected, the transition from work to DI-enrolment - the unconditional DI-probability appeared to be determined both by medical and a diversity of non-medical factors. We used disability indicators that reflect the medical-sociological definition of disablement and, therefore, incorporate the influence of both the nature and severity of impairment and the strenuousness of job requirements.

Having controlled for these prime determinants, we found remarkably powerful impacts of employment opportunities as well as income and leisure considerations on the individual DI-risk. Especially poor (predicted) re-employment probabilities appeared to strongly increase the DI-probability. This finding was supported by significant effects for firm-specific variables (FIRMRISK and JOBPERF) which contain firm-level and individual dimensions of internal employment security.

The size and significance of the variables reflecting income and leisure considerations (LnLOSSLT, ETG, COMTIME) which are core elements in the micro-economic approach, seem to confirm the validity of that approach to disability behavior. Their combined effects, supported by the prominent impact of career perspectives (PROS-PECTS), stress the discretionary aspects of disability behavior. Our results are qualitatively similar to findings in comparable US-studies, although ours are quantitatively more significant. The best fitting value of the discount rate by which the income and leisure streams are depreciated over time appeared to be quite high (.30). On average, therefore, employees tend to employ short time horizons for the evaluation of future income and leisure.

The absence of a significant direct age-effect seems to underscore the validity of our approach to structure the underlying causalities. Its indirect (reduced form) effect, however, has been shown to be sizeable. For instance, summing the indirect effects that run via the instrumental, structural, variables, married men aged 60 run an 11 times larger DI-risk than their 25 years old peers.

We also found a number of unexpected results. Work ethic, for instance, has appeared to be positively related to the probability of DI-entry whereas the effect of job satisfaction is negative but insignificant. Given the insignificance of age and the strong correlation of age with work morale, ethic seems to stand for generation and length of work life.

*The Second Approach: Combining the Unconditional Probability of Long-Term Sickness (PSICK) with the DI-Probability Given Long-Term (5 Months) Sickness (Pr{DI | 5M.SICK})*
As a potentially more accurate and informative approach we also investigated the

DI-process by dividing the 12 months waiting period in two parts: The transition from work to prolonged - 5 months - sickness, and from 5 months sickness to DI-enrolment.

*Step 1: PSICK*

The probability of being on sick leave for more than 5 months has been analyzed using a probit model which has the same specification as the unconditional DI-model. The results appeared to be remarkably similar, both in terms of size and significance. This implies that the occurrence of prolonged spells of sickness is governed by the same set of medical and socio-economic factors that also determine DI-entry. It might also suggest that the second stage in the DI-process is random and has no meaningful structure.

However, analysis of the transition from 5 months sickness to DI-enrolment, using the sick (SB) sample data only, added significantly to our knowledge of the DI-mechanism. Evidently, the SB-sample is select in ways described by the PSICK probit model. Hence, it consists of workers that, apart from their health status, differ from the average insured by, say, lack of labor market success.

*Step 2: Self-Perceptions of Disability*

Given this selection, then, the outcome of the DI-waiting period has appeared to depend on the views and preferences of the three agents involved - the impaired employee, his or her employer, and the gatekeepers of the DI-program. First, we found that self-perceptions of extent of disablement are formed, again, by a combination of medical and non-medical factors. Among the health indicators the views of the treating physicians proved to be very influential. This finding emphasizes their decisive role in legitimating disability behavior.

Next to the impacts of the nature and severity of disablement we found a strong U-shaped age-effect, indicating that self-ratings become increasingly more pessimistic beyond 40. This may reflect feelings of obsolescence.

Moreover, people have shown to feel more disabled the less satisfaction they derive from their job and the less they adhere to a traditional work morale. Unfavorable employment opportunities and the presence of other household income also tend to bias the self-perceived extent of disablement upward. However, the influence of these non-medical factors is much weaker than found for the unconditional probabilities. This is probably due to the fact that the SB-sample is more homogeneous with respect to such motivational elements.

Finally, the reduced form prediction of $Pr\{DI \mid 5M.SICK\}$ appeared to be strongly significant, underlining the endogeneity of self-reported health with respect to retirement. Those with a strong predisposition for DI-enrolment show to be more inclined to declare themselves in poor health.

*Step 3: Expert Ratings of Disability*
In a separate regression the expert - i.e., the program gatekeepers' - ratings of the respondents' extent of disablement were analyzed too. Although these judgments were assumed to be solely based on medical data and age, we applied the more comprehensive specification that was used for the description of self-perceptions. Thus, we purported to test the validity of the expert ratings. The outcomes confirm our expectations and, hence, the validity of the expert ratings. The ratings depend mainly on medical data, including the reports from the curative sector, and on age. In comparison with the self-perceptions the age-effect is stronger. Apparently, similar health data lead to more pessimistic ratings of future work capacity the older the patient.
Moreover, the validity of the expert ratings is reinforced by the insignificance of the reduced form prediction of Pr{DI | SICK}.
*Step 4: The Conditional DI-Probit Model*
The estimation of a structural conditional DI-probit model revealed the relative impacts of self-perceptions and gate-keepers' ratings of disability on the outcome of the DI-entry process. We found equally important contributions of both these parties. This finding stresses the discretion for the insured workers to obtain DI-eligibility and, indirectly, the legitimizing role played by their medical attendants. In their DI-determinations the gatekeepers seem to add age to their medical data represented by their ratings of the extent of disablement. The age-spline for those under 45 is strong and significant; the complementary spline has a small and insignificant effect. Given the policy of explicit labor market consideration in DI-assessments on the one hand, and the insignificance of the variables measuring employment opportunities on the other, the gatekeepers seem to use age as a proxy for labor market opportunities.
The predicted DI-incidence rate in the employing firm is also found to be a moderately important determinant of the conditional DI-probability. To some extent, this effect represents the influence of the employer which adds to the much stronger impacts exerted by employers in the first stage of the DI-process.

**1990-2050 DIS-Population Forecasts (chapter 11)**
We concluded our study by extrapolating the number of disability beneficiaries including civil servants and self-employed - the so-called DIS-population - until 2050. As input data we used the CBS population forecasts.
Our DIS-forecasts are given in several variants. We began by assuming that both labor market and disability behavior would remain unaltered. This scenario was implemented by fixing age and sex-specific labor force participation rates and disability incidence rates at their current level. Due to population greying and a structural inflow surplus, this *central variant* predicts 82.5 percent increase of the

DIS-population from its current size of 753.000 to 1.374.000 in 2020. This corresponds to a 65 percent increase in the disability dependency rate from 0.109 to 0.180 which is partly due to greying of the population at risk and partly to the persistence of an inflow surplus until 2010.

Since an 18 percent dependency rate may well turn out to be unbearable, both for financial and social reasons, we present 6 alternative scenarios by which the demographic wave, induced by the market mechanism or by conscious policy measures, may be prevented from flooding across the DIS-population. First, if due to aging of the labor force the demand for older workers increases, the average disability incidence may remain at its current level. Such a scenario is implemented by the so-called quantile mechanism. Apart from its labor market interpretation keeping the average disability rate constant is a way to control for the effect of aging on the DIS-volume. The resulting forecasts following the *quantile variant* anticipate the DIS-population to grow by 46 percent between 1990 and 2020. From these two forecasts, then, we may conclude that the 82.5 percent growth predicted by the central variant can be broken down into three components:

36.5 percentage points (44 percent) are due to greying of the population at risk; 28.5 percentage points (35 percent) are due to the persistence of an inflow surplus; and the last 17.5 percentage points (21 percent) are on account of labor force growth.

Next, we simulated the effects of strict compliance with the 1987 disability amendments that were aimed at the elimination of labor market considerations from the assessment of disability. We implemented these modifications by introducing a stricter, and simpler, eligibility standard that would deny a benefit to those who are fully capable to perform commensurate work. Using the work capacity estimates discussed in chapter 5, we first lowered both the award and the recovery rates in order to simulate an award policy based on such a stricter definition of disability. By this policy the number of disability beneficiaries was estimated to be 24 percent less than in the central variant, after the demographic wave has flooded across the disability schemes. With a dependency rate reaching 14 percent the results are comparable to those of the quantile-variant.

In a second policy variant we simulated the volume-effects of complete separation of the unemployment component from the DIS-population. This would entail a stricter benefit termination policy on top of enhanced rigor at program entry. In this variant the dependency rate appeared to stay at its current level, suggesting that full compliance with the disability amendments as of 1990, would turn the demographic wave. Upon convergence the DIS-population would be 40 percent smaller than if award and termination policies would not change. This suggest an equally large - 40 percent - unemployment component.

Given the Dutch disability experience full compliance with a strict definition of disability may be too grand a task. As a final exercise, therefore, we presented three scenarios whose outcomes are similar to the second, more rigorous, policy option. These scenarios were based on the unconditional DI-probability model of chapter 10. The first staged a reduction of the prevalence, and extent, of physical disablement by one standard error. The second was based on the assumption that employment opportunities for (mildly) impaired workers might improve considerably. As an alternative to narrowing the gates of the disability insurance programs, such changes may be induced by promoting rehabilitation.

The last scenario staged a modest increase of the income loss due to disability benefit dependency. At the expense of benefit adequacy this option might prove to be the easiest to implement.

## 12.3    Some Policy Implications

In the Netherlands, disability is defined as the incapacity to perform work, commensurate with former vocational status, at the usual market wage. The insured income loss is defined as the difference between the income a person would have earned if not functionally impaired, and the amount of income he or she is able to earn in a job that is commensurate with one's residual capacities and former vocational status. Whether one applies the medical-sociological model of disability or the economic concept of opportunity costs, on theoretical grounds this seems to be a perfectly valid definition of work disability.

Valid as it may be, in actual practice the verification of DI-eligibility by this disability concept seems to pose major difficulties. Our findings suggest that, for lack of a manageable disability standard, DI-enrolment is largely at the discretion of individual employees and their employers. Especially for workers over 45, the DI-program has traits that closely resemble a voluntary early retirement scheme.

By this observation we do not want to imply that those who enter the DI-program are malingerers. On the contrary, nearly all will be functionally impaired to some extent, or at least have been at some stage in the disability process. The issue here, however, is that the allocation of DI-benefits is governed by individual self-selection on socio-economic grounds rather than by uniform adjudications based on unambiguous medical standards.

The process of self-selection as it is pictured by our results, is strongly influenced by pre-impairment vocational disadvantages. Those who enter the DI-rolls appear to have been less successful labor market participants relative to the average DI-insured. Before they reported sick the DI-entrants had higher unemployment and lower re-employment probabilities; were employed in occupational environments which entailed a high disability risk; and had smaller earnings' growth potential.

For all of these reasons it is quite understandable that these socially disadvantaged workers have a relatively strong proclivity to seek income security through DI-dependency. What may be less understandable, however, is that most of the resulting disability claims are honored by full permanent awards. After all, what the multivariate analyses in chapter 10 have clearly shown is that each of these vocational, non-medical, attributes exert a strong and independent influence on the probability of being recognized as disabled. If we combine these results with our estimates of the unemployment component among disability beneficiaries in chapters 5 and 11, we can only conclude that for lack of reliable eligibility standards the Dutch DI-system is, and has been for years, faced with a considerable moral hazard problem.

While it is hard to provide a definition of work disability without arbitrary elements, we like to think that the extent of arbitrariness presently prevailing in the Dutch DI-program and its administration needs to be reduced in order to preserve public support for social disability insurance. Arbitrary elements in social disability insurance will erode the legitimacy of substantial and still increasing amounts of disability transfers. Fading societal support will increase stigma costs for DI-beneficiaries without residual earning capacities and is likely to result in calls for a downward adjustment of the DI-benefit income levels that would leave the totally disabled with inappropriate coverage.

With respect to the definition and measurement of work disability, there seems to be a trade-off between validity and reliability. In our opinion the present performance of the Dutch DI-system calls for measures to improve its reliability at the expense of both theoretical validity and individual discretion on the part of the covered employees and their employers. If we would wish older workers to be treated generously, we may as well make this explicit, for instance by allowing all workers older than say 55 to the DI-program. If this would be considered too expensive, one could consider to narrow down the definition of work disability by reducing the number of disability categories.

For its apparent uncontrollability and arbitrariness the current performance of the DI-program is not at all reassuring. Moreover, the forecasts presented in the last chapter show that a straightforward extrapolation using today's age specific DI-incidence rates would result in continued growth of the DI-population in the near future.

As with many forecasts, ours is unlikely to come true. For one thing, the 65 percent rise in the DI-dependency rate is likely to elicit shortages in labor supply that, in turn, will induce wages to rise and employment prospects to improve, potentially causing a substantial decrease of the annual DI-incidence. Other countervailing powers activated by an increasing dependency rate will be brought about by adjustments in public policies towards the disabled until a bearable DI-dependency rate has been reached.

The effort needed to reduce DI-recipiency depends, of course, on what society considers to be equitable and adequate. Society may wish to enable older workers to withdraw from the labor force through the DI-program, or it may prefer a system strictly targeted at the coverage of "true" disability risks, irrespective of age and employment opportunities. Either option involves its costs and benefits and its own level of DI-dependency.

Whatever the level we collectively would agree on, in any case, transparent standards and criteria are needed to warrant lasting public support for social security disability insurance.

357

# REFERENCES

Aaron, Henri J., *Economic Effects of Social Security*, Washington DC: The Brookings Institution, 1982.

Aarts, Leo J.M., "Bedrijven en arbeidsongeschiktheid", Research Report, Zoetermeer: Sociale Verzekeringsraad, 1984.

Aarts, Leo J.M., "Work Capacity of the Disabled", in Emanuel et al. (1987).

Aarts, Leo J.M. and Hop, J. Peter, "A Dynamic Analysis of the Dutch Labor Market", Unpublished Mimeo, Leiden University: Center for Research in Public Economics, 1986.

Aarts, Leo J.M., Bruinsma, Hilbrand, and De Jong, Philip R., "Arbeidscapaciteit van WAO-toetreders", Research Report, Zoetermeer: Sociale Verzekeringsraad, 1982.

Aarts, Leo J.M., Bruinsma, Hilbrand, and De Jong, Philip R., "Beschrijving van WAO-toetreders", *Sociaal Maandblad Arbeid*, 1982, 37, 560-586.

Aarts, Leo J.M., Bruinsma, Hilbrand, and De Jong, Philip R., "Validiteit en betrouwbaarheid van de gehanteerde variabelen in het WAO-toetredingsonderzoek", Research Report, Zoetermeer: Sociale Verzekeringsraad, 1983.

Aarts, Leo J.M., Paul, Louk, and De Neubourg, Chris, "Arbeidsmarktsegmentatie in Nederland; een empirische benadering", *Economisch en Sociaal Tijdschrift*, 1983, 37, 209-227.

Aarts, Leo J.M. and De Jong, Philip R., "Early Retirement of Older Male Workers under the Dutch Social Security Disability Insurance Program", in Atkinson and Rein (1992).

Aarts, Leo J.M., Burkhauser, Richard V., and De Jong, Philip R., "A Cautionary Tale of European Disability Policies: Lessons for the United States", Policy Paper No. 6, The Maxwell School, Metropolitan Studies Program, Syracuse University, U.S., February 1992.

Addison, J.T. and Siebert, W.S., *The Market for Labor; An Analytical Treatment*, Santa Monica Cal: Goodyear Publishing Company, 1979.

Algemeen Arbeidsongeschiktheidsfonds, *Jaarverslag* (Annual Report), Zoetermeer: AAf, Various years.

Amemiya, Takeshi, "The Estimation of a Simultaneous Equation Generalized Probit Model", *Econometrica*, 1978, 46, 1193-1205.

Andersen, R., "A Behavioral Model of Families' Use of Health Services", Research Report, Chicago: Center for Health Administration Studies, 1968.

Anderson, Kathryn H. and Burkhauser, Richard V., "The Retirement-Health Nexus; A New Measure of an Old Puzzle", *Journal of Human Resources*, 1985, 20, 315-330.

Arrow, K.J. and Hahn, F.H., *General Competitive Analysis*, San Francisco: Holden-Day, 1971.

Ashenfelter, Orly and Ham, J., "Education, Unemployment, and Earnings", *Journal of Political Economy*, 1979, 87, S99-S116.

Ashenfelter, Orly and Layard, Richard, eds., *Handbook of Labor Economics*, Vol. II, New York: North-Holland, 1986.

Atkinson, A.B., Gomulka, J., Micklewright, J., and Rau, N., "Unemployment Benefit, Duration and Incentives in Britain", *Journal of Public Economics*, 1984, 23, 3-26.

Atkinson, A.B. and Rein, M., *Age, Work and Society*, London: Macmillan, 1992.

Bax, Eric H., "De stijging van de arbeidsongeschiktheid in de jaren zeventig", *Mens en Maatschappij*, 1982, 2, 117-144.

Bax, Eric H., De Boer, Thomas W., and Sterrenburg, Kees, "Arbeidsmarkt en arbeidsongeschiktheid", *Economisch Statistische Berichten*, 1979, 64, 540-586.

Bazzoli, Gloria, "The Early Retirement Decision; New Empirical Evidence on the Influence of Health", *Journal of Human Resources*, 1985, 20, 214-234.

Berkowitz, Monroe, Fenn, Paul, and Lambrinos, James, "The Optimal Stock of Health with Endogenous Wages", *Journal of Health Economics*, 1983, 2, 139-147.

Berkowitz, Monroe and Hill, M. Anne, eds., *Disability and the Labor Market*, Ithaca NY: ILR Press, 1986.

Berkowitz, Monroe and Johnson, William G., "Health and Labor Force Participation", *Journal of Human Resources*, 1974, 9, 117-128.

Bijlsma, T. and Koopmans, F., "Ongelijkheid in de WAO: verschillen tussen mannen en vrouwen per bedrijfssector", *Sociaal Maandblad Arbeid*, 1985, 40, 430-455.

Bijlsma, T. and Koopmans, F., "Van ZW naar WAO, verschillen tussen mannen en vrouwen", *Sociaal Maandblad Arbeid*, 1986, 41, 705-719.

Björklund, A., "Unemployment and Mental Health; Some Evidence from Panel Data", *Journal of Human Resources*, 1985, 20, 469-483.

Blinder, A.S., Gordon, R.H., and Wise, D.E., "Reconsidering the Work Disincentive Effects of Social Security", *National Tax Journal*, 1980, 33, 431-442.

Blomsma, Martin and De Vroom, Bert, *Vervroegd uittreden uit betaalde arbeid*, The Hague: HRWB, 1988.

Blundell, R., Ham, J., and Meghir, C., "Unemployment, Discouraged Workers, and Female Labor", Discussion paper, University College, London 1987.

Bolhuis, E.A., Ottens, S.J., and Steenbeek-Vervoort, M.A., "De VUT met pensioen", *Economisch Statistische Berichten*, 1987, 72, 726-727.

Boot, Peter, "Verzpopl, beschrijving van een ALGOL-programma ter voorspelling van het aantal arbeidsongeschikten", Leiden, 1984, unpublished mimeo

Boskin, Michael J. and Hurd, Michael D., "The Effects of Social Security on Early Retirement", *Journal of Public Economics*, 1978, 10, 361-377.

Bruinsma, H., Jacobi, A.M., and Van der Stelt, H.G., "Beëindiging van de WAO-uitkering; het verschil tussen mannen en vrouwen nader bekeken", *Sociaal Maandblad Arbeid*, 1989, 44, 91-105.

Burdett, K., "Search, Leisure and Individual Labor Supply", in Lippman, S.A. and McCall, J.J., eds., *Studies in the Economics of Search*, New York: North-Holland, 1978.

Burdett, K., "A Useful Restriction on the Offer Distribution in Job Search Models", in Eliasson, G., Holmlund, B., and Stafford, F.P., eds., *Studies in Labor Market Behavior*, Stockholm: IUI Conference Report, 1981.

Burdett, K., Kiefer, N.M., and Sharma, S., "Lay-offs and Duration Dependence in a Model of Turnover", *Journal of Econometrics*, 28, Annals 1985-1, 51-70.

Burkhauser, Richard V. and Quinn, Joseph F., Is Mandatory Retirement Overrated? Evidence from the 1970s", *Journal of Human Resources*, 1983, 18, 337-358.

Burtless, G. and Moffitt, R., "The Effect of Social Security Benefits on the Labor Supply of the Aged", in Aron, H. and Burtless, G., eds., *Retirement and Economic Behavior*, Washington DC: Brookings Institution, 1984.

Cain, G.G., "The Challenge of Segmental Labor Market Theories to Orthodox Theory; A Survey", *Journal of Economic Literature*, 1976, 14, 1215-1257.

Carrin, Guy, *Economic Aspects of Social Security*, Doctoral Thesis, Catholic University of Leuven, 1979.

Centraal Bureau voor de Statistiek, *Maandstatistiek van de bevolking*, Voorburg: CBS, 1982, 32, no. 11.

Centraal Bureau voor de Statistiek B, "Statistisch Zakboek", Voorburg: CBS, Various years.

Centraal Bureau voor de Statistiek C, *Bevolkingsprognose voor Nederland 1988-2050*, The Hague: SDU-uitgeverij/CBS-publicaties, 1989.

Centraal Planbureau, *Centraal Economisch Plan*, The Hague: CPB, Various years.

Centraal Planbureau, *Economisch Beeld 1991*, The Hague: CPB (1990).

Centraal Planbureau, "Raming Arbeidsaanbod 1985-2000", Mimeo 35, The Hague: CPB, 1989.

Chelius, James R. and Smith, Robert S., "Experience Rating and Injury Prevention", in Worrall, John D., ed., *Safety and the Work Force; Incentives and Disincentives in Workers' Compensation*, Ithaca NY: ILR Press, 1983.

Chirikos, Thomas N. and Nestel, Gilbert, "Impairment and Labor Market Outcomes; A Cross-Sectional and Longitudinal Analysis", in Parnes, H.S., ed., *Work and Retirement; A Longitudinal Study of Men*, Cambridge MA: MIT Press, 1981.

Chirikos, Thomas N. and Nestel, Gilbert, "Economic Determinants and Consequences of Self-Reported Work Disability", *Journal of Health Economics*, 1984, 3, 117-136.

Chirikos, Thomas N. and Nestel, Gilbert, "Further Evidence on the Economic Effects of Poor Health", *Review of Economics and Statistics*, 1985, 67, 61-69.

Copeland, Loise S., "International Trends in Disability Program Growth", *Social Security Bulletin*, October 1981, 44, 25-37.

Cragg, J.G. and Uhler, R.S., "The Demand for Automobiles", *Canadian Journal of Economics*, 1970, 3, 386-406.

Culyer, Anthony, "Economics, Social Policy, and Disability", in Lees, D.S. and Shaw, B., eds., *Impairment, Disability, and Handicap*, London: Heinemann, 1974.

Danziger, Sheldon, Haveman, Robert H., and Plotnick, R., "How Income Transfer Programs Affect Work, Savings and the Income Distribution; A Critical Review", *Journal of Economic Literature*, 1981, 19, 975-1028.

De Jong, Philip R., "Determinanten van invalideringsfrequenties, een analyse op macro-niveau", Memo 83.12, Leiden University: Center for Research in Public Economics, 1983.

De Jong, Philip R., "Arbeidsongeschiktheidsperceptie en WAO-toetreding", *Mens en Maatschappij*, 1983, 58, 325-359.

De Jong, Philip R., "Voorwaardelijke vooruitberekeningen van het aantal arbeidsongeschikten tot 2030", Research Report, Zoetermeer: Sociale Verzekeringsraad, 1984.

De Jong, Philip R., "Work Capacity and the Probability of Entry into the Dutch Disability Insurance Program", in Emanuel et al. (1987).

De Jong, Philip R., "On the Problem of Endogenous Measurement Error", in Saris, Willem E. and Gallhofer, Irmtraud N., eds., *Sociometric Research, Vol. 2, Data Analysis*, London: MacMillan Press, 1988, 160-179.

De Jong, Philip R., Bruinsma, Hilbrand, Aarts, Leo J.M., and Hop, J. Peter, "Determinanten van WAO-toetreding; een eerste totaalbeeld", Research Report, Zoetermeer: Sociale Verzekeringsraad, 1981.

De Jong, Philip R., Haveman, Robert H., and Wolfe, Barbara L., "Labor and Transfer Incomes and Older Women's Work; Estimates from the United States", NBER Working Paper, no. 2728, 1988.

De Jong, Philip R., Herweijer, Michiel, and De Wildt, Jaap H., *Form and Reform of the Dutch Social Security System*, Deventer: Kluwer Law and Taxation Publishers, 1990.

Deaton, Angus and Muellbauer, John, *Economics and Consumer Behavior*, Cambridge: Cambridge University Press, 1983.

Diamond, P.A., "A Framework for Social Security Analysis", *Journal of Public Economics*, 1977, 8, 278-298.

Diamond, P. and Hausman, J., "The Retirement and Unemployment Behavior of Older Men", in Aaron, H. and Burtless, G., eds., *Retirement and Economic Behavior*, Washington DC: The Brookings Institution, 1984.

Dijkstra, A., "Reduction of the Employee Population of Business Firms and Sickness Absenteeism; A Longitudinal Secondary Analysis", *Sociologica Neerlandica*, 1975, 11, 116-128.

Dijkstra, A., *Determinanten van ziekteverzuim in productieorganisaties voor gehandicapten*, Leiden: NIPG-TNO, 1977.

Douben, N.H. and Herweijer, M., "Arbeidsmarkt, werkloosheid en arbeidsongeschiktheid", *Maandschrift Economie*, 1979, 43, 309-320.

Draaisma, D., "Ziekteverzuim, WAO-intrede en verzekeringsvorm in de ziektewet", COSZ Research Report, The Hague: Ministry of Social Affairs and Employment, 1983.

Draaisma, D. and Smulders, P.G.W., "Ziekteverzuim en het bedrijf", Research Report, Leiden: NIPG-TNO, 1978.

Duchnok, Sandra, "A Measure of Functional Capacity", ORS Working Paper no. 4, Washington DC: Social Security Administration, 1979.

Elbers, Chris and Ridder, Geert, "True and Spurious Duration Dependence: The Identifiability of the Proportional Hazard Model", *Review of Economic Studies*, 1982, 49, 403-409.

Emanuel, Han, "Achtergronden van het arbeidsongeschiktheidsverschijnsel in Nederland", in: Klant, J.J., et al., eds., *Samenleving en Onderzoek*, Leiden: Stenfert Kroese, 1979.

Emanuel, Han, De Gier, Eric H., and Kalker Konijn, Peter A.B., eds., *Disability Benefits; Factors Determining Application and Awards*, Greenwich Conn: JAI Press, 1987.

Emanuel, Han and Vossers, W.J., "De stelselherziening van de sociale zekerheid", *Economisch Statistische Berichten*, 1983, 68, 720-724.

Emanuel, Han, Halberstadt, Victor, and Petersen, Carel, "Disability Policy in the Netherlands", in Haveman, Halberstadt, and Burkhauser, (1984).

Eurostat, *Social Protection Expenditures and Receipts 1980-1988*, Luxembourg, 1990.

Eurostat, *A Social Portrait of Europe*, Luxembourg, 1991.

Eurostat, *Rapid Reports*, Luxembourg, 1991, no. 4.

Feldstein, M. and Poterba, J., "Unemployment Insurance and Reservation Wages", *Journal of Public Economics*, 1984, 23, 141-167.

Fenn, P.T., "Sickness Duration, Residual Disability, and Income Replacement; An Empirical Analysis", *The Economic Journal*, 1981, 91, 158-173.

Fenn, P.T. and Vlachonikolis, I.G., "Male Labour Force Participation Following Illness or Injury", *Economica*, 1986, 53, 379-391.

Ferguson, Robert, "Some Aspects of the Work Environment and Subsequent Disability among Working Age Men", Staff Paper no. 43, Washington DC: Social Security Administration, 1983.

Fields, Gary S. and Mitchell, Olivia S., *Retirement, Pensions and Social Security*, Cambridge MA: MIT Press, 1984.

Flinn, Chris J. and Heckman, James J., "Models for the Analysis of Labor Force Dynamics", in Basmann, R. and Rhodes, G., eds., *Advances in Econometrics*, Greenwich Conn: JAI Press, 1982, 35-95.

Freeman, R.B., "Job-Satisfaction as an Economic Variable", *American Economic Review Proceedings*, 1978, 68, no. 2, 135-141.

Gemeenschappelijke Medische Dienst, "AAW/WAO, Kerncijfers 1987", Amsterdam: GMD, 1988.

Gemeenschappelijke Medische Dienst, *Jaarverslag* (Annual Report), Amsterdam: GMD, Various years.

Goldberger, A.S., *Econometric Theory*, New York: Wiley, 1964.

Gordon, Richard H. and Blinder A.S., "Market Wages, Reservation Wages, and Retirement Decisions", *Journal of Public Economics*, 1980, 14, 277-308.

Goudswaard, Kees P. and De Jong, Philip R., "The Distributional Impact of Current Income Transfer Policies in the Netherlands", *Journal of Social Policy*, 1985, 14, 367-383.

Groothoff, J.W., *Gezondheidstoestand van de beroepsbevolking; een studie naar de indicatoren arbeids- ongeschiktheid, sterfte, gezondheidszorg*, Doctoral Thesis, Groningen University, 1986.

Grossman, M., "On the Concept of Health Capital and the Demand for Health", *Journal of Political Economy*, 1972, 80, 223-255.

Grossman, M. and Benham, L., "Health, Hours, and Wages", in Perlman, M., ed., *The Economics of Health and Medical Care*, New York: Wiley, 1974.

Haber, L.D., "Identifying the Disabled: Concepts and Methods in the Measurement of Disability", *Social Security Bulletin*, December 1967, 30, 17-34.

Haber, L.D. and Smith, R.T., "Disability and Deviance; Normative Adaptations of Role Behavior", *American Sociological Review*, 1971, 36, 87-97.

Hagenaars, Aldi J.M., *The Perception of Poverty*, Amsterdam: North Holland, 1985.

Hall, R.E., "The Importance of Life Time Jobs in the US Economy", *American Economic Review*, 1982, 72, 716-724.

Halpern, Janice and Hausman, Jerry, "Choice under Uncertainty: A Model of Applications for the Social Security Disability Insurance Program.", Mimeo, M.I.T., 1984.

Hambor, John C., "Unemployment and Disability: An Econometric Analysis with Time Series Data", ORS Working Paper, no. 20, Washington DC: Social Security Administration, 1975.

Hartog, J. and Theeuwes, J.J.M., "The Emergence of the Working Wife in Holland", *Journal of Labor Economics*, 1985, 3, S235-S255.

Hausman, J.A., "The Econometrics of Nonlinear Budget Sets", *Econometrica*, 1985, 53, 1255-1282.

Hausman, J.A. and Wise, D.A., "The Evaluation of Results from Truncated Samples; The New Yersey Negative Income Tax Experiment", *Annals of Economic and Social Measurement*, 1976, 5, 421-445.

Haveman, Robert H., "Does the Welfare State Increase Welfare? Reflections on the Hidden Negatives and Observed Positives", *De Economist*, 1985, 133, 445-466.

Haveman, Robert H., Halberstadt, Victor, and Burkhauser, Richard V., eds., *Public Policy toward Disabled Workers*, Ithaca NY: Cornell University Press, 1984.

Haveman, Robert H. and Wolfe, Barbara L., "Disability Transfers and Early Retirement; A Causal Relationship?", *Journal of Public Economics*, 1984a, 23, 47-66.

Haveman, Robert H. and Wolfe, Barbara L., "The Decline in Male Labor Force Participation; Comment", *Journal of Political Economy*, 1984b, 92, 532-541.

Haveman, Robert H., Wolfe, Barbara L., and Halberstadt, Victor, "The European Welfare State in Transition", in Palmer, J.L., ed., *Perspectives on the Reagan Years*, Washington DC: Urban Institute Press, 1986.

Haveman, Robert H., Wolfe, Barbara L., and Warlick, Jennifer, "Labor Market Behavior of Older Men", *Journal of Public Economics*, 1988, 36, 153-175.

Haveman, Robert H., De Jong, Philip R., and Wolfe, Barbara L., "Disability Transfers and the Work Decision of Older Men", *Quarterly Journal of Economics*, 1991, 939-949.

Heckman, James J., "Shadow Prices, Market Wages and Labor Supply", *Econometrica*, 1974, 42, 679-694.

Heckman, James J., "Dummy Endogenous Variables in a Simultaneous Equations System" *Econometrica*, 1978, 46, 931-959.

Heckman, James J., "Sample Selection Bias as a Specification Error" *Econometrica*, 1979, 47, 153-161.

Hermans, P.C., "Vrouwen uit de WAO", *Sociaal Maandblad Arbeid*, 1987, 42, 247-259.

Hermans, P.C., Sas, C. and Schraven, B., "Schat de regering de arbeidsongeschiktheidsschatting juist in?", *Sociaal Maandblad Arbeid*, 1986, 41, 126-136.

Holt, C., "Job Search, Philips Wage Relation and Union Influence; Theory and Evidence", in Phelps, E.S. et al., eds., *Microeconomic Foundations of Employment and Inflation Theory*, New York: W.W. Norton, 1970.

Howards, Irving, Brehm, Henry P., and Nagi, Saad Z., *Disability from Social Problem to Federal Program*, New York: Praeger, 1980.

Johnson, William G. and Lambrinos, J., "Wage Discrimination against Handicapped Men and Women", *Journal of Human Resources*, 1985, 20, 264-277.

Jovanovich, B., "Job Matching and the Theory of Turnover", *Journal of Political Economy*, 1979, 87, 972-990.

Kasper, H., "The Asking Price of Labor and the Duration of Unemployment", *Review of Economics and Statistics*, 1967, 49, 165-172.

Kiefer, N.M. and Neumann, G.R., "An Empirical Job Search Model, with a Test of the Constant-Reservation-Wage Hypothesis", *Journal of Political Economy*, 1979, 87, 165-172.

Kiefer, N.M. and Neumann, G.R., "Individual Effects in a Nonlinear Model; Explicit Treatment of Heterogeneity in the Empirical Job Search Model", *Econometrica*, 1981, 49, 965-979.

Killingsworth, Mark R., *Labor Supply*, Cambridge: Cambridge University Press, 1983.

Killingsworth, Mark R. and Heckman, James J., *Female Labor Supply: A Survey*, in Ashenfelter and Layard (1986).

Kooreman, Peter and Ridder Geert, "The Effects of Age and Unemployment Percentage on the Duration of Unemployment; Evidence from Aggregate Data", *European Economic Review*, 1983, 20, 41-57.

Korpel, J.H., Van der Mark, R.C., and Peters, M.L.A., *Een internationale vergelijking van de minimumlonen, de inkomensverdeling en de minimumuitkeringen*, The Hague: Ministerie van Sociale Zaken en Werkgelegenheid, 1989.

Kovach, K.A., *Organization Size, Job Satisfaction, Absenteeism and Turnover*, Washington DC: University Press of America, 1978.

Lambrinos, J., "Health; A Source of Bias in Labor Supply Models", *Review of Economics and Statistics*, 1981, 63, 206-212.

Lancaster, T., "Econometric Methods for the Duration of Unemployment", *Econometrica*, 1979, 47, 1661-1676.

Lancaster, T., "Simultaneous Equation Models in Applied Search Theory", *Journal of Econometrics*, 28, Annals 1985-1, 113-126.

Lancaster, T. and Chesher, A.D., "An Econometric Analysis of Reservation Wages", *Econometrica*, 1983, 51, 1661-1676.

Lancaster, T. and Nickell, S.J., "The Analysis of Re-Employment Probabilities for the Unemployed", *Journal of the Royal Statistical Society*, 1980, 143, 141-165.

Lando, Mordechai E., Coate, Malmcolm B., and Kraus, Ruth, "Disability Benefits Applications and the Economy", *Social Security Bulletin*, 1979, 42, 3-10.

Lee, Lung-Fei, "Unionism and Wage Rates; A Simultaneous Equation Model with Qualitative and Limited Dependent Variables", *International Economic Review*, 1978, 19, 415-433.

Lee, Lung-Fei, "Identification and Estimation in Binary Choice Models with Limited (Censored) Dependent Variables", *Econometrica*, 1979, 47, 977-996.

Lee, Lung-Fei, "Health and Wage; A Simultaneous Equation Model with Multiple Discrete Indicators", *International Economic Review*, 1982, 33, 199-221.

Lee, Lung-Fei and Trost, R.P., "Estimation of Some Limited Dependent Variable Models with Applications to Housing Demand", *Journal of Econometrics*, 1978, 3, 357-382.

Leigh, Duane, *An Analysis of the Determinants of Occupational Upgrading*, New York: Academic Press, 1978.

Leonard, Jonathan S., "The Social Security Disability Program and Labor Force Participation", NBER Working Paper, no. 392, 1979.

Leonard, Jonathan S.,"Labor Supply Incentives and Disincentives for Disabled Persons", in Berkowitz and Hill (1986).

Levy, Jesse M. and McManus, Leo A., "Functional Limitations and Job Requirements: Effects on Labor Force Choices", in Social Security Administration, *Policy Analysis with Social Security Research Files*, Washington DC: GPO, 1978, 447-460.

Lindeboom, Maarten and Theeuwes, Jules J.M., "Job Duration in the Netherlands: The Simultaneous Occurrence of High and Low Turnover", Mimeo 90.03, Leiden University: Center for Research in Public Economics, 1990.

Lippman, S.A. and McCall, J.J., "The Economics of Job Search; A Survey", *Economic Inquiry*, 1976, 14, 155-189.

Luft, Harold S., "The Impact of Poor Health on Earnings", *Review of Economics and Statistics*, 1975, 57, 43-57.

Luft, Harold S., *Poverty and Health*, Cambridge MA: Ballinger, 1978.

Lynch, Lisa M., "State Dependency in Youth Unemployment: A Lost Generation", *Journal of Econometrics*, 28, Annals 1985-1, 71-84.

Maddala, G.S., *Limited Dependent and Qualitative Variables in Econometrics*, Cambridge MA: Cambridge University Press, 1983.

Marvel, Howard P., "An Economic Analysis of the Operation of Social Security Disability Insurance", *Journal of Human Resources*, 1982, 17, 393-412.

Mashaw, Jerry, L., *Bureaucratic Justice; Managing Social Security Disability Claims*, New Haven Conn: Yale University Press, 1983.

Mechanic, D. and Volkart, E.H., "Stress Illness Behavior and the Sick Role", *American Sociological Review*, 1961, 26, 25-62.

Merens-Riedstra, H.S., *Leven zonder werk*, Doctoral Thesis, Limburg University, 1981.

Ministerie van Sociale Zaken en Werkgelegenheid, "Bovenwettelijke Uitkeringen bij ZW, AAW/WAO, WW, WWV", Research Memorandum, The Hague: Min. SoZaWe, 1985.

Ministerie van Sociale Zaken en Werkelegenheid, *Rapportage Arbeidsmarkt*, The Hague: Min. SoZaWe, Various years.

Moffitt, R., "Unemployment Insurance and the Distribution of Unemployment Spells", *Journal of Econometrics*, 28, Annals 1985-1, 85-102.

Mortensen, D.T., "Job Search and Labor Market Analysis", in Ashenfelter and Layard (1986).

Muller, L. Scott, Levy, Jesse M., and Coate, Malmcolm B., "The Family Labor Supply Response to Disabling Conditions", ORS Working Paper, no. 10, Washington DC: Social Security Administration, 1979.

Muller, L. Scott, "The Impact of Local Labor Market Characteristics on the Disability Process", ORS Working Paper, no. 27, Washington DC: Social Security Administration, 1982.

Mushkin, Selma J., "Health as an Investment", *Journal of Political Economy*, 1962, 70, 129-157.

Nagi, Saad Z., "Some Conceptual Issues in Disability and Rehabilitation", in Sussman, M.B., ed., *Sociology and Rehabilitation*, Washington DC: American Sociological Association, 1965.

Nagi, Saad Z., "Congruency in Medical and Self-Assessment of Disability", *Industrial Medicine*, 1969a, 38, 27-36.

Nagi, Saad Z., *Disability and Rehabilitation; Legal, Clinical and Self-Concepts and Measurements*, Columbus Ohio: Ohio State University Press, 1969b.

Nagi, Saad Z., "Decision Criteria and the Question of Equity and Incentives", in Emanuel et al. (1987).

Nagi, Saad Z. and Hadley, L.W., "Disability Behavior; Income Change and Motivation to Work", *Industrial and Labor Relations Review*, 1972, 25, 223-233.

Narendranathan, W. and Nickell, S., "Modelling the Process of Job Search", *Journal of Econometrics*, 28, Annals 1985-1, 29-50.

Narendranathan, W., Nickell, S., and Metcalf, D., "An Investigation into the Dynamic Structure of Sickness and Unemployment in Britain, 1965-75", *Journal of the Royal Statistical Society A*, 1985, 148, 254-267.

Narendranathan, W., Nickell, S., and Stern, S., "Unemployment Benefits Revisited", *Economic Journal*, 1985, 95, 307-329.

Nickell, S., "Estimating the Probability of Leaving Unemployment", *Econometrica*, 1979a, 47, 1249-1266.

Nickell, S., "Education and Lifetime Patterns of Unemployment", *Journal of Political Economy*, 1979b, 87, S117-S131.

Nickell, S., "The Effect of Unemployment and Related Benefits on the Duration of Unemployment", *Economic Journal*, 1979c, 89, 34-49.

Nickell, S., "Determinants of Occupational Success in Britain", *Review of Economic Studies*, 1982, 43-53.

Nijhuis, F. and Soeters, J., "Werk en ziekte", Research Report, Limburg University, 1982.

Odink, J.G., "Inkomensherverdeling door belastingen en andere overdrachten", *Maandschrift Economie*, 1983, 47, 66-73.

OECD, "Social Expenditure 1960-1990", Social Policy Studies, Paris, 1985.

OECD, "Reforming Public Pensions", Social Policy Studies no. 5, Paris, 1988.

OECD, *The Tax/Benefit Position of Production Workers 1985-1988*, Paris, 1989.

OECD, *Employment Outlook*, Paris, 1991.

OECD, *Labour Force Statistics 1969-1989*, Paris, 1991.

Ombudsvrouw, "Klachtenboek vrouwen in WAO/AAW", Den Haag: Landelijke Stichting Ombudsvrouw, 1981.

Orr, Larry L., "Income Transfers as a Public Good: An Application to AFDC", *American Economic Review*, 1976, 66, 359-371.

Oxley, Howard, Maher, Maria, Martin, John P., Nicoletti, Giuseppe, and Alonso-Gamo, Patricia, "The Public Sector: Issues for the 1990s", OECD, Dept. of Economics and Statistics, Working Papers no. 90, Paris, 1990.

Parsons, Donald O., "The Decline in Male Labour Force Participation", *Journal of Political Economy*, 1980, 88, 117-134.

Parsons, Donald O., "The Male Labour Force Participation Decision; Health, Reported Health, and Economic Incentives", *Economica*, 1982, 49, 81-91.

Parsons, Donald O., "Disability Insurance and Male Labour Force Participation; A Response to Haveman and Wolfe", *Journal of Political Economy*, 1984a, 92, 542-549.

Parsons, Donald O., "Social Insurance with Imperfect State Verification: Income Insurance for the Disabled", Mimeo, Ohio State University, 1984b.

Parsons, Talcott, *The Social System*, Glencoe Ill.: The Free Press, 1951.

Pauly, Mark V., "The Economics of Moral Hazard: Comment", *American Economic Review*, 1968, 58, 531-537.

Philipsen, H., *Afwezigheid wegens ziekte*, Groningen: Wolters-Noordhof, 1969.

Prins, Rienk, "Arbeidsongeschiktheid in internationaal perspectief", *Economisch Statistische Berichten*, 1991, 76, 64-72.

Quinn, Joseph, F., "Micro-Economic Determinants of Early Retirement; A Cross-Sectional View of White Married Men", *Journal of Human Resources*, 1977, 12, 329-346.

Ridder, G., *Life Cycle Patterns in Labor Market Experience*, Doctoral Thesis, University of Amsterdam, 1987.

Ridder, G. and Gorter, K., "Unemployment Benefits and Search Behaviour: an Empirical Investigation", AE-report 11/86, University of Amsterdam, Dept. of Actuarial Science and Econometrics, 1986.

Ris, B.G.M., "Personeelsbeleid en ziekteduur", Research Report, Leiden: NIPG-TNO, 1978.

Roodenburg, H.J. and Wong Meeuw Hing, W.J.M.L., "De arbeidsmarktcomponent in de WAO", Occasional Paper 34, The Hague: Centraal Planbureau, 1985.

Ruser, John W., "Workers' Compensation Insurance, Experience Rating and Occupational Injuries", Mimeo, Washington DC: US Bureau of Labor Statistics, 1984.

Safilios-Rothschild, C., *The Sociology and Social Psychology of Disability and Rehabilitation*, New York: Random House, 1970.

Saunders, Peter and Klau, Friedrich, "The Role of the Public Sector, Causes and Consequences of the Growth of Government", *OECD Economic Studies*, Spring 1985.

Schaufeli, Wilmar, *Unemployment and Psychological Health; An Investigation among Dutch Professionals*, Doctoral Thesis, Groningen University, 1988.

Schechter, Evan S., "Commitment to Work and the Self-Perception of Disability", *Social Security Bulletin*, June 1981, 44, 22-30.

Sirén, Pekka, "Some Tentative Work Disability Models", Mimeo, Social Insurance Institution, Helsinki, 1976.

Slade, Frederic P., "Labor Supply under Disability Insurance", NBER Working Paper, no. 860, 1982.

Smulders, P.G.W., *Balans van 30 jaar ziekteverzuimonderzoek*, Leiden: NIPG-TNO, 1984.

Smulders, P.G.W., *Bedrijfskenmerken en ziekteverzuim in de jaren zestig en tachtig*, Leiden: NIPG-TNO, 1984b.

Sociale Verzekeringsraad, *Ontwikkeling arbeidsongeschiktheid (Quarterly Reports on Disability)*, Zoetermeer: SVr, Various quarters.

Spruit, I.P., *Unemployment, Employment and Health*, Doctoral Thesis, Leiden University, 1983.

Statistical Office of the European Communities, *Eurostat Review 1976-1985*, Luxembourg: European Communities, 1987.

Stern, Steven, "Measuring the Effect of Disability on Labor Force Participation", *Journal of Human Resources*, 1989, 24, 361-395.

Stewart, M.B. and Greenhalgh, C.A., "Work History Patterns and the Occupational Attainment of Women", *The Economic Journal*, 1984, 94, 493-519.

Taubman, Paul and Wachter, Michael L., "Segmented Labor Markets", in Ashenfelter and Layard (1986).

Tazelaar, F. and Sprengers, M., "Werkloosheid en sociaal isolement", *Sociologische Gids*, 1984, 31, 48-79.

Theeuwes, Jules J.M., "Arbeid en belastingen", in *Belastingheffing en belastinghervorming*, Pre-adviezen van de Koninklijke Vereniging voor de Staathuishoudkunde, Leiden: Stenfert Kroese, 1988.

Theeuwes, Jules J.M., Kerkhofs, Marcel, and Lindeboom, Maarten, "Transition Intensities in the Dutch Labour Market 1980-1985", *Applied Economics*, 1990, 22, 1043-1061.

Treitel, Ralph, "Appeal by Denied Disability Claimants", ORS Staff Paper no. 23, Washington DC: Social Security Administration, 1976.

Tweede Kamer der Staten-Generaal A, *(Financiële) Nota Sociale Zekerheid*, The Hague, Various years.

Tweede Kamer der Staten-Generaal B, *Inkomensnota*, The Hague, Various years.

Tweede Kamer der Staten-Generaal C, "Herziening van het stelsel van sociale zekerheid", Vergaderjaar 1982-1983, 17475, nr. 6, The Hague, 1982.

Valkenburg, F. and Vissers, A., *Dubbele arbeidsmarkt in Nederland*, Tilburg: IVA, 1979.

Van den Boom, C.E.M., *De ontslagpraktijk van het arbeidsbureau*, Deventer: Kluwer, 1985.

Van den Bosch, F.A.J. and Petersen, C., "An Explanation of the Growth of Social Security Disability Transfers", *De Economist*, 1983a, 131, 66-79.

Van den Bosch, F.A.J. and Petersen, C., *Aspecten van ziekte en arbeidsongeschiktheid in het stelsel van sociale zekerheid*, Doctoral Thesis, Leiden University, 1983b.

Van den Bosch, F.A.J. and Petersen, C., "De omvang van de verborgen werkloosheid in de WAO", *Economisch Statistische Berichten*, 1980, 65, 52-58.

Van der Horst, F.G.E.M., *Gezondheid en niet werken*, Doctoral Thesis, Limburg University, 1987.

Van de Ven, Wynand P.M.M. and Van der Gaag, Jacques, "Health as an Unobservable; a MIMIC-Model of the Demand for Health Care", *Journal of Health Economics*, 1982, 1, 157-185.

Van der Veen, Romke J., *De sociale grenzen van beleid*, Leiden: Stenfert Kroese, 1990.

Van Ginneken, W. and Park, J., *Generating Internationally Comparability of Statistics on Income Distribution*, Geneva: ILO, 1984.

Van Kessel, J.G.F.M., *Sociale zekerheid en rechtsbeleid*, Deventer: Kluwer, Sociale Zekerheidsreeks nr.12, 1985.

Van Mourik, A., "Ontwikkelingen in de beroepssegregatie tussen mannen en vrouwen, 1971-1985", *Economisch Statistische Berichten*, 1988, 73, 732-736.

Van Opstal, Rocus and Theeuwes, Jules J.M., "Duration of Unemployment in the Dutch Youth Labour Market", *De Economist*, 1986, 134, 351-367.

Van Praag, Bernard M.S., "Ontwikkelingen in arbeidsongeschiktheid", in Van den Bosch, F.A.J. and Petersen C., eds., *Arbeidsongeschiktheid, Een multidisciplinaire benadering*, Deventer: Kluwer, 1981.

Van Praag, Bernard M.S. and Emanuel, Han, "On the Concept of Non-Employability, with Respect to a Non-Homogeneous Labour Force", in N.N., ed., *The Arne Ryde Symposium on Social Insurance*, Amsterdam: North-Holland, 1983.

Van Praag, Bernard M.S. and Halberstadt, Victor, "Towards an Economic Theory of Non-Employability, a First Approach", in Roskamp, Karl W., ed., *Public Choice and Public Finance*, Paris: XX, 1980.

Van Praag, Bernard M.S., Halberstadt, Victor, and Emanuel, Han, "De valkuil der sociale zekerheid", *Economisch Statistische Berichten*, 1982, 67, 1155-59.

Van Praag, Bernard M.S. and Van Weeren, Hans, "The Time Discounting Mechanism in the Formation of Value Judgements on Income", Memo 83.22, Leiden University: Center for Research in Public Economics, 1983.

Van Soest, Arthur, "Minimum Wage Rate and Unemployment in the Netherlands", *De Economist*, 1989, 137, 279-308.

Van Zaal, M.J., "Wat voeren de uitvoerders eigenlijk uit", *Economisch Statistische Berichten*, 1981, 66, 28-34.

Verkleij, H., *Langdurige werkloosheid, werkhervatting en gezondheid*, Amsterdam/Lisse: Swets en Zeitlinger, 1988.

Victor, Richard B., *Workers' Compensation and Work Place Safety*, Santa Monica Cal: Rand Corporation, 1983.

Victor, Richard B., "Experience Rating and Work Place Safety", in Worral, John D. and Appel, David, eds., *Workers' Compensation Benefits; Adequacy, Equity and Efficiency*, Ithaca NY: ILR Press, 1985.

Viscusi, W. Kip, "Imperfect Job Risk Information and Optimal Workmen's Compensation Benefits", *Journal of Public Economics*, 1980, 14, 319-337.

Vrijhof, B.J., "Determinanten van WAO-toetreding", *Economisch Statistische Berichten*, 1981, 66, 1224-26.

Vrijhof, B.J., "Deeltijdarbeid en ziekteverzuim", *Tijdschrift voor Sociale Gezondheidszorg*, 1985, 63, 337-342.

Weaver, Carolyn, L., "Social Security Disability Policy in the 1980s and Beyond", in Berkowitz and Hill (1986).

Wetenschappelijke Raad voor het Regeringsbeleid, *Een werkend perspectief*, Den Haag: SDU, 1990.

Wiersma, D., *Psychosociale stress en langdurige arbeidsongeschiktheid*, Doctoral Thesis, Groningen University, 1979.

Wolfe, Barbara L., De Jong, Philip R., Haveman, Rober H., Halberstadt, Victor, and Goudswaard, Kees P., "Income Transfers and Work Effort; The Netherlands and the United States in the 1970s", *Kyklos*, 1984, 37, 609-637.

World Health Organization, *International Classification of Impairments, Disabilities and Handicaps*, Geneva: WHO, 1980.

Worrall, John D. and Butler, Richard J., "Some Lessons from the Workers' Compensation Program", in Berkowitz and Hill (1986).

Zabalza, A., Pissarides, P.A., and Barton, M., "Social Security and the Choice between Full-Time Work, Part-Time Work and Retirement", *Journal of Public Economics*, 1980, 14, 245-276.

Zola, Irving K., "Socio-cultural Factors in the Seeking of Medical Care: A Progress Report", *Transcultural Psychiatric Research*, 1963, 64-65.

Zweekhorst, W.A., "Verborgen werkloosheid in de WAO", *Intermediair*, June 1981, 17, no. 23, 25-29,48.

# AUTHOR INDEX

371

# SUBJECT INDEX